Stevens in His Physical Prime

THADDEUS STEVENS

BY

THOMAS FREDERICK WOODLEY

THE TELEGRAPH PRESS
HARRISBURG, PA.
1934

Copyright, 1934, by The Telegraph Press

Printed in the U. S. A.

by

THE TELEGRAPH PRESS

Harrisburg, Penna.

THIS BOOK
IS AFFECTIONATELY DEDICATED TO
THE ONE WHO INSPIRED ITS EFFORT
MABEL SLUTTER WOODLEY

"**H**E SEEMED like an eagle, perched alone upon a blasted oak, with sullen and defiant majesty scorning alike the chatter and scream of other birds around him; his eye sometimes covered with film as of down from the passing wing of death, but in a moment shooting into pinions on which he proudly soared to the sun."

From the Remarks of Representative Robinson delivered upon the occasion of the Memorial Services for Thaddeus Stevens, held in the House of Representatives.

PREFACE

Thaddeus Stevens stands well forward in the ranks of the first dozen Americans who have made large imprint on their country's history. Because of his almost enigmatic character, he has been difficult to appraise, and although nearly seven decades have elapsed since his death, his place is by no means fixed.

While he lived, his followers could find no words strong enough to praise him, and his enemies, especially in the South, could find no language bitter enough to damn him. Curiously, biographers and recorders of the generations that followed him appear fair enough in their estimates of his contemporaries. But immediately upon their pens touching the Old Commoner, there seems to be a flare back to the passions of the days in which he lived, and the record made for him is either colored in his favor by his defenders, or unreasonably denigrated by those not sympathetic with his policies.

At any rate, no complete story of Stevens has been written which the longer range historian has not severely criticized as prejudicial. And even a superficial study of the speeches and writings of the man makes all too apparent the reason.

Although he left a small bale of writings, and his utterances cover many pages of the official records of the Nation, a complete reading of all in no way satisfies the investigator that he knows the man. Uniquely parsimonious with words, he never used an unnecessary one, and met loquacious colleagues with a uniformly contemptuous silence. There is not a single writing from his pen that does not show how begrudgingly he

permitted expression. In all his long and active public
life he made but a single explanation of his action, and
that was done more as an argument than for the purpose of disclosing himself.

In spite of the fact that he left a reputation for inherent honesty and outspoken truthfulness that is un-
surpassed by any character in American history, one
feels, nevertheless, that in all he said and wrote, he,
in some adroit manner, concealed the full and balanced
portrait of himself.

The author has interviewed many persons who knew
Stevens, but their appraisals are utterly irreconcilable.

In the days of his might, his acts were constantly re-
current bolts of chain lightning tearing their way across
the troubled skies of the War and early Reconstruction.
They struck at great things and vital ones, and rarely
could their effect be confined to localities or small
groups. His efforts were not the feeble shimmerings
of heat lightning that might concern only those on the
other side of the horizon; they were terrific and in-
escapable strokes that rived themselves into the very
lives and homes of all the Nation. That it was never
known before time how or where or when he would
strike, only made him more effective. Wielding such
tremendous power and striking with devastating effects,
no one could be neutral toward him.

He was either the benefactor who purged the air
and mightily struck down obsolescent and obstructive
landmarks to achieve a better and freer life for the
peoples of America, or he was the ruthless and merciless foe who, in order to promulgate a policy, without
hesitation, sabotaged Constitutional tradition to crush

a civilization. That his personality was oblique, his body deformed and his disposition immobile, only complicates the problem of his analysis.

A biography may be presented in two different ways. If the subject is not too difficult of analysis, it is probably best to present him against a carefully reproduced historic background of his times, as Reynolds might show a character. But occasionally it may be justifiable to treat a person as Rembrandt did in an attempt to translate character subjectively, and without emphasis of the background. To be of real historic value, of course, the former method must be used, but if pure biography is the aim, then the latter may best answer. Between these two methods, all shades of middle ground have been used.

Because Stevens is such a difficult and startling character and was so recognized even by his contemporaries; because he is an wholly sufficient study unto himself, the author here has attempted in the main to follow the latter method of treatment.

The author is convinced that the words a man utters are symptoms of his ego. In several instances, brief verbatim quotations from the pen or mouth of the subject have been used. This was found peculiarly necessary in an attempt to portray a conscientious and truthful picture of the man's character, for master of language that he was, so subtle and shaded are many of his expressions, that accurate paraphrasing is quite impossible.

No attempt at a comprehensive and all-conclusive work can be even thought of in a single volume. Stevens has been practically ignored since his death, and only

PREFACE

now is the demand for further light upon him asserting itself. Without doubt, as time goes on, new material will be unearthed that will amplify, modify, or perhaps even change our present appraisal of him.

In this work, the author has attempted to give a fair and balanced portrait in the light of recently discovered writings and a more or less exhaustive research of unused newspaper reports, especially those concerning the Old Commoner's life up to the age of fifty years, which hitherto has been little known.

Because it has been the custom to accept Stevens as a man almost wholly devoid of the finer attributes of character, it may appear that the author has been overly sympathetic toward him. Such has been neither his aim nor desire. Facts have been authenticated; opinions designated as such. The author has endeavored merely to present the man and permit the reader to develop his own conclusions.

Appreciation is expressed to Dr. Thomas P. Martin and his staff of the Library of Congress; Hon. Donald McPherson and John D. Keith of Gettysburg; William F. Worner, Hon. B. C. Atlee and Miss Gertrude Haldy of the Lancaster County Historical Society for helpful suggestions in the matter of research; to Frank P. McKibben for the use of his collection of Stevens letters, and to Ellingwood Kay and Hon. William H. Kirkpatrick for assistance in reading and correcting the manuscript.

East Bangor, Pa., August, 1934.

CONTENTS

Book One
PROLOGUE

Book Two
CRUSADER

Book Three
CONGRESSMAN

Book Four
DEFENDER

Contents

Book Five

Helmsman

Book Six

Dictator

Book Seven

Epilogue

ILLUSTRATIONS

[xiii]

"I HAVE done what I deemed best for humanity. It is easy to protect the interests of the rich and powerful. But it is a great labor to protect the interests of the poor and downtrodden. It is the eternal labor of Sisyphus, forever to be renewed. I know how unprofitable is all such toil. But he who is earnest heeds not such things. It has not been popular. But if there be anything for which I have entire indifference; perhaps I might say contempt, it is the public opinion which is founded on popular clamor.

"I see nothing in my political career, especially in my action with regard to human freedom which I wish to have changed or expurged. I believe that every man must finally answer for the deeds done in the body; and that patriotic deeds will be among the accounts. I desire to take to the Bar of that dread account the record which I shall make on the question of human rights."

From a holograph writing of Stevens found among his preparatory notes of a speech delivered in Congress on the Fourteenth Amendment. *McPherson Collection, Library of Congress No. 53590.*

BOOK ONE

PROLOGUE

Thaddeus Stevens

Book One—Prologue

I

CLUBFOOT

SHORTLY after two o'clock in the afternoon of February 22, 1868, a sick old man, lame from birth, leaning heavily on a stout hickory cane, was recognized by Speaker Colfax to the Floor of the United States House of Representatives in Washington. His presence was commanding, his dark eyes piercing, his personality overpowering. He spoke barely ten minutes, but the mighty meaning of his simple words electrified the country. His speech was clear and incisive, but not strong, for perpetual pain racked his body and drained his energies.

As he spoke that dreary Saturday afternoon, the crowded Floor of the House, liberally sprinkled with United States Senators, listened in stirless solemnity; the packed galleries bent forward in awed silence.

At that point of time there was concentrated in the speaker the unrelenting force of a majority of the peoples' representatives determined to remove the incumbent from the highest office in the country, in order, as they believed, to secure the unconsolidated victories of the War of the Rebellion. The mightiest man on the continent was speaking. His report closed with the words, "Resolved, that Andrew Johnson, President of the United States, be impeached of high crimes and misdemeanors."

More than ten months past his seventy-fifth birthday, the Finger of Death had already beckoned him and
he knew it. Deformity, disease, years of pain, grievous
disappointments mourned for alone, and the cumulative weight of his years bore heavily upon him, but
a stupendous will that only death could subdue drove
him on.

This, however, was not the first time impeachment of
the President had been proposed to the House. General Ashley, Representative from Ohio, had offered a
similar resolution fourteen months before. But then
the proposer was James M. Ashley; now it was Thaddeus Stevens. Ashley's proposal was defeated by a
vote of one hundred eight to fifty-seven. Stevens'
resolution was carried two days after it was offered by
a vote of one hundred twenty-eight to forty-seven. For
the first and only time in history, the President of the
United States was impeached.

The day after the vote was taken, he appeared with
another Congressman before the Senate. With pallid
face, whose deathlike hue was exaggerated by the fire
of his deep-sunken, brilliantly dark eyes, gaunt, bewigged and tottering, but fully realizing the stupendous importance of his mission, he paused at the entrance of the Upper Chamber. A doorkeeper called
out, "A message from the House of Representatives;"
and a bewildered Senate struck into silence at the announcement, turned to the portentous messenger to
hear him say:

"Mr. President: By order of the House of Representatives, we appear at the bar of the Senate, and in
the name of the House of Representatives, and of all

the people of the United States, we do impeach Andrew Johnson, President of the United States, of high crimes and misdemeanors in office; and we do further inform the Senate that the House of Representatives will in due time exhibit particular articles of impeachment against him, and make good the same; and in their name *we do demand* that the Senate take order for the appearance of the said Andrew Johnson to answer to said impeachment."

No man in all the country's history had ever made such dread pronouncement in that forum, and the country, as well as the Senate, trembled at its impact.

Born a cripple and poor, in the rugged mountain country of Vermont where, at the time to obtain the bare requirements of life was a task demanding an all-exclusive attention, he emigrated in early manhood without means and without promise to a distant state. There among strangers, a clubfooted newcomer without friends, he staked his future. Unbecomingly shy, embarrassed by his infirmity, he labored and studied.

The years made him a local leader. He became a member of the General Assembly of his adopted State. Here he is seen by the crushing weight of his argument and a terrible earnestness, driving the Legislature of a great Commonwealth into a position where it was forced to vote against an overwhelmingly popular bill to repeal the Free School law, thereby making his name as immortal as the public school system.

Scandalized as have been but few men in our history, going to Congress for the first time well past middle life, and there rising to a pinnacle of near absolute legislative power; dictating the country's policy through its greatest crisis; preparing the path for one of the Nation's greatest Presidents and forcing him to follow it; impeaching the highest official of a great government, he died in the peaceful quiet of a Washington summer's midnight, under the eyes of the Nation with a negro Catholic Sister of Charity soothing him into finality.

Who was this Master of the early reconstruction; this dictator of the House of Representatives; this greatest of American Parliamentarians; this baffling stalwart of the fighting heart; and by what merit or method did he rise?

Rarely an orator, yet words were his only weapons; long in politics, yet never catering to the public will and frequently bluntly opposing it; never loved, yet having thousands who would stand by him to the bitter end; charitable to the extent of self-denial, yet called the most violently vindictive man in our history; never holding executive or judicial power to punish or reward, yet the absolute dictator of his party; tenderly sensitive, yet outwardly frigid; frequently flashing an unique wit and sometimes a gentle humor, yet always convincingly serious; reared in a Puritanical environment, yet broad and liberal in faith and practice; cynic, yet showing an unbounded faith; author of volumes of writings and speeches, yet concealing much that was himself; unsympathetic toward churches, yet remembering them among the first in his Will.

One who recently wrote a history of our country, referred to him as "perhaps the most despicable, malevolent and morally deformed character who has ever risen to high power in America." [1] Yet he did more for a whole race than any man in all history. A Protestant minister believed him to be an inspired force for universal good and prayed for him daily. To the masses in the North, he was affectionately known as the "Old Commoner," but the bitter opinion throughout the white South was that he was a vicious demon incarnate, and one great American newspaper went so far in its fiery hatred of him to say, even after his death, that he had been the author of more evil and mischief than any other inhabitant of the Globe.[2]

* * * * *

In early April of 1792, as the patiently awaited winds from the South were freeing inland Vermont from its winter bound isolation, the wife of a dissolute shoemaker in the little crossroad settlement of Danville, gave birth to a fourth and last child. Father and mother were of peasant English ancestry, differing but little from the run of the ordinary there. The black-eyed baby boy, not overly strong,[3] came into the world marred with a clubfoot. Inflicted upon his sensitive nature, this ever-assertive deformity scarred his life and sealed his destiny.

The official records at Danville give the birth date as April 4, 1792, but other authorities make it the corresponding day of 1793.[4] The date is of importance because of its pertinence to stories concerning his paternity. Gross scandal, a threatening spectre that dogged him all his life, touched him even before he was born. According to stories which gained wide currency in his later years, he was the natural child of his mother and the French Count Talleyrand DePerigord.[5] It was even said that there was documentary proof in ex-

[7]

istence showing conclusively that these allegations were true.[6]

Although the Count, a master intriguer, left what purported to be his original papers and records, he is at times difficult to trace. One of his recent biographers says that in spite of assertions that the duplicates made of Talleyrand's memoirs were exact copies of the original documents, "the more famous historians and critics are of the unanimous opinion" that the papers left by him have been greatly modified; pages have been omitted and many statements changed.[7]

Upon our point, however, we are able to follow him through collateral references. He went on a confidential mission for his government during the French revolution, to England, arriving there in January of 1792.[8] He remained only a short time, when he returned to France, but left on a second mission to the same country in April of the same year.[9] Fearing a second return to France, he remained in England, apparently satisfied to live there indefinitely. But his intrigues made him obnoxious to the British Government, and he was notified to leave the country late in January of 1794.[10] He sailed upon his first trip to America on February 3 of that year.[11] The date of this departure from England is accurately fixed from the sailing records, and although his arrival here cannot be determined precisely, we know he was in England as late as February of 1794.

Therefore, even if the more recent date given as that of Stevens' birth is the correct one, the record proves beyond doubt, the physical impossibility of Talleyrand's paternity of him. The story, like many another sordid one that clustered about his name, is a fabrication of the gossips.

Although there were three other children, each was normal physically. Only the baby, blemished with a clubfoot, was a cripple. There is nothing in the entire record to indicate that Thaddeus was of an intelligence superior to his brothers or of more inviting personality, but nevertheless the mother early determined to educate him and send him to college if she could.[12] The mother's life, from the earliest, seemed pointed toward advancement in life for little Thad and her letters indicate her concentrated interest in him. Because this disproportionate division of affection was apparent from the time Stevens was tiny, there are but two reasonable bases to found it. Either it was because Thaddeus was her youngest, or because he was crippled, or both.

A careful study of her writings leaves no doubt that the overshadowing reason for the outpouring of her love on the baby was the realization of his physical handicap. Maternal love is the strongest one, but when to it is added a mother's compassion for undeserved torment which her child must inevitably endure, the emotion is magnified to dimensions that only a mother so affected can measure. Life, as Stevens was born to it, was hard enough for a normal person; for a sensitive cripple, and no one understood better than she how exceedingly tender the boy really was, the wise parent knew that the direst of hardship must lie ahead.

Here was inflicted upon Stevens' nature a mother's pity, which, when fully comprehended by him, incalculably influenced his life. He was quick to understand that the emotion was inspired by his physical disfigurement, and it was but natural that a part of his reaction was embitterment at his fate. But there was nothing in him that was weak. Though that deformity might preclude much in life there still was something left. His mother's pity so patent at all times fired his early ambitions, steeled his character and begrimed his determination to succeed. As it emphasized unduly his blemish it brought him to believe that normal social intercourse especially with the other sex would be conclusively barred. It made him a lonely being. On the other hand, it served as an anchor to windward through his long and stormy life and created in him a devotion for his mother rarely surpassed in a son. His genuine love for her was the only real affection that he ever showed toward any individual of all humanity.

The clubfoot began to take its toll as soon as the boy could walk. Because of the deformity, he could not run and play as other children of his age did, but was compelled to stand aside. Crippled, he was not encouraged to join in their games, and his inherent modesty prevented him from injecting himself. One who knew him well in those days remembered him as "still and quiet-like, different from the rest of the boys," who would "laugh at him, boylike, and mimic his limping walk."[13] He was, even at that early age, extremely delicate of feelings and easily hurt, and his playmates' snubs cut the little fellow to his heart.[14]

In spite of his reputation in later years for being a grim, determined and cold-hearted man, Stevens was intrinsically an unusually sensitive being, sentimentally sympathetic with all unfortunates, and prodigally charitable. His appearance of hardness was but an acquired veneer, product of a determined Spartan discipline of himself.

The physical deformity not only made him a hobbling cripple; its charge was infinitely more. Had he been able to accept it for merely what it showed, his life might have been larger and fuller. But before he was old enough to appraise it at its proper weight, it had eaten into the very vitals of his ego, upset a normal emotional balance, and done irreparable damage. It certainly created a modified inferiority complex and his reaction to that deep-grounded and lifelong infliction showed in all the ambitions that motivated him. In his case, the natural adjustments early in life crystallized into an exalted humanitarian attitude which made him the Equalitarian.

His incapacity to mingle unhampered and play with children forced retreat to his mother's company. He became her constant companion, went regularly to church with her, and at times they together visited the sick of the neighborhood.[15] But going to church and visiting could fill only part of his play time. Finding him constantly in her company, the mother was quick to take advantage of her precious opportunity. Books and learning would open the way for Thaddeus, and books and learning he would have. When but a tot she taught him to read, and devout Baptist that she was, naturally used the Bible for most of her teaching. She wanted him to become a minister but admonished him not to attempt to preach until he had first become a "thorough Christian."[16]

In later years, he seemed reluctant to discuss this

phase of his early life. On an occasion in Gettysburg,
when his superior knowledge of the Bible attracted the
attention of one to whom he was speaking, his listener
asked if he had not at one time prepared for the min-
istry. Stevens' noncommittal answer was, "Well, I
have read the books." [17]

At any rate, reading was substituted for play, and
this fitted satisfactorily into the mother's plans to train
his mind. Slowly and patiently she encouraged him
along lines of thought and learning, and gently pressed
upon him the importance of mental development. Not
only did he placate himself through his idle hours by
reading as a pastime, but we find him very early developing a real interest in books. On that little clubfoot
he frequently hobbled for miles to borrow one, for his
modest home had little besides the Bible and a few volumes of commentaries upon it. [18]

In Stevens' native county of Caledonia in the latter
part of the Eighteenth Century, there were two rival
towns; his birthplace, Danville, and Peacham. The latter held control of the county. The country was recovering from the shock of War and forward looking citizens were effecting a political structure. The County
was about to select its shire town so that a Court House
could be allocated and erected. With the fairminded-
ness typical of the pioneer, it was understood that of the
two towns, one should have the Court House and the
other an academy. Holding political advantage, it
would of course, be for Peacham to take her choice.
There were many town meetings and much discussion,
some of it quite heated. Business and financial interests wanted the Court House. Those who thought more

of learning sought the School. The latter group finally had its way. Peacham became the situs of the academy and to the neighboring town of Danville was allotted the Court House.[19]

Interested more in schools than she was in Court Houses, Mrs. Stevens had kept a watchful and interested attention upon the proceedings and their outcome. As soon as the decision was reported, she lost no time in moving from the Court House Settlement to the Academy Town.[20]

As early as 1795, citizens of Peacham had organized for the purpose of founding some type of school. An academy was built in 1797, and opened the latter part of that year. It was a modest two-story structure substantially constructed with plenty of windows. The Trustees had specifically directed that "the building be thirty feet long and forty feet wide; the upstairs to be used for school purposes and public rooms and the first floor for church services." Plain, unpretentious, and roughly finished inside, it had a single fireplace to temper the extreme cold of New England winters. There was little equipment and no refinement. Handhewn benches for desks; a few of the standard classics; several copies of texts and a globe—such was Stevens' first school.[21]

The single instructor, who was also Principal, was a disciplinarian, harsh and severe. Certainly there was little that was inviting and nothing that could be entertaining to a child of tender years. But the wistful crippled boy did not look for entertainment. In her burning ambition to educate him, his Mother had persistently encouraged him in his studies and fortified as he was with her early instruction in reading, that

crude school room was a haven where the clubfoot faded
into the background. Here for the first time he could
at least be on a level with his fellows. Little wonder
that he liked it! There was intellectual warmth and a
friendliness about it. Anything that would remove even
partially the paining hurts of his infirmity would receive welcome in his little heart. Here began an attachment to the school. Here was planted within him the
idea that education was one of the necessaries of life in
a Democracy. He was the ardent advocate of Public
Schools from then on until the day of his death.

We have no record of his rating as a student in his
first school, but we do know that while there, he founded
a Junior Library.[22] Some six decades later, when he
came to write his will, that Juvenile Library Association "founded at the Caledonia County Academy," was
his first beneficiary.[23]

The purpose of the founders of Stevens' first school
was to establish a free school for all children in Caledonia County, but they soon realized that the cost was
greater than they had anticipated. A levy on the students was found necessary by November of 1797, and
the Trustees imposed a charge of "one shilling per
month in advance, for procuring wood for winter, purchasing a book of records and other contingent costs."
Next year, they voted that "each pupil pay twenty-five
cents per quarter for the purpose of procuring globes
and for other necessary expenses." [24]

At the annual meeting of 1799, the first mention of
tuition is made when the Board assessed for it a charge
of "seventeen cents in advance for each quarter." While
Thaddeus was in attendance at the academy, fees for

instruction ranged from this amount up to twenty-five cents per month.

The only official writing that remains at the school today mentioning Stevens is a minute of the Trustees. Strangely enough, that record is mute as to his standing as a scholar, but, without indicating ability or lack of ability, indicts him for having taken "part in a tragedy by candlelight." In 1811, which was Stevens' last year there, school regulations provided that annually there should be "an exhibition in which the male scholars shall be the only performers and that the pieces to be spoken shall be selected by the preceptor and submitted to the inspection of the prudential committee." But the rule had been twice amended, first by the proviso "that there be no performances by candlelight," and secondly by a restriction excluding "tragedies, comedies and other theatrical performances."

The record shows that not only did Thaddeus and his fellows violate the rules by doing something that was forbidden, but they also refused to perform a part of their duties, and by their impudence, forced an irritating delay of the ceremonies. Whether it was a mere schoolboy prank or a willful assertion designed to register objection to what was considered too narrow regulations, will never be known. The meager record permits no elaboration.

But that Board of Trustees was made up of stern, Puritanical men who regarded discipline so important in the formation of character that they practiced it freely, not only upon those over whom they exercised control, but even upon themselves. Certainly the malefactions of their students would not be overlooked, especially in a case as this one where a willful breach openly flaunted was aggravated by an arrogant indifference which kept that dignified body cooling its feet and warming its temper through an entire day, awaiting the pleasure of its subjects. The remarkable feature of the incident is that the punishment was so mild.

When the Board next met, after naming Stevens and twelve companions, it resolved that "their action in refusing on the day of public exhibition, being the fourth of September, last, to proceed in their exhibition in the daytime while the authorities were waiting to see their performance, was conduct highly reprehensible. And that their proceeding to exhibit a tragedy in the evening of the said day, contrary to the known rules and orders of the School, and the express prohibition of the preceptor, was a gross violation of the rules and the by-laws of the institution."

Accordingly they were required to subscribe the following admission, viz: "We, the subscribers, students in the Academy at Peacham, having been concerned in the exhibition of a tragedy on September 4, 1811, contrary to the known rules of the Board of Trustees, on reflection are convinced that we have done wrong in not paying a suitable respect to the authority of the Board and hereby promise that as long as we continue students at this Academy, we will observe such rules as the Board may prescribe."

Two of the miscreants refused to sign the paper, but Stevens subscribed, and apparently without compulsion. Certainly he was not so obligated in order to remain in school, for at about that time, he left it to enter

An Early Letter of Stevens which is Among the Most Legible of His Writings

college. It is the single record that remains of his long life in which he admitted publicly that he had acted in error. The crippled stripling who, in that little village school agreed not again to take part in a "tragedy by candlelight," just a half century later was taking a leading part in one of history's greatest tragedies, for which a Nation was the stage and the civilized world the audience.

It is interesting to note in passing that in 1810 the Board had voted "No person shall be admitted to learn to write who cannot write a legible hand." If this rule were practiced before it was formally enacted it is consoling to one who has tried to translate Stevens' letters to believe that he could at one time write a legible hand. More likely, however, he wrote in those days about the same hand that he did in later life, and the regulation might have been invoked so that no other who wrote as badly as he should gain admission to the school.

All his life Stevens was a notoriously illegible penman. The many thousands of. sheets of holograph material he left are puzzlingly done in a hurried scrawl requiring, as a rule, an expert to decipher.

His correspondents frequently admonished him to write more clearly. An old Quaker friend of his "would be very willing to know what thy opinion is, if thou could write so I could read it." [25] A representative of the Cumberland County, Pa., Dunkers, acting for his society, asked Stevens to send them his suggestions concerning a political matter. But inasmuch as he desired the answer "to be passed around for general perusal, and as your chirography would be all Latin to them," he asked that Stevens dictate his reply to one who could write legibly.[26] In all the great field of the letter writers of his age, Stevens stands unchallenged as the most undecipherable.

However, he completed his studies at the Caledonia Academy sometime late in 1811. The school minutes indicate that the Board of Trustees did not pass the above-quoted Resolution until October 7. Stevens therefore signed his pledge after that date, and it seems reasonable to conclude that he must have been a student at the school when he signed it. His name appeared in the Annual Catalogue of Dartmouth College dated October, 1811, but how it got there is not clear, nor can the Dartmouth College authorities explain it.[27]

It may be that in his well-planned procedure to obtain a college education, he had applied for admission long enough before October, 1811, to get his name in the lists of that date. At any rate, it is certain that he did attend Dartmouth for a time later in 1811, and a part of 1812.[28]

During that year and the succeeding one, 1812-13, he also attended the University of Vermont. While there, the Federal Government took over the buildings of the University to use as barracks for its soldiers of the War of 1812. Suddenly deprived of college facilities, Stevens returned to Dartmouth in the fall of 1813, and graduated from there in August of the next year.

All was not well with him at Dartmouth, but time has erased the reason. In a letter to his aunt, Mrs. Smith, which Stevens wrote from Littletown, N. H., in March, 1813, he expressed doubts about getting back to college. He said he then had been studying three months with a Mr. Carpenter, "the minister of the

place," who "has expressed willingness to give me testi-
monials of good behaviour at any time. He even offered
to write to the Faculty of the College and try and get
me back at the commencement of the spring term, but
I told him I thought it would be of no avail. He has
several times told me that my conduct has been perfectly unexceptionable since I had been here." Further
on in the letter, the crippled boy wrote, "It had been my
intention not to write to you again until I had gotten
back into college and in case I did not get back, not
to let you hear from me again."

It therefore appears that Stevens' trouble at Dartmouth was not one concerning his studies, but one concerning his conduct.

Already he had decided to emigrate from Vermont.
On January 5, 1814, in one of his longest letters, he
inquired of his former teacher, who had moved to York,
Pennsylvania, the prospects of obtaining employment
in that State. To "Preceptor Merrill" he wrote, "unless
honored with degradation, I shall graduate next August, and shall be at that time under the necessity of
entering into a school. If you know of any vacancies
and could assist me without trouble to yourself, you
would do me a favor."

In this early correspondence, he shows an already
strongly formed democratic attitude and an animadver-
sion to secret societies. Among the other "news," he
reported: "Charles Leverett has entered into the service
of the aristocracy, in the capacity of scullion; and it is
expected as a reward for his services, he will be
Knighted, that is, elected Phi Betian. Those fawning
parasites, who are grasping at unmerited honors, seem

for once to have blundered into the truth, that they must flatter the nobility, or remain in obscurity; that they must degrade themselves by sycophancy, or others will not exalt them. The democracy rule in the Fraternity. The aristocracy make threatening grimaces, but it is only sport for us poor plebians."

In lighter manner: "Friend Sam, I assure you, you can hardly conceive the anxiety your friends feel for you, in that distant country. Considering you exposed to the invincible charms of those fair Dutch wenches, with their dozen pair of petticoats they are really afraid, that you will lose your heart or get lost, with Goodie Twiller's ladle, in one corner of their pockets; that filthy lucre will induce you to become the son-in-law of some Ten Breeches; and then we shall despair of seeing you again; for I suppose it as much impossible to transport those 'fair lumps of earth' into another climate as it would be to people America with crocodiles, by way of the frozen regions." [29]

The answer to this letter was apparently the encouragement which brought Stevens to Pennsylvania. Although diligent search has been made, it has not been found.

Stevens arrived in his adopted State in the late summer or early autumn of 1815, and began teaching in the Academy at York, Pennsylvania, where Merrill had gotten him a job. As soon as he was settled, he turned in spare moments to his legal studies which he had started under Judge John Battocks in Vermont. Almost immediately he formed a contact with David Cassett, Esquire, one of the outstanding members of the York County Bar under whom, in his spare time, he industriously followed his new course in law.

A rare comment on his personality in that day is preserved as a recollection of Amos Gilbert, a fellow teacher at York. He regarded the Vermonter as "one of the most backward, retiring and modest young men" he had ever seen. He also noticed that the newcomer was a "very close student." [30]

It soon became known that the lame school teacher had ambitions to enter the County Bar, and that Association, for some reason, immediately took steps to block him. A resolution was passed prohibiting entrance to membership of those who followed any other vocation whilst preparing for admission. It seems that the action was aimed directly at Stevens. [31]

If this were the fact and he knew it, or if he ever suspected that it was, he gave no indication of offense at the time. He just ignored it. Assiduously but serenely, he labored on to the end of his course. Then, on a hot midsummer day late in August of 1816, he rode out of York on horseback and the next day appeared at the Court House of Harford County, at Bel Air, Maryland. Here, where it was said that "if the gate did not stand open, its latch was loose," he petitioned for admission to the Bar. [32]

A committee was appointed to examine him and the ordeal was held after supper at the hotel. As a condition precedent to the questioning, "young Stevens was notified that two bottles of Madeira, which must pass the committee's test, must first be supplied on the table before the Judges by the party to be examined." With this condition he immediately complied. He was asked what law books he had read and replied that he had

studied Coke on Littleton; Gilbert on Evidence; Black-
stone, and a work on Pleading. He was next required
to distinguish between a contingent remainder and an
executory devise. This he did to the committee's satisfaction and was then advised that before the examination could be concluded, he must produce two bottles
more of Madeira. This he also did. His certificate
was signed.

Although he met the test of his legal understanding,
he apparently did not qualify as well in a game of cards
afterward. Sitting in a game of "Fip-Loo," for the
greater part of the night, he lost, and when he had paid
his bill the next morning, he had but $3.50 left from
$45.00 he began with the evening before.[33]

The Court minutes for the next day bear the following record: "Upon application of Stevenson Archer,
Esquire, for the admission of Thaddeus Stevens, Esquire, as an attorney of this Court, the said Stevens is
admitted as an attorney of this Court and thereupon
takes and signs his several oaths prescribed by law, and
registers and signs a declaration of his belief in the
Christian religion."

Wasting no time in Maryland, he left Bel Air next
morning for Lancaster, famed as one of the great inland towns of the country, prosperous, pious and proud.
On the journey, he narrowly escaped being drowned
while crossing the McCall's Ferry Bridge, then in course
of construction. Reaching Lancaster before noon, he
dined at its leading hotel and afterward took a walk
about the town carefully studying what his prospects
might be if he located there.

Amos Gilbert's appraisal of Stevens as backward,

retiring and modest, was here vindicated, for a stranger, young, poor, crippled and friendless, he was overwhelmed with the smug, cold aloofness of the aristocratic Lancaster of that day. The city was too big and impregnable for him. He just could not bring himself to challenge it.

Burying his admitted defeat in the lonesomeness of himself, he decided to chance the future in the much smaller town of Gettysburg, County seat of Adams, where the struggle might not be so hard. The act of the York County Bar Association apparently had hurt him for not only did he not return there from Maryland, but he refused to consider the place even as second choice. York was just another town on his cheerless way from Lancaster to Gettysburg.

Why he selected this location remains a mystery, for so far as diligent research develops, he was acquainted with not a single person there. It was just a sprawling county town and none could know that a half century later it was to give its name to one of the most decisive battles of all history.

The fertile lands of the prosperous farmers of Adams County must have conveyed some note of promise to him as he approached Gettysburg. Those fields by which he rode, heavy with grain in the hush of summer's noon were eloquent of peaceful quiet. The lame man on horseback could not look ahead to the forty-seventh time the grain would again ripen there to see those very acres drenched with the blood of more than forty thousands of his slain and wounded countrymen who there met in the most tragic War of modern times.

From that very road in July of 1863, one could see

locked in a grip of death, the armies of the North and South, spectacularly fighting a three days' battle which marked the high point of Southern invasion of Northern soil and ending on the anniversary of Independence Day in utter defeat of Lee's forces, broke the heart of the South.

But shadows of uncertainty too must have occupied part of the future Stevens may have contemplated on the journey to his new home, where all were strangers.

Arriving, he lost no time in getting started. He took a room in the old McClellan House,[34] now the Gettysburg Hotel, and with a few books, opened the door of a law office and the way to a stormswept life.

Under date of September 24, 1816, the Court minutes bear the simple record, "Thaddeus Stevens is admitted to practice before the Adams County Court." It was customary in those days, as it is today, to have a member of the Bar move the admission of an applicant, but the entry indicates Stevens did the unusual in obtaining entrance on his own motion.

There were six other lawyers practicing in Gettysburg at the time, and how much better it would have been to present himself to one of them and have him move the admission. Such an acquaintanceship might have proved inestimably valuable in the new town. But it was characteristic of the newcomer never to ask either favor or courtesy. This was the first showing of that quirk in Stevens' make-up which undoubtedly cost him more than one appointment to high office.

He inaugurated a novel form by inserting his professional card in the local newspaper.[35] But the advertisement could not have been considered unethical, for in January of 1817, two of the other lawyers adopted the practice, although none had used it before Stevens.

His funds at the time were practically gone. All the money he had in the world was what he had saved while teaching at York. Some of this had gone for a few law books, and some for board bills since he stopped teaching. An absolute unknown in the town,[36] shy and hypersensitive, he made friends slowly. Patiently he waited for clients, studying the meanwhile. But the little business that came to him was hardly enough to live on.

His first appearance was as attorney for plaintiff, in the case of David Little versus Samuel King, filed under date of October 9, 1816. It was submitted to arbitrators who, in February of 1817, ordered that defendant pay plaintiff the "sum of $10.00 damages and costs of suit." Stevens was victorious in his first case. In the suit he was opposed by John McConaughy, Esq., one of the then leaders of the Adams County Bar.

His next case was his first jury trial. In it he was opposed by the same eminent counsel, and was again victorious, obtaining a verdict for his client in the amount of $330.00 "and six cents damages and six cents costs." [37] Between times he acted as attorney for execution creditors in some small collections. His fees from these were extremely modest. An example of the type of suits he worked upon in those years is one which was appealed from a Justice of the Peace Court.

McConaughy represented the plaintiff and Stevens the defendant. Judgment of the Justice was "that plaintiff pay the costs of suit in the amount of $5.82." From this plaintiff appealed and the Referees who heard the case found "for the plaintiff in the amount of $12.68; plaintiff to pay one-third of the costs and defendant the other two parts." [38]

There were a few other trivial matters which came to him, but if fees were in proportion to amounts involved, they must have been pitiably small. His income accordingly continued less than enough for support. Under these circumstances, it was characteristic of him to lose hope, and so disheartened did he become at the time, that he told an acquaintance "he could hold out no longer and must select a new location." [39]

Shortly after this, however,[40] a mentally unbalanced farmhand committed a murder near Gettysburg. Apparently without cause, he had attacked with a scythe and cut the throat of a fellow worker. The victim died immediately. The community was enraged against the alleged murderer, and condemned the act as so repulsive that none of the local lawyers would represent him. In seeking counsel, he finally gravitated to Stevens. The case was hurried to trial [41] and although Stevens surprised everyone, including the Court, with the very earnest and able defense which he raised in his client's behalf, it was of no avail. He pled the mental unsoundness of defendant, and on it made a good showing. But it was not enough to convince the jury. The unfortunate was quickly convicted and summarily hanged.

Many years later in discussing the case, Stevens stated that in his career, he had represented more than fifty defendants charged with murder and that in many of them where insanity was raised as a defense, the defendant was acquitted; in fact, he said, this was his only client tried for murder who was hanged, and oddly enough, this fellow he would always believe was the only one really insane.[42] Legend has it that for his work in the case, Stevens received a fee of $1500.00, but this appears to be exaggerated. He did, however, receive a substantial sum; the exact amount is of little importance.

The significance of the event as it affected the young lawyer's life was in the great recommendation it gave him as a sturdy fighter and competent, resourceful lawyer. The atmosphere in which he tried it was anything but sympathetic. In the first place, he was a newcomer to the community. Worse, he lacked the easy, pleasing manners which invite a friendly support. Furthermore, he had dared to stand between the community and the perpetrator of a hideous crime, who, in the eyes of his fellows, had no defense and ought to have been unceremoniously executed.

The profession itself gave him neither help nor encouragement. Since he had come to town, it had been the custom for the other attorneys, when they did not care to take an obnoxious suit, or one in which little or no fee was involved, to contemptuously suggest, "There is a lame young lawyer by the name of Stevens in town, who, if you see him, may attend to your case."[43] For a long time he was looked upon by his fellow attorneys as one who had forced himself in their midst.

As an uninvited guest, he was treated with anything but cordiality, shown no favors and given little consideration. Tender-hearted and profoundly sensitive, he took the treatment painfully but in silence, cloaking his feelings with studied calm and masked contentment. However, he needed no assistance after this first

murder case. He referred to it frequently in later
years, and always spoke of it as the turning point in his
early career.[44] Business came to him, slowly at first
and small in kind, but it was work and that was all
he needed. His cases were his opportunities and his
reputation grew as they increased in number.

He soon established himself financially and the year
1818 found him the owner of a house and a one-half lot
in Gettysburg assessed at $2500.00. Also he had ac-
quired a horse, which, for tax purposes, was valued at
$50.00.[45] Being fond of physical exercise, and espe-
cially riding, the clubfooted man on horseback was,
from this time on for the next decade, a familiar figure
along the country roads of Adams County.

In May, 1822, he was elected to the Borough Council
and unanimously chosen its president. As councilman,
he immediately became active in improving the facilities
for the local volunteer fire company and proposed the
installation of a municipal water system. Law work
was coming to him rapidly, and not only was he gaining
a reputation as a lawyer, but also he was accumulating
property.

The next year the assessors' books show him the
owner of three houses and lots and two other pieces of
land in the town, the aggregate assessment of which
was $4,060.00.[46] He was returned to the Borough
Council in 1824-25, but there was little of important
business to be transacted. One regular meeting left
an only minute of employing a man "to wind the Town
Clock for one year at $10.00."

Nine years after he arrived there, Stevens was the
largest individual holder of real estate in Gettysburg.

His property was assessed at $11,420.00, on which, incidentally, the total tax was but $10.58. Intermittently, he continued a member of the Borough Council until 1832. He was the highest assessed individual in the town from 1829 forward through the next decade.

During these years he relaxed at cards and was especially fond of the old game of euchre. But he had a strict habit never to indulge in any card game until a full days' work was done. Many anecdotes of his card playing days are still current in and about Gettysburg. One frequently told has him playing his favorite game one evening in a hotel room fronting on the street. A tenant farmer of his drove up with a load of hay. Two or three times he called in to Stevens, but the lawyer, engrossed in his game, paid little attention. Finally in answer to the farmer's repeated question of what he should do with it, Stevens shouted, "Bring it in and bet it on the ace."

He enjoyed the local political discussions and generally was the center of the group debates. Occasionally he went to the races at Hagerstown, Maryland. His lurid humor and incisive wit, together with his ability at the Bar, were attracting attention. He was making some friends and gaining a large acquaintanceship. His law practice had grown by leaps and bounds until by 1833, he was a prominent member of the Adams County Bar, and by 1837, in trial work had become its generally accepted head.

The "lame young lawyer" had found himself.

II

POLITICS

Stevens stepped from municipal to county politics in 1830, when he attended the State Anti-Masonic Convention at Harrisburg as a delegate from Adams County. For the decade prior to this, he had been interested in what was going on politically in the county and state, but had never had a constituency beyond the little town of Gettysburg. The man seemed pointed to a political career in spite of many traits of character which, in an average person would have prohibited it.

Even then he was learning that such a course would expose him to more than an ordinary amount of abuse but that seemed no deterrent. He had early learned to assimilate such treatment and well that he had. From the time when, as a tender child, his playmates had ridiculed him for his deformity, and "mimiced his limping walk," [1] 'til he died, a bitterly hated man, his life was riddled with defeats, reverses, and a never ceasing barrage of attacks.

Quitting York because of the unfriendly attitude of the County Bar Association, he had come to Gettysburg. Plodding along alone, nearly starving, it was unfortunate that his first opportunity to distinguish himself as a lawyer came in a case where the feelings of the entire community were angrily concluded against his client. [2] His staunch defense of the accused not only did not add to his popularity, but created a fertile soil in which the weeds of ugly slanders against him could flourish. Insults and humiliations cut deeply, but he never showed that he felt them.

He apparently resolved early in life to permit neither praise nor abuse to influence his course in the least. Always indifferent to personal popularity, frequently antagonizing his electorate without necessity, spurning utterly the politician's wiles to please his followers, he furnishes an intriguing study.

If a close friend would not support what Stevens viewed as a noble principle, he hesitated not a moment to turn upon him. When Bingham, one of his Radical co-workers, wanted to modify a reconstruction measure, Stevens harshly condemned him, saying for immemorial record, "In all this contest, I do not propose either to take his counsel, recognize his authority, or believe a word he says." [3] On the other hand, he would just as readily commend unstintingly an enemy. After his battle with Johnson had become a public matter, he paid a sincere tribute to the President with the words, "I honor his integrity, patriotism, courage and good intentions. He stood too firmly for the Union in the midst of dangers and sacrifices to allow me to doubt the purity of his wishes." [4]

Sometimes he appears unusually defiant of those about him, and even of his own constituents, as was the case when he led a minority opposition against repeal of the Pennsylvania School Bill after he and his co-assemblymen had been almost unanimously instructed to support it. At other times, he gives a near pathetic appearance of one who, courageously laboring for a principle, believes he is forever doomed to be hopelessly misunderstood.

He seems to have wanted the respect and good will of people, but indicates in subtle manner that such was more than unfortunate he, could expect. So stalwart, however, was his make-up, that nowhere is he heard to complain or seek sympathy. Whatever came in the line of attack upon him, whether deservedly or undeservedly, from fair opponent or coward, he received with adamant exterior, permitting none of it to swerve him from his way. Irretrievably handicapped in the unbending personality and ungracious presence that nature gave him, he distinguished himself in spite of them. A chaste honesty, accurately geared to a fine mind, overcame all that he lacked in the pleasantries, conventions, and diplomacies of life.

Ever unyielding, appearing always somehow to challenge, at times really obnoxious, engaging unrestrainedly in the kind of politics that engender vituperation, the inevitable resultants soon appeared.

Because his deadly counter attacks were so generally feared, few dared cross him openly. Nevertheless, occasionally someone tried it. But no foolhardy contender ever repeated his reckless act.

A new member of the Pennsylvania Legislature from Uniontown, who had heard of his reputation was anxious to engage in argument with him. He seized the first opportunity which came while the Gettysburgian was commenting on a measure before the Assembly. He interrupted to call out, "Mr. Speaker, the gentleman from Adams does not understand this Bill." Calmly, but without hesitation, Stevens turned toward him and in slow, clear voice, answered, "Oh! Very likely, very likely. Balaam's ass saw the angel when his master did not." [5] The challenger was heard no more.

On another occasion in Congress, Roscoe Conkling,

Reproduced from the Gettysburg College Eicholtz painting.

Stevens as his Legislative Career Opened in 1833

then a young man, attempted to chide him during one
of his serious speeches. Conkling had just come from
the barber shop adorned with a corkscrew curl, beauti-
fully arranged on his forehead. In the midst of
Stevens' speech, he imperiously demanded that Stevens
explain certain irrelevant collateral matter. The
speaker did not appreciate the interruption nor the
manner in which it was made. Turning to Conkling, his
resourceful mind immediately showed him the vulnerable point. "Young man," said he quietly, "unscrew
that curl so that you can get your feet flat on the floor,
and I'll talk to you." Sinking in his seat, young Conkling forgot what there was to talk about.[6]

None who knew him cared to invite such withering
rebuffs and those who opposed him politically or disliked him personally, fearing to meet him in verbal encounter, adopted a common but cowardly method of
combat. There were murmurings against him, ugly
stories, and vicious slanders. Before the Yankee lawyer
had been ten years in Gettysburg, he was accused of
every crime in the calendar from fornication to murder.

Long before he had become a candidate for county
office, he wrote the Governor of the State saying, "For
the last six or eight years, as the election approaches,
he[7] has regularly charged me by innuendoes and intan-
gible insinuation, with the crime of murder."[8] It was
but an example of the scandal mongers' art, and they
practiced untiringly and unceasingly upon him both
in and out of season, throughout his life, and even after
his death. Less than a year before he died, in a letter
to a friend, he summed up his unfortunate lot by stating, and no doubt correctly so, that few men "had re-

ceived more slanders or been charged with more vices or malignant crimes." [9]

And so, with a make-up that seemed to invite personal calumnies, Stevens' advance to the larger field of county politics in 1830, carried with it the incidental enlargement of the zone from which he must meet attack. The gates were now opened through which the political tides, ebbing and flowing throughout his life, were to bring their flotsam and jetsam of personal obloquy upon him. In hardly more than a year, the feeling generated against him by his Anti-Masonic position culminated in a violent newspaper attack which gave rise to the famous Lefever law suits and prosecutions, which are set forth in detail in the succeeding chapter on Anti-Masonry.

Strange it is that the crippled Yankee, even during the last five sick years of his life when accusations were most venomous, was never overcome. Still stranger it is that he never made the slightest attempt except in the Lefever and Hunter cases, to prevent the spread of the fiendish stories against him. "I have seldom noticed them," he wrote, "never to contradict them unless they affected my moral character aside from politics, or unless a contradiction was required by the interest of others." [10] The scandals must take care of themselves; his attention was given to his work.

His prodigious activities from 1830 up to his temporary retirement in 1842, make an impressive record. It was the period in American History when political conventions were in their hey-day. Old parties were breaking down and the people, in their efforts to discover foundations on which to build new ones, resorted

to the Convention method where free discussion could
be had and some attempt to crystallize opinions could
be made. During these twelve years, in addition to representing his county in the Lower House of the Legislature for six terms, and keeping up an extremely busy
law practice, he attended, as a delegate, no less than
sixteen state and national conventions, the Constitutional Convention of 1837, and made scores of political
addresses.

A reporter in Adams County remarked that his Lancaster County neighbor, James Buchanan, spent the
whole year in laborious preparation to make three or
four speeches in Congress, while Stevens in that time
made a hundred, each "abounding in wit as well as wisdom." [11]

In most of the conventions, especially the earlier ones,
he was able to dictate his ideas.[12] But as time moved,
opposition to him became better organized and frequently was strong enough to defeat him.[13]

Stevens cannot be recorded as the ardent advocate
of any party in his early days in Gettysburg. If he
is to be classified on the basis of complexion of political
views, then, of course, he must be deemed a Federalist.
In a law case in which they were opposing counsel in
1827, James Buchanan had advised him to support
Jackson for the Presidency, but Stevens never saw eye
to eye with Jackson, and remained aloof.

The first faint stirrings of the Anti-Masonic party
appealed to his democratic leanings, and although it was
a narrow position to stand in, Stevens adopted it. He
made enough of it in Adams County to obtain convey-
ance upon its ticket into the State Legislature in 1833,

and several succeeding years. But its platform was never an appealing one to cool minds, and although grounded on a principle of pure democracy, was too restricted to serve as party foundation in any large way or for any substantial time. In 1835, its existence in Pennsylvania was seriously threatened and it owed its extension of life there mainly to the prodigious work of Stevens.[14]

Keenly understanding the situation, he watched the infant Whig Party rapidly gain supporters, many of whom were moving from Anti-Masonic ranks. Between the Whigs and the Anti-Masons the struggle by that time was already well begun, and under the standard of the victor, would gather the various groups opposed to the Democratic, or as it was then called, Van Buren Party.

In essence, Stevens was probably a good Whig, but a situation had arisen that created an absolute bar to his joining the parade into Whig lines. Many of those leaders were Free Masons, and for him to support them would mean admission that he had not been sincere in his Anti-Masonic position. Furthermore, it involved the yielding up of a fight with what might be interpreted as a show of weakness, and that was not in him.

As early as 1829, he made contact with gubernatorial candidate Ritner. Although badly defeated in the elections of that year, it is significant that Stevens' county of Adams went for him. The same was true in larger measure in the succeeding election of 1832, in which Ritner was defeated by but three thousand votes.

When Stevens went next year as one of the representatives of his County to the Pennsylvania Legislature, he lost no time in becoming active there. The House Journal fairly bristles with his name and the reports of his work. It is indicative that one of the very first matters in which he became interested, even before his Anti-Masonic work, was the cause of education.[15]

His single standing committee appointment was the one on the Judicial System, but that did not restrict him. In the few months that the Legislature was in session, he presented hundreds of petitions and proposed legislation in fields varying from soldiers' pensions and divorces to Orphan's Court procedure and depositories for the public monies.

It was in this session that he inaugurated in the Legislature the Anti-Masonic Party's campaign against Free Masonry. He was regularly returned with swelling majorities to the next two sessions, and in his second term, made his memorable defense of the public school system which immortalized his name in the educational records of Pennsylvania.

In 1836, lulled into a sense of safety by his prior majorities and the further fact that his opponent was not thought to be a strong one, he suffered his first and only defeat at the hands of an electorate. He awoke too late to find that he had been defeated by less than twenty votes.[16] Later in commenting upon it, he said he "had never been defeated in an election except by a nobody." A month later, however, he retrieved his political leadership through election to the State Constitutional Convention as a delegate from Adams.

The year of 1836 was a dull one for him, in spite of the fact that it was a Presidential year. With Anti-Masonic support on the wane, and Clay, Webster, and

Harrison in the field opposing Van Buren, Stevens was puzzled. Clay was everywhere known as a Mason and Stevens had attacked him as such. Moreover, he differed fundamentally with Clay on the slavery question. Webster seemed too inclined to compromise in what Stevens thought were matters of principle.

Late in 1835, he had opened a correspondence with Harrison to learn his position on Anti-Masonry. He asked the candidate two succinct questions: first, "Do you believe that Free Masonry and all other secret oath bound societies are evils and inconsistent with the genius and safety of Republican Government?" Second, "Will you join your Anti-Masonic fellow citizens in the use of all constitutional, fair and honorable means for their final and effectual suppression?"

Harrison answered that he "believed in Anti-Masonic principles, but although" he was "far from asserting that evils arising from Masonry do not form a proper subject for the deliberations and actions of some constituted authorities of the country," yet he "was certain that there exists no such power, either in the whole Government of the United States or in any of its Departments, and that the attempt to exercise it would constitute a usurpation of power, pregnant if tolerated by the people with mischiefs infinitely more fatal than those which it was intended to remedy." [17] This reply was entirely unsatisfactory to Stevens, and there is some reason for believing that he was tempted to oppose Harrison and support Webster.[18] However, he seemed to lose interest in the campaign and took no assertive part for any candidate.

Through the panic year of 1837, he busied himself

half-heartedly with the Constitutional Convention, which is treated in a separate chapter. Here he met his first real repudiation. It came because of utter inability or positive refusal on his part to take men into his confidence and deal with them personally and individually and that trait burdened him through his whole public life. He just could not or would not sit down quietly with one or two, tell them his program, and ask their support. It was not his way. He surely knew how tremendously advantageous and effective it was to be supported by immediate and scattered approvals over the Floor, once he had proposed a course of action to a body. But prodigally, he would have none of it.

He preferred to keep his own counsel, trust nobody [19] and when the time came, suddenly launch his plan. This he generally supported with a short, forceful, and well-prepared speech. Because of his blunt manner, much of what he would do often appeared inconsistent or radical, and it was not strange that uninformed as they were, even his close friends and followers frequently hesitated to rally to him. This strong-headed determination to thrust his ideas before a body of delegates or representatives with absolutely no preparation for reception, was an innate weakness of the man and one which cost him dearly.

Frustrated in the Convention, but not vanquished, he returned to Adams County as candidate for the State Legislature in 1837. His organization there stood him in good stead and by a clear-cut victory, he wiped out the stigma of the prior year's defeat. His friend Ritner was still Governor and if he were Ritner's Dictator, as the opposition newspapers so frequently contended, he would enjoy the fruits of it at the State Capitol. Back to his Anti-Masonic fight in the forum of the House, even more assertive than before and engaging a stronger opposition. The catastrophe of the next two years at Harrisburg where he met an all engulfing defeat, was cast out of the Legislature and nearly murdered, is told in the story of the Buckshot War.

But 1840 was another Presidential year and political defeat was but an incident in a politician's life. In 1836, he had supported Harrison for want of a more fitting candidate and carried his county for him. It was said that his support at that time was half-hearted, but there could be no doubt about it now. So vigorous was he in the campaign that the Van Buren newspapers concentrated their attack upon him. One of these at Harrisburg grew so scurrilous that he had the editors arrested for criminal libel.[20]

The paper had accused Stevens of taking part "in the administration of the Sacrament to the followers of Old Tip," in a meeting of the Tippycanoe Club at Gettysburg, which the clubfoot lawyer had organized. Furthermore, it stated that he had taken part in blasphemous "Tippycanoe prayers." It is a curious note in Stevens' life that he could stand any kind of abuse and would tolerate having anything said about him except where it affected his religious beliefs.[21]

There is little doubt that this reaction was closely coupled and incident to his tender feelings for his mother. She was a very religious woman and kept in contact with the doings of Thaddeus through the Pennsylvania newspapers. Nothing would have hurt her more than to think of her son as a blasphemer.

Stevens prepared the case carefully. Democratic friends of the editors were fearful of a conviction, claiming that "the man from Gettysburg" was "prosecutor, witness and counsel," and that "the Judge was his political and personal friend and companion, and the jury his Anti-Masonic lead-supporters and admirers." [22]

The authorities lost no time in calling the case for trial. The accused plead not guilty, a jury was called and sworn, and the witnesses were in Court ready to testify. At that moment, counsel for the defendants stepped forth, exhibiting, to the surprise of everyone present, and the utter chagrin of Stevens, a full pardon of the alleged offense from the Free-Mason Governor of the Commonwealth. [23]

The procedure was unique, to say the least, and although Stevens attempted to attack it, he got nowhere. The Harrison newspapers created quite a stir in their unfavorable comment of the Executive's action, but the Democratic journals supported him, claiming that he had good precedent in the matter. [24] Less partisan newspapers considered the Governor's untimely intervention arbitrary, on the ground that he had arrested proceedings at law and prejudged the case. [25] Stevens passed the incident as merely corroborating his oft-repeated accusation that a Mason could be counted upon to extricate from trouble his brother, whether right or wrong.

But Harrison was elected and his Adams County majority was more than double that of 1836, in spite of his refusal to take the positive stand against secret societies which Stevens demanded. However, the Commoner had a real reason for giving an whole-hearted support to him in 1840. While the Whig National Convention was meeting in Harrisburg in December of 1839, to choose from among Clay, Harrison and Scott a Presidential candidate Harrison sent an autographed letter to Stevens, voluntarily proposing that if he should be nominated and elected President, Stevens would be made a member of his Cabinet.[26] Not only was Harrison nominated by the Convention, but it was brought about largely through the Gettysburgian's influence.[27]

Stevens relied on the promise and gave all that was in him to the General's campaign. He neither saw nor heard from Harrison from the date he received the letter until the inauguration. Of strictest honor in matters of promise and pledge, he expected as much as he gave. After election, having the word of the President-elect in writing, he saw no reason why further assurances should be asked. So oddly secretive was he that he never even mentioned the matter to his close friend Burrowes who headed a Pennsylvania delegation which went to Washington for the sole purpose of urging the appointment of Stevens to a cabinet position.

That Stevens wanted the office cannot be doubted. Having an absolute confidence in the soldier President he probably thought of it as already within his grasp. As is always the case, there were at the time several minor Pennsylvania aspirants for a place in the new Cabinet. However, all were close to Stevens and had he gone to them and shown the letter, he in all probability would have obtained their willing withdrawals. But his unbending and unconfiding nature permitted no such procedure. Not only was he silent and seemingly indifferent; he was positively injurious to his own cause.

Wholly without excuse he permitted an open warfare to break out between himself and his former friends.

Penrose, former stalwart of his, labelled Stevens a "bold, bad man," and Stevens in turn, through his Gettysburg *Star,* referred to the Pennsylvania Senate over which Penrose presided, as a "pie-bald Senate, the rottenest piece of human architecture ever thrown together." [28]

In due time Harrison announced his official family. The Pennsylvanian's name was not there. The place had gone to Francis Granger of New York. Stevens' disappointment nearly overwhelmed him. He had relied upon the agreement volunteered by a man who was made the Chief Executive of the Nation. That man had broken his word. And nothing could be done about it. Just how Harrison reconciled his conduct in the matter, if he ever attempted to do so, has never been disclosed. He knew all the facts,[29] was in the key position, and regardless of what was happening in Pennsylvania, certainly should have acted in a bigger and fairer way to Stevens.

He had pledged his solemn word to the man; the Gettysburgian had unstintingly fulfilled his part; President Harrison deliberately and without notice, breached his agreement. Years afterward, Stevens attributed Harrison's action to the influence of Clay and Webster.

It was rumored at the time that as a consolation, the Pennsylvanian "had been tendered a foreign mission," [30] but if true, nothing ever came of it.

Harrison died a month after his inauguration and Tyler succeeded him. Because of vehement opposition to the new President, Stevens immediately took up the cause of General Winfield Scott. That the election was three years off did not seem to matter.

He went to work vigorously. It was said that through his Gettysburg *Star,* he even proposed "that the Whigs and Anti-Masons of the Union hold a Convention in Baltimore in the early part of next summer to instruct Captain Tyler to resign." [31]

At any rate, under date of October 20, 1841, Stevens wrote General Scott saying that "by resolution of citizens of this County who are desirous of electing you to the Presidency, it is made the duty of myself . . . and others to present your claims to the people of this Commonwealth." He asked the General to send him "in confidence" a short biography of himself setting forth "mainly incidents" of "greatest charm for the people" so that some campaign literature could be made up and circulated. [32]

Scott replied on November first, saying that he had already sent "a little draft circular," adding, "I see evidences of your power in many and important quarters. On account of many friends, more than my own, I hope to do nothing that may not be for the best; and in matters not involving high principles, I shall always be found sufficiently docile and practicable." [33] In another letter of November 4, Scott explained his attitude "in respect to rotation or removals of office holders," saying that he "would retain no political opponent in office who had not a very high degree of merit—taking care not to bring into the same office . . . too many green hands at once—that is to say, I would turn out gradually political opponents of mediocrity for political friends of superior merit." [34]

On November 15, at a meeting of the friends of the General held at Harrisburg, Stevens was appointed Chairman of the Scott State Central Committee.[35] The Gettysburg *Compiler,* commenting upon this selection says, "This settles the matter beyond all shadow of doubt that General Scott will be the opposition candidate for President in this State and that the Whippables (Whigs) must support him—they dare not go contrary to the wishes of Mr. Stevens. His will is their law; and like obsequious menials, they must obey."

Scott remained in communication with Stevens, discussing political plans and elaborating his idea of the distribution of federal patronage through a considerable correspondence. In spite of his being "oppressed with official honors," he sometimes wrote Stevens two long letters in the same day.

During the year, Stevens continued to organize Scott meetings throughout a number of counties in southern and southeastern Pennsylvania, bending his every effort to drawing the Whig support solidly behind the General. While engaged in the work, Stevens moved his home, but this interfered in no way with the state-wide Presidential campaign which he led.

The year before, over the protest of his friends, he had refused to be a candidate for the State Legislature. He was then giving full faith to Harrison's offer and concentrating his energies upon the Presidential campaign to the exclusion of his own candidacy. But that dream had turned to ashes. The next year, salvaging what was left for him politically, he accepted the office of Legislator in lieu of the lost Cabinet position.

While in Harrisburg, the conviction that he must

move from Gettysburg shaped itself. Many circumstances demanded it and with little comment, in the
summer of 1842, he quit Gettysburg for larger fields.
Past fifty years of age, he cut himself off irrevocably
from a good law practice and political leadership there
on the chance of finding a more lucrative and better
future in Lancaster.

This change of home, requiring abundance of courage, was one of the bravest and most intelligent acts of
his life.

BOOK TWO
CRUSADER

THADDEUS STEVENS

The Old Commoner at the Outbreak of the War

BOOK TWO—CRUSADER

I

ANTI-MASONRY

FOR ten years after locating in Gettysburg Stevens was known only as a local attorney. He first achieved State-wide and to some extent National prominence as a crusader in the cause of Anti-Masonry.

By the year 1800, Free Masonry had made itself a power in the political life of England and on the Continent. Naturally its foes were neither inactive nor silent. In 1798, a libellous volume against it was published in England, professing to set forth its secret ceremonies and oaths. The latter were regarded by many as being more binding upon the member than judicial oaths, and it was charged that a Mason would protect a brother Mason even against the interests of the community and the Government.

By the end of the first quarter of the last century, the Lodge in this country counted as members a majority of outstanding men of the Nation. Rumblings against the Order were heard; some politically inspired, but most of them expressions of sincere conviction. As early as January, 1821, the Presbyterian Church Synod of Pittsburgh condemned Free Masonry "as unfit for professing Christians." [1]

Office seekers were quick to capitalize the situation. Frequently a non-Mason used an Anti-Masonic position to attack a Masonic opponent. However, their assaults upon the Order were sporadic and unorganized. With little to concentrate upon that interested the pub-

[49]

lic, the condemnations seemed hardly more than politically inspired speeches and the beratings of reformers.

But in September, 1826, a happening in New York State gave the Anti-Masons their long desired opportunity, and they seized it eagerly. One William Morgan, a Free-Mason of Batavia, disappeared. According to the Anti-Masons, he was about to expose the Order through publication of its secrets and oaths. They charged that he had been kidnapped and "done away with" by members of the Batavia Lodge. This, of course, was vigorously denied by the members, but the fact remained that Morgan had mysteriously vanished and was never heard of again.

One Masonic explanation of the disappearance was that it was caused by David C. Miller, a fellow conspirator who was to print the exposé, and John Davids and Russel Dyer, who were to finance the enterprise. The three had given Morgan their one-half million dollar bond in the matter, guaranteeing his share in the contemplated profits.[2]

At any rate, the incident was given great newspaper attention. It was heatedly discussed and throughout northeastern United States created extraordinary excitement. In a surprisingly short time, the long repressed resentments against the Order flared forth. Meetings of citizens were held in which groups were appointed to examine into the doings of the Fraternity. "Committees of Safety" were selected to protect the communities from it. Charges were made that it was unrepublican and subversive of our form of Government, and that it contained the seeds of a movement to dominate politics, imperil the freedom of American citizenry and destroy its equality before the law. By the very nature of the movement the Order was placed upon the defensive from the outset and could do practically nothing to stem the tide of animosity that surged over it.

The parties involved in the Morgan episode were tried in the New York State Courts and some received minor sentences, but the murder charge was never proven.[3] To the student of today it appears that the trials, accounts of which were widely published, aroused more interest and caused more excitement than the disappearance itself.

Public sentiment against the Order became so strong that a political party formed upon it. Naturally it made its appearance in New York State where, in 1827, it polled about 33,000 votes which increased the next year to 70,000.

There had been some agitation in Pennsylvania against Masonry as early as 1820. Stimulated by the Morgan incident, the movement in 1828 had numerous adherents. Pamphlets were published, speakers lectured on the subject, and even newspapers were established to promulgate the Anti-Masonic platform. The Anti-Masonic *Herald,* established by Theophilus Fenn, later State printer, and Dr. Thomas W. Veazey at New Holland, Lancaster County, in June, 1828, was the first party newspaper to make its appearance in the State.[4] Others followed closely.[5]

The party made its first formal appearance in the Keystone State in 1828, when William Heister of Lancaster County ran as a candidate for Congress on its ticket.[6]

Because the Federalist Party at the time was rapidly

disintegrating, many of its constituents joined the new group along with a lesser number of Democrats. Among the first in Pennsylvania to appear in the new movement was Stevens. Due to his early position as a Federalist, he had little in common with the principles of the Democratic Party and was in no personal sympathy with its local leaders. To him the indictments laid against the Masonic Order, and he believed them, were fuel to the flame of deep seated convictions, which made him fight to extremity all that tended to human inequality.

He did not champion the cause of Anti-Masonry nor adopt it. Its expressed purpose was an inherent part of his being, which until then had showed but slightly. It was there, strong, steadfast, and unalterable, awaiting opportunity for expression. It was impossible for him to take any position except that of a zealot to advance it. If there was one conviction in him, it was the unswerving one that any artificial distinction between mankind making for discriminating preferment on any ground but merit alone, was fundamentally wrong.

It was the key to his life behaviour. Nothing can give a more genuine picture of his work than to sum it up as a crusade of five decades to eliminate unjust class distinctions among men and establish equal rights, equal punishments, and equal opportunities for all.

True, the new party presented itself at a most seasonable time for him. With Federalist disintegration and an impossibility of association with the Democrats, satisfactory political affiliation without the appearance of another party would have been difficult. The Anti-Masonic movement fitted perfectly.

When Stevens entered the new party, he did it as was characteristic of him, earnestly, vigorously, and unrestrainedly. In his denunciations of the Order, he was outspoken, strenuous, and at times vitriolic. In a very short time he had antagonized the Masons of Adams and all neighboring counties.

In the bitter strife of his early Anti-Masonic days, he was frequently charged with having become the violent crusader that he was because he had been refused admission to the Order. These stories persist to this day in York, Adams, and Lancaster Counties of Pennsylvania, and in at least one reputable writing it is actually stated that he was denied membership in the Lodge.[7]

Diligent search of the complete records of the Masonic Lodges, both locally and in the Grand Body, shows no entry of Stevens' application for admission. It can be authoritatively stated that if he ever sought membership, it was not done formally. It is possible that oral inquiries were made by him and a refusal returned, but the answer to this seems beyond recovery.

By his forceful advocacy of Anti-Masonry, he soon placed his county of Adams in that party column politically. In the Fall elections of 1828, he carried it for Adams for President as opposed to Jackson, when but three other counties of the State voted that way. This was his first engagement of county-wide moment.

He early made known his opposition to Free-Mason Governor Wolfe and in 1829 again asserted his political strength by carrying his county for Ritner for Governor against him.

Stevens had not confined his Anti-Masonic advocacy

[53]

of Ritner to Adams County, but had campaigned in
the several adjoining ones. Although defeated, Ritner
polled 49,000 votes and carried seventeen counties, receiving a heavy vote in seven more.[8] The election
showed beyond question that a new and energetic party
had appeared in Pennsylvania. Its sudden rise seemed
phenomenal. But under the surface, currents had been
moving for some time which, when united in a common
flow and brought to the surface, appeared remarkable
in dimensions.[9]

Advocates of temperance had opposed the Masonic
Order, charging that it used wine in many of its ceremonies and thereby spread the drinking habit. Some
Protestant churches opposed it, believing the Order
attempted to usurp its place in religious instruction,
was blasphemous and sacriligeous in its rites. Moreover, a feeling was gaining foothold among the masses
that it was dangerously undemocratic. Stevens, with
a few lieutenants, skillfully organized and propagated
these forces.

When their combined political effect was expressed,
it astounded many. An indication that the party was
strong enough to assert itself in the Legislature was
evident in the passage of a law removing the Masonic
Hall in Philadelphia from tax exemption. The measure
was carried in the Lower House by a vote of fifty-three
to thirty-one.[10]

*   *   *   *   *

From the seeds which he sowed in his early Anti-
Masonic campaign grew Steven's first crop of enemies.
Because he was the local leader and a forceful one, he

became the center of assault for newspapers of opposing political views.

Aware from the outset that a newspaper was necessary to advance the party, he assembled a group in 1829 for the purpose of establishing one in Gettysburg. Offers were made to subsidize the two existing there, but both refused.[11] Unperturbed and with the financial help of his first substantial client, George Himes, who lived near Gettysburg, he immediately launched the Anti-Masonic *Star* which continued as the party mouthpiece as long as Stevens remained in Adams County.

All local newspapers were openly partisan, not too modest to laud their own cause, nor too backward to denounce the others'. It was the era when men and movements were assailed in the daily journals, and it was not unusual to see caustic and sometimes violent personal assaults made through the medium of a published, unsigned letter. An example was one appearing in the Democratic Gettysburg Compiler of June 21, 1831, directed at Stevens, which resulted in his bringing both civil and criminal suits against the Editor. The cases were of more than local interest because the charges and the defenses raised covered the disputed ground between Masons and Anti-Masons. The story is enlightening of the time and involved Stevens as a principal.

Having entered wholeheartedly into a cause close to his very being, he did not confine his politico-anti-masonic activities to Pennsylvania. On the fourth of June, 1831, at the invitation of "several citizens of Hagerstown, Maryland," he delivered an address to a large group of his partisans who had met there. The meeting, which was a public one, naturally attracted many of opposite views who were curious to hear him. His thesis contended that Free Masonry was inconsistent with pure morals, true religion and the permanent existence of liberty. The only way to suppress the evil was "by opposing it politically."

He began with the Morgan incident in New York. Next he set forth at length what he said were the obligations of the first three degrees of Masonry.

Stevens' verbal bombs had jagged edges, well calculated to tear into whatever they landed upon. Because of the way he said it, friend, foe and neutral had to notice what he said.

In one of them he charged, "the presiding officer personated the Almighty God, while the hood-winked candidate is made to represent Moses! And then, amid the lurid glimmerings of their midnight den, this feeble band of lowly reptiles aspire to enact the sublime and terrific scene before which mortals veiled their faces and Mt. Sinai trembled to its center."

Describing an alleged scene in the Knight Templar's degree, he said, "twelve tapers were placed in a triangle. The candidate was made to extinguish one of them, which he was told represented Judas Iscariot, who betrayed his Master, and that such would be the fate of all those who betrayed the secrets of Free Masonry. The chief officer led the candidate into what he called the Sepulchre of our Saviour—read to him several passages from Scripture—brought him forth, and showed him Jesus ascending into Heaven, by and through the influence of Masonry!

"Then," continued the Pennsylvanian, "the candidate was made to drink five libations of wine, the last of which was administered out of a Human Skull!"

History presented but "one parallel to this revolting atrocity. When Cataline, with a band of profligate associates, conspired against the lives and liberty of Rome, they sacrificed a Man, and ate of his flesh, as a pledge of their secrecy and fidelity! No other case, where the objects and the pledge are so nearly allied, can be found to disgrace the annals of barbarity!"

Another charge was made that in the Royal Arch degree, they swore "to extricate each other from every difficulty, whether right or wrong," and "to keep each other's secrets, murder and treason not excepted." To him this was laying the axe at the root of the tree of morality. It was the perversion of all social principles; the breaking up of the elements of society.

It meant to Stevens that the Lodge was a chartered band of lawless incendiaries, invited to the commission of crime by immunity from punishment. A corporate body, associated for the purpose of bidding defiance to the law and mocking at justice! Free Masonry was not only "immoral and irreligious," it was inconsistent with permanent Liberty! If they intended nothing but legitimate and fair objects, there could be no cause for secrecy; no one would molest them for pursuing such purposes.

Secrecy, therefore, was not only the cause, but the evidence of iniquity in such self-constituted assemblies. He accused them of swearing "to promote each other's political preferment," made the sweeping charge that "four-sixths of all the high and profitable offices in the State and general Governments are held by Masons";

[57]

that "more than twenty of the twenty-four States are governed by the Fraternity"; that "your President is Grandmaster of Tennessee, the Secretary of State is Great-Grand High Priest of the Union"; that "all the heads of departments are of the same Order and that no one is permitted to be nominated for the presidency but a Mason." He mentioned Henry Clay by name to note that he "is the present Grand Master of Kentucky."

"Surely," said he, "they do effectually promote each other's political preferment."

Moreover, "signs of distress" were used in court rooms by culprits, which robbed "justice of its due and honesty of its rights." The people should refuse to trust adhering Masons with any office of trust or profit until they were shorn of their locks and became like other men. "Let the means by which they seek to monopolize all power, be the cause of their defeat. Turn their own weapons against them. They cannot complain. Haman was hanged on the same gallows which he had erected for another and none ever condemned the sentence."

He exhorted his hearers not to be afraid of joining the Anti-Masons, but wanted "no hireling forces." Those who addressed themselves to this warfare, must do it from love of country. "Who," he asked, "would not rather sleep in honor in the Spartan's grave, side by side with Leonidas, and his little band of martyred patriarchs, than ride triumphant o'er a prostrate world with the principles and company of Neroes and Calligulas?"

The people would act in time. With the faith of the true Crusader, he was certain all would be righted.

Truth and justice would triumph, and the "walls of this unholy city fall before the 'sword of the Lord and Gideon.' "[12]

In the issue of the Gettysburg Compiler for June 21, 1831, editor and owner Lefever printed, under the head of "communicated," an unsigned letter dated June 12, which had as its subject, "Stevens' Maryland Speech." The orator was described as "a stout man, about forty years of age, with bald head and lame." You had "but to see the man and hear him speak in private or public to be satisfied, as I am, that he is incapable of feeling a-right upon that, or any other matter." His speech was the worst "compound of vile slander, barefaced falsehood, and pandemoniac malignity against a large and respectable portion of our citizens that ever fell from the lips of any man."

But "any men who attempt to change our course, must come to us with pure hearts and clean hands. If they talk to us of crimes and murder, we must know that they have no blood on their skirts.[13] If a change in politics or religion be their object, we must have assurance that they are honest. Those must not come, in whose wake is heard the wail of the widow and orphan, or rioting in the spoils of the unfortunate."[14]

The writer rejoiced that the men who got up the proscription could not claim Pennsylvania as the place of their birth. They had been imported from that part of our country "proverbial for tricks and gauds and vendors of the most worthless and deceptive of commodities; flannel sausages, wooden nutmegs and horn gun-flints." The name of Washington was "enough to bury their whole faction in the dust."[15]

After reading the libel, Stevens did not hesitate. On the twenty-third of June, he filed an action in trespass on the case against Lefever, for damages. A criminal suit was also immediately instituted, charging the editor with criminal libel. The latter moved swiftly. Lefever was convicted on August 24; sentenced to pay a fine of fifty dollars and costs, and undergo imprisonment for three calendar months in the Adams County jail.

But the confinement was soon ended. A few days after he entered prison, George Wolfe, Free-Mason Governor of Pennsylvania, as Stevens said in his paper, "extricated his brother from difficulty" by pardoning him.[16] Governor Wolfe would hear from Stevens later.

However, the latter believed, as did many others, that Lefever who was easily led, had published the libel at the inducement of certain of his friends who were Stevens' enemies, having himself, little or no feeling in the matter.

The civil suit for damages dragged for years. There were three counts in the Statement of Claim or "Narr" as it was then called. To two of these defendant pled justification by which the truth of the allegations were put directly at issue.

The case attracted more than passing attention. Able counsel appeared on both sides. Commissions were taken in five different states, and the action was finally called for trial in August of 1835. The jury found for the defendant on the second and third counts, but for the plaintiff Stevens, in the amount of Eighteen hundred dollars damages on the first count.[17]

The Anti-Mason was more desirous of learning the author of the libel, however, than he was of recovering

money damages. Accordingly, after judgment against
the Editor was entered, he filed of record a proposal
that if Lefever would give up the name of the person
who wrote the letter, he would "exact no more of the
verdict against defendant than will cover actual expenses." Weak-willed though he might have been, Lefever was firm enough not to yield. After some newspaper communications between the parties, the matter
was dropped and Stevens never learned the name of
the actual libellant.[18]

The vindication which the clubfoot lawyer received
in the two cases seemed enough to satisfy him, for after
buying in Lefever's property under the Sheriff's execution, he magnanimously left it with him and assigned
the balance of the judgment remaining unsatisfied, to
Lefever's wife.[19]

In February of 1830, a State Convention of the new
Anti-Masonic party was held at Harrisburg to elect
delegates for a national gathering. Future Governor
Joseph Ritner presided and Stevens was present for his
county.[20] His formal appearance as a leader of the
Party was looked upon as "an event of greatest significance to the cause in Pennsylvania." [21]

That year he was unsparingly active in many counties
in behalf of the movement which was now becoming of
importance politically. In the Fall, his party arrived.
From the elections it harvested six Congressmen, four
State Senators, and twenty-seven members of the
House. It claimed to have polled fifty-four thousand
votes.[22] Anti-Masonry that year furnished a rallying
ground for independent opponents of the Democratic
Party, and in addition, had some effective liaison with

the Clay adherents.[23] When the Pennsylvania House organized, Ner Middleswarth, Anti-Masonic colleague of Stevens, was easily elected speaker.[24]

In September, 1831, the young Party introduced an institution novel to American politics by meeting in National Convention to select candidates. William Wirt was made its nominee for the Presidency, and Stevens' close friend Amos Ellmaker, was chosen for the Vice-Presidency. Only ten states sent representatives and if its success must be measured solely by the national interest shown, it was anything but startling. But it is important in American History in a way little reckoned by the delegates. The National Convention idea to pick candidates was sooner or later adopted by all other parties. It was the single contribution of the Anti-Masonic Party to the formal political procedure of the Nation.

In spite of the publicity given the National Meeting with its attendant promise of country-wide significance, the Party in the Fall [25] was able to elect only two State Senators and twenty Assemblymen.[26] It was an off year for the new politicos and even with all his effort, Stevens was unable to carry his county for the Anti-Masonic ticket.

It was a time of natural reaction to the new cause, and assisted by a general dissatisfaction with the Democratic national administration which revivified the National Republican Party, substantial numbers of votes that had priorly been Anti-Masonic moved to Republican columns.

During 1831-32, little of importance developed in or from the ranks of the crusaders. The leaders went ahead with their organization, establishing newspapers, especially in German sections of the State, and distributing their party literature. They kept in close touch with their partisans through local meetings, where spirited party speeches were the order.[27]

It was to be expected, that the terrific efforts of the Anti-Masons would show results sooner or later. In Pennsylvania, it began in 1830. Local Masonic Lodges began to disband. Notices of dissolution were frequent. The one at Gettysburg,[28] organized in January of 1825, was able to survive only until December of 1832.

It was customary for the suspending Lodge to issue a statement and many of these showed on the part of the Order, a highminded and unselfish attitude. They explained their action as taken not because of any truth in the charges, but solely in the interest of the public welfare. For example, the members of the Gettysburg Lodge stated that to avoid strife, they had "felt it their duty to yield to solicitations of their friends and the opinion of those who were honestly opposed to the Institution." [29]

The crusaders kept at their work unrelentingly. By 1838, over seventy warrants for Lodges in Pennsylvania had been vacated, so that only forty-six were left. In New York State, upwards of four hundred had been dissolved, which left a bare third of the original number in operation.[30]

In 1832, Ritner was again a candidate on the new Party ticket for the governorship against Wolfe, but lost election by some 3,000 votes.[31] In the offices of Congressmen, State Senators and Assemblymen, the Anti-Masons held approximately their previous position,[32] but suffered a severe defeat in their presidential vote, Jackson obtaining 24,000 votes more than his opponents. Stevens was able to hold Adams and adjoining Franklin County in line, but only seven other counties in Pennsylvania remained in their company.

The set-back gave great concern, and various devices were used in explaining it. Chief among them was what they called the "all prevailing popularity of Jackson." In spite of concentrated efforts made upon them, "the German Anti-Masons deserted their own electoral nominees and went to the polls hurrahing for 'Sheneral Shackson as in 1824 and 1828.'"[33] Other reasons ascribed were the late date of the Clay ticket withdrawal, and desertion of Clay men.

In that election, the blow had been struck which marked the beginning of the end of Anti-Masonry in New York State, where it had enjoyed a remarkable strength, and in practically every other state except Pennsylvania. In spite of the Southwicks and Weeds, Anti-Masonry outside the Keystone State lacked a leader powerful enough to save it. In Pennsylvania, Stevens stolidly absorbed the blow for the new party and determinedly carried on. Manifesting utter confidence in its principles, he stood on its platform as candidate for the Legislature.

Ignoring the party defeat and the apathy of its constituents, with coolly bitter and persistently aggressive campaigning, he whipped his followers in Adams County into action and emerged successful in his first real campaign. He had now reached the stage in his political career where the record is more nearly accurate and considerably more comprehensive.

Stevens
vs
Lefever

No 21 of August Term 1831 —

Th. Stevens proposes to Defendant, that if he will give up the name of the author of the Libel or which said was bought in this case, and will ... against him as a witness and testify; and if said author be a man of fair standing and responsibility, and resident in the County of Adams, said Stevens will meet as now of the ... = dict against Defendant then will come actual ...

August 27th 1835

T. Stevens

From the original court records.

Having Convicted Lefever, Publisher of the Libel Upon Him, Stevens Attempted to Identify the Author of it

In Harrisburg, as soon as the House cleared itself of perfunctory details, he lost no time in opening the Anti-Masonic matter. Surrounded by the falling ruins of his party in neighboring states, he still appeared undismayed. It had been a struggle to get his fight into the Legislative Halls of a great State and now there, he could not falter. It required courage to introduce as he did on February 10, his famous resolution for a committee to "inquire into the expediency" of making Masonic affiliation a good cause for peremptory challenge of jurors in all cases where one of the parties was a Lodge member and the other not. He would disqualify a Masonic Judge from acting in a case where one and only one of the litigants was his fraternal brother, and apply restrictions upon a Free Mason Sheriff in the summoning of jurors. To give effect to his resolution, he asked that the "committee have power to send for persons and papers." [34]

Newcomer there, his method was novel. He made no long address. He neither rehearsed the party arguments nor reviewed its history. His short supporting speech was strongly worded, terse and pointed. But the House was not ready for such stringent action, and his motion was lost by a vote of 31 to 45. Astute enough to know from the outset that his proposal would not carry, he made use of it to designate of record the position of each member of the House. His strategy was to force opponents into the open. He believed that a principle as democratic as the Anti-Masonic one must appeal to the common people and if they could be won, their influence would finally force the legislators to his side. He received some support for his motion from

the Whigs, but charged the Democrats with shielding
the Masons from his attack.

In one of his speeches, he said the vote would show
who and what party were the protectors, the fosterers
and guardians of Free Masonry. Those who opposed
the resolution could never afterwards, "by all their
sophistry and denials, persuade a watchful and intelligent people that they are not the Masonic Party." [35]

He waited just a week after the decisive defeat of
February 10 [36] and then tried a skillful parliamentary
move. He presented "three memorials from citizens of
this Commonwealth" seeking the same end as his lost
resolution. Inspired, no doubt, if not really drawn by
himself, they were in the terms he wished. Under the
regular procedure of the House, they were referred to
the committee of which he was chairman.[37] He saw to
it that they got immediate attention. His committee,
after outlining a plan, attempted to exercise the power
granted "to send for persons and papers." Following
the accepted method, it "gave a praecipe for a subpoena for witnesses to the clerk of the House to be by
him issued and . . . signed by the speaker." All of
which was at least annoying to the Conservative groups.
But there was a way to stop him; the subpoena was refused.[38]

Undismayed, on February 24, he presented similar
petitions and again asked permission "to send for persons and papers." Fighting almost singlehandedly, the
odds against him were tremendous. The House was
cold and haughty. With no one to second it, he withdrew his motion. Nevertheless, his persistence was
alarming his adversaries. Something must be done to

check him. The withdrawal of his motion gave an opportunity.

Patterson, Democrat, began the counter-attack by presenting a petition for a committee to inquire "into the evils of Anti-Masonry and the extent and influence of its injustice and wicked operations upon the community." Oddly enough, as soon as he sat down, Stevens moved that it "be referred to a committee with power to send for persons and papers." [39] He had asked the subpoena power for his committee investigating Masonry. It had been refused. Everyone knew no real investigation could be conducted without it. So with eminent fairness he would grant it to opponents, even though they had denied it to him. [40]

The attitude of the House toward the whole matter was one of extreme caution. When the Anti-Masons having been refused subpoena power, asked permission "to take the testimony of such witnesses as may voluntarily appear before them," the House refused even that. [41]

Denied the means of getting any first hand testimony, Stevens' efforts seemed entirely nullified. But he could always salvage something. In dogged earnestness, he reported for the committee as best he could on March 20. What he filed read more like a piece of propaganda than a committee report. It was an excellent brief for campaign purposes. Petitions had been presented to the Legislature, setting forth the belief that the Masonic Fraternity was associated for purposes "inconsistent with the equal rights and privileges which are the birthright of every freeman." Members were bound together by "secret obligations and oaths, illegal, immoral, blasphemous, subversive of all public law and hostile to the pure administration of justice."

When the committee on the matter met, "the members could not hesitate as to their right to do that for which they had been especially appointed. Nor did they suppose," Stevens' report very reasonably continued, "that they had been commanded by the House to perform such duty without being clothed with the power asked for by the petitioners and indispensably necessary and incidental to its faithful and intelligent discharge."

The refusal of the House to grant the subpoena power was a plain intimation of that Body's unwillingness to have the secret designs, principles, and practices of that institution authentically established and made known to the people. Bound by that refusal and treating it with the respect which was "always due the wish of this Body," the committee felt themselves constrained to make use of whatever proof was accessible, even though taken in other States, to develop the Lodge's alleged iniquities and establish the identity of Pennsylvania and New York Masonry.

Stevens' enemies in the House thought they had strangled his inquisitors by denuding it of the power to investigate. But he constructed his report so skillfully that he was able to incorporate testimony taken in other jurisdictions, certainly as damaging as any that could be gotten in Pennsylvania. And all this he did in such a plausible way that it appeared wholly permissible. Defending his committee's procedure, he said it had hoped to examine the Masonic members of this House and the Cabinet. And Stevens went to high places.

The Governor of the Commonwealth[42] was scheduled to be a witness and have a full opportunity of explaining under oath, the principles and practices of the Order of which he was a conspicuous member. It was thought that papers in his possession might throw much light on the question of how far Masonry secured political and Executive favor. Their inspection would have shown whether it was true that applications for offices had been founded on Masonic merit and claimed as Masonic rights; whether, in such applications the 'significant symbols' and mystic watch-words of the Order had been used; and in how many cases such applications had been successful in securing Executive patronage.

It might not have been unprofitable also to inquire how many convicted felons who had been pardoned by the present Governor were brethren of the 'mystic tie,' [43] or connected by blood or politics with members of that institution; and how few of those who could boast of no such connection had been successful in similar applications.

In its sweeping innuendo, the Committee did not overlook the Judiciary. They might "have deemed it necessary, in the faithful discharge of their duty" to call before them some of the many Judges who were Masons to ascertain whether, in their official positions, the 'grand hailing sign' had ever been handed, sent, or thrown to them by either of the parties litigant; and if so, what the result of the trial had been. Perplexed as they admitted they were in attempting to carry out their duties, the committee reported a bill to prohibit in the future, "the administration of Masonic, Odd Fellows, and all other secret extra judicial oaths, obligations and promises in the nature of oaths."[44]

Certainly the report was in bad taste, and perhaps unfair. But in the encounter with a majority that far outnumbered him, Stevens was, on the whole, the victor. The House avoided his carefully drawn document as though it were laden with contagious plague and killed the proferred bill by refusing even to consider it.

On April 1, the committee to investigate Anti-Masonry filed a majority report in which the Party was variously assaulted and ridiculed. It found that the movement owed its origin to the same latitude which produced the "celebrated blue lights, blue laws, golden Bibles, Mormon Religion, and sins akin to those perpetrated against the fairer sex at Salem for witchcraft, who were tied by the legs and arms and thrown into deep water; if witches, to swim and be burnt; if innocent, simply to drown."

Anti-Masonry came from the land of notions and was quite unadaptable to the climate, common sense and sober feelings of Pennsylvania. It was charged with forcing a "belief of slanders which would unhinge our government and destroy the power and efficiency of all legal authority in the land." No facts had come to the Committee's attention which established or imputed guilt "on any Mason in Pennsylvania." What happened in other states was a matter for those States' attention. If crime were committed here, the Courts were the proper forum in which to proceed.[45]

The minority filed a flowery report attacking the Fraternity and defending Anti-Masonry, and appended purported oaths for the first four degrees of Free Masonry.[46] Because the committee reports were pertinent to questions heatedly discussed at the time, all three were printed and widely used by the Parties for the Fall elections.

When the Legislature adjourned in April of 1834, two facts were established; first, that Anti-Masonry had to be reckoned with as a political power in Pennsylvania, and secondly, that Thaddeus Stevens had become a figure of state-wide importance. But in the October voting, the Democrats again proved their Party the most powerful one. They elected more State officers than the Whigs and Anti-Masons combined.[47] Stevens was returned to the Legislature by a substantial majority, although a continuing bitterness against him prevailed at home.

Early in the December Session, he offered his famous resolution of high indictment against the Masonic institution. It sets forth the position and platform of Anti-Masonry at its peak in the most concise and authentic manner that is to be found in the records that have come down to us.

"Whereas, it is alleged and believed by a large and respectable portion of the citizens of this Commonwealth, that the Masonic institution is injurious to the rights and dangerous to the liberties of the people;

"That it imposes on its members oaths and obligations unauthorized by, and inconsistent with, the laws of the country;

"That it binds the members to give a preference to each other in all things, over the rest of their fellow-citizens;

"To 'apprise each other of all approaching danger,' whether such danger arise from the legal prosecution of their own crimes and misdemeanors or otherwise;

"To conceal the secrets and crimes of each other, not excepting even murder and treason;

"To espouse each other's cause, and if possible, extricate them from all difficulties, 'whether they be right or wrong';

"To avenge even unto death the violation of any of the Masonic oaths and the revelation of any of their secrets.

"That the rights and ceremonies of the lodge are of a degrading, immoral and impious character.

"That the candidates are stripped nearly naked and led to the imposition of their awful oaths hoodwinked and with a rope or cord around their necks, called a 'cable tow.'

"That in the Royal Arch degree, they affect to enact the sublime and sacred scene of God appearing to Moses in the burning bush of Mt. Horeb.

"That in order to impress the conscience of the candidate, with the 'sealed obligation' which is a renewal of all his former unholy Masonic oaths and obligations, they administer to him the Sacrament out of a human skull; and compel him to invoke upon his soul in addition to death on earth, eternal damnation in the world to come, as the penalty of violating any obligation which he may theretofore have taken, is then taking, or may thereafter take, in relation to any degree of Masonry or order of Knighthood.

"That it is anti-republican, and an insidious and dangerous enemy to our democratic form of government.

"That it creates and sustains a secret order of Nobility in violation of the spirit of the constitution.

"That it is a regularly organized Kingdom within the limits of this Republic, assuming and secretly exercising all the prerogatives and powers of an independent Kingdom.

"It has established a central and controlling government, extending its branches all over the civilized world, which they denominate the 'Holy Empire;' the seat of this Government in America is what in Masonic language is called the 'Valley of New York.' This branch of Masonic power is called 'The Grand Supreme Council of Most Puissant Sovereign Grand Inspectors General of the Thirty-third degree at the Grand Orient of New York.'

"It sends ambassadors to, and receives them from all the Masonic Kingdoms of the earth.

"It secures an undue, because an unmerited, advantage to members of the fraternity over the uninitiated farmer, mechanic and laborer, in all the ordinary business transactions of life.

"It prefers a corrupt 'brother' to an honest citizen in appointment to office.

"It prevents the wholesome enactment and due administration of laws.

"It enters and corrupts our legislative halls, our executive offices, and our courts of justice.

"The trial by jury instead of being the palladium of our rights, it converts into an engine of favoritism and Masonic fraud.

"Its whole tendency is to cherish a hatred of democracy and a love of aristocratic and regal forms and power.

"The truth of all these things has been repeatedly proclaimed to the world under the signatures of thousands of honest men, by authentic documents procured from the Lodges themselves, and by the testimony under oath of numerous adhering Masons of good character, and it has never yet been contradicted by the sworn testimony of a single witness.

"Therefore, be it resolved, That the committee on the judiciary system be instructed to bring in a bill effectually to suppress and prohibit the administration and reception of Masonic, Odd Fellows and all other secret extra-judicial oaths, obligations and promises in the nature of oaths."

Not only was it laid on the table, but the House still showed its fear of even touching the subject. It refused to pass the usual motion to have it printed.[48]

Yet against such odds the "Arch Priest of Anti-Masonry," as Stevens was so often called by the Masons, kept unceasingly at it, meeting every rebuff of the House with another patient attempt. His tenacity was finally rewarded on March 14, when the Body passed his resolutions against "secret extra judicial oaths." Still cautious, the Legislators amended his preamble by striking out the words Masonic and Odd Fellows and inserting "all secret societies."[49]

But no other major legislation on the matter was considered.

*　　*　　*　　*　　*

The "Arch Priest" with all his labors at Harrisburg, did not permit legislative work to usurp his attentions to the party welfare. He was making contacts over the

State and actively, though quietly, campaigning for Ritner for Governor.

Under his confident leadership, Anti-Masons were becoming amalgamated. The usual frown of fortune which the Crusaders by this time had grown to expect, relaxed into a fleeting smile early in 1835, when friction developed in the Democratic ranks between the "strong Wolfe (Andrew Jackson) men" and the "Van-Buren supporters." [50]

When the Democratic Nominating Convention met on March 4, many delegates were determined to nominate Rev. Henry A. Muhlenberg for Governor.[51] But they were not strong enough to make their will that of the Convention. After many speeches and much haranguing, Governor Wolfe was nominated. Muhlenberg delegates would not acquiesce and withdrew. In their "rump" meeting, Muhlenberg was declared the nominee of the Democrats.[52] The struggle assumed such proportions that President Jackson wrote a letter to Muhlenberg asking him, in the interest of harmony, to withdraw.[53]

Muhlenberg, however, insisted on standing and this gave Anti-Masonry its real opportunity. When the votes were counted, Ritner had a decisive plurality. He became the first and only Anti-Masonic Governor of the Commonwealth.[54]

Moreover the young Party also elected enough Legislators so that with the Whigs they held seventy-two out of the one hundred seats in the Lower House, and although in a minority in the Senate, could control both Houses on a joint vote.[55]

That Stevens' party would be prominently recognized and practically important during the new Governor's administration, was indicated in his inaugural address. He said significantly, "the Supremacy of the laws and the equal rights of the people, whether threatened or assailed by individuals, or by secret, sworn associations, I shall, so far as may be compatible with the constitutional power of the Executive, endeavor to maintain as well in compliance with the known will of the people, as from obligations of duty to the Commonwealth. In these endeavors, I shall entertain no doubt of zealous cooperation by the enlightened and patriotic Legislature of the State. The people have willed the destruction of all secret societies, and that will cannot be disregarded." [56]

Assured by the Executive, and counting a strong support in the House, Stevens saw no reason to delay. The Legislature convened on the first day of December. On the second he gave notice "that he would on tomorrow, ask leave to bring in a Bill entitled 'an Act to suppress secret societies bound together by secret and unlawful oaths.' " [57]

His request was granted and a committee appointed of which he was chairman "to prepare and bring in a Bill accordingly." Four days later he reported. For substance to work upon, he presented five petitions praying for an investigation of Free Masonry. On December 19, these together with all others which had accumulated up to that time, he had referred to his committee. All important to Stevens, he now had power "to send for persons and papers." [58]

Free Masonry was again in battle for its life. Never had the Institution a better equipped, more adroit or more dangerous antagonist. Stevens had succeeded in harnessing the tremendous power of a sovereign state to the task of demolishing the organization. Masonry shuddered. But astute Anti-Masons understood that this also was their Party's supreme effort. Failure now, they knew, meant destruction of Anti-Masonry and no end of personal ridicule for its proponents. Interested partisans all over the Nation followed the proceedings at Harrisburg.[59]

The "Arch Priest" in possession of the power he had sought and dreamed of for years, showed his encouragement in the pouring forth of a stupendous energy devoted, as he believed, to constructive measures over a wide field. He was the busiest man in the Legislature.[60] Behind him was his party, well organized in its strongholds through the State. His colleagues were easily able to control the Lower House; had at all times a substantial power in the Upper House and their endeavors were ever smiled upon by a friendly Chief Executive. While opportunity was at hand, no time was to be lost and the investigating Committee, therefore, fixed January 11 as the day to begin the taking of testimony.

Subpoenas were accordingly issued to prominent Masons, among whom was Ex-Governor Wolfe. People flocked to the scene of battle. The day had come when the strongly guarded secrets of the greatest Secret Society on earth would be opened to the light of day. But all was not so easy; the Masons would fight. Witnesses refused to appear before the committee and challenged its authority in the premises. Checkmated, Stevens next day reported this status to

the House, and asked the Body "to compel the attendance of the witnesses before the Committee." [61]

The Ex-Governor and another prominent Mason,
John Neilson, had written to the Committee, setting
forth their positions in refusing to appear. Wolfe's
letter especially was a fine argument in his behalf. He
wanted to know where in the Constitution the House
obtained the power to institute such an investigation.
"What article of that venerated instrument forbids the
people from associating together 'in pursuit of their
own happiness?' If the association is criminal or in
violation of any principle of the Constitution or laws,
the mode and manner of suppressing the unlawful combination must be in accord with the Constitution and
laws. I have yet to learn that an inquisition at whose
shrine the rights and liberties of the citizens are to be
invaded is authorized by the principles of our institutions; or that any power exists by which citizens can
be coerced to give testimony before any tribunal or for
any object other than the investigation of matters at
issue affecting the rights of persons or of things . . .
If no law has been violated, why call upon an individual
to give evidence touching a lawful association? If unlawful, why call upon him to criminate himself?" [62]

The argument was pointed, but Stevens, exhibiting
a fine sense of fairness, moved that both letters be
printed and made of record in the House Journal.[63]
In spite of a solid party backing priorly apparent and
a promise of success in prospect, some followers began
to weaken. They thought that in his earnestness,
Stevens was going too far. But next day, when he
came back to the House insisting on the execution of

a power already given the committee, it was still
friendly. "If we let George Wolfe go," he argued,
"every small cur of the Masonic kennel will demand
with some kind of propriety the same privilege." [64] The
House sustained him, directing that attachments issue
against the delinquent witnesses.[65] Consequently, the
arm of the State reached out and brought in those who
had refused to appear.[66]

Deep interest was everywhere apparent and the large
crowds that had come to Harrisburg were agitated and
excited. The Democrats tried ridicule. They called
Stevens the "Chief Inquisitor" and the "Arch Priest"
of Anti-Masonry. They likened him and his man-
euvers to those of "Salem Witchcraft days."

When the witnesses were called, each Mason took the
stand but refused to be sworn. Many of them read prepared statements, protesting against the proceedings,
and setting forth the grounds for their positions. Some
used strong language. Surprised by their defiance, the
committee was puzzled to find its way out. Even
Stevens was helpless.

One of the witnesses, a Reverend Dr. Sproal, when
called, refused to take the oath "on the grounds that
it would wound his conscience as a Christian" and
violate "his Constitutional rights as a man." Drawing
forth a pretentious looking paper, he quickly began
reading "with much pathos and impressiveness, deline-
ating with great force and beauty of language and of
metaphor what he conceived to be the nature of the
attempt to coerce him into repudiating his moral obligations and civil engagements." Stevens could stand
it no longer. Showing an unusual impatience, he

ordered the witness "to hold his tongue and not utter another word." But the Reverend gentleman "desired to explain anything that might have given offense." Non-plussed, Stevens thought it best to get rid of him, and peremptorily announced "the committee would not hear another syllable." [67]

Several newspapers [68] said the Inquisitor had lost his temper but what they took for anger was probably only embarrassment. In a rough and tumble battle of words, he was invincible, but against a modest and verbose clergyman whom he would not offend, he was neutralized.

The investigation, which had begun so auspiciously for Anti-Masonry was blighted. Something had to be done to prevent stalemate, which for the investigators would be failure. No one knew this better than Stevens. Back in the House on January 21, he asked that the witnesses be committed to the custody of the Sergeant-at-Arms for contempt in refusing to answer the Committee's questions.

The House showed no enthusiasm. Some attempted ridicule. One Legislator would instruct the Speaker to "apologize to the prisoners at the Bar." A newspaper editor who was present, believed that the House was really and seriously in doubt at the moment "whether to commit the prisoners or apologize to them." The crisis had come. Stevens had been given his opportunity and had made his greatest fight up to that time. He lost.

By a vote of fifty to forty-three,[69] the prisoners were discharged and Stevens' defeat sealed. He knew that all was over for Anti-Masonry in that session, and perhaps forever. The Whigs had turned upon the Cru-

From the author's collection.

A Stevens Letter Written in the Heat of his Anti-Masonic Campaign

saders and that was but another bit of evidence to
justify Stevens' conviction that the two could never
get along together. It firmed his determination to fight
Whig absorption of his Party to the end.

But defeat to him did not mean surrender. The following month, he succeeded in having the House pass,
by a single vote, his bill making membership in the
Masonic or Odd Fellow Orders good cause for peremptory challenge of a juror in trials where one of the
parties was a Mason or an Odd Fellow.[70]

In March, he was confident that the people would
soon understand that there was before them no question
other "than Masonry or Anti-Masonry." [71] Again he
was willing to "go home in a minority" and calling upon
the people would "either succeed in crushing that pol-
luting Order, which sustains itself by trampling over
the best interests of the country, or go down to the
grave never faltering in a righteous cause." [72]

In his speeches outside the Legislature, he was bitter.
In one of them, he said, "The Lodge is a chartered iniquity, within whose jaws are crushed the bones of immortal men, and whose mouth is continually reeking
with human blood, and spitting forth human gore. If
you were to raze the lodges to the ground and hang the
Masons, this banded brotherhood would have no reason
to complain, because you would be acting in accordance
with the principles which they themselves have inculcated." [73]

At the Anti-Masonic Convention in Harrisburg, he
felt he was "coming to the funeral of an object upon
which the affection of his whole soul had been fixed for
years." [74] When his fellow partisans in supporting

Harrison, had boasted of their strength, they reminded him of "faithless servants who talked to their Master of life and stripped him before he was cold." [75] Yet he held fast. The crystal jewel of devotion to his cause flashed brightest in adversity.

In his party's extremity, he was the most loyal Anti-Mason of them all. His resolutions, which were adopted by the conferees of Franklin and Adams Counties, boldly set forth that his group would "support no man not an avowed political Anti-Mason, form no coalitions, and persevere in opposition to secret oath bound societies," holding that its "party's success is desirable only because it promotes the welfare of the country." [76] In September, candidate on the ticket of the party that had been bludgeoned so severely, he would not shift to a more popular issue. Opposition to secret societies was still the outstanding plank in his platform.

Defeated at the Fall elections, he retrieved his seat in the Legislature in the following year. The Governor, still a good Anti-Mason, again urged upon the Legislature the necessity of a law to prohibit the administration of all extra judicial oaths. [77] The recommendation was referred to a committee of which Stevens was chairman. But the times were inauspicious; effort was useless. Even the "Chief Inquisitor" of the former investigation could do nothing.

Political warfare upon secret societies in Pennsylvania was over. Anti-Masonry in that State, following its course in others, had gone into deterioration and history. It originated at a time most fortunate for Stevens and on its crest, he had gone to the Legislature and there gained National attention. When it suddenly burst forth as a political group in Pennsylvania, Stevens was without party affiliation, and had it not come when it did, in all probability, he would not have been in the Legislature in 1834-5. Were that true, Pennsylvania might be less advanced than it is today, due to lack of early common schools. Although they surely would have come later, in fairness it must be recorded that Stevens brought them to Pennsylvania in 1835. There appears to have been no one who could have substituted for him at that crucial time.

Anti-Masonry meant more than a political vehicle to Stevens. It aimed at making men equal before the law, which was the bed rock of true democracy. He never modified his conviction that Masons were pledged to and did "promote each other's political advancement in preference to a Non-Mason." The year he died, suspecting Masonic combination in the impeachment proceedings, he wrote the Clerk of the House of Representatives, requesting the names of Free Masons who were members of the Congress.[78]

The movement, as the name implies, was a political war on Free Masonry. The Party was short-lived, had no congressional career of consequence, and attained significance in only five or six states. Although at times it was induced to enlarge its field of attack to include Odd Fellows and other secret societies, Masonry bore the brunt of its onslaught. In the light of history, it was ephemeral and except for the national convention technique contributed little to our national ideas or ideals.

Its appeal, although truly Democratic, was in no way comprehensive enough to gather and hold together

any substantial number of people. Unless one studies
the times, it is difficult to understand how a scheme so
restricted could support a party at all, for its purpose
was essentially destructive.

But the country then was only a half century from
the Declaration of Independence, and less than that
from the vigorous debates upon the Federal Constitution. Some remembered what the Fathers there had
said about ranks, titles and secret affiliations. Furthermore, it was the day when inflaming literature was current. The people had been aroused by such books as
Bernard's Light on Masonry, Allyn's Ritual, and Morgan's Illustrations, all of which presumed to set forth
the secrets and evils of the Lodge.

The Fraternity was painted as a bound band of blood
brothers pledged on most terrible oaths in awful solemnity and secrecy to advance each other regardless of
merit, and shield each other even though the accused
might be guilty of high crime against society. Em-
phatically the Anti-Masons insisted that in a true democracy there could be no place for such groups. The
cause skillfully implanted found some sustenance in the
temper of the people at the time, and with sturdy champions was able to endure an evanescent existence.

Anti-Masonry is a curious relic in the history of the
Nation. Thaddeus Stevens was its picturesque leader
in Pennsylvania.

II

ANTI-SLAVIST

Human slavery was a firmly established and commonly assented to, institution in the ancient, medieval and modern structures of the social system. Older than our so-called civilization itself, by Stevens' time the masses had come to view it as but a natural product and many thinking people accepted it where races were concerned as but the assertion of superior intelligence.

It required the daring of the radicals who precipitated and took part in the French Revolution to give it substantial challenge. True it was that Lord Mansfield twenty years before Stevens was born, had written it as the law of England that human slavery was contrary to the statutes of the realm and could not lawfully obtain there. [1] No one argued that the finding of the Justice was not good law, but on the other hand no one hurried to obey it.

The American colonies of that time existed by virtue of grants or charters which required that their laws be "not repugnant to those of England." Long before 1772, they had recognized slavery. When Mansfield's decision came, they paid not the slightest attention to it.

Most of the New England States which later became hot beds of Anti-slavery, had early in their history viewed the institution with favor and legalized it; Massachusetts in 1641, and Connecticut and Rhode Island in 1650. Virginia had taken a similar action as early as 1620. New York followed in 1656, Maryland in 1663, and New Jersey in 1665.

At various times, individual writers and lecturers and

some insignificant groups raised a sporadic opposition, but the complaints were vague and ill-defined, resting mainly on the intangibles of human revulsion toward it.

As early as 1672, the Assembly of Virginia searched for some way "to get rid of the great evil." [2] In one of his drafts of the Declaration of Independence, Thomas Jefferson had charged the King of England with waging "cruel war against human nature itself, violating its most sacred rights of life and liberty in the persons of a distant people who never offended him." [3]

In 1775, a Georgia Convention registered its protest against the institution. Two years later, Stevens' native State of Vermont, first in the country to do so, abolished slavery. Pennsylvania followed in 1780 with an act for "gradual abolishment" and by 1804, all the Northern States had either outlawed it or adopted measures for its future banishment. [4]

In the National Constitutional Convention of 1787, many delegates were disposed to preclude slavery, but found themselves in minority. The compromise finally agreed upon provided for gradual elimination of the slave trade, to be consummated by January 1, 1808.

In the year of Stevens' birth, Whitney had invented the cotton gin. For some years prior, slavery had been on the down grade in the United States, due to the fact that in most places where it existed, it was not profitable. But this new device gave it a vigorous rebirth. Separating the seeds from the fibre by hand, was an extremely slow and tedious process, and most planters had reached the conclusion that it could not be done gainfully.

The new gin provided the solution and the cotton states rapidly increased their acreage for the staple.

This created, an enormous demand for serf labor to prepare the ground, sow, care for, and harvest the crop, and the business of importing slaves to the United States experienced a sudden revival and an increasing prosperity.[5]

In the early nineteenth century, many prominent Americans were conscientiously opposed to the institution, but their remonstrances were still mild and gave little general concern. Although it was of economic importance in the Southland, representing huge underlying investments and property interests there, there was nothing then to indicate that the problem could not be solved without appeal to arms. Great Britain had abolished her slave trade in 1807, and by a compensated emancipation, freed all her West Indian, slaves in 1833.

Many reasonable methods were suggested here. One was the liberation with payment to owners, by either the State or Nation or both. The so-called "Ohio plan" was submitted. It provided for gradual emancipation and farm colonization.[6] 'Most any of the proposals could have been worked out, and if an intelligent man of those days had been told that no peaceful means would be found by the United States to adjust or determine the slave question, and that it would cause an all engulfing sectional war, he hardly would have believed it. One of the striking facts of our history is that no peaceful solution could be found.

The Anti-slavery movement in America began to assume substantial proportions in the early 1830's. Stevens' home county of Adams bordered on the slave state of Maryland and sentiment there, up to this time, as was true of all the border land region of the north, was extremely tolerant of the institution. The people could see without going out of their way the pitiful escape attempts of slaves and the frequently practiced cruelties of slave-catchers. Although an angry disgust would occasionally show itself, the weight of public opinion regarded the latter as permitted by the Constitution and recapture of escaped blacks as a lawful procedure under the Fugitive Slave Acts. Furthermore, the sincere desire to prevent conflict between the North and South was a tremendous check to the periodic resentments that flared.

It was the day when the colonization movement was being experimented with. The first record we have of Stevens' public appearance in opposition to slavery was at a meeting of the Young Men's Colonization Society of Pennsylvania held in the Gettysburg Presbyterian Church in July, 1835. His name headed the list of a committee appointed by the meeting "to solicit donations in aid of the cause." [7]

For a number of years he had assisted the individual slave in every manner possible. In spite of a very busy law practice, he always had time to take the case of an escaping black [8] and although the then existing laws gave no jurisdiction over the fugitive to the Pennsylvania Courts, Stevens generally managed by some method (frequently the one of identification) to obtain a hearing for the captive.

When all other methods failed, it was his custom to use his not abundant means to purchase the freedom of his client. His conduct along this line was not popular, but he persisted in it. [9]

Sometime after taking up residence in Gettysburg,

Stevens started on a trip to Baltimore to purchase some
law books, stopping overnight in a Maryland Hotel
"kept by a man with whom he was well acquainted."
Next morning, a negro woman, in tears, appealed to
him to prevent the sale of her slave husband. Stevens
asked who her husband was, and she answered, "Why,
Massa, he is the boy who took your horse to the stable."
The Gettysburgian remembered the "boy" and went
immediately to his owner, the landlord, requesting him
not to make the sale. But the man was adamant. After
some discussion Stevens offered to pay him $150.00—
half the price demanded, if he would free the slave.
But the Proprietor was "inexorable." All the while
Stevens had known that the slave was the landlord's
son, but had carefully refrained from any reference to
it. Finally, in exasperation, he turned upon the owner
and asked bluntly, "Are you not ashamed to sell your
own flesh and blood?"

But the slave owner was unshaken, and in matter-of-
fact manner, answered, "I must have money and John
is cheap at $300." Realizing that there was but one
way to prevent the heartless sale, Stevens paid the
owner $300 and manumitted John. To the young
lawyer, then but a few years at the Bar, that sum was a
considerable amount and quite exhausted his resources.
He returned home without books but content with his
expenditure.[10]

In September, 1835, he spoke at a meeting in the
County Court House in Gettysburg, called to express
sentiments on slavery. His remarks were unusually
mild.[11]

But it should be remembered that he was then a member of the Legislature and a candidate for reelection the following month.[12] His temperate language meant only that he viewed the occasion as unripe for more forceful assertion and can in no sense be taken to indicate that he was afraid to express himself. He had a keen appreciation of when to talk and when not to talk.

In October, he was easily returned, and his candidate, Ritner, was victor in a three-cornered fight for the Governorship.

The Legislatures of the slave states were now beginning to take action against the assaults of the Anti-slavery men and abolition societies. Various Southern States transmitted resolutions to the North, setting forth that their alleged interference with a wholly Intra-State question (slavery) was unjustifiable and apt to lead to serious consequences. A direct appeal was made to stop the irritating literature and newspapers which were called "incendiary," at their source.

Communications received by Pennsylvania were turned over, by the Governor, to the Legislature.[13] That body referred them to the Judiciary Committee of which Stevens was Chairman. He filed a report on May 30, 1836, and its verbiage stamps it with his personal authorship.

The committee was in agreement with the part of the resolutions asserting that the State alone had the right to control domestic slavery within its limits but it could not "concede that individual freemen are, or can be prohibited from discussing the question of slavery in all its bearings upon the morality, religion and happiness of a people and the expediency and duty of abolishing it by constitutional means."

As to the demand of the Slave States that legislation be immediately enacted to prohibit the publishing and circulating of what they called "seditious or incendiary publications," calculated or having a tendency to operate on her population, the committee reported "that it denied the right of Virginia or any other State to claim from us any legislation" of the character. Every citizen, regardless of where he lived, had "a right freely to think and publish his thoughts on any subject of national or state policy" without confining "his remarks to such subjects as affect only the state in which he lives."

For instance, any citizen "may attempt to show that usury laws of New York or Pennsylvania or the laws regulating negro slavery in Virginia or Mississippi, are immoral and unjust and injurious to the peace and happiness of the respective states. His arguments may be weak, foolish and false, but it would be tyranny to prohibit their promulgation." The committee differed with the contention set forth in the resolutions that Congress had no power to abolish slavery in the District of Columbia or the territories, stoutly maintaining that such power was constitutionally granted and that the abolishment of slavery and slave trade there was expedient.[14]

The findings were too advanced for the conservative Legislature, however, and although adoption was frequently moved, the House at length, rid itself of the troublesome matter by voting an indefinite layover of the whole subject.[15] This report marks the first official expression of Stevens against slavery.

Pennsylvania rejected it then but the country adopted it three decades later. A few newspapers [16] gave the incident passing notice. The radical Chambersburg *Whig* said the report "will form a bright gem in the history of a statesman and patriot." But generally the subject was deemed too dangerous for official discussion, and the entire matter of Slave State resolutions was quietly smothered.

Abolition leaders had for some time noted that the Southern borderland of Pennsylvania was quite intolerant of them, and felt that some missionary work should be done there. One of their prominent speakers of the day, the Reverend Jonathan Blanchard, of Cincinnati, who later became an intimate friend of Stevens, was sent to Gettysburg in March of 1837.

The Commoner, while in Harrisburg, gave the preacher a little practical support before he started on his Pennsylvania tour by handing him ninety dollars in bank bills. "Take that," said he, "and go down to Adams County and lecture, and if they Morganize you, we will make a party out of it." Blanchard first declined the contribution, but Stevens prevailed with, "never mind, I am one and twenty in such things and know they cannot be done without money." [17]

Blanchard's mission was to lead a public free discussion of the irritating slavery question. The bare announcement of his coming created a general excitement in the community for at the time, an Abolition lecturer would have been "just as welcome in Maryland as in the border counties of Pennsylvania." [18] But Blanchard came and spoke. When he finished, two prominent citizens of Gettysburg arose and answered him. [19] The meeting then promptly passed resolutions condemning further agitation on the subject. Furthermore, it was plainly indicated to Blanchard that he was no longer welcome in the community, "a hint which in those days was very generally understood." [20]

All this happened while Stevens was attending the Legislature at the State Capitol. As soon as he learned of the incident, he hurried to Gettysburg and called another meeting at the Court House. He was enraged at the occurrence, not because of the group's attitude on the slavery question, but because he felt Blanchard's right of free speech had been violated. Arranging to have someone move reconsideration of the previous resolutions, Stevens took the floor.

He scrupulously avoided mention of slavery, but forcefully championed the right of an American citizen to speak. While Blanchard was delivering his address, a County Judge had called out to him, "we have no slaves! Why come here to disturb our Borough with a discussion of slavery?" The same Judge was present at the second meeting. Turning to him, Stevens said, "so then human liberty is become a local question and must be discussed only in particular localities." Referring to another lecturer who had spoken in the town a few days before Blanchard, he said the Judge would "quietly hear a Universalist deny all the doctrines which Christ and the Apostles preached and allow him to pass on. But if a man comes to speak for universal liberty, him you answer with violence and rotten eggs. Shame! Shame! Shame! What freeman does not feel himself covered with burning blushes to find himself so surrounded?"

And so Stevens continued until "the poor old Judge broke through the crowd and fled from the Court House." [21]

The resolutions of the previous meeting had been unanimously adopted and although the constituents of both meetings were nearly identical, no one could be heard now bold enough to defend them. On the contrary, another set affirming the right of free discussion and inviting Blanchard to continue his labors were unanimously passed. There were no more pro-slavery gatherings in Gettysburg. [22]

The Convention to amend the State Constitution was scheduled to meet in May of this year. Stevens was to represent Adams County in that body. But because of his bold Judiciary Committee Report above cited, slavery sympathizers feared what he might do. Democrat M'Giffin, who had succeeded in carrying his motion for indefinite postponement of Stevens' Anti-Slavery resolutions, conceived a well-planned device to weaken the Gettysburgian and make him ineffective in the Convention. His scheme was to convene a Body of Representatives, calling themselves "friends of the integrity of the Union." They would show that the overwhelming sentiment of the people was opposed to abolition and anti-slavery movements, because such would foment strife and ultimately break up the Nation. Then it would be a simple step to brand Stevens as a dangerous agitator.

M'Giffin's idea was ridiculed by the Whigs, but in a very short time, more than seven hundred delegates claimed by some manner or other to have been elected. At first Stevens ignored it. In his paper he said, "we learn that a meeting secretly got up is to be held during the week to send Representatives from Adams County to a Convention called by persons representing themselves as 'friends of the integrity of the Union.' "

He advised honest "citizens to take no part in it, for it is but a new scheme of the Lodge to destroy Anti-Masonry." [23]

When the day came for the convention to assemble, so well had M'Giffin and his Anti-abolitionist friends advertised it, that the Court House in Harrisburg was "densely packed." Blanchard, deeply concerned, was there. He has left us the best description of the meeting: "I managed to squeeze in, and stood behind a pillar to sketch and write out a report of that remarkable melee. Mr. Stevens came in late and his coming was greeted by the dense crowd with looks of fear, hatred and wrath."

Soon after the meeting had been called to order, a preacher from Pittsburgh rose and said: "Born in Tennessee, raised in Kentucky, I am an exile from my native state on account of slavery; yet I have come to this convention ready to peril my all in the cause of our National Union."

As soon as he sat down, Stevens rose from his seat. "In an instant every spitbox was kicked and rattled. Hundreds hissed and mouths that did not hiss groaned and howled. It was Bedlam uncapped. For a moment I was stunned; then I looked at Mr. Stevens. He turned with calm haughtiness around and looked that storm of howls and hisses in the face! Then, with an emphasis utterly indescribable, above the uproar, he said, 'Mr. President, we're not slaves here in Pennsyl-

vania and if, (slowly and solemnly) sir, the attempt is
made to make us such, there are some of us in this
Court House who will make resistance enough to let
Pennsylvanians outside know the doom that awaits
them.'

"The House was now so still that you could hear the
clock tick. He turned toward the preacher and, imitating his drawl, said, 'Sir, I deeply sympathize with
my respected friend over the way in all that he has
done and suffered in the cause of our glorious Union
which we have now first met to promote. Indeed, sir,
so moved am I at beholding him an exile from his native
state, driven out by slavery, that I am ready to join
this convention in a vote of reprobation of that foul
institution which drives men from their homes to wander
as exiles in distant states."

The latter statement, uttered in Stevens' well-trained
voice with impressive mock solemnity, was met with a
roar of applause. Some of it from those who had but
a few minutes before hissed the speaker. He continued
to ridicule the pseudo-patriotism of the preacher whom
it appears published a pro-slavery newspaper which he
was desirous of advertising.

"Imitating the preacher's voice and manner, Stevens
extended his mock commiseration for him and launched
his terrible satire on the pro-slavery leaders of the crowd
whom he assumed were all anti-slavery as he was."
Blanchard reports that the Gettysburgian "so overwhelmed them by the drollery, wit, and fearless justice
of his argument, that from that time he had the meeting wholly under his control."

He had devised an effective method of stalemating

Gettysburg nov 5. 1839

Jh^d Dunlop Esqr
President ~~Bank~~ U. S.

Sir

A statement is going the rounds of the news-papers charging your citizen, and his canal commissioners with having embezzled about £64.000 of the money received to repair the breach ~~above~~ in the public works at Huntingdon dam. Justice requires that the amount actually recd for that purpose should be known. It was all drawn from the Harrisburg bank of the Bank of the United States. Will you be so good as to inform me how much was recd from the B. U. S. for that purpose? Whether any part of it was drawn by the governor, or canal commissioners? And whether the whole was not paid to the superintendant Jones Steel Esqr? And further, whether your bank has rendered its account for the money in question to the present state treasurer, or Auditor general?

With much respect
your obt serv^t

Thaddeus Stevens

Jh. Dunlop &c
P. B. U. S.

Stevens Asks for Facts Concerning Political Propaganda in the Campaign which Led up to the "Buckshot War"

the Convention. Everytime M'Giffin would offer his pro-slavery resolutions, Stevens would move to amend by adding words in favor of human liberty from the Pennsylvania Constitution and Bill of Rights which the body dared not vote down.

With the ingenuity of his procedure and the force and satire of his speech, he ridiculed the convention into absurdity. He convinced the fairminded members that such a meeting could do nothing constructive and soon gained their acclaim at his single-handed victory. He had "turned the whole thing into a farce and they broke up in a roar of laughter." [24]

But if Stevens were victor here, M'Giffin and his friends had not long to wait to accomplish their revenge. When the Constitutional Convention met shortly afterward, the tables were turned.

III

CONSTITUTIONAL CONVENTION

Pennsylvania, with Benjamin Franklin presiding, created her first Constitution in 1776. The framers, meeting a problem that was wholly new, did a surprisingly good job. But its shortcomings were soon apparent and in 1790 a more comprehensive substitute was adopted.

In the next few decades the Commonwealth experienced its most rapid growth. Population figures climbed abruptly, its virgin acres yielded unheard of returns, mineral wealth in abundance was uncovered, and hundreds of lusty new industries sprang up. The need soon made itself felt for a Constitution that permitted more refined and more up to date legislation.

In the fall of 1835, the people expressed their desire for a new document and the next year elected delegates. They assembled in the Capitol at Harrisburg early in May of 1837, with Stevens one of the representatives from Adams County. Because of his forensic ability, and his great influence with Governor Ritner, he was a power in the Commonwealth.

His Anti-Masonic-Whig combination had been in control of the State Government since late in 1835. Prior to that time its leaders had advocated Constitutional changes which, in the main, would limit executive appointments. But quite naturally, their accession to office tempered their demands. On the other hand, the Democrats, who while in power prior to 1835, saw no necessity for amendments, now became convinced that such reform was of high importance. Conforming to

[98]

the rule as old as party government itself, the group in power was conservative, and those out of power progressive.

Some of the latter were really radical. George M. Dallas, a Democratic candidate for delegate to the Convention, in speaking of what that body might do, had written that "it might reorganize our entire system of social existence . . . restore the institution of slavery amongst us, make the penal code as bloody as that of Draco, withdraw the charters of the cities, supersede the judiciary with a plan of occasional arbitration and umpirage, prohibit particular professions or trades, permanently suspend the writ of Habeas Corpus and even take from us trial by jury." [1]

The position taken by these extreme Democrats caused a mild dissension in their party.[2] But in the regular elections of 1836, they were successful in carrying the Lower House of the Legislature, although it was by a greatly reduced margin. The next month, they were able to elect a bare majority of delegates to the Convention.

Stevens' case is an example of the evenly matched strength of the political parties. In October he was defeated for the Legislature by fourteen votes and the next month, elected as delegate to the Convention by two hundred votes.

Although the Democrats had elected sixty-seven and their opponents only sixty-six of the delegates to the Convention, when the Body assembled, the figures were reversed, due to the death of a Democrat, whose position had been filled by a Whig.[3] This turn put Stevens and his group in control of organization and the advantage, of course, was not lost. John Sergeant, an eminent Whig lawyer, who paid dignified obeisance to Stevens, was made President of the Convention, and another friend, Shoch, Secretary. The Pennsylvania *Reporter* discoursed at length upon the "tactics by which Stevens, the Drill Sergeant, organized the Assembly." [4]

The efficient method that the Adams County leader used was something between the workings of a steam roller and an instrument of precision. Before his opponents realized what was going on, and with the advantage of but a single vote, he swept into control.

Charles Ingersol, a Democratic member from Philadelphia, complained that "it was very painful to him to observe the effects of party organization, as demonstrated by forcing the President into office by a party vote, so unlike the Virginia and New York Conventions, where it was done by unanimous vote." Stevens chided him as having "no right to complain, although he sympathized with him as to the painful feelings he experienced." Partisan feelings had been shown by Ingersol and his friends in as striking a manner as by those he complained against, for "if he and his friends had voted for Mr. Sergeant, they need not have complained of his being placed in the chair by party vote of the majority." [5]

Happy in his victory, Stevens jokingly announced, "if the Democrats had a majority the Federalists would cheerfully give them an equal share of the offices and honors, but being a majority and *no politicians* the conservatives would be content with taking the whole." [6]

The Adams County delegate had approached the work of the Convention in the fulsomeness of good faith. Through his newspaper, he had said, "in such a body, all party bickerings should be laid aside." [7] Although in favor of no extreme Constitutional modification, he did desire certain changes which he believed were forward looking. Still active in his Anti-Masonic fight, he wanted an amendment prohibiting secret societies in the Commonwealth. In spite of the fact that the Governor was an intimate of his, Stevens advocated curbing the Executive's appointive powers, and restricting his term to three years in six, instead of nine in any twelve, as was then permitted.

Because Legislators from the larger cities consistently voted in groups, giving rise to block legislation, Stevens thought that representation allowed those municipalities should be materially reduced and permanently limited. The question of state banks was much agitated at the time, but Stevens' expressions on the subject made in his contemporary speeches and through his newspaper, do not set forth clearly just what his attitude was. [8]

Oddly enough, the proposition which became the outstanding one with the Gettysburgian, and which in the end caused him to wash his hands of the whole Convention, was not anticipated. It was the matter of suffrage restriction on a color basis.

As the Convention organized, it looked as though Stevens would assume a lead position, and through personal influence, reinforced by the State Governmental machinery, control the proceedings. He himself no doubt felt assured of this, as is indicated by his more than usual good humor in the early discussions. But auspicious as it seemed at the opening, he was soon to learn that it held for him little more than abuse and defeat. Defeat not only of himself, but also of what he believed were constructive and beneficial measures.

Less than four years before, he had gone to Harrisburg as an Assemblyman. There he had opened his fight on secret societies, concentrating his blows on Free Masonry. Many members of the Fraternity of highest character and honesty, had noticed his attacks from afar. Some of them, now delegates, were convinced that Stevens' conduct was extreme, even vicious, and motivated solely by political ambition.[9] They had taken courage at his unsuccessful effort to force them to testify before the Legislative Investigating Committee the previous winter.

Furthermore, Stevens had ridiculed the Democrats into a stalemate in the M'Giffin Convention immediately before, and his biting satire was fresh in the minds of many of the delegates who had been members of that Assembly.

Then also, there were a number of men not strict partisans who saw Stevens' bold abolition stand as a menace to harmony between the states.[10] They, too, awaited occasion to crush him. In addition to these more or less organized groups, there were delegates who disliked him simply for his brusque and tactless manner, and his frequently offensive speech.

It didn't take long for these adversaries of the Adam's County delegate to appreciate their strength. Having once sensed a substantial resentment toward him, and convinced that he had now become vulnerable, they were ever watchful from that moment on to seize every chance to embarrass, belittle, and if possible overwhelm him.

Immediately after the presiding officer had been elected, they showed their hand. Knowing that he was a satellite of Stevens, an attempt was made to deny him the usual power of appointing committees. But so irregular was this move that it could not be carried.[11] Stevens was given responsible Chairmanships on the Committees on the Governor, public improvements, loans and debts of the State, and secret societies.

The Whig-Anti-Masonic combination, if it could be held compactly together, had enough votes to dictate its desires. Stevens, in control as he was on the opening day, by the exercise of a little political dexterity, could have held his supporters in line. But his utter weakness in this respect showed itself glaringly. On July 7, he admitted that he was already on the defensive, when he notified the Democrats that to pass any measures, "they must concede something." [12]

Within the month, he not only had lost his Whig supporters, but their leader, Meredith, turned fiercely upon him in the most savage personal encounter of the Convention. Whether or not Stevens could have avoided it, is difficult to say.

It came about through his desire to limit cities, regardless of size, to six Representatives in the Lower House. The Adams County delegate had quoted Jefferson's words that "great cities were sores upon the body politic." [13] He was careful to say that he made no charges against individuals or communities, for he "respected their moral character." But he did believe that if the present tendency was continued in, within a few years, three or four counties would rule the destinies of the whole Commonwealth. His objection was not to majority rule, but quite the opposite. Representatives from the cities organized while those from the outlying districts did not. As everyone knew, this frequently gave rise to what was really minority legislation. His years at Harrisburg had made this all too plain to him, where the tactics of the solid city groups had often forced laws which he considered inequitable and even injurious.

Especially was he irritated by the block voting on public improvements. For example, the Philadelphia contingent consistently opposed improving the Susquehanna River for commerce,[14] fearing, of course, that creating such an outlet would deprive their city of that trade. In spite of Stevens' making clear that his whole argument was upon a matter of principle, and for a fair balance of representation, Meredith had whipped himself into a fury by the time the Adams Countian concluded his address.

Seizing the floor, before his passion could subside, his answer did him no credit. Aiming at the person rather than the argument, he said, "no man was ever more over-rated than Mr. Stevens . . . A broad front, stentorious voice, and impudent looks and actions, form the true basis of his greatness. He has a schoolboy readiness in using the obsolete machinery of heathen oracles, gods and goddesses, and in quoting everyday threadbare scraps from the ancient classics; all of which he has at his finger's ends from having long exercised the vocation of pedagogue."

Dubbing Stevens the "great unchained of Adams," he accused him of knowing nothing of the use of argument, but pouring "forth torrents of declamation for

the one-shilling galley which his toad leaders present as
the climacteric of eloquence and which, if uttered in a
modest tone and manner, would set his hearers asleep or
to reading newspapers." [15]   And so on at length.[16]

Stevens was really taken back by the distempered
blow. But he managed to reply, "the extraordinary
course of the gentleman from Philadelphia has aston-
ished me. During the greater part of his concerted
personal tirade, I was at a loss to know what course had
driven him beside himself. I could not imagine on
what boiling cauldron he had been sitting to make him
foam with all the fury of a wizard who had been con-
cocting poison from bitter herbs." But the Gettysburgian said this was all explained when Meredith referred to Masonry. Being a votary and tool of the
"Hand-Maid" he felt and resented the injury she had
sustained.

However, as the speaker had often before endured
such assaults from her subjects, he would permit no
personal abuse, "however foul or ungentlemanly" to
betray him into passion, make him to forget to command his temper, or induce him to reply in similar strain.
"I will not degrade myself," said he, "to the level of a
blackguard to imitate any man, however respectable."

Meredith had referred to him as having "venom without fangs." He needed not that gentleman's admoni-
tion to remind him of his weakness. "But I hardly need
fangs, for I never make offensive personal assaults;
however, I may, sometimes, in my own defense, turn
my fangless jaws upon my assailants with such grip as
I possess. But it is well that with such great strength
that gentleman has so little venom. I have little to

boast of, either in matter or manners, but rustic and rude as is my education, destitute as I am of the polished manners and city politeness of that gentleman, I have a sufficiently strong native sense of decency not to answer arguments by low, gross abuse. I sustained propositions which I deemed beneficial to the whole State. Nor will I be driven from my course by the gentleman of the city, or the one from the county of Philadelphia. I shall fearlessly discharge my duty, however low, ungentlemanly and indecent personal abuse may be heaped upon me by malignant wise men or gilded fools." [17]

But the proposal of Stevens to limit representation in the areas of heavier population and by so doing, curb evils of block legislation, got nowhere. Sensing the temper of the Convention, he soon dropped it.

His position was rather anomalous in his insistence on executive appointment of the higher judiciary, and election of the minor ones. A key to his stand is probably furnished in his statement that "out of the four thousand Justices of the Peace, more than two thousand were members of the Society (Masonic) sworn to give judgment in each other's favor, and they belonged to a class too likely to give heed to oaths. It was not to be supposed," said he, "that the more important judicial officers were influenced by these secret obligations—they were above it." [18]

He would countenance no modification of the then obtaining method, by which the Governor appointed judicial officers for life.

When a compromise measure providing for Executive appointment "by and with the advice and consent

of the Senate" was approved, he was exasperated.[19]
He said when the Act embodying pains and penalties
against the Queen had passed by small majority, the
English House of Lords immediately adjourned and
the Ministers never called it up again. It had been
his fate once or twice in the Legislature to hear the
death of a member announced when the House instantly
adjourned to be withdrawn from reflections unsuited
for the mournful occasion. Now they had just passed
by a small margin [20] a bill of Pains and Penalties upon
a thing that was sacred to us all. By a bare majority
"we have destroyed the Constitution."

He trusted therefore that the Convention would now
adjourn so that members might not have their minds
disturbed by any trivial matter. When an opponent
chaffingly suggested "that the members do wear a
crepe," Stevens replied that he would "accept the suggestion, did he not know there was a majority against
it. Under the circumstances, he would as soon think
of making a motion to wear crepe as to recommend
it to a boy whom he saw dancing upon his mother's
grave." [21]

Defeated in the main issue, he had the meager consolation of having the Convention adopt his Amendment to have the Senate "sit with open doors" in acting
on executive nominations.[22]

Before the Convention had been two months in session, Stevens realized that he was completely vanquished. Early in July, he had thought the opposition
must make some concessions [23] but by the middle of the
month, he admitted they "had strength enough to do
what they pleased." [24]

Whenever he spoke, his enemies missed no opportunity to strike, so that he finally referred to himself in debate as being something "like a man who, in riding through a town, is beset by all the dogs, big and little, fat and lean." [25]

He complained constantly that the body was wasting time, and getting nowhere.[26] Evidence to corroborate this accusation appeared on his proposal that "no member of the Convention shall hold office under the amended Constitution." [27] One of the opposition moved to modify by adding the words "except those from the County of Adams." Strangely enough, this was accepted by the body by a vote of thirty-five to thirty-four.[28]

In debate, much ado was made of the matter, and in pseudo-seriousness, Stevens was made the butt of ridicule. After he had been toyed with and embarrassed to the satisfaction of his adversaries, the whole thing was dropped by permitting him to withdraw his original proposal.

All through the discussion, the Gettysburgian pressed with unusual vigor to sustain his amendment so that one wonders if it was an adroit move with ulterior motives. By this time he was plainly discouraged and disgusted. Perhaps his aim was to force adoption, even though the delegates opposed it privately. Embodied in the proposed Constitution, it would be so distasteful in excluding them from all offices, that they might oppose the whole set of amendments at election time, rather than bar the doors of their political futures. If such were his plan, it was masterful strategy, but in the end the Convention out-maneuvered him.

When the Body was about to adjourn from Harrisburg to Philadelphia, he submitted a resolution to pay the Clergymen who had officiated as Chaplains and extend to them its thanks.[29] A freakish opposition arose which Stevens thought was so hateful that when the motion to employ other Clergymen was introduced at the opening of the Philadelphia session, he moved to postpone its consideration indefinitely. He did so, not because he was opposed to having Clergymen open and close the session, but "because the members had shown before the Convention left Harrisburg that they did not consider the services of the Clergymen worth a farthing. . . . The debate on that subject was disgraceful." Whether listening to prayers "where they are so much needed would be productive of a dangerous union of Church and State," he left others to decide.[30]

But he was allowed a few crumbs. Largely through his efforts, the provision depriving one engaging in a duel of the right to hold any office of honor or profit in the State, was accepted.

For many days he remained inconspicuous, and then determined on one last grand effort. It exemplified his usual lack of tact. Obtaining the floor, he further offended the members by dubbing the Convention a "sluggish body."[31] Calling attention to its operating cost of $1,100 per day [32] he demanded action. He presented his own idea of a schedule of amendments. They differed from those before the Convention in that he would not modify the suffrage clause then obtaining for granting the vote to "every free man." He would cut the residence requirements from two years to one year, and would limit the State Debt never to "exceed the sum of thirty millions of dollars."

He would retain the method of filling judicial offices but provide for election of county officers and also Justices of the Peace and Aldermen. After suggesting a new method of amending the Constitution, he presented an article which would submit to the people the question whether or not the Convention should reconvene after election. His thought was that if proposed Amendments were adopted, the Convention should then adjourn. If the people were not satisfied, they would so signify, and the Body could continue at work. His scheme was an excellent one to expeditiously incorporate the will of the electorate.

A striking omission from his proposed modifications was his pet one prohibiting secret societies. Probably he had real hope of the Convention adopting what he submitted, and because it had already refused the one against secret orders, he was willing, in a spirit of compromise, not to insist upon it.[33] But all to no avail. The delegates, now grown openly hostile, made short work of his offer. They heard his suggestions and then quietly sent them to oblivion by moving the previous question.[34]

On an article submitted which would prohibit free and slave negroes from coming into Pennsylvania, Stevens' first motion to postpone its consideration was lost, fifty-two to fifty-nine, but with considerable effort, he finally gained his point.[35]

He presented a petition praying that "trial by jury should be extended to all." [36] Equalitarian Stevens had gotten to that rule of fair play before Pennsylvania.

But the proposal received only scattered support, and the Convention made no change in the old Constitution.

He would compel no citizen to bear arms in time of peace, but required all to do so in time of war; conscientious objectors to pay an assessment to the Government or be fined.[37] This too was ignored.

When an attempt was made to refuse reception of a petition from some free negroes in Pittsburgh by sending it to Committee, he took the Floor to say that "those who petitioned this body, whether black or white, had a right to be heard, whether on this or any other subject relative to the business before the Convention." He asked that the prayer be given respectful consideration. To receive it was not only a matter of common courtesy, but of duty, and he wondered what it was "that should operate on our minds to make us forego our duty."[38]

When the Convention met, the Pennsylvania Constitution extended the right of suffrage "to every free man of the age of twenty-one." The Democrats were determined to modify this. The Whigs and Anti-Masons were just as valiantly bent on retaining it. In the early days of the session, while the latter were in control, no effort looking toward a change was made. But when the former felt their strength increasing, they moved to restrict suffrage to "white men." On the first test, they were defeated by a vote of forty-nine to sixty-one. The vote was roughly on party lines with the Democrats as proponents.[39]

But by the middle of January, with the Convention well in hand, they had the limiting word inserted by a vote of seventy-seven to forty-five.[40] The position of

[111]

William R. Meredith, a Whig leader in this matter [41] illumines the way in which Stevens' forces, who constituted a majority at the opening of the session were pared into a minority. Although Meredith showed plainly by his later outspoken remarks that he strongly favored restricting the suffrage, yet as long as the Anti-Masons and Whigs worked together in the union that had been effected prior to organization, he seemed content to withhold his feelings, in order that the combination might rule. But after the breach came he took a leading part in the battle to limit voting to white citizens. Very probably his bitter debate with Stevens referred to above ruptured the alliance and gave control to the Democrats.

On July 14 the Convention adjourned until after the Fall elections and Stevens went home to repair his political fences.

When the delegates reconvened in October, he had been returned to the Legislature. All the great hopes that he had when the Convention opened for constructive and forward looking amendments, were by now annihilated. Convinced that he could accomplish nothing, he absented himself from most of the sessions, although he did at times put in a reluctant appearance.

When the Convention concluded its none too striking labors, its recommendations were submitted to the members for their signatures. Stevens was one of the very few who refused to sign. [42] He left no record of the reason for withholding his name, but it was generally understood that it was because the word "white" had been inserted in the amendments, restricting the right of franchise to Caucasians. [43]

Stevens' opportunity to distinguish himself in the Convention which appeared so promising at the outset, had been strangled by bitter personal enmities, and his enormous lack of tact.

The combination of enemies now organized against him, opened the way to his crushing defeat in the Buckshot War, and except for a single term in the Legislature, forced him from public life for nearly a decade.

IV

BUCKSHOT WAR

Pennsylvania has always been recognized as a Commonwealth where politics receives at least, its due notice. Even before the days of the Camerons and Quay, it was the subject of careful planning and intricate stratagem and intrigue.

Early in 1838 the Parties of the Keystone State began vigorous preparation for the October election. The chief prizes at stake were the Governorship and a United States Senatorship.[1]

The Commonwealth still operated under its Constitution of 1790 which gave the executive a vast field of official and judicial appointments. The Democrats had enjoyed the fruits of this office for a number of years prior to 1835, when Governor Ritner was elected on a Whig Anti-Masonic ticket in a three cornered battle in which the Democrats were divided. They felt their loss sorely and determined to retrieve it.

Because Stevens had early championed Ritner, carried Adams County for him regularly and had great influence with the Governor it was widely printed that he could have had any office in all the realm of executive appointments. But the Gettysburgian seemed to desire nothing officially. During Ritner's term, he served two years in the legislature and one as a delegate to the State Constitutional Convention.

Ritner was a wholly unoffending and non-aggressive personality. Stevens was blunt, determined and threatening to political adversaries. It was good politics for the Democratic newspapers to center their partisan attacks on the defeated "Arch-Priest of Anti-Masonry."

Beginning soon after Ritner's inauguration, they had blatantly announced that the Executive was the willing servant of Stevens who was the real Governor of Pennsylvania.[2] But as long as he held no office to work through, he was only limitedly effective. Official position might make him dangerous.

His appointment by Ritner as President of the Board of Canal Commissioners in May, 1838 therefore, created consternation among the Democrats. The office was of importance because of huge expenditures under the Board's control, and a statewide authority in allocating water routes of commerce. The reason for placing the sagacious Stevens in such office, at the time, seemed obvious to opposition newspapers. The Pennsylvania *Reporter* for June 1, said editorially, "No one doubts that the public interests are to become, under the auspices of Messrs. Stevens and Dickey, but a secondary consideration; that we are to have a Board (of Canal Commissioners) perambulating the State, endeavoring to purchase up votes, etc." [3] And there is little doubt that Stevens was placed in this position to marshal forces for the approaching election.

Complaints were soon heard that supporters of the Democratic gubernatorial candidate, David R. Porter, were being discharged from the improvement work under the jurisdiction of the new Commissioners,[4] and that workmen favorable to Ritner were being moved to politically strategic points. Moreover the Board was charged with attempting to raise a "missionary fund from the contractors for use at the next election." [5]

The Whig and Anti-Masonic press vigorously denied these accusations, claiming that all the Canal Commissioners did was done for efficiency in the construction and administration of all the public works.[6]

In the October elections, a vote was to be taken on the proposed amendments to the State Constitution and partisans did not hesitate to distort them as issues. Violent factional speeches were made and the public prints of the day sullied their pages with low-grade abuse against political opponents. Never in Pennsylvania's history had its newspapers printed such sordid matter as the heat of this campaign generated.

For example, Governor Ritner was called "a damned old Dutch hog."[7] Base caricatures representing him as engaged in unwholesome acts were given wide currency.[8] The Democratic candidate, Porter, was accused in the notorious Rebecca Beaty affidavits which were broadcast in the Whig and Anti-Masonic newspapers of being the father of her two colored children.[9] In another instance, he was called a "fraudulent, insolent, and perjured knave,"[10] and again openly referred to as "the father of yellow children."[11]

Bets on the outcome of the election were laid in large amounts and on a scale never before known and never since approached.[12] Most of the wagering was done with money, but if that were not available, so wrought up were the people that they bet their horses, farms, and even their canal boats.[13] Stakes in the amount of ten thousand dollars were not unusual,[14] and even a staid newspaper offered to risk that amount on General Porter's election.[15]

The Democratic papers accused Stevens of using his office to import into Pennsylvania, workers from other states in order that they might vote his ticket. To this counter charges were made by the Whig Anti-Masonic papers that Porter's friends were importing voters to the state for a similar purpose.[16] Partisan ardor was agitated to highest pitch and violent speeches, coupled with vicious attacks in reputable newspapers, inflamed the feelings of the voters of the whole Commonwealth. Many good citizens, feeding their convictions on the generally malignant propaganda of one or the other side, actually believed that if opponents were victorious, nothing less than calamity impended.

After the partisan proddings, vituperation, calumniation and abuse of this heated and long drawn out campaign, one could not expect a quiet yielding by the loser, especially where it was commonly known that irregularities had been engaged in by both sides. Returns were unusually slow coming in and even when compiled were inconclusive because of alleged frauds and threatened contests.

Although at first the Ritner partisans questioned Porter's election as Governor, their position was never seriously maintained and they soon acknowledged defeat in that field.

On the matter of the Constitutional amendments there seemed more doubt. Among the principal political effects of their acceptance were the restrictions placed upon the appointive powers of the Governor. Porter's friends did not immediately recognize defeat on the amendments, and he appeared at the State Capitol in December, presumably to take office under the old Constitution.[17] However, his friends finally conceded passage of the Constitutional modifications, which victory in curtailing the Governor's patronage, went as a consolation prize to the Whig Anti-Masonic group.

The Senate was admittably Whig Anti-Masonic, but a struggle ensued for control of the Lower House. Neither faction could count a majority without its Philadelphia contingent where a contest was laid. From this encounter came the so-called "Buckshot War."

The immediate trouble arose over the election returns from the Northern Liberties and Spring Garden Districts of Philadelphia County.[18] Charles J. Ingersol, the Democratic, or as he chose to call himself, Van Buren Congressional candidate from that district, played a leading part in precipitation of the struggle.

As soon as he learned of the returns from these precincts, the net result of which was to defeat him, he claimed that gross frauds had been perpetrated. The election was held on the second Tuesday of October, and between that time and the succeeding Friday, on which day the Board of Return Judges were scheduled to meet, Ingersol and his followers by hand bills and newspaper notices, had notified the people of his charges and called upon them to attend the meeting at the State House, "in order," as they said, "to see that justice be done them and their friends." [19]

Ingersol appeared before the Judges and demanded that he be given an opportunity to prove alleged irregularities in the voting of the questioned districts. Among the major charges on which he based his demand to throw out the Northern Liberties vote, was the one that an election clerk had lost the tally sheets. That the clerk was a member of Ingersol's own party and officiated in a ward in which he and his party had received a substantial majority, seems not to have mattered.[20]

Specific violation was charged in only this district, but under a general charge of fraud, and because the voting for all the precincts was done in the same building, he demanded that the entire vote of approximately fifty-three hundred be thrown out.

The Board was composed of seventeen members, one representing each district of Philadelphia County. Ten were Democrats and the remaining seven were either Whigs or of a Whig-Anti-Masonic complexion. Ingersol himself was permitted to argue his case before the Board. It was most unusual for a candidate to be heard by returning judges on the validity of votes to be returned.

It was clearly illegal for the judges to go into the matter of alleged fraud for the purpose of determining the validity of those returns. Although it appears that all of the Board understood this, nevertheless by a strict party vote of ten to seven, the demand of Ingersol was granted and the entire vote of the Northern Liberties district was thrown out.

After this determination of the majority, the seven Whig and Whig-Anti-Masonic members comprising the minority withdrew. The majority continued its meeting, composing its returns upon the basis of ten of the seventeen districts. One copy of its report was properly deposited with the Prothonotary of the County. The law required that the other copy be delivered to the Sheriff and by him or his deputy returned to the Secretary of the Commonwealth. For some unknown reason (probably a suspicion that the Sheriff was aligned with their political opponents) the ten return judges did not see fit to follow the regular requirements for getting the record to the Secretary of the Commonwealth.

At any rate, the copy to be forwarded was sent to that official, contrary to law, by a passenger on a steam train.

In the meantime, the minority members of the Board, who had retired to another room in the State House, proceeded to formulate their returns for the six districts comprising the Northern Liberties and one Spring Garden district. These reports they certified and followed the correct statutory procedure in filing both copies.[21] No time was lost by the Sheriff in getting this minority return to Harrisburg in consequence of which it was the first received by the then Secretary of State, Thomas H. Burrowes.

But he was also Chairman of the Whig Central State Committee [22] and his sympathies, of course, were with the minority group of the returning judges. He quickly discovered that their report was the only one that had come to his hands in the regularly ordained manner. This proved a particularly fine argument for treating it as the only return.

On the fifteenth day of October, as Chairman of the Ritner Central State Committee, he addressed an unusual letter "to the friends of Joseph Ritner" in which he said that "the general election has resulted in a manner contrary to all our reasonable calculations and just expectations." If, he went on, "it had been fairly produced, we as good citizens would quietly, if not cheerfully, submit. But there is a so strong possibility of malpractice and fraud in the whole transaction, that it is our duty peacefully to resist it and fully to expose it."

He questioned the majority of Porter for Governor and referred to "the votes of whole districts" which had been "rejected without shadow of law or justice." On behalf of the State Committee of Correspondence and Vigilance, he suggested, "an investigation."

He admonished that it should "be done determinedly and thoroughly, but peacefully and with a resolution to submit to the results whether favorable or unfavorable to our wishes. But, fellow citizens," he concluded, "until this investigation be fully made and fairly determined, let us treat the election of the ninth instant as if we had not been defeated, and in that attitude, abide the results." [23]

The propriety, at least, of such a declaration by an officer of the Commonwealth must be questioned. The Democrats already feared gravely what Burrowes might do in his office of Secretary of State in returning the election results to the Legislature, and this statement of his served only to deepen their suspicions.

Leading newspapers, instead of attempting to calm the people, seemed to intensify partisan hatreds and by the time the Legislature convened on December 3, a party bitterness that can hardly be appreciated today stirred much of the State. Some even prominent editors, in their ardor did not restrict themselves to the truth. For example, speaking editorially in its issue of December 12, the reputable *Keystone* (Democrat) said, "Everyone knows that Mr. Burrowes has issued a proclamation ordering all his friends to *treat the election as though it had not happened.*"

As Burrowes really stated it, the appeal was a wholly

legitimate one; as the *Keystone* distorted it, it was an invitation to revolution.

The Whigs [24] challenged that "their members from the County of Philadelphia *will* have their seats—peaceably if possible, but forcibly otherwise." [25] The Democrats threatened that if their members were "not seated on the first day" the Legislature met, "twenty thousand bayonets would bristle at Harrisburg." [26]

Under the law, the Legislature was scheduled to convene on Tuesday, the fourth of December. As early as the Saturday previous, outsiders poured into Harrisburg in unusual numbers. By Monday evening, the hotels and lodging houses were filled. Groups of uneducated men and those of the type not usually interested in Government, crowded the bar rooms and streets. A Democratic Legislator, in reporting the conditions confidentially to his home, said, "You can form no idea of the degree of excitement that prevails here. It is thought by many there will be a riot in the Hall."[27]

Much loose talk was vented and many threats of personal violence were made against Stevens, Burrowes and Penrose, the presiding officer of the Senate. Some even went so far as to state "they would be satisfied with nothing less than Stevens' heart's blood!" [28]

Most of the visitors were from Philadelphia, although other parts of the State were represented.[29] Stevens depicts the Philadelphia contingent as made up of "rough, ferocious, crude looking men, ignorant, desperate, and addicted to the lowest habits and vices." [30]

In another instance describing them he said,[31] "The most respectable of them—the 'Captains of Tens,' were keepers of disorderly houses in Kensington. Then came journeymen butchers, who were too worthless to find regular employment—next professional boxers who practice their pugilistic powers for hire and low gamblers who infest the oyster cellars of the suburbs. A portion of them consisted of a class of men whose business you would hardly understand—dogkeepers who in Spring Garden and Southwark, raise and train a ferocious breed of dogs, which they fight weekly for wages and for the amusement of the 'indignant people.'

"Their troop was flanked by a few professional thieves and discharged convicts. These men gathered up from the dens and hovels were refitted with such cast-off clothes as their employers could command and hired at fifteen dollars the head and freight to come to Harrisburg, instruct the Legislature in their duties, and *protect their rights.*"

Long before the convening hour of eleven o'clock on Tuesday morning the galleries, lobbies and halls of the House of Representatives were packed to overflowing.[32] Bullies and strong arm men of both parties were conspicuously present "to see that their party friends obtained their constitutional rights." [33] Stevens was the center of abuse, being blamed for Burrowes' statement and feared for what his political generalship might accomplish in organizing the House.

When the hour arrived, the House was in utter confusion. The mob not only occupied the galleries, lobbies and halls, but crowded over the Floor of the House itself. Stevens wrote, "the aisles and open spaces in front of the Speaker's chair were choked up with rude looking strangers and the chairs of several members were surrounded with rough, brawny bullies. My seat had the honor of being guarded by eight or ten of the most desperate brawlers of Kensington . . . Most of them wore coats with outside pockets in which their hands were generally thrust and, as I afterward satisfactorily ascertained, were armed with double-barreled pistols, bowieknives and dirks. Men of a similar description and similarly accoutred occupied the platform around the speaker's desk." [34]

After the clerk had called the House to order as best he could, Burrowes handed him the "official returns of the late election for the members of the House of Representatives." [35] No objection was made as he began reading them. But when he reached the names of the Philadelphia contingent, Charles Bray, one of the Democratic claimants, arose and stated that the returns that were being read "were false." [36]

He handed the clerk a paper which he had taken from his pocket, declaring that it "was a certified copy of the true returns" and asked that it be read as such. On motion of Hopkins, the clerk put the question to the members to ascertain if both sets of returns should be read. A Philadelphia member by the name of Smith rose and objected to the House voting on any question of the legality of the returns until it was organized, "as until that time the members were not competent under the Constitution and laws, to decide the rights in contests of its seats nor take any other vote as a House of Representatives."

The question, however, was put. The clerk ruled that the motion to read both sets of returns had passed and proceeded accordingly.

After he had finished reading all the names, includ-

ing those for the sixteen contested seats, Stevens took
the floor to say "that a difference of opinion as to the
legal mode of organizing the House was likely to arise
but as this was a government of laws," he trusted no
difficulties would disturb orderly procedure. If either
party erred in its judgment of the law, that error
could be "peaceably corrected by the proper tribunals."
He was willing to trust his case to these bodies and
hoped his "opponents would see the propriety of following the same course and do nothing to disturb the peace
or sully the honor of the Commonwealth."

He proposed that the House organize by electing a
speaker. He argued that the returns presented by the
Secretary of the Commonwealth being sealed, were the
only ones that could be considered in the first instance
because they were the only ones that had reached his
hands through legal channels. His sole duty was to
transmit them. Those returns of course "might be false
or the persons therein returned as elected might have
been unduly elected."

But the law supposed such cases might happen and
had provided the remedy in accordance with the Constitution. However that remedy could not be applied
at the moment because the issue could not be made until
the members returned to the Secretary and by him to
the House had been duly sworn.

Until then no parties existed between whom to form
the issue. It was absurd to say that the prima facie
decision of the contested seats in the House of Representatives could be postponed until all the disputed
returns were read, and then those members decide the
disputed ones, because until the speaker was elected

and the members duly qualified, they were not a body competent to entertain any question. Everything anterior to that was a mere consentible agreement among so many gentlemen.

By the Constitution and laws, there must be "one hundred members capable of voting for speaker and taking their seats at the organization. If the disputes are to be postponed until such organization is perfected, it would be easy to defeat it altogether by contesting all the seats and leaving none as umpires. This, however, is an entirely false view of the matter....There must, in every instance, be sitting members upon the returns furnished by the Secretary of the Commonwealth; and the only way by which they can be unseated is by a petition presented by the claiming members complaining of a false return or undue election of the returned members—and that petition referred to a committee selected by lot according to the Act of 1791, whose report is final and conclusive."

This position is impregnable to legal attack, but had it been accepted, there is little doubt that the Whigs would have been permanently seated and the Democrats excluded. However, Stevens suggested that "if any gentleman thought any other mode legal, he call such names as he pleased and if in so doing, two speakers should happen to be chosen, the House certainly would be courteous enough to find room for both on the speaker's platform until the law decided between them." [37]

Presumably, therefore, the sixteen contesting members were all seated. This arrangement gave either faction a clear majority if it counted those eight seats and ignored the corresponding eight of its opponent.

Stevens proceeded to nominate Thomas S. Cunningham for speaker and his arch enemy, Democrat McElwee, member from Bedford County, nominated Hopkins. Two separate elections then took place simultaneously. The Cunningham tellers made the first report, announcing that Cunningham had been duly elected speaker with fifty-two votes. Amid the "hisses of the multitude," he was conducted to the chair.

But soon after he arrived there, the other tellers reported Hopkins duly elected speaker with fifty-six votes.

Upon this announcement, loud cheers arose from the galleries and stamping feet shook the floor. His partisans escorted Hopkins to the chair and although some "elbowing" was done, it marked the extent of personal encounter.

Both Cunningham and Hopkins were sworn in as speakers.

With Democratic supporters in control of the House, and "bullies crowding around the speaker's chair," Cunningham, overawed, and in fear of bodily harm, withdrew. It was said in the testimony taken later before the Senate Investigating Committee that had he not quietly retired in good time, he would have been "thrown in the Susquehanna River."

Soon afterward, a motion was made for the Cunningham House to adjourn to the next afternoon.[38] After some perfunctory procedure and speeches the Hopkins House adjourned to meet at ten o'clock the next morning. However, when they retired, the Hopkins followers posted a guard to prevent the Cunningham faction from using the House chamber for any purpose.

The Senate meeting was set for the afternoon of the same day. Fearing that Body which was decidedly Whig, might recognize the Cunningham House, Democratic partisans crowded the Senate galleries and lobby, to again "see that justice was done." Senators had great trouble in getting through the packed corridors and entrances to the Floor. It was known that two Philadelphia seats in the Senate were contested but this could have no great weight in organization for the Whigs had a clear majority without them.

As the first Whig contestant was called to be sworn the crowd in the galleries began their disturbance. Charles Brown, Democratic contender for the seat, arose. Speaker Penrose advised him that he could not be heard for at the time he was not a member of the Senate. Upon the Speaker's ruling, loud cries were raised in the galleries and in the lobbies of "Brown, Brown; hear him; we will hear Brown! We will have our rights or we will have blood! Down with Penrose, Burrowes and Stevens." [39]

The disturbance became so great and the threats upon Penrose so serious that he retired from the chair.[40] Brown was then granted the Floor and made a peculiar speech, not calculated to soothe or quiet the mob. After addressing the Chairman, he turned to face the galleries and the lobby.

Asserting that he was but a private citizen, that they were in the midst of a revolution; that the Constitution was at an end and the people must take the government into their own hands, he asked his partisans in the gallery if "in order to defend their rights," of which and forfeited all claims to the belief of the public in any statement he may hereafter make.

PORTER AND PERJURY.

Two weeks ago we offered to bet $500, that we could prove David R Porter a PERJURED KNAVE. The banter not being taken up, we last week offered to DOUBLE THE BET. As the Loco Focos have not seen fit to take this banter, we now offer to bet

2,000, Dollars.

that David R. Porter is a perjured knave, to be proven in a court of justice, agreeably to our propositions of last week and week before.— Now then, if the statements of the Stone-bereakers and others are false, as the Loco Focos would like to make appear, why do they not close in with the offer? The answer is, because they BELIEVE THE CHARGE TO BE TRUE. We have also charged David R. Porter with being guilty of PERJURY TO DEFRAUD HIS CREDITORS, and invited him to prosecute us, if it is not true.

From Pennsylvania Telegraph, September 5, 1838.

A Prominent Newspaper is Concerned About the Character of the Man Whom Two Months Later was Elected Governor of the State

they have been robbed by "Burrowes, Stevens and Company," they were "ready to drench the Senate Chamber with the best blood of the State?" The mob quickly and loudly affirmed its readiness so to do, and Brown, having apparently gotten the answer he desired, artfully commented, "I hope not." [41]

When he retired, Penrose joined Stevens near a fireplace in the Senate Chamber. Reports came to them constantly from friends that dire threats were being made on their lives and as Stevens said when word came from "most reliable sources" that they were about to be "stabbed or knifed," he, with Penrose and Burrowes, withdrew to a side room and escaped through an open window." [42]

This retreat of the three Anti-Masonic-Whig Generals of the Buckshot War from the mob that had boasted it would kill them, was certainly nothing of which to be ashamed. Yet Stevens' enemies throughout life got no end of satisfaction in constantly referring to it, orally and in writing. The vanquished leaders who had so unceremoniously departed, had not gone a moment too soon, for while they were still hiding in the shadows of bushes a few feet from the building, the mob rushed around the corner.

Enlightened by the open window, the leader in disgust, shouted, "By God, they are gone!" Another member complained, "If we had not gone in to see what that fracas was about, we might have accomplished our design." [43]

With ruffians surging over the Senate floor, not even the semblance of order could be maintained and the body adjourned in confusion shortly after dusk, amid cries of "Put out the lights."[44]   Harrisburg and the State government were now given over to the mob.

Democratic legislator Flenninken, eye-witness, in his letter of December 5, wrote, "We here are doubtless in the midst of a revolution.   The town of Harrisburg is crowded with the most excited population, beyond all control. Yesterday they drove out the Senate....I fear that blood will flow freely in this devoted place, and that the days of Stevens, Burrowes and Penrose are numbered."

Democratic ire was concentrated against the clubfoot Legislator who walked with a cane. He was called the Arch Conspirator and had he shown himself, there is little doubt that he would have been murdered. An unbiased observer, in recording the matter thirty years later, said that his assassination had been "deliberately planned and its execution was only prevented by a mistake on the part of the persons who intended to do it." [45] The same recorder says that although Stevens knew from the very first day of the Buckshot War that his life was in real peril, yet during the whole time he acted with "most perfect coolness and deliberation." [46]

Excitement was spreading and the intensity and fury of the mob increasing. It would have taken very little in the way of collision between the parties to initiate civil war. Fortunately, at this moment, the Democrats felt it important in furtherance of their cause to meet together and accordingly a large number of them retired to the Court House.

Here violent speeches were made and the furor was not abated. Spokesmen announced that there was "no government" and the group accordingly proceeded to

construct a "provisional one" under the "denomination
of a Committee of Public Safety." [47]   After appointing
a subcommittee to obtain the election returns from the
Secretary of the Commonwealth, the meeting adjourned to the next morning.[48]

By this time, all who knew the facts realized that if
neither side yielded, serious consequences might follow
quickly. The Governor was afraid to go to his Chamber
and the leading Whigs dared not show themselves.[49]

Believing there was no chance of peaceful adjudica-
tion of the inflamed situation, Governor Ritner, on December 5, issued a proclamation in which he said that
because "a lawless, infuriated and armed mob have
assembled at the seat of Government, with the avowed
object of disturbing, interrupting and overawing the
Legislature of this Commonwealth,"....he was compelled to call upon the "civil authorities to exert themselves to restore order to the utmost of their power, and
upon the military force of the Commonwealth to hold
themselves in readiness to repair to the seat of Government, and upon all good citizens to curb this lawless
mob and reinstate the supremacy of the law." [50]

At the Democratic meeting next morning, the speakers urged a calmer attitude, and the resolutions adopted
were considerably moderated. But in the afternoon,
there was a bloodless battle of bullies for possession of
the State arsenal. The immediate trouble, however, was
adjusted with no serious consequence, although it in no
way cooled the temper of the participants.

Stevens' name had been used as one of the parties
to the compromise, but in a letter to the editor of the
Pennsylvania Telegraph, dated December 6, he vigor-

ously denied having anything to do with it, saying that he had "uniformly deemed it disgraceful to treat with the rebels on any subject or do any act, either now or hereafter, on their demand." Such would be "disgraceful to myself personally and an infamous surrender of the rights of the people of the Republic."

The Hopkins House had met at ten o'clock on the morning of the fifth, and after some inconsequential business, adjourned.

As the Cunningham House, which by the Democrats was called the "Stevens Rump," was adjourned to two-thirty o'clock that afternoon, Spackman, a member from Philadelphia, went to the House at that time and attempted to adjourn it to the next day. He was prevented from doing this by Democratic guards there and Representative McElwee, who told him that if he attempted to adjourn the House, he (McElwee) who then seemed to be in charge, "would not be responsible for his safety."

Flenniken wrote his constituents, "I have the greatest apprehensions that before tomorrow night the blood of our fellow citizens will flow in the Capitol and in the streets of Harrisburg. Members are arming themselves with the weapons of death, and what is to be the consequence, God only knows." [51]

With excitement unabated, Governor Ritner called upon the Federal troops at Carlisle to come to Harrisburg "for the suppression of the insurrection and for the preservation of our Republican form of Government, agreeably with the Constitution of the United States." The officer in charge answered that "as the disturbance at the Capitol of this State appears to proceed from political difference alone, I do not feel that it would be proper for me to interpose my command between the parties."

The Governor, therefore, on December 7, wrote President Martin Van Buren, informing him of the "domestic violence" existing at Harrisburg and requesting him to take measures to protect that State.[52] Through his Secretary of War, the Democrat President replied in very much the same tone as the commander at Carlisle had done.

With all hope for Federal help removed, Ritner called upon the State militia to report at Harrisburg, and the first contingent arrived on the evening of the ninth.[53] General Paterson in command, on December 7 issued his famous order for the troops to "assemble in winter uniform, with knapsacks, provided with thirteen rounds of buckshot, cartridge, etc." And from this order the "War" took its name.

The movement of militia toward the Capitol had a decidedly quieting effect on the rioting elements there. The Senate was permitted to meet without disturbance on the eighth. The Hopkins House had continued to gather in the House Chamber and the Cunningham House, or 'Stevens Rump,' met at a hotel room until it was locked out, when it gathered once or twice in the Supreme Court room.[54]

When the Democrats learned that the Governor had actually called out the militia, their speaker appointed sergeants-at-arms and the Democratic sheriff of the county, sympathizing with them, appointed additional deputies, which groups together numbered approximately one hundred twenty-five men. However, Ritner

was scrupulously careful that the soldiers in no way
interfered with the procedure of either of the legislative bodies. He notified General Paterson on December 8 that the object of the militia's presence was
"exclusively that of preventing violence and bloodshed"
and forbade the use of weapons by troops for everything "except maintenance of the public peace."

Two days later he ordered the General to "permit
no officer or private in uniform or armed to enter within
the enclosure in which the State Capitol stands." [55]

On the nineteenth day of December, the Whig Senate
refused to deal with the Hopkins House. But six days
later, after some defections from the Cunningham
group had reenforced it, the Upper Body, by a seventeen to sixteen vote, recognized the Hopkins House.
The 'War' was over.

Stevens, however, was not among those who admitted
defeat. In a letter to his constituents dated December
26, he explained that some of his fellows who with him
had constituted the Cunningham House, "unwilling to
forego the advantages of local legislation and despair-
ing of obtaining justice for their constituents without
their personal attendance" . . . had "determined to submit to the mortifying necessity and enter the illegal
House."

But that was their choice, not his. With their course
he said he found "no fault." However he believed his
Adams County constituents "preferred the permanent
interests of our whole country to your own temporary
benefit." Such could be preserved only by refusing to
yield anything to lawless rebellion. "I find no difficulty
in choosing my own course in selecting between an asso-

ciation with successful insurgents or withdrawing from office. Such voluntary association would sanctify or at least palliate their treason. Preferring retirement to dishonor, I withdraw from the Legislature to mingle again with you and wait upon your decision on my conduct. I shall take another occasion to give a more extended account of the alarming acts which have disgraced the last month, and wounded, I feel, irrevocably, the very heart of *freedom.*"[56]

One of the conditions on which the Senate acknowledged the Hopkins House was that Hopkins, the speaker, should resign as soon as the House was recognized. This he did, but was immediately reelected.

Stevens conscientiously believed that his position was the only legal one and that the Democrats had succeeded in organizing the House unlawfully and by force alone. Realizing that if he submitted and took his seat, he would be in the midst of not only bitter political enemies whom he considered a "band of rebels," [57] but a host of deserting supporters, he absented himself from Harrisburg. The Legislature continued in session until March 27, when it adjourned to May 7.

In the meantime, at a mass meeting in Gettysburg,[58] his constituents, although they staunchly supported him in his refusal to take his seat in the House, requested him to attend the next session, believing he "could be of service to the Commonwealth."

In his answer, he said he had not changed his opinion of the legality of the Hopkins House, still believing it to be a "usurping body, forced upon the State by a band of rebels who have shaken to their fall the pillars of our Constitution. But," he added with unusual grace,

[135]

"I owe too much to the kindness and steady confidence of the people of Adams County to disobey their wishes, however delicately intimated. I shall therefore conquer my repugnance to it and enter the House at the adjourned session. I shall feel happy if, contrary to my expectations, I shall be able to be of any service to you, the Commonwealth at large, and the liberty of the people which I fear is doomed to a short existence."[59]

However, the fires of party hatred were still burning at Harrisburg, and when on May 8, Stevens' colleague from Adams County announced that Stevens was then "in his seat and ready to take the requisite qualifications," his old political enemy, McElwee, offered a resolution in bar of his admission.

Under the proposal a committee of five was appointed "to investigate the claims of Stevens to a seat in the House of Representatives of Pennsylvania, and whether he has, if duly elected, forfeited his seat by malconduct."

Accordingly, on May 11, the committee was appointed, but its composition was prophetic in that of its five members, four had already voted to refuse Stevens his seat.[60]

Thirty-eight members of the House, among whom were some Democrats, filed of record their reasons for protest against the House's refusal to seat Stevens. They were convinced such procedure was irregular and illegal.[61]

Stevens was duly invited to appear before the investigating committee but refused. In a letter to them under date of May 13, he said, in referring to the remarks of McElwee on the resolution to refuse him his

seat, that the "grounds of such forfeiture as set forth by
him consist in non-user, mis-user, contempt of the
House by calling it an illegal body—the offspring of a
mob, and sundry personal improprieties."

He was on firm legal ground when he continued,
"no Constitutional disqualification was or is alleged,
and for none other can the House, without an illegal
exercise of arbitrary power, prevent a member elected
from taking his seat. Expulsion for good cause after
admission stands on different grounds, and is authorized by the Constitution," but "until a member-elect has
taken the requisite oaths, he can no more participate
in the proceedings of the House, nor is he any more
subject to its jurisdiction, than a private citizen."

Although he still considered the Hopkins House a
"usurping body," nevertheless, "like all other usurpers
having possession of the government de facto, its acts
will be binding for good or evil on the State. Hence
my constituents have thought it proper to ask me to
take my seat and attempt to moderate the evil which
is now without remedy."

While he had been at home in Gettysburg, a warrant
had been sworn out for him on an information charging him with fornication and bastardy.[62] His enemies
in the House made much of this. But if the Committee
was to sit in judgment on such matters, Stevens would
further object, for he could not "admit the intellectual,
moral or habitual competency of McElwee, his compeers, coadjutors and followers to decide a question of
decency and morals." [63]

On May 20, the committee reported that Stevens
"having resigned his office, is not entitled to a seat in

the House" and recommended that the speaker issue a "writ of election to fill the vacancy." [64] The House adopted the majority report and the speaker acted accordingly, fixing June 14 for the special voting.[65]

On May 25, Stevens addressed a letter to his constituents in which he reported the refusal of the "tyrants who have usurped power" to seat him. He said, "if they are permitted finally to triumph, you hold your liberty, your life, your reputation, and your property in their will alone.... Both my inclination and my interest require me to retire from public life, but I will not execute that settled intention when it will be construed into cowardice or despondency. To refuse to be a candidate now would be seized upon by my enemies as an evidence that I distrust the people and I am afraid to entrust to them the redress of their own wrongs."

He called for restoration of that which he had "been robbed by those who 'feel power and forget right,'" and appealed to "every freeman of his constituents, regardless of party, to rebuke tyranny in that great tribunal of freeman—the ballot box." [66]

He was overwhelmingly reelected, appeared in the House and subscribed to the oath on June 19. The session lasted but a few days, and when it adjourned on June 27, Stevens hastened home. Besides his regular law practice, there were two matters that required his attention.

One was the indictment against him which the Grand Jury had found in his absence. He had entered bail to answer the charges at the next term of Court. While in Harrisburg, his old friend McPherson had written him from Gettysburg that he would be glad to do what he could to help him in the criminal matter. Stevens thanked him and told him he had been informed that five men in the home town were at the bottom of the trouble. He gave their names and said that they had often, through the winter, visited the girl's father "and urged him by all manner of arguments to bring suit... assuring him that he could recover twenty thousand dollars and offering to back him with money."

The only thing that surprised Stevens in the whole matter was that one of the names mentioned was that of a gentleman with whom he had always been on most friendly terms.

He flatly denied guilt in the affair, saying that he would show "beyond doubt that the girl was courted —and worse than merely courted—by a man who turned out to be married at the time. Nevertheless, I wish the cursed matter were ended. But I shall never make advances. I shall carry on the war in the same spirit in which it was begun; and regret it more for the sake of the weak girl—the instrument of her father's cupidity, than for my own." [67]

When the case was called at the next term, Stevens was absent. It was continued and bail renewed. Before the succeeding term came around, the action had been withdrawn and closed. Rumor had it that Stevens had compromised the suit, but no record remains, not even newspaper insinuation, that he effected a settlement.

The second matter that he wished to attend to was the criminal prosecution that he and his followers had instituted against the Democratic leaders of the Buck- shot War. The cases had first been called in April [68]

when the defendants, through their counsel, challenged
the array of jurors on the ground that it had not been
properly drawn. They were sustained in their contention and continuances granted.

When the actions were called a second time, objection was made again to the jury panel on the ground
that the Commissioners had discriminated in their selections. With the Democratic newspapers shouting
"packed juries," the Court again sustained the defendants' motion.[69] A week later when called for a third
time, the prosecuting witnesses were not present and
the defendants were discharged.[70] Thus died the last
echoes of the Buckshot War. And with it died the
political power of the Whig-Anti-Masonic alliance.
The Democrats by the margin of a hair's breadth had
retrieved control of the State Government, and en-
trenching themselves, held it for the next decade.

For Stevens, it was utter route and in one phase at
least, irremediable ruin. It was well understood in
Pennsylvania in the latter part of 1838 that if the Anti-
Masonic-Whig combination was successful in gaining
control of the Legislature, that Stevens would be the
next United States Senator.[71] With Democratic success, these hopes which had been based on excellent
prospects, were shattered irrevocably.

Had he gone to the Senate at that time, the history of
our Nation might read much differently today. Perhaps the War of the Rebellion would have come much
earlier, or with a firm hand in control in place of the
weak ones which guided the Nation's action, especially
in Buchanan's administration, the terrible War might
have been entirely averted.

In light of the ease with which he was able to continue himself in Congress from one election to another, it is reasonable to suppose that he could and would have continued himself in the Senate of the United States when once he had arrived there. The conjecture may be interesting to speculate upon; the fact was that for Stevens the Buckshot War spelled repudiation, retirement, and temporary political oblivion.

V

EDUCATOR

The present outstanding public school system of Pennsylvania is the product of the genius of no single man or group of men. Its development from the time when William Penn in his first "Frame of Government" gave the Governor and Provincial Council the power to "erect and order all public schools" to its creditable position of today, is an interesting study of progressive group attitude.

But interesting as it might be to trace the vaguely expressed and evolving desire of the early settlers for education of their children which crystallized in 1776 in the constitutional mandate to the legislature "to establish schools in each county," and a somewhat similar enjoiner upon the legislature in the constitution of 1790 "to establish schools throughout the state;" to note the firm and consistent advocation by the governors for the next forty years to carry out the constitutional direction and follow the gropings of the legislators to discover the will of the people in the premises, such is outside the scope of this work.

In no state or colony in the Union was the task of establishing public schools as difficult as it was in Pennsylvania. The problem of the Keystone State, in large measure, was due to the heterogeneous texture of her people which consisted of a greater number of religious, political, and national groups than that of any other state. There could be no uniform feeling, and it was practically impossible to definitely ascertain the composite, popular will in the matter.

The astounding fact about it all is that Pennsylvania did develop a fairly good public school system as early as it did. It was not a copy of any other nor did it spring into being fully developed. Slowly taking form through a score of decades, it stands today the sublimated result of the thought and labor of many farsighted educators, legislators and patriots. Credit for it can be given to no individual, but if a single person should be designated who has contributed most toward that great public school system, the honor goes to Thaddeus Stevens.

Earliest settlers in Pennsylvania were compelled to devote most of their time to acquiring the necessaries of life. There was but little time and scant equipment to educate their children. Of the many varied groups who came first to Penn's Province, everyone had been accustomed to associate education with the Church. Secular instruction was embraced within the brackets of religious training as one of its component parts, and that idea had been ingrained through the generations. This proved the first great barrier to public schools. Practically all religious sects joined hands in opposing the severance.

Especially assertive in this position were the Friends, Mennonites, Lutherans and Reformed. But this was a new country where new ideas found easier expression. In the homelands, few would have thought of independent schools. Nevertheless, in Pennsylvania several had been established by the Dutch and Swedes before Penn came. They were, of course, under church supervision and control, but the idea was clearly an advance. More were opened within the half century after the

Founder's arrival, as were also a few academies. By 1725, it was not unusual in Southeastern Pennsylvania to find a schoolhouse operated in conjunction with a church, where both used the same room or building. People were slowly becoming accustomed to a program that used a community building for church services on Sunday, and school purposes through the week.

In the Pennsylvania Constitution of 1776 was a provision that "a school or schools shall be established in each county by the legislature for the convenient instruction of youth, with such salaries to the master paid by the public as may enable them to instruct youth at low prices; and all useful learning shall be duly encouraged and promoted in one or more universities." In this the authors were laying the ground work for free schools, but if they saw it at all, it was only in the dim distance. Their plan was scarcely an advance upon "Pennsylvania's Frames" submitted nearly a hundred years before, and from which it seems to have been modeled.[1] Many schemes for public instruction of youth had been suggested through the intervening years.[2]

The first legislation carrying into effect the school mandate of the 1790 Constitution was passed in 1802. But here the Legislature itself raised a second barrier in providing "instruction for poor children only." The Executives showed a greater breadth of vision in recommending schools impliedly for the use of all. But the lawmakers, checked by the popular will, vitiated the school enactments by confining their benefits to children whose parents could not otherwise provide for their education.

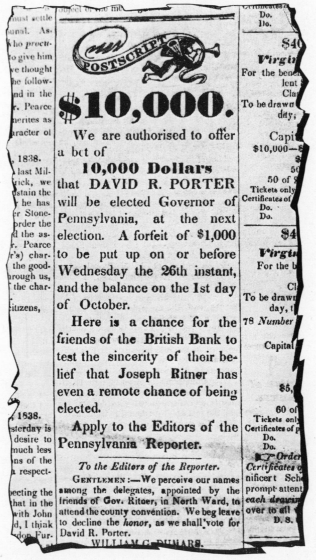

From the Harrisburg Reporter and State Journal, September 21, 1838.

An Example of the Election Betting in the Campaign of 1838

No community took advantage of the 1802 enactments. Two years later, another act was passed, aiming to "more effectually provide education for the children of the poor gratuitously." This also was ignored, and in 1809 a further law was passed "to teach the children of the poor gratis." Although clearer and sounder, it defeated its own purpose, for it required parents to mark their children as paupers in order to obtain free tuition. Public registration of their inability to pay for the schooling of their children was grossly offensive to citizens, who were of Anglo-Saxon and German origins.

It is not surprising that little was done under any of these enactments, and in 1824 all were repealed and another substituted. This was in turn repealed in 1826, and the Act of 1809 reinstated. Such, briefly, was the history and status of the school laws when Stevens became a member of the Legislature.

His zeal to extend educational opportunities to the masses, early showed itself and continued with uniform intensity throughout life. It was a necessary corollary to his ambition for human equality in the matter of liberties, rights and punishments. To him, education was the best means afforded to humankind to obtain equal opportunity in life, and he never veered from his staunch conviction that public schools were a fundamental requisite for the maintenance of our form of Government.

Municipally provided instruction was, for a long time, most unpopular in Stevens' home county of Adams. But he untiringly agitated for it. As early as 1825, he believed he had convinced his town of the advantages of public schools and felt confident that a vote

would so indicate. But he was too optimistic. When
the ballots were counted, it showed that eighty-two had
voted 'No Schools' while only sixty-eight voted 'For
Schools.'[3] This in spite of the fact that the vote was
taken under the direction of Stevens and his committee
who favored free schools.[4] In fact every township in
the county showed a decided opinion in opposition.[5]
He kept up his propaganda, however, and at public
gatherings where toasts were offered, his would be
"Education—May the film be removed from the eyes
of Pennsylvania and she learn to dread ignorance more
than taxation." [6] Against a majority opposition, he continued preaching his beliefs and materially aiding
academies and seminaries.[7]

If forced to choose between the cause of education
and his political ambitions, he never hesitated to sacra-
fice the latter in favor of the former. When he first
entered the Legislature in 1833, he well knew from his
many soundings of public opinion that his constituents,
by a great majority, disapproved of state financial aid
to colleges. But, as he saw it, the voters were wrong,
and whether or not it antagonized them, he would do
his duty. He supported to the limit a measure appropriating money to Gettysburg College, and with full
understanding of what it might mean to his public
career, staunchly defended his action.

When severely taken to task for it, he did not retire
to the defensive. His people had rebuked him; he put
in plain words his feeling toward them. "But what was
the surprise of the Legislature and my mortification, to
see a large number of remonstrances presented against
it, signed by the citizens of the very county in the midst

of which it is located. Nor was that mortification lessoned when I learnt that an organized political party, as such, had in a formal meeting resolved to oppose it, and that that party was the one to which it was my pride to belong. You say," he went on, "you pledged yourselves as my friends that I would oppose the college. I deny that I ever authorized such pledge, nor indeed do you assert it." Defiantly answering his Anti-Masonic Party's threat to defeat him for his stand, he said, "painful as it is, if such must be the consequence of bestowing a blessing upon your children and the state at large, *let it come*. I would sooner lose every friend on earth than violate the glorious dictates of my own conscience—the clearest commands of my official oath."

"Pardon me, therefore, while I tell you I cannot obey your orders. I will not sacrifice your posterity to selfish view. Gentlemen, to you in your company I dared to make war upon a powerful and revengeful institution. If, to secure the country from moral treason, I consented to part with old and valued friends; if I did not shrink amidst the most malignant prosecutions that ever man endured, you will scarcely expect me to yield now, when ignorance and avarice and bigotry are sweeping over you in a blasting whirlwind."

The letter gives a superb flashlight picture of his character. Where principle was involved, there was no hesitating, no mincing of words even when his own party, creature of his thought and work, was on the other side. It might hurt beyond expression; it might precipitate him with breath-taking swiftness to private life and even forever bar his return. But all that was of no weight against his seeking for the right as it appeared to him. He showed the courage that was inherent in him when he concluded, "I have already resolved that the sight of my name shall never again burthen your ticket. I will withdraw active part in your political discussions. And if it be necessary to the wellbeing of our country, dear to me as are my friends and constituents, I shall withdraw from your county to some place where the advocates of *Anti-Masonry* may still be the advocates of *knowledge*." Relaxing, he quaintly signed the letter, "your faithful, if not obedient servant, Thaddeus Stevens." [8]

Bitter hardship had attended his own efforts to obtain an education, and no one knew better than he the obstacles ahead of the poor youth who desired to learn. To finance himself in college he had taught school for two or three of the short winter terms in Vermont and so knew how few educational advantages were offered. In Gettysburg, he had given up his position on the Borough Council to become a school director. He was vigorous, farsighted, and broad in his educational outlook. Whatever he could do to encourage learning was done with all the concentrated power of his dynamic being.

Although a few prominent educators had located in and about Gettysburg, community feeling toward education was not in advance of its time and lack of public instruction was as much felt there as elsewhere. Through the years, Stevens, as school director, as lawyer, as borough councilman, as business man, and as public speaker, used all the weight of his influence to further the cause of education of the masses. He aided academies in debt,[9] supported professors [10] in Gettysburg, and loaned his books to schools.[11] He was among those instrumental in obtaining a charter for Pennsylvania College in 1832, and from the time of its establishment, assisted it in all ways possible. He permitted one of its buildings to be erected on his property, and then deeded the land to the College for a nominal amount.[12] It is notable that during his first term as a member of the Pennsylvania Legislature, he obtained for this College over vehement protest and remonstrance, an appropriation of $18,000.

When his colleague from Adams County, Patterson, obeying the commands of their constituents, opposed the grant, Stevens found himself pointedly between his instructions and his desires. Patterson had made a vigorous speech opposing aid to colleges [13] and when he sat down, the members turned curiously to Stevens. He arose slowly to "congratulate the House and country on the possession of at least one man who, in stern and cold integrity, rivals the Roman father who sat in judgment and passed sentence of death upon his own son." But "if such punishment must beset those who ought to be dear to us," Stevens felt "the blows should be dealt by some other hand."

He was certain "that the creation of literary institutions, the establishment of common schools, and the spreading of means of information throughout the Commonwealth, are as necessary to the permanency of our free institutions, to intellectual enjoyment and respectability, as food is to the existence of animal life. Until this is done, Pennsylvania will never hold rank which the integrity, industry and wealth of her citizens entitle her to in the Councils of the Nation."

Berating his colleague for opposing expenditure of money "only when it goes to the improvement of the mind," he said Patterson and "those who think with him, deem it of much more importance that mudholes in their roads should be filled up, that their horses may go dry-shod to mill, than that the rubbish of ignorance should be cleared away from the intellects of our children." He suspected that real hostility to the bill was founded on latent dread of learning. "When a boy in a distant part of the Union, I read in a newspaper what purported to be an extract from a speech delivered by a member of the Pennsylvania Legislature. He said 'I hate learning and I hate learned men.' . . . No man would venture to utter, although I fear too many entertain that sentiment."

He cared not that their constituents directed them to oppose the bill. "In matters of doubtful propriety of mere local concern, the will of our constituents clearly expressed should be obeyed," but when they were manifestly in error, it was the duty of representatives to resist their will and do them good, however ungrateful they may be for it.

The ancients believed that for the success of any great enterprise, some victims should be offered up on their altars; and it might be that the great cause of education in Pennsylvania required that some victim be offered up on the altar of ignorance and avarice. If "I could be deemed a sufficient propitiation, I know of no one whose sacrifice would be less regretted, whose immolation would break fewer ties." If a single individual dared aspire to such high immortality, he

would press forward to that honored post of martyr-
dom, and "most willingly say, 'let it come to pass,' and
on my devoted head be the concentrated vengeance of
diluted error and infuriated avarice."

True it might be that Stevens was ambitious; he would
be proud to rank among statemen, but he scorned to
degrade himself to the level of demagogues. His ambition did not consist "in the desire to be the idol of
fools, and his noblest enjoyment the propagation of
their folly." If the agitators of ignorance outnumbered
the advocates of knowledge, he would not change his
course, "and demagogues might note it for future use
and send it on the wings of the wind to the ears of
everyone of my constituents." He would rather "hear
the approving voice of one judicious, intelligent and
enlightened mind than be greeted by the loud huzzas of
the whole host of ignorance." His course was "fixed.
Let others shape theirs as they please. If they desire
it, let them so vote as to secure, for another blessed year,
the privilege of resting upon the cushions of this envied
Hall. It is far easier to secure such a resting place
than to repose with honor upon the bosom of future
ages. For my part, I shall be amply rewarded, if my
exertions shall have earned the benedictions of the
friends of learning, and the poor man's children." [14]

During that term, he was unceasingly active in enlarging and bettering the conditions of every educational institution that sought aid.

Although he has been frequently referred to as the
father of the common school system in Pennsylvania,
the appellation is not exactly correct. He can be more
strictly designated as its "saviour." In order to better

understand the situation existing at that time, it is necessary to note that the Public School Act of 1834 was signed by Governor Wolfe on the first day of April. So intense and widespread was the feeling against the law that it formed the main issue in the Fall elections. Nearly all Legislators were elected on a platform committed to repeal or received specific instructions to that end.

Before the matter was presented to the new Legislature early in 1835, hundreds of petitions favoring repeal had poured into the House of Representatives. The official report said that nearly 32,000 [15] persons sought repeal of the statute while only 2,500 favored its continuance. Leading reasons for objection to the law were the extra taxes that would be necessarily incurred; that it removed instruction from religious control, and ridiculous as it may sound today, an argument used with much effect, was that it would force the whole group to pay for instruction to benefit only that part of the group who had children in school.

Stevens was absent on a committee investigation when the repealer was called up in the Legislature. It met no opposition in the Senate, and no one believed any member had the temerity to oppose it in the House. Informed that it was about to be called up in the Assembly, the Gettysburgian hurried to Harrisburg. His Adams County colleague, McSherry, met him to report that he had again sounded out their constituents and was clearly convinced that practically all of them determinedly insisted upon the repealer, and that he would so vote.

The fact was, McSherry reported, that a test vote

had shown that there were but few in the House who would vote against it and "that the friends of the law had consulted and agreed that it was useless to oppose the repealer." [16] But the Governor had indicated that he would veto the repealer and this no doubt fortified Stevens. He was the only member in the entire Legislature courageous enough to defy the steamroller of public opinion.

Shortly after noon of the eleventh of April, the bill was called up in the House. Word went round that in spite of what looked like an already lost cause, Stevens would address the House in defense of it. The galleries were filled. Nearly every member was in his seat and many of the Senators, hearing of his bold plan had come down to the House. Appearing as advocate before a goodly and attentive audience, for what he believed to be the noblest of causes, Stevens thrilled to the occasion. His speech on that memorable occasion and in that great debate, carried him to the heights. It was his first great opportunity to test the power of his spoken words.

He arose in that impressive assembly and began in plain, straight from the shoulder manner: "I will briefly give you," he said, "the reasons why I shall oppose the repeal of the School Law. To repeal it now, before its practical effects have been discovered, would argue that it contained some glaring and pernicious defect, and that the last Legislature acted under some strong and fatal delusion, which blinded every man of them to the interests of the Commonwealth. I will attempt to show that the law is salutary, useful and important; and that consequently the last Legislature acted wisely in passing, and the present one would act unwisely in repealing it; that, instead of being oppressive to the people, it will lighten their burdens, while it elevates them in the scale of human intellect."

Asserting that he deemed no formal argument necessary "to prove the utility, and to free governments the absolute necessity of education," he reasoned, "if, then, education be of admitted importance to the people under all forms of government, and of unquestioned necessity when they govern themselves, it follows, of course, that its cultivation and diffusion is a matter of public concern, and a duty which every government owes to its people. In accordance with this principle, the ancient republics, which were most renowned for their wisdom and success, considered every child born subject to their control, as the property of the State, so far as its education was concerned; and during the proper period of instruction, they were withdrawn from the control of their parents, and placed under the guardianship of the Commonwealth."

Indicative of his real democratic attitude, he praised the old-time method where "all were instructed at the same school; all were placed on perfect equality, the rich and the poor man's sons; for all were deemed children of the same common parent—the Commonwealth. Indeed, where all have the means of knowledge placed within their reach, and meet at common schools on equal terms, the forms of government seem of less importance to the happiness of the people than is generally supposed; or rather, such a people are seldom in danger of having their rights invaded by their rulers."

With sound logic, he argued that, "if an elective republic is to endure for any great length of time, every elector must have sufficient information, not only to accumulate wealth and take care of his pecuniary concerns, but to direct wisely the Legislature, the Ambassadors, and the Executive of the Nation; for some part of all these things, some agency in approving or disapproving of them, falls to every freeman. If, then, the permanency of our government depends upon such knowledge, it is the duty of government to see that the means of information be diffused to every citizen." This he thought was sufficient answer to those who "deem education a private and not a public duty—who argue that they are willing to educate their own children, but not their neighbor's."

To those alarmed at the supposed burdensome cost of operation, he said that, "a little judicious reflection, or a single year's experience, would show that education, under the free-school system will cost more than one-half less and afford better and more permanent instruction, than the present disgraceful plan pursued by Pennsylvania."

He explained how the Act of 1834 would result in a saving of nearly five hundred dollars per annum per township over the costs of administration under the school laws then in force. Opposing the amendment then before the House in substitution for the then existing law, he said, "It is, in my opinion, of a most hateful and degrading character. It is a reenactment of the pauper law of 1809. It proposes that the assessors shall take a census, and make a record of the poor. This shall be revised, and a new record made by the County Commissioners, so that the names of those who have the misfortune to be poor men's children shall be forever preserved as a distinct class, in the archives of the county!"

The teacher, too, would be compelled to keep in his school a pauper book and register the names and attendance of poor scholars; thus pointing out and recording their poverty in the midst of their companions. "Sir, hereditary distinctions of rank are sufficiently odious; but that which is founded on poverty is infinitely more so. Such a law should be entitled, 'an act for branding and marking the poor, so that they may be known from the rich and proud.'"

To answer those opposed to the necessary taxes as not benefiting themselves, he pointedly remarked that "their attitude was a mistake. It is for their own benefit, inasmuch as it perpetuates the government and ensures the due administration of the laws under which they live, and by which their lives and property are protected. Why do they not urge the same objection against all other taxes? The industrious, thrifty, rich farmer pays a heavy county tax to support criminal courts, build jails, and pay sheriffs and jail keepers, and yet probably he never has had and never will have any direct personal use for any of them.

"He never gets the worth of his money by being tried for a crime before a court, allowed the privilege of a jail on conviction, or by receiving an equivalent from the sheriff and his hangmen officers! He cheerfully pays the burdensome taxes which are necessarily levied to support and punish convicts, but loudly complains of that which goes to prevent his fellow-being from becoming a criminal, and to obviate the necessity of those humiliating institutions."

His logic was equally forceful when he turned to another class of opponents. "This law is often objected to because its benefits are shared by the children of the profligate spendthrift equally with those of most industrious and economical habits. It ought to be remembered that the benefit is bestowed, not upon the erring parents, but the innocent children. Carry out this objection, and you punish children for the crimes or misfortunes of their parents. You virtually establish castes and grades, founded on no merit of the particular generation, but on the demerits of their ancestors; an aristocracy of the most odious and insolent kind—the aristocracy of wealth and pride."

He deemed another objection of sufficient importance to remark, "It is said that its advantages will be unjustly and unequally enjoyed, because the industrious, money-making man keeps his whole family constantly employed, and has but little time for them to spend at school; while the idle man has but little employment for his family, and they will constantly attend school. I know, sir, that there are some men whose whole souls are so completely absorbed in the accumulation of wealth, and whose avarice so increases with success, that they look upon their very children in no other light than as instruments of gain—that they, as well as the ox and ass within their gates, are valuable only in proportion to their annual earnings."

Under the then existing system, the children of such men were reduced almost to an intellectual level with their co-laborers of the brute creation. The 1834 law would be of vast advantage to the offspring of such misers. If they were compelled to pay taxes to support schools, their very meanness would induce them to educate their children in order to get the worth of their money. Thus it would extract good out of the very penuriousness of the miser. "Surely a system which will work such wonders ought to be as greedily sought for and more highly prized than that coveted alchemy which was to produce gold and silver out of the blood and entrails of vipers, lizards, and other filthy vermin!"

In comparing the relatively backward schools of Pennsylvania with those of his own New England, he asked, "Why, sir, are the colleges and literary institutions of Pennsylvania now, and ever have been, in a languishing and sickly condition? Why, with a fertile soil and genial climate, has she, in proportion to her population, scarcely one-third as many collegiate students as cold, barren New England?" The answer was obvious: "Pennsylvania has no free schools. Until she shall have, you may in vain endow college after college; they will never be filled, or filled only by students from other States.

"In New England free schools plant the seeds and the desire of knowledge in every mind, without regard to the wealth of the parent, or the texture of the pupil's garments. When seed, thus universally sown, happens to fall on fertile soil, it springs up and is fostered by a generous public, until it produces its glorious fruit. Those who have but scanty means, and are pursuing a collegiate education, find it necessary to spend a portion of the year in teaching common schools. They impart the knowledge which they acquire and raise the dignity of the employment to an honorable rank which

it should always hold in proportion to the high qualifications necessary for its discharge.

"Because they devote a portion of their time to acquiring the means of subsistence, industrious habits are
forced upon them, and their minds and bodies become
disciplined to a regularity and energy which is seldom
the lot of the rich. It is no uncommon occurrence to
see the poor man's son, thus encouraged by wise legislation, far outstrip and bear off the laurels from the
less industrious heirs of wealth. Some of the ablest men
of the present and past days never could have been educated except for that benevolent system.

"Not to mention any of the living, it is well known
that the architect of an immortal name who 'plucked
the lightnings from Heaven, and the sceptre from tyrants' was the child of free schools. Why shall Pennsylvania now repudiate a system which is calculated to
elevate her to that rank in the intellectual, which, by the
blessing of Providence, she holds in the natural world
—to be the keystone of the arch, the 'very first among
her equals?' I am aware how difficult it is for the great
mass of the people, who have never seen this system in
operation, to understand its advantages. But is it not
wise to let it go in to full operation, and learn its results from experience? Then, if it prove useless or burdensome, how easy to repeal it!

"I know how large a portion of the community can
scarcely feel any sympathy with, or understand the
necessities of the poor; or appreciate the exquisite feelings which they enjoy, when they see their children
receiving the boon of education, and rising in intellectual superiority above the clogs which hereditary poverty

had cast upon them. It is not wonderful that he whose fat acres have descended to him, from father to son, in unbroken succession, should never have sought for the surest means of alleviating it. When I reflect how apt hereditary wealth, hereditary influence, and perhaps as a consequence, hereditary pride, are to close the avenues and steel the heart against the wants and the rights of the poor, I am induced to thank my Creator for having, from early life, bestowed upon me the blessing of poverty. Sir, it is a blessing—for if there be any human sensation more ethereal and divine than all others, it is that which feelingly sympathizes with misfortune."

He came to the general unpopularity of the then law. "Has it not always been so with every reform in the condition of man?" he demanded. "Old habits and old prejudices are hard to be removed from the mind. Every new improvement which has been gradually leading man from the savage, through the civilized, up to a highly cultivated state, has required the most strenuous and often perilous exertions of the wise and the good.

"But, sir, much of its unpopularity is chargeable upon the vile arts of unprincipled demagogues. Instead of attempting to remove the honest misapprehensions of the people, they cater to their prejudices, and take advantage of them, to gain low, dirty, temporary, local triumphs. I do not charge this on any particular party. Unfortunately, almost the only spot on which all parties meet in union, is this ground of common infamy!"

So much for the general attack on the repealer. With his merciless barbs he had set the whole Legislature to thinking. His problem now was to rally support to sustain the 1834 law. His method was a striking mixture of force and threat on the one hand, and appeal to intelligence on the other. Governor Wolfe had never been Stevens' friend, but the man from Gettysburg took advantage of the Executive's support in a subtle bid for the votes of his followers.

"I have seen the present chief magistrate of this Commonwealth violently assailed as the projector and father of this law. I am not the eulogist of that gentleman; he has been guilty of many deep political sins. But he deserves the undying gratitude of the people for the steady, untiring zeal which he has manifested in favor of common schools. I will not say his exertions in that cause have covered all, but they have atoned for many of his errors. I trust that the people of this State will never be called upon to choose between a supporter and an opposer of free schools. But if it should come to that, if that should be made the turning point on which we are to cast our suffrages, if the opponent of education were my most intimate personal and political friend, and the free school candidate my most obnoxious enemy, I should deem it my duty, as a patriot at this moment of our intellectual crisis, to forget all other considerations, and I should place myself unhesitatingly and cordially, in the ranks of him whose banner streams in light!"

He rebuked his own Anti-Masonic party for yielding principle to popularity. "I would not foster or flatter ignorance to gain political victories, which, however they might profit individuals, must prove disastrous to our country. Let it not be supposed from these remarks, that because I deem this a paramount subject, I think less highly than heretofore of those great, important cardinal principles which for years have controlled my political action. They are, and ever shall be, deeply cherished in my inmost heart. But I must be allowed to exercise my own judgment as to the best means of effecting that and every other object which I think beneficial to the community. And, according to that judgment, the light of general information will as surely counteract the pernicious influence of secret, oathbound, murderous institutions as the sun in heaven dispels the darkness and damp vapors of the night."

He turned to those Representatives who owed "their election to their hostility of general education" and others who "lost their election by being in favor of it." Referring to two of the latter class, Stevens said he believed they "did fail of reelection on that ground only. They were summoned before a county meeting, and requested to pledge themselves to vote for its repeal as the price of their reelection. But they were too high-minded and honorable to consent to such degradation. The people, incapable for the moment of appreciating their worth, dismissed them from their service. But I venture to predict that they have passed them by, only for the moment. Those gentlemen have earned the approbation of all good and intelligent men more effectually by their retirement, than they could ever have done by retaining popular favor at the expense of self-humiliation. They fell, it is true, in this great struggle between the powers of light and darkness; but they fell, as every Roman mother wishes her sons to fall, facing the enemy, with all their wounds in front."

Of two other wavering members who were defeated
for somewhat similar reasons, he regretted, "that gentlemen whom I so highly respect, and whom I take pleasure
in ranking among my personal friends, had not possessed a little more nerve to enable them to withstand
the assaults which were made upon them; or, if they
must be overpowered, to wrap their mantles gracefully
around them and yield with dignity. But this, I am
aware, requires a high degree of fortitude; and those respected gentlemen, distracted and faltering between the
dictates of conscience and the clamor of the populace,
at length turned and fled; but duty had detained them
so long that they fled too late, and the shaft which had
already been winged by ignorance, overtook and pierced
them from behind. I am happy to say, sir, that a more
fortunate fate awaited our friends from York. Possess-
ing a keener insight into futurity, and a sharper in-
stinct of danger, they saw the peril at a greater distance,
and retreated in time to escape the fury of the storm,
and can now safely boast that 'discretion is the better
part of valor' and that 'they fought and ran away' and
'live to fight'—on t'other side."

To any member, and there were many, who consented
to base his election on hostility to general education,
Stevens remarked that "if honest ambition were his
object, he will ere long lament that he attempted to
raise his monument of glory on so muddy a foundation."
But of those elected on a platform to obstruct the diffusion of knowledge, "it is but justice to say that they
fitly and faithfully represent the spirit which sent them
here, when they attempt to sacrifice this law on the altars
which, at home, among their constituents, they have

raised and consecrated to intellectual darkness; and on which they are pouring oblations to send forth their fetid and noxious odors over the ten miles square of their ambition!"

"But," he inquired, "will this Legislature—will the wise guardians of the dearest interests of a great Commonwealth—consent to surrender the high advantages and brilliant prospects which this law promises, because it is desired by worthy gentlemen, who, in a moment of causeless panic and popular delusion, sailed into power on a Tartarean flood? A flood of ignorance, darker and to the intelligent mind more dreadful, than that accursed Stygian pool, at which mortals and immortals tremble! Sir, it seems to me that the liberal and enlightened proceedings of the last Legislature have aroused the demon of ignorance from his slumber; and maddened at the threatened loss of his murky empire, his discordant howlings are heard in every part of our land."

Vigorously he contended that it was the duty of Representatives not to cherish and obey the prejudices and errors of their constituents, but, "instead of prophesying smooth things, and flattering the people with the belief of their present perfection, and thus retarding the mind in its onward progress, to create and sustain such laws and institutions as shall teach us our wants, foster our cravings after knowledge, and urge us forward in the march of intellect. The barbarous and disgraceful cry which we hear abroad in some parts of our land, 'that learning makes us worse—that education makes men rogues,' should find no echo within these walls. Those who hold such doctrines anywhere would be the objects of bitter detestation if they were not rather the pitiable objects of commiseration. For even voluntary fools require our compassion, as well as natural idiots!"

Of those who, desiring popularity, had sought repeal, and thereby fame, he asked if they had "looked back and consulted the history of their race, to learn on what foundation and on what materials that popularity is built which outlives its possessor—which is not buried in the same grave that covers his mortal remains? Sir, I believe that kind of fame may be acquired by deep learning, or even the love of it, by mild philanthropy or unconquerable courage. And it seems to me, that in the present state of feeling in Pennsylvania, those who will heartily and successfully support the cause of general education can acquire at least some portion of the honor of all these qualities combined; while those who oppose it will be remembered without pleasure and will soon pass away with the things that perish."

He counselled his fellow legislators that "by giving this law to posterity you act the part of the philanthropist, by bestowing upon the poor as well as the rich the greatest earthly boon which they are capable of receiving; you act the part of the philosopher, by pointing out, if you do not lead them up, the hill of science; you act the part of the hero, if it be true, as you say, that popular vengeance follows close upon your footsteps. Here, then, if you wish true popularity, is a theatre in which you may acquire it. What renders the name of Socrates immortal but his love of the human family, exhibited under all circumstances, and in contempt of every danger?

"Courage, even with but little benevolence, may con-

fer lasting renown. It is this which makes us bow with
involuntary respect at the names of Napoleon, of
Caesar, and of Richard the Lion-Hearted. But what
earthly glory is there, equal in lustre and duration to
that conferred by education? What else could have
bestowed such renown upon the philosophers, the poets,
the statesmen, and orators of antiquity? What else
could have conferred such undisputed applause upon
Aristotle, Demosthenes, and Homer; on Virgil, Horace,
and Cicero? And is learning less interesting and important now than it was in centuries past, when those
statesmen and orators charmed and ruled empires with
their eloquence?"

He admonished those who would acquire popularity
"to build not your monuments of brass or marble, but to
make them of ever-living mind!" He encouraged the
members to sustain the then law. Any who would oppose it, either through inability to comprehend the advantages of general education or from unwillingness
to bestow them upon all his fellow citizens, even to the
lowest, to the poorest, or from dread of popular vengeance, seemed to him to lack either the head of the
philosopher, the heart of the philanthropist, or the nerve
of the hero.

In conclusion, he demanded, "who would not rather
do one living deed than to have his ashes forever en-
shrined in burnished gold? Sir! I trust that when we
come to act on this question, we shall take lofty ground
—look beyond the narrow space which now circum-
scribes our vision—beyond the passing, fleeting point
of time on which we stand—and so cast our votes that
the blessing of education shall be conferred on every son

of Pennsylvania—shall be carried home to the poorest
child of the poorest inhabitant of the meanest hut of
your mountains, so that even he may be prepared to act
well his part in this land of freedom, and lay on earth
a broad and solid foundation for that enduring knowledge which goes on increasing through increasing eter-
nity."

The address marked the greatest single effort of his
entire Legislative career. It was the solitary attempt
at oratory in his long life. Reading his words from
printed page can give but faint idea of the striking
impressiveness of its delivery. Those who listened were
awed by his courage, and stunned by the terrible sincerity of his grave endeavor. Scarcely a man in that
Chamber but realized he was battling grimly for a
righteous cause. Fighting unselfishly for an opportunity for the generations to come; fighting to have the
State see to it that because a child were born poor,
poverty should not bar his way to a fair education.

Every listener knew that he had thrown his political
fate in the balance. Willingly, even eagerly, in the
knowledge that what he pled for was overwhelmingly
unpopular.

Extracts of the speech as they above appear are the
best account we have of what Stevens said, but unfortunately, as no means were provided in those days, it
was not recorded as delivered. Afterward, there was
such general demand to have it in writing, that Stevens
who had spoken from but few meager notes, reconstructed it as best he could.[17] Doubtless, what we have
is but a poor reproduction, for setting it down after the
crisis had passed, it must necessarily lack the ardor and

earnestness of the appeal when the decision was being pled for.

Before Stevens spoke, there was little doubt in any one's mind who knew the situation, but that the repealer would pass. The day before, when the resolution was before the Senate on third reading, it was approved without record vote and even without debate.[18] If Senators, whose term of office was four times as long as that of Representatives, were so sensitive to the popular demand, then certainly in greater measure must the members of the House have felt that pressure, and the more especially because many of them had specific instructions for repeal.

The weight of the Commoner's speech is convincingly shown by the fact that the Upper House, most of whose members heard him, very shortly afterward rescinded their action and joined the House in supporting his substituted amendment, which not only approved, but strengthened and enlarged the school law of the year before.

His majestic appeal jolted Pennsylvania back to her good senses. It was the single instance in his life when partisan newspapers of the bitter opposition manfully credited him. The fiercely Democratic *Pennsylvania Reporter* of Harrisburg, which in those days rarely missed an issue that scathed him, approved it as "particularly fine" and felt "assured that a more beautiful effort at oratory was never listened to within the walls of this or any other Legislative Hall." [19]

A contemporary historian [20] politically opposed and unfriendly to Stevens, who went so far as to impugn Stevens' motive in defending the Free School System,[21]

said, "his speech had a magical effect upon the sentiments of members . . . All, without distinction, whether
enemies or friends, acknowledged the overpowering superiority of it. Many who had determined to favor
repeal changed their opinions and voted to sustain the
Law of 1834. This speech ranked its author henceforth,
as one of the first intellects of Pennsylvania." [22]

It marked the highpoint of Stevens' early life and
gained for him admiration and praise from political
friends and foes alike as long as he lived. It brought
him the name of "Father of the Common School System
of Pennsylvania," and although that is but roughly
correct, it was fairly earned and well-deserved. In
1866, James A. Garfield, then a Representative, paying
fine tribute to its author, had a portion of it read into
the Congressional record. [23] Henry Ward Beecher, a
year before Stevens' death, referred to it as "founding
a system of common schools which disenthralled that
State from its ignorance and brought it by knowledge
to the stature and power of a gigantic Commonwealth." [24]

It was widely printed in and out of Pennsylvania and
so devastatingly did it do its work that for years no
attempt was made to change the law in any way. The
opposition which had been so loud and powerful, subsided into silent helplessness. Stevens, single-handed,
had challenged a majority [25] whom he believed was
wrong. After the contest, the majority admitted it.
With a reversal of public opinion Free Schools soon became popular, and increased in number from eight hundred in 1834 to approximately thirty-four hundred in
1837, while at the same time, the number of students

rose from thirty-two thousand to one hundred fifty thousand.[26]

Stevens' next great public effort for education was his speech in the Legislature in March of 1838, supporting a bill to establish a School of Arts in Philadelphia, and endow other educational institutions generally. His first battle had been concerned with public schools of the elementary class. His battle now was to encourage and aid higher educational institutions. Again he summoned the power of his school speech three years before. The occasion required all that was in him, for opponents who had been smothered in 1835 were still reactionary. They had lost their fight to prevent the common school but that did not mean they would not still oppose state aid for colleges. As on the former occasion, his speech showed conclusively that he was capable of moving a body to his side solely by the power of his argument.

He spoke in the House on the appropriation bill on Saturday afternoon; the vote was taken immediately and the bill passed with forty-six favoring it and thirty-two against it. The members had gone on record with Stevens' speech still ringing in their ears, and the opposition went to their week-end out-voted but still fighting. On Monday, they moved to reconsider the vote of Saturday, and with that time intervening from Stevens' speech, defeated the bill by six votes. The incident bears tribute to the stark force of Stevens' words.

In the Constitutional Convention of 1837, he opposed restricting education to children; he would broaden the power to include "every person who was conscious of his being ignorant and desirous to obtain instruction.[27] . . . Educational institutions should be open to all without inquiring into their wealth or their poverty, and a system, which in its fundamental law laid down those lines of distinction, was not in accordance with that spirit of liberty which should prevail in every free country.[28] . . . There is nothing in the Constitution so important . . . nothing which affects so deeply the good or evil government of the country as this very subject of education. It is second to none in magnitude and second to none in its influence upon our social system. I shall, therefore, give my anxious attention to this first above all other matters claiming our consideration." [29]

Democratic newspapers had said Stevens was made a Canal Commissioner purely for political purposes. If that were so, he used the office in a larger way. While visiting the public works of the State, he noticed that the families who had been drawn to the places of construction, often found no schools available for their children. Using the weight of his position, he "respectfully suggested to the contractors of all the public works, when children of laborers are not within convenient distance of free schools, to establish temporary schools for their instruction." He realized the Board had no legal authority to enforce this arrangement, but recommended it "to the judgment and liberality of the contractors." [30]

While in Congress, he had little opportunity to do anything officially for education, because the Federal Government could have nothing to say of those matters within the States. In the only field where the Nation has jurisdiction, that is the District of Columbia, he agitated continually for a system of common schools. Time after time he attempted to get through the House a bill that would give the District a good, free school system. But always that Body seemed to show not the slightest interest in it. It is significant, however, that his last substantial writing, done in faltering hand,[31] just a month before he died, was a draft of a bill to provide for schools there.

In his Will, after endowing the Juvenile Library Association at Peacham, and making a few family bequests, he gave the bulk of his estate to trustees to found a refuge for the relief of homeless, indigent orphans. Prominently set forth is the direction that "all be carefully educated in the various branches of English education . . . with no preference shown on account of race or color in admission or treatment."

To be credited with the actual establishment of a free public school system in a great Commonwealth is certainly signal honor, but to have succeeded in that establishment against stupendous odds and over-awing popular opposition, is sufficient claim for historic recognition. Stevens always treasured privately what he had accomplished for education, but was extremely modest about whatever tribute was paid him. He would feel himself "abundantly rewarded for all my efforts in behalf of universal education, if a single child educated by the Commonwealth would drop a tear of gratitude on my grave." [32]

UNITED STATES BANK AND
"THE TAPEWORM"

When President Jackson in 1829, expressed his doubt of the constitutionality of the Bank of the United States, its owners and officials were notified of his purposeful opposition to it. Well-knowing the determination of the man, they realized that he would do everything in his power to end it when its Charter expired in 1836, if he could not in the meantime destroy it.

Stockholders of the Bank had applied for renewal of Charter in 1832, but the Bill granting it, which was passed by both Houses of Congress was, as expected, vetoed by him. Thereupon, Nicholas Biddle, President of the Bank, took up the idea of a State Charter.[1]

Located in Philadelphia, Pennsylvania, was the logical State in which to seek a Certificate. Working obscurely through the Whig Party, representatives of the Bank appear to have reached an understanding that in exchange for support of Ritner for Governor in 1835, they were to obtain a State grant, in event of Ritner's success.[2] In any event, immediately after the election, and before the new Governor had taken office, there was open discussion of the matter.[3]

When the Legislature convened, Stevens' Anti-Masonic friend, Ner Middleswarth, Speaker of the House, appointed committees sympathetic toward the institution. The Committee on Banks wrote Biddle, saying that they had been informed that the stockholders of his Bank would accept a Charter from the

State, and requested him to inform them of the terms on which this could be effected. In his answer, Biddle outlined what the Bank desired and urged the Committee to lose no time, so that action could be taken at a meeting of stockholders scheduled for the near future.[4]

Biddle had written on January 7. Twelve days later, the Committee on Inland Navigation and Internal Improvements introduced through Stevens a Bill to form the Bank.[5] Oddly enough, it was entitled, "an act to repeal the state tax on real and personal property, and to continue and extend the improvements of the State by railroads and canals and other purposes."[6] The original title made no mention of the United States Bank, but this was later inserted.[7]

The Bill was ingeniously conceived and skillfully drawn. At the time, the State debt was so appalling that an especially obnoxious tax had been levied on several kinds of personal property as a temporary relief measure. Stevens' Bill would repeal that tax, obtain more than its equivalent from other sources and, in addition, bring millions into the Treasury of the Commonwealth. It would please the people by materially reducing taxes; it would gain the support of Legislators by allocating public improvements to their districts. Biddle's agent, William B. Reed, had suggested that as far as Legislative support was concerned, "the temptation of a turnpike or a few miles of canal and railroad as a beginning on a favorite route, is nearly irresistable."[8]

The proposal was long and involved. In exchange for a thirty year Charter, carrying with it exemption from taxation on its dividends, the Bank was to pay to

the Commonwealth a bonus of two million dollars; to
loan it up to six million dollars at low interest, and
subscribe six hundred seventy-five thousand dollars to
various designated internal improvements. Furthermore, and of paramount importance to Stevens, the
Institution was required to pay a bonus of five hundred
thousand dollars in 1837 and one hundred thousand
dollars annually thereafter for twenty years, all of
which was to be used for the benefit of the State's newly
established system of public schools.[9]

Another section which endeared it to Stevens, was
the one allocating two hundred thousand dollars to begin work on his pet railroad, which would run west from
the town of Gettysburg. He had been agitating in behalf of this construction for years, and his persistent determination to effect it, brought him no end of
opprobrium. Dubbed "The Tapeworm" because of its
necessarily circuitous route, it is treated more particularly hereafter.

The proposed legislation was something new for
Pennsylvania. The idea of the Commonwealth obtaining the larger part of its monies by means other than
taxation of its citizens, was intriguing. But Stevens,
charmed with the public school and railroad features,
rushed it through. Under his direction, with few unimportant amendments, it passed by a vote of fifty-seven
to thirty.[10]

Only a scattered opposition showed itself, and that
was easily overcome. Attorney-General Todd, who
had developed an antipathy for Stevens, tried to persuade Governor Ritner that the Bill was dangerous,
in the great privilege granted for a term so long as

[175]

thirty years. But the mover amended it so that the Legislature might recall the Bank Charter "whenever it was found injurious to the interests of the people." This satisfied the Governor.[11]

While the measure was in the Legislature, Biddle, through his agents, kept in close touch with its progress. In one of the reports, his representative said, "I have never seen a Bill so ably managed as this was this afternoon by Mr. Stevens."[12] Not only did he father it in the House, but with the aid of his partisans, he engineered it through the Senate, all the time seeing to it that the Governor continued in sympathy with it.[13] Another report to Biddle quoted "Mr. Stevens as saying 'the Governor will sign it as soon as requested.'"[14]

Democratic supporters of Jackson in the Senate viewed the contemplated grant as partial nullification of Jackson's victory in abolishing the Federal Bank and heatedly opposed it. Their newspapers saw it as an effort of "that arch traitor to Pennsylvania, Thaddeus Stevens, to sell the liberties of the people."[15]

Through masterful engineering, Stevens and his associates attracted the help of eight Van Buren (Democratic) Senators who had supported Muhlenberg. In order to vote for the Bill, some of them were forced to repudiate their stand supporting Jackson, and at least two of these had openly stated that they were opposed to such Charter.[16]

This was Stevens' first substantial test as a leader of majority forces in the Lower House, and he acquitted himself nobly from a politician's standpoint. Enough opposition arose to prove his mettle, but with the application of his stern discipline, it withered before him.

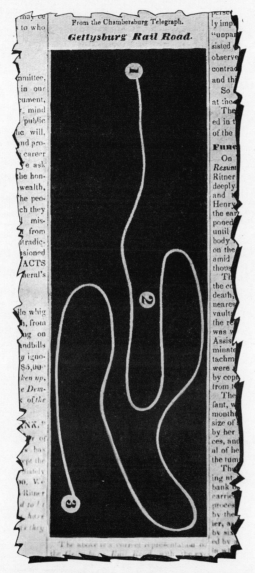

From the Pennsylvania Reporter and State Journal, August 17, 1838.

Route of the "The Tapeworm" Railroad.   (1) Origin; (3) Presumed Terminus; and (2) Stevens' Iron Furnaces

A House member of Stevens' party asked him when he introduced the Bill if its purpose was to incorporate the United States Bank. Stevens answered it was, whereupon the interrogator said, "That will never do." "Won't it?" challenged the Master, "all you have to do is take your seat and vote for it." [17]

Stevens allowed a minimum of discussion, and when it came up for final vote in the House, a single Whig and a single Mason voted against it. [18] The Democrats unable to withstand the clubfoot legislator's steam-roller method of driving the Bill through, and sensing a liaison between bank officials and the Whig-Anti-Masonic combination, raised charges of bribery. This delayed Senate action until an investigating committee looked into the matter.

The Committee found no evidence of bribery, but were convinced "that a deliberate plan was concocted beyond the limits of Pennsylvania, to control the deliberations of the Legislature by the pressure of the people acting under an excitement created by incendiary falsehoods, sent forth upon responsible authority, charging the Bank with bribery, and the Senate with interested treachery." [19]

Less than a month after Stevens introduced it, the Bill became a law. [20] Whether the legislation was wise or not, is unimportant now. Certainly no lasting harm came through it and it did relieve the almost bankrupt State. Some students have thought it "completely unbalanced the financial sense of the Commonwealth" from which it recovered "only after a long and painful period of impotence." [21] If this opinion is correct, then Stevens must be charged with a large part of responsibility for the novel scheme of governmental financing.

One fact, however, remains. Although Pennsylvania did not receive the full amount of bonus, nevertheless, the measure furnished a solid financial bottom on which to propagate the Commonwealth's great system of public schools. Furthermore, Pennsylvania, in granting the Charter, did only what other states were anxious to do; one going so far as to offer, instead of demand, a bonus.[22]

Banks and banking were among the important matters to be considered by the Constitutional Convention which met late in the year. As might be expected, Stevens contended that Andrew Jackson was wrong in holding that a United States Bank was not authorized by the Federal Constitution. One of the most interesting incidents in the whole Convention resulted from Stevens' discussion of the matter. It indicates how powerful he might have been in the Convention, had he used even a bit of tact.

He was known everywhere as a champion of banks. Naturally, the Democrats were opposed. He stunned them by proposing an amendment that "no branch or branches of the State Government nor all of them combined, shall have the power to establish any bank or banks within this Commonwealth."[23] To his opponents, this was an amazing faceabout. Surely this was the man who had been the moving spirit in the grant of a State Charter to the United States Bank in the prior Legislative session. He was the personal friend of nationally known banker Nicholas Biddle. His proposal must be part of some subtle strategy to out-general them. Fearing that he might trick them in some mysterious way, the Democrats opposed and voted down the amendment, which in a measure embodied their own widely flaunted policy.

In this, Stevens' adversaries admitted an ability in him greater than they claimed for themselves. What a name he might have made for himself in that Convention, and what a promising future he might there have opened, had he dealt patiently, graciously, and courteously with the members.

But the amendment was not so much a reversal of Stevens' bank ideas as would first appear. Astute, competent student, he already saw the evils that must come from multiplication of State Banks and their paper. In fact, he proposed that "here on the threshold of the Constitution, a barrier be set up to protect the country from the almost insupportable evils of paper currency, and local banks." Said he, "the Banks sit like an incubus upon all the States of the Union, and until we throw them off, we never can flourish." A thoroughgoing lawyer, he believed "that the Constitution withholds from the States, the power to create banking corporations, or in any other way, to issue bills of credit."

But he admitted long usage and acquiescence, as well as judicial decisions "had sanctioned the exercise of such power by the States." So long as the States erected banks and authorized paper issues, just "so long shall we be disposed to sudden and calamitous fluctuations of the currency." [24]

Already he was convinced, in spite of Jackson, that a National currency was the only intelligent solution. His proposals a generation later in the Congress were but reiterations of what he here advocated in 1837.

"If we restore the exercise of the power to the National Government, where it properly belongs and was intended by the framers of the Constitution to be, it could establish a banking system under which the currency would be rendered uniform and stable throughout the country, exchange facilitated and funds of the Government transmitted in a single week from Maine to Louisiana, without disturbing the regular business. Where," he inquired, "on the face of the globe, was there a currency equal to that which we had when the Federal Government exercised a power over it through a National Bank?" [25]

But he was thirty years ahead of the Country. It required those three decades of time, losses of billions, and the shock of a devasting War, to advance the Nation to him.

In December, on the banking subject, he made his longest speech of the Convention. He chided Jackson for destroying the Federal Institution and laid this as one of the causes of the then expanding panic. He painted a vivid picture of Pennsylvania's financial chaos before it passed the United States Bank Bill.

The Commonwealth owed twenty-five million dollars, with an additional million dollars due for internal improvements, no single dollar of which had been "provided for by law or was to be procured from the Treasury." The people were burdened with annual taxes of nearly a half million dollars, and the State was borrowing a million dollars a year to pay interest on the public debt, as well as three or four million more to continue public works.

"Thus the Commonwealth was paying in addition to the ordinary interest on her debt, an enormous compound interest upon it, all of which, in a less space of time than twenty years, would have overbalanced her with a debt of one hundred million dollars, and for the repayment of which every man's house and property must have been mortgaged."

He lauded the Governor and the Legislators for the way they had met the crisis. He praised the "patriotic, enlightened, and proud hearted Pennsylvanian" who then presided over the Bank, in accepting at the hands of the State, the Charter for which "the price was high and extravagant, and the terms hard."

But what a blessing to the Commonwealth! "The State tax was instantly repealed. Interest on the public debt was paid, public improvements continued, and Pennsylvania, for the first time since the public works were undertaken, exhibited one of the noblest systems of internal improvement that ever distinguished any people on earth—and that too without taxing her people a single cent, without borrowing a dollar to pay the interest on her State debt, and without attaining any permanent increase of obligation."

He defied "the wisdom of the whole agrarian tribe to point out any means by which those great ends could have been attained other than those by which they had been attained." He confessed he felt "a proud satisfaction in the reflection that he had some little agency in the passage of that law." [26]

The second feature of "that law" which enthused Stevens, was a handsome allotment to construct a railroad from his native town westward. Gettysburg was so hemmed in with mountains that railroad approaches were unusually tortuous and correspondingly expensive. The engineering problem was so difficult that he could not at first even suggest a terminal. What he wanted was an outlet for the town south and west, but because the mountains had been unexplored by engineers, no committment could be made as to just where or with what the railroad should connect.

The opposition newspapers were not long in turning Stevens' problem to ridicule. They referred to it as a railroad "to commence in the woods and end nowhere." [27] But to him, that did not conclude the matter. It meant only that getting the railroad would be a little harder work.

He had begun his agitation in 1831, when at a mass meeting he had himself appointed chairman of a committee to appear before the Legislature in behalf of the project. It listened and promptly forgot. Although he kept constantly demanding it, he was unable to do anything until the Bank Bill in 1836 so unexpectedly furnished pregnant and luscious opportunity.

In command of the Bill, he was not too modest to seek and obtain a substantial allotment. Two hundred thousand dollars, his enemies wailed, to build a railroad "when no exploration had been made of the route—no estimate of its cost, no information obtained of its usefulness, and no limit assigned to its westward termination." [28] Even if it could be constructed it would be "circuitous, full of high grades, dangerous to travelers, and good for nothing. Its costs would run into indefinite millions." [29]

No one knew much about his scheme in 1836, but

Stevens had two great levers to get it through. If the Bank Bill, as he drew it, were not passed, all the numerous appropriations to turnpikes and railroads through the State, would be endangered. With ingenious distribution of funds provided for by the Bill, the various legislators were forced to support it as it was to obtain the respective allotments and benefits appropriated to their individual localities. They were willing to join in a little "log-rolling."

Furthermore, even if the man from Gettysburg were not the actual Governor, as the Democrats claimed he was, it was generally understood that the Governor would not sign the Bill unless it conformed to Stevens' wishes. He had seen to it that in the Executive's annual message, he approved the operation.

The Bill passed. Work on the railroad was started. It aimed in a generally southwesterly direction; and was to "cross the route of the Baltimore and Ohio Railroad and connect with the Chesapeake and Ohio Canal at some point in the State of Maryland, at or west of Williamsport." [30]

One part of its route seemed certain. Stevens had become interested in the Maria Iron Furnace in Franklin County, and there was little doubt in anyone's mind that if he continued to control it, it would pass near that operation. It was blatantly published that his main object in pushing it through was the personal profit he was to derive from it. [31] Transporting ore and coal by horse and cart was a great deal more expensive than hauling it by railroad. Furthermore, its propinquity would also materially increase the value of some of his real estate. [32]

That he did get some practical benefit from the operation is conclusively shown by the election returns. In those days, the voting laws required no long residence, and a thousand workers, if properly instructed, could do great "good" at the polls.[33]

The work went on, but as annual appropriations were made and the railroad grew, the problem of a definite route became pressing. Oddly enough, its proponents were unable to give any map or plan. They had some engineers survey the terrain, and submit a map, but it looked so crooked and winding that even though they had promised to publish it, they were afraid to, when they saw it.[34] Somehow the Democrats obtained a copy and got much pleasure circulating it in the fall of 1838. It disclosed a most tortuous route and took little imagination to see an outline of "The Tapeworm." And "The Tapeworm" it was ever afterward, to them.[35]

From Gettysburg to Waynesboro was eighteen miles in direct line, and twenty-two miles by road, but by the proposed railroad, it was no less than thirty-five. It meandered up mountains "some seven or eight miles," and turned on itself no less than four times.[36] But just as the work was nicely started, the Democrats came into power in the Lower House.

They determined to end it by cutting off appropriations. A Committee from each branch of the Legislature was appointed to investigate. The House Committee, with Stevens' arch enemy, M'Elwee as Chairman, found it "an isolated work" passing through "a barren waste without fertility, presenting the general features of an American Siberia," and recommended that it should not be prosecuted to completion, but that "all operations on the road be immediately suspended."[37] Even the minority concurred that the "work ought to be abandoned for the present." [38]

The Senate Committee reported that "the railroad will not justify the expense which must inevitably be incurred in the construction thereof, and therefore, the sooner it is suspended, the better it will be for the State. It was folly to commence it; to persevere in it at this time will be madness." [39] Stevens said nothing. When the Legislature met that Fall, it passed a bill making an appropriation for work already done, and directed suspension "after the first day of January next." [40]

That was on December 19, 1837, but before the Governor signed it, the Legislature adjourned temporarily. It reconvened on January 9, 1838, and on that day the Governor signed the Bill and returned it to the Legislature with a message. Again Stevens had out-maneuvered his opposition. Had the Bill become a law, as the Legislature intended, work on the railroad would have stopped on December 31, 1837. With Stevens' manipulation the Legislature itself permissively continued it a full year.

The work went on but because of exhausted appropriations, the workers could not be paid. It was a State operation, with the faith of the Commonwealth pledged to the contractors. Democratic Governor Porter found the bills before him and could do nothing but borrow the money to liquidate them.[41]

But five millions of costs was insurmountable.[42] Stevens was out of the Legislature and could give no help in getting through a life-saving appropriation. "The Tapeworm" died. In the fall of 1842, the State advertised it for sale, and the Democratic newspapers celebrated. Under an editorial of "Bargains! Ho! Bargains!" the *Keystone* proclaimed "The 'Tapeworm' for sale! Those who have been adventurous enough to hazard life and limb in exploration of its localities, have repeatedly given the public assurance that Satan's flight from the regions of Paradise to the caverns of Pandemonium could not possibly have been half as serpentine. The moral and political career of its illustrious patron is not more full of twistings, windings and contortions than is this most extraordinary of all projects, ancient and modern." [43]

So expired the public improvement which was close to Stevens' heart. No one can argue that it would not have benefited him materially and substantially. The real question of whether or not it was in the public interest is doubtful. After being bought by another railroad, it is today in useful operation as a main artery of traffic to and from Gettysburg.

BOOK THREE
CONGRESSMAN

BOOK THREE—CONGRESSMAN

I

LANCASTER

THE year 1842, was a critical one in Stevens' life. By the time his last term as Legislator was completed, his closely guarded deliberations had determined him upon a radical change. He would move to Lancaster. With a single act, he severed himself from a law practice that he had labored a generation to build, and unostentatiously abandoned the only home he had ever known. The abrupt movement which necessarily involved a beginning over again, showed real moral courage, for he was then past fifty years of age.

Just what reasons dictated this act were never made known through those thin, firm lips of his. The man had no enlarged ego and as was usual with him, he no doubt thought the world had little concern in why or how he acted. And so announcements and explanations concerning them would be of no use or interest.

We know of one fact which might have influenced his decision. Some years before, he had invested in an iron business just west of Gettysburg, but it had failed so miserably that at the time it was more than $200,000 in debt with a net failure of greater than $90,000.[1] In the enterprise he had a partner who was just as legally responsible as was he for the debts. When the insolvency came, the partner went into bankruptcy and cleared himself. A friend suggested to Stevens that he do likewise. The Commoner paused a moment, looked piercingly at his friend, and then in measured words, through

which showed a rugged determination long arrived at,
answered, "yes I could. I may be forced to take advantage of the bankrupt laws in the next world, but
that I will never do in this." [2] In his letter to Blanchard,
he said he knew "of no way out of such things but to
pay the uttermost farthing."

If this were to be done, some change had to be made.
Adams County was a prosperous region, but only
sparsely settled. Lacking industrial centers, its legal
business involved no large amounts. Returns from his
practice there could never be made sufficient to liquidate his obligations.

Some twenty-five years before, he had fixed upon
the old inland city of Lancaster as a place in which he
might like to build his fame and fortune. But the
crippled Yankee youth, after seeing it, could not muster
the courage to intrude himself. He who a half century
later hesitated not to challenge the highest executive of
the Nation had been unable to face a city of Lancaster's
proportions. But during his Gettysburg years the iron
that was in him, through exposure to the fires of battle
and heavy blows upon it, had been changed to steel.
Battered, buffeted, abused—sometimes brutally, he had
not given up. Time after time he had faced hostile
audiences, conventions and legislatures, and through
the driving power of his argument, brought them to
his side. True, Lancaster had challenged him in his
youth and overwhelmed him. That fact must have always been a deep-seated sore within him. To him, as
long as it remained, it was an acknowledged defeat.
And it was of the kind that struck most deeply. It
admitted lack of moral courage.

Yes, he was a cripple physically, as the world could see, but in the depths of his own self-consciousness, he liked to think himself possessed of a stupendous moral bravery that so far outweighed the physical deficiency that the latter was belittled comparatively to nothingness. To prove himself, he could never rest until in real trial he had met the challenge of Lancaster. The larger field that it offered, where debts could be paid the sooner, appears on the surface as the immediate cause of his moving. But a study of the character of the man indicates that the real reason for his act was his unyielding desire to overcome the stinging rebuff he had experienced on his first visit to the city in the summer of 1816.

Local politics weighed but little in the decision. In 1841, he had notified his party that he would no longer be a candidate on its ticket for the Legislature, but at the same time, he was carrying on an important political conversation of national proportions.

Salmon P. Chase, then a growing figure in Ohio, had become interested in, and effected organization of a group in that State which styled itself the "Liberty Party." [3] Stevens' old friend Blanchard, who was associated with Chase in the movement, suggested that he get in touch with Stevens. Accordingly, Chase wrote the Pennsylvanian from Cincinnati in April, 1842. "Although a stranger," he explained, "I have determined to write you on a subject in which I feel a deep interest, as frankly as I would talk to an old acquaintance. What I hear of your character leads me to believe that you will take what I say in good part."

He reported the Convention of the Liberty Party

which had assembled in Columbus in the prior December. Careful to point out to Stevens the difference between Abolitionism and the platform of the new Party, he said, the former "seeks to abolish slavery everywhere —the means which it employs corresponds with the object to be asked—they are of a moral nature—argument, persuasion, remonstrance and the like," but "the Liberty Party seeks to abolish slavery wherever it exists within reach of the Constitutional action of Congress; to restrict it within the slave states and to deliver the government from the control of the slave power."

Chase felt that it would be "absurd to make abolitionism a political test, for it seeks the extinction of slavery, not only where it can be reached by Congress, but in the States and everywhere," and its object therefore could not be effected by political power.

On the other hand, it would be equally absurd not to make his Party's doctrine a political question, for "it has reference to subjects on which the political power of the country may, should, and must be brought to bear, and that speedily. Or they would see....slavery, escaped from constitutional limits and stalking at large through the whole country, striking....down whatever is most valuable in the institution which our fathers have bequeathed to us." He asked Stevens to take ground with him and his followers, and wondered if he could "not bring the old Anti-Masonic party of Pennsylvania on to the Liberty platform." After discussing their party nominees, he requested the Commoner to weigh the matters he had submitted and send him his views of them.[4]

The above letter reads as follows:

If you have not yet addressed letters to the persons of whom we spoke, please defer it until I write you again. Will you allow me one consultation with anti-masons elsewhere, to suggest a formula of letter to use? If so, we will devise one to bring them up to the chalk.

I shall probably learn this forthwith this afternoon. This is not quite certain, as I may be detained by business in Cumberland County. If so, I shall not be there until the session commences.

Next day, Blanchard wrote Stevens, indicating that he knew of Chase's letter, saying "I thought I would write you a word or two respecting the men who are embarked in the organization" of the Liberty Party. One of them was "a lawyer, a Methodist preacher, and an honest man—three extremes which rarely meet in the composition of one man." He wanted Stevens to "help Chase displace the name of Birney and substitute that of Seward or J. Q. Adams as Anti-slavery candidate for the Presidency; and that in a way will prevent a break between western and eastern abolitionists." [5]

Stevens waited more than a month to reply to the letters. At heart he was an abolitionist out and out, although he had early recognized the Constitutional difficulties of reaching that end politically. The Liberty Party platform, at best a compromise with institutions so fundamentally wrong as he felt slavery was, was stench in his nostrils. Just what reply Stevens did make is not clear, but a good insight into his attitude may be gathered from a draft presumably a copy of a letter which he addressed to Blanchard in May.

In it he said he had delayed answering the letters because he "had not determined exactly what answer to give." Chase had held his appeal to support for the Liberty platform. Blanchard spoke of outright abolitionism. Stevens said significantly, "I need not say to you how entirely my views and wishes accord with your own in the object you have in view."

While these communications were passing, he effected his courageous change of home. What regrets he left at Gettysburg or what hopes he took to Lancaster, were

securely sealed in that continent but virile mind of his.
In the Adams County town, he had lived an unusually
active, vigorous, and at times vehement life. Looking
back over the years, some monuments of accomplishment marked their passing. There were successes at the
Bar, constructive achievements in the Legislature, some
political success, and an outstanding accomplishment
which he treasured above all, his majestic victory against
overwhelming odds in saving the Free School System
in Pennsylvania, and grounding it on such secure base
that it could not be destroyed. One real asset he had.
Study and industry in his practice had made him an
excellent lawyer, able to compete in any forum with
the best.

Fame, after a fashion, was his. Generally acknowledged the leader of Anti-Masonry in Pennsylvania his
name had been broadcast throughout her borders. But
all was not happy in these years—they had brought
the pressing burden of a host of personal as well as
political enemies. His courageous battle against secret
societies had been irretrievably lost and the party demolished. He had accumulated some property in the
town, but all of his worldly wealth had been more than
wiped out in the miserable failure of his iron mines.
It was just two and one-half decades since he had come
to town. Down that old high road on horseback, the
crippled Yankee had ridden inconspicuously into town,
unannounced and unwelcome. He had come unknown
and alone. He would leave well-known—but still alone.

He had arrived friendless and although practically
every adult in Adams County must have either known
or heard of him at the time of his leaving, there is noth-

ing to indicate that all those years had brought any real friends. There was no ceremony as he packed the simple furnishings of his home, boxed his law books, took down his shingle, and locked the door of the little brickfronted office, two steps up from "The Square." It was characteristic of him to make no remark upon it. What he had done in Gettysburg would speak for itself. Whatever Lancaster might bring too, must bear its own record. He simply moved.

Lancaster gave no great promise. A few Anti-Masonic friends, including Ellmaker and Burrowes lived there, and it might have been significant that the first person in Pennsylvania to come out for Congress under the Anti-Masonic standard was from Lancaster County. Perhaps the place might hold some little warmth for him on account of those old Party ties. But that was all, and as far as business was concerned, he could count on nothing.

In the new city, he lost no time in opening his law office and inserted, as he had done in Gettysburg, his professional card in the newspapers. Only one of them received him cordially, stating editorially, "this distinguished legal and political gentleman has commenced the practice of law in our city. His reputation as a powerful speaker, ingenious and profound lawyer, and as an accomplished statesman, has already preceded him. We cannot doubt his professional success." [6]

It could not be expected that the city would be especially enthusiastic at his coming, nor that it would immediately accord him high place, for if it were true that there was in the hey-day of the Anti-Masons, a virile group of them in Lancaster, it was also true that

[195]

in numbers that group was at all times largely over-
shadowed by those of opposing views. And since 1836
Anti-Masons had been rapidly disappearing.

Lancaster in those days was a self-contained old
city, and its distinguished social and professional strata
held many conservatives, and for that matter, Masonic
leaders. They, of course, not only differed with Stevens
politically, but openly viewed him as a Yankee invader
of Pennsylvania soil, recklessly ambitious and heatedly
partisan.

But with no noise he went to work. With careful
preparation of cases, his dynamic appeal to juries and
his terse but accurate summing up of the law, he slowly
forged ahead at the new Bar. Because he was a State-
wide figure and enjoyed a personal acquaintanceship as well as a respectable status in the Appellate
Courts, some members of the Bar found it of value to
have him associated in their cases. Although it cannot
be denied that for a long time there was personal dis-
like of him by several substantial members, the Bar,
as a whole, after he had proven himself, accepted him
at his fair worth as a lawyer and gentleman, and ac-
corded him a decent hospitality.

Stevens never was a social figure. He lacked the
graces; was so made that he just could not repeat the
appropriate but meaningless forms of etiquette, and the
last thing on earth in which he could indulge was pleasant flattery. In business contacts, he never became
intimate, and made no appeal to the individual. Whatever support he gained in life, came from those who
saw him as the champion of their ideas, or ideals. In
all his long years, nothing came because of personal

friendship—of this he was either incapable or had no
desire to accomplish. His entire life is eloquent of his
lack of personal appeal. There is little doubt that
had he been adorned with such asset, he would have
sat in Harrison's Cabinet and probably Lincoln's.

Stevens brought to the Lancaster County Bar a
wealth of experience and a good legal reputation. But
he held himself in no great esteem. When a defendant
appeared in the Criminal Court without an attorney, it
was the custom in that County, as in every other, for
the Court to appoint as counsel, some younger member
of the Bar who wanted the experience. As a newcomer,
Stevens ranked himself with the novices. His first case
in the new County was one in which he volunteered his
services to a negro who had been indicted for assault
and battery with intent to kill. His client was convicted
but the new lawyer made a favorable impression on the
Court and those who heard him.[7]

It wasn't long until he was among the leaders. In
the appeal cases which came before the highest Court
in Pennsylvania in 1844, his appearance was entered in
several of the most important.

He is credited with one innovation at the new Bar
which was viewed with favor by the Court, but not by
the lawyers. The custom there had been for counsel to
address the Court and jury in long and tiresome
speeches. Stevens never wasted words. His speeches,
in refreshing contrast, were unusually short, and restricted to one or two points on the matter at issue.
Under steady pressure from the Bench, the Bar was
reluctantly brought to the Stevens' method.[8]

When he began practice in Gettysburg, he was timid,

untried, and without confidence either in himself or his
legal ability. When he came to Lancaster, he was
poised, afraid of no man nor matter, and fortified with
an abounding confidence of his knowledge and skill in
the devious ways of the law. Within five years, he had
gained a respected position as one of the able members
of the Bar of his newly adopted County. His practice
was large, of good grade, and yielded him twelve to
fifteen thousand dollars per year.[9]

But to gain prominence in the politics of his new
home was not so easy. By this time he was forced to
the realization that his Anti-Masonic Party, so dear
to him, if not dead, was rapidly dying. Without
a party, he was adrift on political seas. Lancaster was
predominantly Whig. They were in unquestioned control of the County and neither needed nor welcomed
outside assistance. Accordingly, he was not invited to
their counsels, encouraged or even recognized. Whig
leaders whose call he longed for, simply ignored him.
Advances to any of the parties he had fought, was more
distasteful to him than to the ordinary man. There
was but one thing left. He must salvage what was left
of his old party and make battle. This he did.

He labored hard and long to resurrect the disinte-
grated and worn out Anti-Masonic Party for the elections of 1843. But he labored in vain. It didn't matter
that his faction polled fifteen hundred votes and divided
the opposition to the Democrats. The Whig ticket was
elected in spite of the breach.

The unnecessary battle which Stevens raised against
the Whigs in no way brought them closer to him. They
marked him as an extremist. It appeared as though

he would again be forced to withdraw from politics.

Clay, however, had just been nominated for the Presidency and Pennsylvania was an important state. To win, the nominee's supporters knew he must carry the Keystone State. Stevens, years before, had been close to Clay, but when disappointment came to him in the Harrison Cabinet appointments, he held the Kentuckian partly responsible for it. Lancaster County Whigs, satisfied that as a result of the last election they could get along without Stevens, rejoiced in the way they had smothered him. They were convinced he was not nor would be a factor in politics. The state leaders thought otherwise. They knew Stevens for what he was; a vigorous and effective campaigner who had a peculiarly democratic appeal to the voters. They ordered the Lancaster County leaders to bring Stevens behind Clay.

Stevens was adamant. The Kentuckian had no political appeal for him and furthermore, he couldn't easily forget the old injury. As a last resort, Clay sent word to him that if he were elected, "atonement would be made for past wrongs." [10] A fortunate circumstance had again smiled upon Stevens. But the smile was a fleeting one. Stevens accepted Clay's promise in all good faith, and immediately started on a state-wide speech-making tour for him. All to no avail. The "Mill Boy of the Slashes" was defeated for the Presidency and again Stevens' vision for a Cabinet position collapsed like another bubble.

However, affiliation with the political machine of the County and his appearance with its leaders, not only gave him valuable contacts, but brought him before the voters of the majority party under correct sponsorship. His law business was prospering and through it, he was gaining a wide acquaintanceship and hosts of supporters.

He carried to Lancaster a practice he had early started in Gettysburg, of being especially deferential to all young members of the Bar. Not only that, but he rendered all assistance possible to those men who sought the law as a profession. He is reported to have had more students in his office than any member of the Lancaster Bar.[11] It was the custom, in those days, for the aspirant to pay for his training. Stevens didn't apply it too rigorously. When a young man wrote to ask what his terms were to study law in his office, he replied, "Two hundred dollars. Some pay; some don't." [12]

While in Lancaster, more than a score of young men studied law under him and he moved the admission of fourteen.[13] Nowhere in the records can any indication be found that he ever refused a young man an opportunity to enter his office as a student, regardless of what his ability to pay might have been.

By the early part of 1848, Stevens had made such progress in the politics of the County that he felt he could aspire to a seat in Congress. In those days, party nominations were made through the caucus system and in its decision lay Stevens' destiny. By midsummer of that year, he was already being addressed by committees and organizations inquiring what position he would take on certain matters if elected to Congress.

In reply to a Free Soil Committee, who had asked if he would in the event of his election, stand "to exclude slavery and involuntary servitude from newly acquired territories," and "support a bill for the extinguishing of slavery wherever Congress had jurisdiction over it," he said, "I answer both your questions in the affirmative. I will further add what perhaps your letter does not require; that I will vote for no man for any office whom I believe would interpose any official obstruction to the accomplishment of these objects." [14]

He was active in support of General Taylor for the Presidency.[15] There was wide demand for his speeches at political rallies [16] and a prolific shower of letters to newspapers calling for his nomination as Representative.[17] His fame had reached to Buffalo, where one of its papers, in referring to him, said, "He is one of the best debaters in the United States, and being distinguished for independence and firmness, would soon acquire a commanding position in the House. As a controversial debater, he has no equal in the House, nor do we believe there is his match in the Senate with the exception of Mr. Corwin....He is a man of great and varied abilities, capable of accomplishing as much in a legislative body as any individual in the country." [18] The Auburn, New York, Journal said, "His are the services the North needs and now is a crisis that demands them."

When the County Convention met late in August, three names were before it for Congress. Stevens was nominated on the third ballot against a prominent Whig of high standing and old family in the County, by a vote of twenty-three to seventeen.[19] Democratic newspapers viewed his rapid rise in popular esteem with no little concern. Realizing that he would make a strong opponent, they were uneasy about his nomination. In accounting for his selection over the objection of some strong leaders of the old Whig machine, one said, "the nomination of this gentleman for a seat in the National Councils against the earnest remonstrances of those to whom the Whig Party has been long accustomed to resort to for counsel, is doubtless the homage paid at all times and by all men to preeminent and distinguished talent." But it assailed him as "the sworn foe of the South" who would "foment internal discord ....like some fell spirit of Pandemonium....and so widen the breach which every patriot should seek to heal." [20]

The candidate immediately began an intensive campaign addressing scores of rallies and political gatherings. When the votes were counted, he had over 9,500 and his Democratic opponent less than 5,500.[21] In fact, so popular had he become with the voters, that he was "warmly urged" to fill an existing vacancy in the office of United States Senator.[22] This boom, however, was confined to a few counties and as Stevens in no way attempted to give it momentum, soon collapsed. But his rapid rise to political prominence in his newly adopted County opened the way to a forum where his virile ruggedness of thought was to mould and lead a congressional majority which saw in the blazing fury of war, opportunity to substantially modify the Constitution itself.

II

IN AND OUT OF CONGRESS

When the Thirty-first Congress, to which Thaddeus Stevens had been elected, convened on December 3, 1849, it faced a combination of critical sectional differences which, many believed, actually threatened a break-up of the Union.

For more than a decade, far-sighted men of the South had realized that the North was steadily out-stripping it in power in the National Councils. The simple cause lay in the fact that the population of the North was increasing much the more rapidly. When the first wave of the Anti-slavery movement swept the country in the early 1830's, the slave power was put on notice that there existed potential opposition that could and might overwhelm it. From that time until the convening of this Congress, Southern leaders viewed with grave concern the vigorous growth of a possibly hostile North and pondered all methods it could conceive to eliminate or overcome it.

Various superficial reasons were given for the fiery attitude that the South had shown to the North from 1835 on, but the real and fundamental one on which all others reposed, was the fear and alarm which struck the South when she realized that she was becoming a minority power in the Federal Government. Calhoun touched the heart of the matter in his last great speech of March 4, 1850, when he said that the great and primary cause of the universal discontent that covered the entire South was that it realized "that the equilibrium between the two sections had been destroyed."

[203]

The industrial North soon would have a larger Congressional representation than the agricultural South. Unless the growing Anti-slavery feeling in the former could be checked by some means or other, it was but a matter of time until the latter must bow before it. One device adopted was an attempt to intimidate the North. Through many Congresses, loyal but fiery Southerners laboring to preserve the dominant status of the slave domain, had accused the North of aggression in its attempts to interfere with slavery, and had, time after time, threatened that if it were not speedily stopped, they would move for secession.

The journals of the two Bodies bear witness of the extent to which the South was wrought up by the propaganda of Northern abolition societies. They are liberally sprinkled with feverish speeches actually advocating withdrawal from the Union as the only redress.

By the end of 1849, several new and troublesome problems had arisen to increase the strain between the sections. Texas had been admitted against Anti-slavery opposition which feared with some real basis that the motivating cause was the creation of new ground for slavery expansion. That vast area which the United States had obtained from Mexico under the Treaty of Guadalupe Hidalgo, thrust itself forward as a prize for the slave power and its contenders to battle over. California was knocking at the door of the Union. Under a bonafide vote of its citizens, it had declared against slavery, which meant if admitted, it should be as a Free State. Slave state representatives, who always held themselves forth as champions of popular sovereignty, dared not argue otherwise.

A custom had been established of admitting the states in pairs; that is, a slave state and a free state would come in at approximately the same time, and so preserve a near equilibrium in the Senate. But there was no slave state ready for entrance at the time.

Consequently, Southerners could leave no stone unturned in resisting California's application. The Wilmont Proviso that "neither slavery nor involuntary servitude, except in punishment of crime" should ever exist in any part of the territory acquired from Mexico, had been voted down. Its thorough and heated discussion in the Congress and throughout the country had instilled in the minds of many Northerners a determination to insist upon it.

Further complications were added by the feeling of a substantial number of moderates, that the Missouri Compromise, which prohibited slavery north of the southern boundary of that state, should be enlarged so as to carry that line of demarcation westward to the Pacific. Abolition of slavery in the District of Columbia was being agitated; Northern radicals were pressing for prohibition of interstate slave trade, and the South insisted that the Fugitive Slave Laws were being nullified. In addition, State Legislatures of the South were passing fiery resolutions and Southern Governors were issuing irritating proclamations charging the North with aggressive hostility to slavery, unauthorized by the laws and Constitution. All these circumstances combined made the outlook alarming.

To add to all this a heated discussion in the widely circulated newspapers of the right of Congress to prohibit slavery in the territories, furnished more grist for

the mill which was grinding out ill feeling between the
sections. The country realized that it was approaching
a crisis. Could it be hoped that Congress would in some
way abate the intense sectional feelings or would its
meeting merely provide a battleground for the clashing
elements and so intensify the rapidly expanding ill-will?

The day came when Congress met. The atmosphere
was one of dire tension. Much had been said and much
had been planned by both North and South on the
strategy of procedure. Unless slavery could be engineered into the extensive new domains of the Southwest, domination of the Federal Government must
gradually be relinquished to the Abolitionists. The
North appreciated this situation as fully as did the
South. Prohibition of slavery in the new areas would
be a wholly efficient means of ultimately strangling it.

The first important item of business was the election
of Speaker. Because he would appoint the Committees,
the matter was of greatest concern. Each group, feeling
its way was highly cautious of its own actions and suspiciously watchful of the other's. Day after day the
House met and balloted to elect a presiding officer, but
could get nowhere.

Venable, of North Carolina, had early notified the
House that he had pledged "himself to his constituents
to vote for no Free-Soiler or Abolitionist for Speaker,
and he meant to adhere to this pledge whatever might
be the result." He charged that the anti-slavery forces
had combined for the purpose of effecting "by indirection, that which could not be openly obtained."

Many speeches were made, principally by Southern
members who demanded concession or compromise on

the part of the North, and resorted to all sorts of argument to forestall legislation curbing slavery. Much of this was couched in heated language, and although the speakers talked of conciliation, their words could have been no different had it been their deliberate purpose to infuriate.

The session was barely ten days old when Stephens of Georgia, later to become Vice-President of the Confederacy in a flaming attack on the North, said he "never expected to live to see the day when" he "should be called upon to discuss the question of the Union of the States," but he challenged: "I tell this House, whether the people of the North believe it or not, that the day in which agression is consummated upon any section of the country, much and deeply as I regret it, this Union is dissolved." He preferred "that the Southern country should perish. . . . that all her statesmen and all her gallant spirits should be buried in honorable graves," rather than submit for "one instant to degradation."[1]

On the same day, Meade of Virginia, offered to support a Speaker from either side of the House if it could be first agreed upon that no anti-slave legislation would be attempted. But if measures of that kind were to be passed, there would be but one determination in the South, one solemn resolve—to defend their homes and maintain their honor. "Let the issue come when it may," the North would "find every Southern sinew converted into a spring of steel." He did not "utter this as a threat, but," said he, "gentlemen will find a difference between men contending for their firesides and the robbers who are seeking to despoil them of their rights

and degrade them before the world." If laws restrain-
ing slavery were to be passed, he solemnly stated, "I
trust in God that my eyes have rested upon the last
Speaker of the House of Representatives." [2]

Incandescent Toombs of Georgia voicing the Southern attitude, said, "Conviction is forced upon my mind
that my section of the Union is in danger, and I am
therefore unwilling to surrender the great power of the
Speaker's chair without obtaining security for the
future." He had "as much attachment to the Union of
these States, under the Constitution of our fathers, as
any free man ought to have. I am ready to concede
and sacrifice for it whatever a just and honorable man
ought to sacrifice but I do not hesitate to avow before
this House and the country and in the presence of the
living God, that if, by your legislation, you seek to
drive us from the territories of New Mexico and California, purchased by the common blood and treasure
of the whole people, and to abolish slavery in this District, thereby attempting to fix a national degradation
upon half the States in this Confederacy, I am for disunion; and if my physical courage be equal to the maintenance of my convictions of right and duty, I will devote all I am and all I have on earth to its consummation."

Correctly, Toombs stated, "a great Constitutional
right which was declared by a distinguished, Northern
Justice of the Supreme Court to be the cornerstone of
the Union, had already practically been abrogated in
all of the non-slave-holding states." He referred to
the recapture of fugitive blacks, and challenged every
Northern man to answer him if it were not true that

"that great right indispensable to the formation of the Union" had been taken away.

With sincerest conviction, he declared, "we are denounced out of doors as recusants and factionists, and indoors we are met with the cry of 'Union, Union.' Sir, we have passed that point. It is too late. I have used all my energies from the beginning of this question to save the country from this convulsion. I have resisted what I deemed unnecessary, hurtful agitation. . . . I hoped against hope, that a sense of justice and patriotism would induce the North to settle these questions upon principles honorable and safe to both sections. We must arouse and appeal to the Nation. We must tell them boldly and frankly that we prefer any calamities to submission to such degradation and injury as they would entail upon us; that we hold that to be consummation of all evil. . . . These are the principles upon which I act. Give me securities that the power of the organization which you seek will not be used to the injury of my constituents, then you can have my cooperation, but not till then. . . . Grant them, and you prevent the recurrence of the disgraceful scenes of the last twenty-four hours, and restore tranquillity to the country. Refuse them, and as far as I am concerned, 'let discord reign forever.' "

When Baker of Illinois, chided Southern members by stating "he did not believe the South was in earnest as to her determination to leave the Union" if anti-slave measures were enacted, Colcock of South Carolina assured him that although something approaching the "fervid and impassioned language . . . of Southern gentlemen today might have been heard in the

House before, that now the South was really in earnest."

He regarded secession in all its solemnity and importance, and with a full view of all the consequences that surrounded it. But he believed that now "the South is prepared to teach the North that she is really serious." Said he, "I here pledge myself that if any bill shall be passed at this Congress abolishing slavery in the District of Columbia, or incorporating the Wilmot Proviso in any form, I will introduce a resolution in this House declaring in terms that this Union ought to be dissolved."

Thoughtfully brooding, Stevens sat patiently through all this inflammatory eloquence and wrangling, all these arguments and threats. Strict parliamentarian, the irregularity of procedure irritated him. Nothing was before the House but the election of Speaker. The Representatives were going far afield in their campaigning. Difficulty, of course, had been expected in the election, but no one anticipated such furious talk.

Robert C. Winthrop of Massachusetts, had been Speaker of the prior session, and was in nomination here, but because he could not obtain the combined votes of Whigs and Free-Soilers, was unable to attain a majority.[3]

Stevens supported the choice of the party that had elected him, although there is little doubt that his sympathies were with the Free Soilers. For the first forty ballots he voted consistently for Whig candidate, Winthrop; then switched, casting the only vote for Duer, of New York for eight ballots, returning then to give all of his remaining votes to Winthrop.

It was no small tribute to Stevens that in this, his

first appearance in the House, he was among those nominated for Speaker. The vote for him was not only complimentary, but quite respectable. On December 17, it reached its high point of twenty-seven, and among those voting for him were Horace Mann and Joshua Giddings.

The Body just could not find a candidate strong enough to obtain a majority of votes, and in exhaustion, after sixty-three ballots, agreed to make the candidate who received the highest number of votes on that ballot, Speaker. Cobb, of Georgia, got the office. This was the first time in our history that a Speaker of the House was elected by plurality vote.

Characteristically no compromiser, the Lancastrian did not vote on this measure. Already recognized by the slave power as one of its most dangerous opponents, he was noticed as little as possible in the organization of the House.[4]

Because the impassioned words that had passed while the House was attempting to elect a Speaker were entirely irregular, Stevens disdained to answer them out of order. He waited until the President's message was before the House on February 20. Then, on his motion to lay it aside in order to take up the special message on the admission of California, and in approved parliamentary sequence, he delivered his maiden speech in that forum.

If proper remarks on that occasion should have aimed to soothe and pacify, then Stevens' speech was most highly improper. For years and decades it had been the custom of the Southerners in milder fashion to challenge and threaten the North and to intimidate

them with strong words of secession and disunion. No
representative of the North up to that time had in any
substantial way dared to meet them in their own manner. But no prior Congress had had a Thaddeus
Stevens.

Believing in human liberty, just as zealously and perhaps just as fanatically as any Southerner believed in
slavery, Stevens would not remain on the defensive.
He would carry the battle to the South. Not only
would he talk in their own terms, but, master of language that he was with subtle blend of crushing words,
irony, wit and sarcasm, he would punish them with
more of the strong man's speech than they had ever
heard a Northerner utter. He would chastise them ver-
bally until they literally squirmed in their seats.

From the beginning he was accurate but irritating.
"For a considerable time, after our meeting," said he,
the organization of the House was obstructed and since
organized, a large portion of time has been occupied
by speeches on the subject of slavery when no practical
question to which they could apply was before us."
There was, no doubt, a well defined object in this;
partly to intimidate Congress and partly to occupy its
time so that no legislation could be matured obnoxious
to those gentlemen.

"In one of these speeches, the gentleman (Clingham)
in opening the debate in behalf of human bondage dis-
tinctly notified us that unless Congress as a condition
precedent submitted to settle the slavery question, according to southern demands there should be no legislation even to the passage of the ordinary appropriations necessary to sustain the government." He did

not doubt that the speaker had the full support of the majority of southern representatives "before he ventured on so high a threat." It was, therefore, " a well defined and palpable conspiracy of southern members combined to stop the supply necessary to the existence of the government, disorganize and dissolve it until the bands that bind the Union together are severed." Well might the gentleman anticipate that the country and posterity "would pronounce this treason, rank treason against the Nation!"

He doubted if there was "another legislative body in the world where such sedition would not be followed by prosecution and punishment. But in this glorious country where nearly two-thirds of the people are free, we can say anything within these walls or beyond them with impunity, unless it be to agitate in favor of human liberty—that is aggression!"

What was the grave offense, the mighty wrong of the Nation which would justify a challenge of such portentous consequences? It was solely the refusal of Congress to extend slavery. "Will intelligent and free posterity," he asked, "believe it when impartial history records that the only cause for this high threat was the apprehension that the Congress of this free republic would not propagate nor permit to be propagated, the institution of human slavery into her vast territories now free?" Yet such was the simple fact.

Slavery "was a great evil which ought to be interdicted" and which "we should oppose as statesmen, philanthropists and moralists." But the Commoner was still a good Constitutionalist, and so made himself of record. However, he made it clear that he would no longer permit the North to be on the defensive in Congress. But bitter and determined as he was, he would restrict the fight to conform to the Federal pact, and "while I thus announce my unchangeful hostility to slavery in every form and in every place, I also avow my determination to stand by all the compromises of the Constitution and carry them into faithful effect." Some of these he greatly disliked and were they then open for consideration, they would never receive his assent. But "I find them in a Constitution formed in difficult times and I would not disturb them."

He regretted that due to those clauses, Congress had no power over slavery in the states, for if it had, he said he "would go over all threats, for some legal, just, safe and certain means for its final extinction." He knew of no one who claimed the right or desire to "touch it within the states" but in the territories he believed it the duty of the Congress to act "if it believes it will contribute to the prosperity, power, permanency, and glory of the Nation." Did slavery, he inquired, contribute to any of these?

From the standpoint of political economy, he found the system badly wanting. Virginia was a desolate example of the retrogression that slavery had brought, although by nature she had capabilities equal if not superior to any state in the Union. "There is scarcely a new town . . . within her borders, her ancient villages have the appearance of mournful decay, her minerals and timbers are unwrought, her water power is but partly utilized, her fine harbors are without ships, except from other ports and her seaport towns are without commerce. . ."

Slavery "prevents or destroys education and enfeebles a nation in war as well as peace." It was impossible that a nation of masters and slaves could be as powerful and formidable either in offensive or defensive war as a nation of free men. A large portion of her population must remain at home to prevent the rebellion of those who were constantly in a state of latent warfare with their oppressors. "I know, sir, we have had a most alarming description of the prowess of slavery. We have heard the cannon roar, seen their bayonets bristle, heard the war-cry of the charging chivalry and seen the bowie knives gleam within this hall, in the vivid picture of the terrible gentleman from North Carolina."

He opposed the "diffusion of slavery because confining it within its present limits will bring the states themselves to its gradual abolition. Let this disease spread, and although it will render the whole body leprous and loathsome, yet it will long survive. Confine it and like the cancer that is tending to the heart, it must be eradicated or it will eat out the vitals. The sooner the patient is convinced of this the sooner he will procure the healing operation. Confine this malady within its present limits; surround it with a cordon of free men so that it cannot spread and in less than twenty-five years every slaveholding state in this Union will have on its statute books a law for its gradual and final extinction."

To those who held that slavery was a matter between the slaveholders and their own consciences, he said, "I trust it may be so decided by impartial history and the unerring Judge that we may not be branded with that great stigma and that grievous burden may not burst

upon our souls." But could one hope for that justification if now when he had the power to prevent it, he
permitted the evil to spread over thousands of square
leagues then free and settle upon unborn millions?

"Sir, for myself, I should look upon any northern
man enlightened by a northern education who would
directly or indirectly by omission or commission, by
basely voting or cowardly skulking, permit it to spread
over one rood of God's free earth, as a traitor to liberty and recreant to his God."

Meade of Virginia, had said that Southerners though
"in numerical minority in the union for fifty years," had
"during the greater part of that period, managed to
control the destinies of the union." Stevens would
not complain of that statement; it was both candid and
true. But he could not listen to its recital without feeling the burning blush on his countenance "that the
North with her overshadowing millions of free men has
for half a century been tame and servile enough to submit to this arrogant rule.

"How often," he wondered, had "these walls been
profaned and the North insulted by insolent threats that
if Congress legislated against the Southern will it would
be disregarded, resisted to extremity and the Union destroyed? During the present session, we have been more
than once told amid raving excitement that if we dared
to legislate in a certain way the South would teach
the North a lesson." With a cool defiance, pregnant
with warning, he closed; "you have too often intimi-
dated Congress. You have more than once frightened
the tame North from its propriety and found dough-
faces enough to be your tools. But the dough-faces

were an unmanly, unvirile race, and incapable according to the laws of nature of reproduction. The old ones were deep in political graves, and had left no descendants. Moreover, there would be for them no resurrection, for they were soulless." [5]

This great speech of Stevens' stands out as a monumental landmark in the legislative record of the times. It marked the first appearance in Congress of a Northerner fearless enough to hurl back at the South its own challenge. Southern members were stunned.

Until then, the North had been on the defensive; throughout the balance of this session and the next one, that is, as long as Stevens served in the Congresses of the period, he was aggressor. Before, the South had always found the North yielding when it talked of disunion. Here came a man who dared them to carry out their threats. They had defended slavery on legal authority. Stevens indicted it on higher grounds. With all the force of admitted facts carefully marshalled, he proved to the limits of conviction that the institution was not only unethical and immoral, but dangerously threatening to the welfare of the Nation and even to the Union itself.

Priorly, their secession threats had always gotten what they sought. Now came one to whom their strong language was so much shouting and no more. Southerners had always appeared to answer objections to their desires by argument, but here was a stranger whose words struck so mightily and so accurately, that they could find no argument to refute him.

Nevertheless, with his biting speech ringing in their ears, they could not remain silent. Millson of Virginia, attempted a reply. He opened with ornate language, but soon realizing his inability to cope with Stevens' argument, had to be content with "quiet loathing and disgust." The best he could do was point to a portrait of Washington "and rest his case upon that patriot." [6]

The debate degenerated into a personal arraignment of the Lancastrian. Marshall of Kentucky, censured him for what he said was insulting language "better suited to a fish market." Harris admired his "frankness and candor" but criticized his determination to curb slavery in the light of his statement that he believed there was no power in the Constitution to do so. To him, Stevens was attempting that end by "insidious and assassin-like steps of indirection." [7]

Stanley of North Carolina accused him of using in his speech "language that Southern gentlemen would not use to a respectable negro." Referring to Stevens' early activities in Anti-Masonry, he said that since it would "no longer answer for a hobby-horse, the gentleman must preach against the horrors and despotism of slavery." He hoped the Northerner's next speech "would be fit to read in the families of Pennsylvania farmers and that he would find some other Morgan to frighten grandmothers and children with." All he asked was that Stevens and his group be shown no interference. If the Abolitionists were "let alone, they would in a few years be universally despised and buried with the burial of an ass, drawn and cast forth beyond the gates of Jerusalem." [8]

Of course the Lancastrian got no comfort from the Democratic Representatives of Pennsylvania. His colleague, Ross, openly rebuked him for the speech, saying had Stevens "raised his eyes to the portrait of Washington which hung before him, he would have seen the indignant frown at his ignoble attempt to excite one section of the Union against the other; or if the heart of that member had throbbed with even one patriotic impulse, he would have shrunk back to his seat covered with shame and remorse for his libel upon the Government of his country."

Surely "language so offensive, and impudence so unblushing have never before been heard or seen in any respectable assemblage of men. But," he consoled the House, "Pennsylvania knows that member, and with deep humiliation, she acknowledges the acquaintance. His history has been the history of her wrongs and her misfortune." Through the tinsel of what flowed from him as many fine words he concluded "that Pennsylvania had affixed a brand on the Lancaster Representative as deep and indelible as the wrongs she suffered at his hands were grievous and intolerable." [9]

Some Pennsylvania newspapers took offense at Stevens' speech; one holding that his "falsehoods were most insulting." [10] Another thought that although he was unquestionably a man of great talent, his speech "at this crisis can do only mischief." [11] A third felt that his speech had "excited the special indignation of all 'Niggerdom.' " [12] Most Northern newspapers commenting on the address, rebuked mildly some of the language used, but took no pains to cover a sly approval of Stevens' stand.

So great a resentment did the speech cause in the House that it was constantly referred to and frequently quoted from for several months after it was delivered.

Two hundred thousand copies of it were printed in pamphlet form and circulated over the country.[13]

Stevens, remarkable in his restraint, sat quietly through all the ugly comment of his colleagues. They seemed unable to find even the weakest of argument to answer him; their billingsgate he characteristically ignored. One fact stood out. Two months before he was an absolute stranger to the Congress and it to him. After his first address, the House was shocked into the realization that in its entire membership no one could match him in the devastating manner of his argument. That House held many able veterans but so much the better for Stevens. He was not long in properly appraising his relative ability in verbal encounter in the new forum. From that day forward, he had no fear of any man who rose to gainsay him. It was an excellent base on which to build a Congressional dictatorship.

The speech made him leader of the Anti-slavery cause in that Congress, and formed a rallying point for unorganized Abolition sentiment. It is significant historically as the first real challenge to the long held Southern domination of the Union.

As the session proceeded, Stevens busied himself with other matters. From the first he was an ardent advocate of high tariff, and frequently remarked in favor of it. He presented a number of petitions and resolutions for assistance of soldiers of the War of 1812, and engaged himself with a study of Post Office Departmental organization, and matters concerning the census. The latter had an especial interest because of the slave representation then allowed in the House, and his diligence was applied to find a method of legitimately reducing it.

On June 10, 1850, while the House was again in committee of the whole considering the part of the President's message relating to California, Stevens made his second important speech. He discussed the extent of the Congressional authority to legislate for the territories and admit new states into the Union, agreeing with Jefferson that the Constitutional power extended only to new states formed out of territory previously belonging to the Nation. "For sixty years and upward," said he, "after the passage of the Ordinance of 1787 and the adoption of the Constitution no one seriously doubted the right of Congress to control the whole legislation of the territories—to establish government there, create courts, fix the tenure of the judges and other officers, and exercise all acts of municipal as well as political regulations."

This authority had been exercised over the Northwestern and the Southwestern Territory, Louisiana, Florida, and Oregon. The policy had been approved of by Presidents, Congresses, and repeated decisions of the Supreme Court of the United States. "It is only," said Stevens, "since our dismemberment of the Mexican Empire that this question has been opened, and found able and apparently sensible statesmen to totally deny the power."

He charged that the real purpose of obtaining new territory was to enlarge the slave domain. But when the South unexpectedly found opposition to slavery in the new provinces, Southern statesmen discovered that the only chance they had of carrying out the original

design was to deny the power of Congress to pass laws
excluding slavery. They then abandoned the position
sanctioned by themselves and by the prescription of
sixty years, and boldly assumed this new attitude.

He argued that Congress has full and absolute
power to legislate for the territories. It was contended
that although it had exclusive, it had not unlimited,
jurisdiction in the territories, and that although bound
to legislate to protect slavery, Congress could not prohibit it. Clay had taken a middle position, holding that
Congress could "abolish, prohibit, or establish slavery
in the territories."

Stevens could not agree to either of these propositions. His argument was that under the common law,
a slave escaping from a slave state into a free state became free. Although that principle was prevented
from operating in the states by a clause in the Constitution, it was nevertheless in full force in the territories
to which the provision did not extend. The master,
therefore, who took his slave into free territories, had no
vested rights or property in him which could be impaired. "The slave becomes a man and has a vested and
inalienable right to liberty." Consequently, though
Congress had the "right to prohibit and abolish slavery
in those areas, it does not follow that it has the power
to establish it."

He reasoned that the Bill of Rights of the American
Nation declared "liberty to be an unalienable right."
The Constitution gave Congress no power to restrain
or take away this right except in the case of fugitives
from labor into other states. That led to the same conclusion; Congress, although it might abolish or prohibit

slavery wherever it had exclusive jurisdiction could "establish it nowhere."

Referring to his February speech, he said he expected to be assailed by the defenders of slavery when he gave his opinion of the real conditions and evils of that institution. He recalled how John Quincy Adams, "that greatest, most honest, and most fearless of modern statesmen," had been made the object of the "bitterest abuses in this House" for denouncing the horrors of slavery. No motives were too foul to impugn to him, no crimes too atrocious to charge upon him for taking such stand.

Of the many assaults upon himself, he said, "I do not remember one of the numerous gentlemen who have referred to my remarks who has attempted to deny one of the facts or refute one of the arguments. They have noticed them merely to vituperate their author." He would not retaliate, but if he were looking for a response with such weapons, he could "find them any day by entering the Fish Market. However," said he, lapsing into his own acid words, "I beg those respectable fish ladies to understand that I do not include my colleague from Bucks County (Ross) among those whom I deem fit to be their associates. I would not so degrade them. There is in the natural world a little spotted, contemptible animal which is armed by nature with a foetid, volatile, penetrating virus which so pollutes whoever attacks it as to make him offensive to himself and all around him for a long time. Indeed, he is almost incapable of purification. No insult shall provoke me to crush so filthy a beast! But" he quickly added with seeming regret, "that was more than I in-

tended to say." Regaining his poise, he apologized to
the chair and trusted he would "never again be betrayed
into a similar digression, even to brush off these invad-
ing vermin."

Back to his subject he noticed "comparisons have
been instituted between slave and laboring free men,
much to the advantage of slavery. Instances are cited
where the slave, after having tried freedom, had voluntarily returned to resume his serfdom." He turned to
irony and ridicule. "Well, if this be so, let us give all
a chance to enjoy this pleasure. Let the slaves who
choose, go free and the free who choose, become slaves.
If these gentlemen believe there is a word of truth in
what they preach, the slave-holder need be under no
apprehension that he will ever lack bondsmen." Their
slaves would remain and many free men would seek
admission into this happy condition.

"Let them be active in propagating their principles.
We will not complain if they establish societies in the
South for that purpose—abolition societies to abolish
freedom. Nor will we rob the mails to search for incendiary publications in favor of slavery, even if they
contain seductive pictures and cuts of those implements
of happiness—handcuffs, iron yokes and cat-o'-nine-
tails."

It could not be denied that for two centuries, the
North had contributed to secure to a particular race
the whole advantages of this blissful condition of slavery; and at the same time had imposed on the white
race the cares, the troubles, the lean anxieties of freedom. This was a monopoly inconsistent with Republican principles and should be corrected if it would save

eader will observe in the above picture, that the rotundity of th
ten, and he is represented as rather slender. 'The followin
on another page, represents him again with Falstaff proportions

The Governor waylaid and almost murdered by a Royal Arch
ge 21 another allusion is made to religion, and the Governor i
Buren, "*let him take the followers of St. Paul, we are con
of Moses!!!*" On page 22, a letter is given as coming from
of the Governor, in which a fling at the Germans is made as

From the Pennsylvania Telegraph, August 15, 1838.

Anti-Mason Governor Ritner Appears to be Bested in Encounter with an Alleged
Member of the "Fraternity"

the Union. Then let the "gentlemen introduce a compromise by which these races may change positions; by which the oppressed master may slide into that happy state where he can stretch his sleek limbs on the sunny ground without fear of deranging his toilet; when he will have no care for tomorrow; another will be bound to find him meat and drink, food and raiment, and provide for the infirmities and illnesses of old age. Impose, if you will, upon the other race as a compensation for their former blessings all those cares and duties and anxieties."

He asked Reverend Hilliard, rabid slavist and others, "if the ethnological research of the past and present, whether drawn from the physiology or the philology of tribes and nations of men," did not all corroborate the recorded fact that "He hath made of one blood all nations of men" and that their present great varity in color, form, and intellect is the effect of climate, habit, food and education.

The white man who would exchange position with the slave should not despair on account of the misfortune of his color. If he took his "stand in the swamp, spade and mattock in hand, and, uncovered and half-naked, toiled beneath the boiling sun, and then went to his hut at night to sleep on the bare ground and then go forth in the morning, unwashed, to his daily labor, in a few short years or a generation or two at most, he will have a color that will pass muster in the most fastidious and pious slave market in Christendom."

Holly was authority for the statement that the moment a man became a slave, he lost half himself, and a few short years of apprenticeship expunged all the rest except a "faint gleaming of an immortal soul. Your shape will gradually conform to your condition. Your parched and swollen lips will assume a prominent and permanent thickness of the most approved style. Your feet, unconfined by shoes and accustomed to marshy soil, will shoot out behind and side-wise until they will assume the most delightful symmetry of slavery. Deprived of all education, cut off from all ambitious aspirations, your mind would soon lose all foolish and perplexing desires for freedom, and the whole man would be sunk into a most happy and contented indifference."

The "numerous clergymen who defended slavery and praised its comforts and advantages," next received his attention. He would not answer their "absurd and blasphemous position," but he would say "that these Reverend Parasites do more to make infidels than all the writings of Hume, Voltaire, and Paine. If it were shown that the Bible authorized, sanctioned and enjoined human slavery, no good man would be a Christian!"

As an example of slavery's "comforts and advantages," he cited an 1808 statute of Virginia, providing that any slave who would not be reclaimed from the disorderly courses of "going abroad in the night or running away and lying out, by common methods of punishment might be dismembered and punished in any other way not touching life as the Court should think fit." But if the slave should "die by means of such dismembering, no forfeiture or punishment shall be thereby incurred." Stevens said he would not read the act himself, but gave it to the clerk to read lest it should make "Southern gentlemen blush."

Because of the injustice of slave representation, he would not consent to the admission of another slave state into the Union. The fact that there were then twenty-five gentlemen on the Floor veritably representatives of the blacks alone and having not one free constituent, was unjust to the free states and an outrage on every representative principle.

As to the Southern demand for compromise, he said that when that word was applied to human and Constitutional rights, he abhorred it. When the Congress assembled it was well known that a large majority were in favor of prohibiting slavery in the territories and admitting no new slave states, but terror, treason and threats were used to compel the majority to yield to a turbulent minority. "The wiles of preaching, the recklessness of ambition, and the corruption of party were all used to bring about this compromise of Constitutional rights. He who regarded his oath to support the Constitution, could not thus surrender." Clay's Compromise Bill "was the most extraordinary conspiracy against liberty, and if it should survive its puerperal fever the House would have another opportunity of knocking the monster in the head."

When he said "the proposal to pay Virginia $200,-000,000 to transport her slaves to Africa away from the land of their birth to the land of strangers, was a proposal not fit to be made," Averett of that State asked him if New England had not sold slaves. Stevens answered, "Yes, she had; she was very wicked, but has long since repented. Go ye and do likewise."

But he said he did not reproach the South. He honored her courage and fidelity; "even in a bad, a wicked

cause she showed a united front. All her sons were
faithful to the cause of human bondage because it was
their cause. But the North, the poor, timid, mercenary, grovelling North has no such united defenders
of her cause although it is the cause of human liberty.
None of the bright lights of the Nation shone upon her
section. Even her own great men had turned her accusers. She was the victim of ambition which preferred
self to country, and personal aggrandizement to the
high cause of human liberty. She is offered up a sacrifice to propitiate Southern tyranny—to conciliate
Southern treason."

He attacked Clay's criticism of enforcement laws for
fugitive slaves in the free states, and ridiculed Webster's charge of aggressions of the North in that particular. He assailed the 1793 Act, charging that it gave
a slave owner a more enforceable property right in a
slave than it did in a horse. Under it the slave was
denied trial by jury and was unable to obtain a writ
of Habeas Corpus, and by summary examination could
be sent to hopeless bondage. It should be repealed.

He cited the case of a slave family from Maryland
which escaped into Pennsylvania, and there obtained
the reluctant consent of a farmer to sleep in his barn.
A week later the owner captured them, and the State
Court held the farmer liable for the full value of the
slave besides a $500 penalty. The Lancastrian of-
fered it as an example of the application of laws then
in force, which "these great expounders of Constitutional freedom hold to be too mild."

Clay's proposition was nothing less than vicious. Any
negro alleged to be an escaped slave might easily be

able to prove that he was born free and had spent his entire life in a free state, but he could not even be heard. A mere affidavit which might have been made hundreds of miles away would be absolutely conclusive against him. Under the measure, "the tide-waiters and country postmasters who make no pretentions to legal learning" would be compelled to decide, that the affidavit of a distant soul-dealer was evidence of slavery which could not be gainsaid. "Behold what a court and jury are to pass upon human liberty! An overseer, with a power of attorney, the affidavit of a professional slave-dealer; an itinerant postmaster from Virginia signing judgment in a barroom, the defendant a handcuffed negro, without counsel, witness or judge. Verily, a second Daniel has come to judgment!"

He did not object to the proposed law so strongly because it doubled all the penalties; "its most obnoxious feature was that it expressly recognized slavery in the territories."

Clay's demand that bystanders aid in the capture of fugitive slaves was more than Stevens' constituents would ever grant. They would abide strictly by the Constitution. "The slave-holder may bruise his slave among his own myrmidons unmolested except by their frowning scorn, but no law which that tyrant can pass will ever induce them to join the crowd and cry after the trembling wretch who has escaped from unjust bondage. Their fair land shall never become the hunting ground on which the bloodhounds of slavery shall course and play and command them to join in the hunt.

"Names of the great" had been associated with Clay in support of his Compromise Bill, and this was drawing the country to it. When the ordinary man erred, no great mischief was caused, but when those in whom "the people were accustomed to confide" were mistaken, it was "fatal." If "in this crisis of the fate of liberty, any of the renowned men of the nation shall betray her cause, it were better that they had been unknown to fame. It need not be hoped that the brightness of their past glory will dazzle the eyes of posterity, or illumine the pages of impartial history. Few of its rays may still linger on a fading sky; but they will soon be overwhelmed in the blackness of darkness. For unless progressive civilization, and the increasing love of freedom throughout the Christian and civilized world, are fallacious, the Sun of Liberty, of universal Liberty, is already above the horizon and fast coursing to his meridian splendor where no advocate or apologist of slavery can look upon his face and live." [14]

After Stevens had delivered his speech, someone handed him a treatise by a former theological professor at Andover who spoke of the "blessings and comforts of slavery." His comment was that the "work was able and contained very glowing eulogy on Daniel Webster, and a rather faint one on the Bible." [15]

Although a staunch, bitter, and sometimes vitriolic opponent, Stevens early came to be respected as a straight-forward and outspoken antagonist. He never misrepresented nor attempted to achieve his end through indirection or subterfuge.

On June 15, when the California amendment was under consideration, he said he did not want to hold out the idea that he would compromise with slavery by voting for the amendment, for he desired to deal "frankly, even if offensively with them." He would not agree to the admission of any state in which the institution prevailed, for every such one admitted would be entitled to a representation in the Federal Congress based upon slave population in the proportion of five slaves for three free men.[16]

Texas at the time was insisting on its ownership of a large area in New Mexico. Inasmuch as the former was slave territory and the latter not, it was only natural for Stevens to oppose Congressional approval of the Texas claim. The Lone Star State had its vociferous advocates in Congress, while New Mexico, because of her territorial status, had no one to speak for her there. Stevens thought she should at least be heard and moved to admit Hugh Smith, a delegate from the Territory, for that purpose.

Did the House mean to try the question ex parte, with Texas alone represented? Was it a doctrine of justice that the one party because great and powerful was to be heard, and the other party, equally interested, because weak and defenseless, would not be heard? This was not English or American justice but "more the part of Rhadamanthus, the King of Hell—to condemn without hearing." [17]

The proposal before the House also provided for the payment of ten million dollars to Texas. Stevens defended President Taylor who saw no right in such a measure. The great State in the Southwest had made known its demand in no uncertain language. But in spite of the "most fearful consequences predicted" and "the most terrible vengeance threatened" and in spite of the fact that "civil war disorders and bloody desolation" were the "mildest figures garnishing their discourses" he would say nothing to these impotent threats and gory predictions. Why pay Texas ten million dollars for a part of New Mexico to which she had no shadow of title? The payment was proposed "to buy peace from armed rebels. If any one state or a portion of a state choose to place themselves in military array against the Government of the Union, I am for trying the strength of the Government of the Union. . . . I will not be persuaded by any intimation of spilling of blood. If blood is to be spilt, by whose fault is it to be spilt?"

He would do full justice to Texas and not take a foot of land which belonged to her, but on the other hand, he would give her no land to train her slaves upon, nor pay her money to purchase peace. "Pass this bill," he warned, "and instead of bringing repose it will be the cause of constraint, agitation, and sedition fruitful of future rebellion, disunion, civil war and final ruin of the Republic. Do your duty firmly," he admonished his colleagues, "show that you are fit to be a Government and this Union will be perpetual." [18]

His motion to lay the new Fugitive Slave Bill on the table was easily defeated, and the measure passed by a vote of one hundred five to seventy-three. Many representatives unwilling to go on record had absented themselves from the Floor when they saw the vote was called. As soon as it was announced Stevens suggested that "the Speaker send a page to notify Northern members the Fugitive Slave Bill had been disposed of and they may now come back into the hall."

While Clay's compromise program was still pending,

Stevens had to make up his mind whether to retire or stand for reelection. From debates and votes taken on incidental features of the measure it required no prophet to understand that the main features of the bill would be enacted into law. Stevens' opposition would surely be of no avail. In his home district he had some support for his stand, but the conservative wing of his party and the Democrats joined in rebuking what they termed his dangerous policy of resistance to compromise.

His business obligations were still worrying him [19] and he was beginning to believe that instead of remaining in Congress where he must labor in an already defeated cause, he should "devote his time to paying his debts and making a living." [20] The Whig papers gave him little encouragement.[21] The Lancaster *Intelligencer,* which liked to refer to itself as independent in politics, was "sure that there are many Whigs in Lancaster County who do not sanction his course, and yet he appears to have them so completely under his control that they dare not raise a finger against him." Its editors saw Stevens as "a bold and reckless politician who follows the bent of his own inclinations without regard to the wishes of the people. He takes his position and adheres to it, not caring a fig whether it pleases or displeases his constituents." [22]

Nevertheless, when the Whig Convention assembled in August, Stevens was nominated "by acclamation." [23] His party was so predominantly powerful that even with some dissent in it, he was reelected without effort.[24]

The great compromise measures of 1850 became law in the last term of the Thirty-first Congress. Stevens realized that any speeches he might make in opposition would be merely wasting words, and that was not his practice. Had he believed that the country was against the measure, no Congressional majority in favor of it would have deterred him from attack upon it. The fact that he had little to say is indicative of his conviction that the people approved the compromise program.

Returned to the Thirty-second Congress, he was again nominated for speaker. On one ballot he received sixteen votes and was fourth high. Mann and Giddings consistently supported him. In spite of a country-wide criticism, he was not a pariah among his fellows. The people through their Representatives had simply chosen an adjustment with slavery instead of a firm stand against it. It must be said to Stevens' credit that throughout the entire session he seemed willing to give the Clay measures fair and thorough trial. Remaining in the background, he engaged himself with the small business of presenting memorials and petitions from his constituents.

One question at least had not become sectional, and that was the tariff. He spoke on it in June. The speech is interesting mainly because it is a typical Stevens speech. No outstanding new arguments were used but the old ones were adroitly marshalled and colorfully and spicily stated.

Among the facts used were those pertaining to iron which was of considerable interest to him, because of his iron works in Franklin County. He attacked a free trade attitude and reciprocal laws and held they could be practically used "only when nations are equally

advanced in skill, capital, and power of production."
You may impose on a full-grown man a task of carrying a hundred pounds weight; "reciprocity" required
that a boy of ten years should carry a like burden,
though it crush him to the earth. Such was the operation of the theory between old and young nations. It
was well illustrated in the article, cotton fabrics. In
1850 we imported cotton goods from England to the
amount of $19,096,530; England imported of the same
article from this country, $50 worth! "Twenty millions
of dollars against fifty dollars is the effect of free reciprocal 'trade.' Let the people reflect on these things and
elect such rulers as will pursue a wise and prosperous
policy." [25]

That autumn the country must choose a president.
Thoroughly disheartened with the whole political aspect,
Stevens attempted to do his duty as a good Whig and
an American. He knew that his party was hopelessly
divided on the slavery question and saw the Southern
members rapidly moving to the Democratic side. He
was too wise to think that there was any possible means
of bringing them into the ranks of the Northern faction, as long as the slave question existed. He passed
them as "a small fragment of the Democratic Party
which had deserted the colors and gone over, with what
little political material they could collect, to the camp
of the enemy." [26]

Legislation affecting the question had been passed
and was being tested, but that did not conclude the issue.
He struck and struck squarely. "In the North where
a majority believed that slavery was a great moral, religious and political evil, a disgrace to the nation and a

reproach to humanity, they nevertheless, obeyed the Constitutional provision and tolerated it. But opinion was by no means uniform there; in the larger cities where more men are mercenary and where princely fortunes beget kingly appetites, many men were found whose dispositions naturally inclined to domination, and who sincerely believed that a portion of the human race was created for no other purpose than to be servants of others; that a part of mortal clay was of finer texture and nobler mould than the rest."

In the South, Whigs and Democrats were slaveholders, but even there many were found who condemned the institution. The Whig Party permitted its members to differ in opinion upon slavery. It had never been a party issue, but now, its proponents, having grown stronger, demanded on the part of the presidential candidate, a sympathetic attitude toward their institution, in the absence of which they would concentrate against him. This had been tried successfully once before and "is now being tried upon that superpatriot (Scott) who never yet quailed before the dictate of mortal man."

In the early meetings of the Thirty-first Congress, the slave advocates had raised a "furor and clamor within this Hall which could hardly have been justified had the Republic been in flames." The object of that disgraceful turmoil "was to compel both political parties to incorporate into their party creeds the defense and propagation of slavery."

He accused Southerners of making the slavery question the one of highest importance and forcing all other great issues to the background. The South had come to support General Pierce because it believed "that slavery would be much safer in his hands than in those of General Scott." Faulkner of Virginia, had charged Scott with "expressing" sentiments hostile to the institutions of fifteen states of this Union.[27] In the same letter, the General had also said that he was persuaded that it was the high obligation of masters in slave-holding states . . . to meliorate slavery even to extermination. "That letter," said Stevens, "was General Scott's sole offense and for this he is opposed by the bigots of slavery."

Faulkner claimed that Scott had not given sufficient pledges for him to trust the General. Stevens said the South would not trust Scott because he was not "in favor of the perpetual bondage of the human race."

He referred to Mexico's offer to make Scott President of the Mexican Republic at a salary of a quarter of a million dollars a year which the General rejected and "returned poor and persecuted to his native land," yet "the politicians who have never shown their devotion to their native land except by long orations and the possession of offices dare sit in judgment upon the fidelity of this mutilated hero." He reminded the Southerners that by rejecting General Scott they were raising a sectional issue. If the South forced this issue did she believe that the North, tame as it was, "when so often trod upon would never turn?"

The answer that Southerners would vindicate themselves by a separate Confederacy could not avail, for the South with its increasing slaves and enlarging burdens, was not sure that it could protect itself against foreign foes and servile threats.

He warned them to consider well the danger confronting a separate Nation, and although what might happen to it was painful reflection, "no candid and intelligent statesman can calmly contemplate passing events and exclude from his saddened mind these fearful forebodings." He hoped that "the sound sense and true patriotism of the American people would arrest the headlong career of reckless men." [28]

The Whig Party, attempting to straddle the breach that slavery had made between the North and the South, found itself torn in twain by the opposing sections. General Scott was finally made its candidate for the presidency, and the Democrats picked Pierce to oppose him.

There was at one time some hope that the Free Soil Party, which had nominated John P. Hale of New Hampshire, might divide Scott's opposition far enough to elect him. But such was not the outcome. Webster, the little man with the lion heart and Clay, the pacific adjuster, were both dead. With no leader who could attract a national support, the sectionally rent Whig Party fell upon its death-bed in that election.

Pierce became President; those favoring compromise strengthened their hold on the Government, and Stevens, tired and disheartened, turned his face toward Lancaster.

III

BACK HOME

The Thirty-Third Congress, which convened in December of 1853, had every reason to hope for a quiet session. The Compromise Measures then recently enacted, promised at least a temporary peace. And of no less importance as it affected harmony in the House of Representatives, Thaddeus Stevens was absent.

While the Congress had before it issues largely involving human rights, he was eager to be a member. But when it concerned itself only with routine legislation, he had little desire to be present.

The storm that threatened the country when he went to Congress in 1849, seemed to have been completely dissipated. With sectional differences adjusted, agitation of any kind which would disturb the peace would be out of place. Stevens realized this and even though he believed, as always, that sometime the test must come, he would not precipitate it.

He could not support the Compromise, because he was convinced that human rights were involved and in such matters he would not barter. But so long as a middle-of-the-road policy would maintain national harmony, he was fair enough not to challenge it. Under the circumstances, his unyielding type had no place in Congress. It was best that he retire to the quiet of private life, and quite sensibly he so decided.

As the Thirty-Second Congress was about to close, he had inserted a personal explanation of a "pleasantry" he had passed which "might look grave on paper and be misconstrued." He noticed it because it was "more than probable that hereafter I shall never meet any member here or elsewhere officially, and I desire to part with no unfriendly feeling toward any." [1]

Back in Lancaster, the sixty-one year old lawyer would devote his remaining days to his profession, through forever with politics.

Although he spent nearly all of the previous four years in Washington, he had kept a firm hand upon his law business. In 1851, he appeared as counsel for the defense in a case growing out of the Fugitive Slave Laws. It attracted national attention.

The little settlement of Sadsbury in Stevens' own Lancaster County was hardly ten miles from the southern boundary of Pennsylvania, which marked the northern limit of slave domain. Nearly every home there was a part of the Underground Railroad System [2] which assisted escaped blacks in their northward flight to freedom. Some fugitive slaves had been sheltered overnight in the village by a free negro named Parker. When the owners with their man-catchers and United States Deputies Marshal arrived, they were met by a crowd, largely composed of blacks armed with axes, pitch forks, corn cutters and hoes. In the attack upon Parker's house, the slave owner Gorsuch was killed and his son seriously wounded.

All known participants were arrested, including Castner Hanway and Elijah Lewis, two prominent citizens who had never concealed their abolition sympathies. They retained the "Old Commoner" who took a leading part in the preliminary hearings in Lancaster. [3] Four white men, Hanway, Lewis, Scarlett and Jackson, and twenty-five colored men were indicted later by a Fed-

nothing to blame but his own zeal and
want of honesty in the Loco Foco cause.

REBECCA BEATTY.

The Loco Focos are making great efforts
to create a belief that the statements of Rebecca Beatty, and her son, are not entitled to
credit, because she is a degraded woman.

That she is degraded no one pretends to
dispute. But who made her so? Here is the
rub. Who led her from virtues path into
degradation? It was DAVID R. PORTER.—
If she be degraded, as she undoubtedly is, David R. Porter, is morally MORE so, for he is
THE AUTHOR OF HER DEGRADATION.

The Loco Focos are welcome to prove Rebecca Beatty as abandoned as they please.—
Porter shares the dishonor with her, and
while it does not alter or disprove the fact
that he is the father of a son and daughter
of hers, it shows who was HIS COMPAN-
ION AND ASSOCIATE IN CRIME, for it
is a fact that no one pretends to dispute, that
Rebecca Beatty, abandoned or worthless as
she may be, had TWO CHILDREN BY
DAVID R. PORTER.

EXTRAORDINARY ABSENCE OF MIND.

From the Pennsylvania Telegraph, August 15, 1838.

Accusations Against the Democratic Candidate for Governor

eral grand jury at Philadelphia for treason. They
were charged with having made war against the United
States by resisting the Fugitive Slave Law and ob-
structing the United States Marshal in executing due
process of the law.[4]

At the trial, a prominent Democratic lawyer of Philadelphia, John M. Read, acted as chief counsel for the
defense. Stevens dominated the entire proceedings,
and just why he preferred to remain in the background
is not clear.[5]

The case lasted three weeks and at its end, the Senior
Judge delivered a searing lecture against fanatics and
demagogues who stirred up feeling against, and counselled forcible opposition to the laws of the United
States. But having done what he deemed his duty,
he instructed the jury that as a matter of law, the acts
of the defendants did not "rise to the dignity of treason
or a levy of war against the United States." His directed verdict acquitted them.

The incident is known to history as "The Christiana
Riot" and marks the first bloodshed in resistance to, or
enforcement of the Fugitive Slave Law.[6] It is significant of Stevens' continuing interest in the subject
as well as indicating the extent of public feeling in the
North against the Slave Act.

The next few years mark the third and last period
of Stevens' full attention to the law, unhampered by
public office. The reports of the appellate courts
yield him a fair share of space and, having reached a
position of eminence in the Lancaster County Bar, he
was able to enjoy a lucrative practice of the more interest because it reached into all the varied fields of

the profession. No matter seemed too small for him to take up and none seemed large enough nor strange enough to make him seek the help of associate counsel.

Records of cases in which he was called in to assist other lawyers, are abundant, but nowhere does the reverse appear. There was but a single line of work which he would not accept, and that was special counsel in the prosecution of a capital case. It was generally known that he was opposed to the death penalty, but in those years he gave as his reason for refusal, his belief that prosecution in criminal matters was exclusively the duty of public officers.[7]

Because of a tendency to invest largely in real property it is not strange that he sometimes found himself a party to litigation. On those occasions, instead of retaining counsel, he acted as his own lawyer.

About the time he moved to Lancaster, he became involved in a law suit in which he and a neighbor both raised claims to the same iron ore property. The Lower Court found against Stevens but on the appeal, arguing his own case, he had the decision reversed. The other claimant, Hughes, permitted Stevens a quiet enjoyment of the disputed premises for sixteen years, and then brought another action in trespass. Again the County Court decided against Stevens, and again he appealed. Still champion of his own cause, he obtained in the Supreme Court a reversal of the Lower Court's decision and a new trial.

When the action was retried, Stevens was awarded $500 damages. Under the law, the Court was empowered to assess treble damages if in its opinion the case warranted. The same Judge had presided at both trials. The first time, when Stevens had lost, he was not pleased with the peremptory way the Court had decided against him. Now with the Appellate Court's decision a second time in his favor, he attempted his little joke.

On the weakest of legal grounds, he promptly moved for an assessment of treble damages against the defendant. The Judge, apparently giving undue heed to the Supreme Court's opinion, raised the damages awarded to $1,500 and entered judgment in that amount. Of course, defendant appealed, and although Stevens' assistants tried to dissuade him, he insisted on answering it. He agreed to make the argument himself. But when the time came for it, he could not be found. His assistant, doing the best he could, heard the inevitable decision against Stevens, and hurried home to report it. The Old Commoner merely smiled, saying that he had expected such an outcome, but had wanted the Supreme Court to see "what an utter damned fool the Judge below really was."[8]

Defending himself in the law courts was nothing new. Some ten years after he had come to Gettysburg, he involved himself in a matter from which he heard echoes to the day of his death. An old member of the Bar by the name of James Dobbins, through age and dissolute habits, had become deranged and was the sport of the boys and heartless men of the town. Under his father's will, he had come into possession of a farm, encumbered by certain legacies. His thriftless and untempered ways led him to the inevitable sheriff's sale. Under the execution and at public sale, Stevens purchased the farm and the old man's library. When

Stevens took possession of what he had bought, Dobbins raged like a madman.

The story went out that the club-foot lawyer had defrauded the old man who was unable to take care of himself. An action was brought to set aside the sale on the ground that Stevens had professionally advised a prospective bidder that the property was subject to liens of certain legacies. This opinion it was alleged had caused Stevens' client to refuse to bid. Because Stevens had himself bought the property, it was charged that this was a fraud on his part. The Lower Court sustained that contention but the Supreme Court of the State commended Stevens' legal opinion and vindicated his act wholly.[9]

Until the matter was finally adjudicated, Stevens remained aloof from old Dobbins, permitting him to say and do his worst. But when the contest was concluded in his favor he was free to show his real nature. Mentioning not a word about it to anyone, and, in spite of the fact that the old man had profaned him as only a deluded one can, Stevens paid the old fellow's board for a time and when he became unmanageable, saw to it that he was taken to a comfortable room in the almshouse.

To have proposed the removal would have driven old Dobbins violent, but Stevens handled it masterfully. He was at the time attorney for the Directors of the Poor. He resigned this position and had old Dobbins appointed to it with the understanding that he would have Stevens' office at the institution. The room was fitted up and Dobbin's old library moved in. Stevens thereafter did the work but the poor old man "lived and died in the pleasant delusion that he was again a lawyer of importance." [10]

Stevens, whose judgment in matters of this kind was eminently fair, never felt that he had wronged Dobbins. However, he did not feel that way about all of the properties that he had purchased at sheriff's sales. In an outstanding paragraph in the codicil of his Will, he said, "I bought John Shert's property at sheriff's sale at much below its value. I want only my own. All except $300 the proceeds of it and the interest, I direct shall be returned to the estate."

Some of his cases he tried more because of the principle involved than for the fees obtainable. The Seventh Day Baptists who had colonized in Franklin County, were frequently in conflict with the old Pennsylvania statute of 1794, which prohibited "worldly employment or business" on Sunday. They believed that Sunday was the seventh day of the week instead of the first and found no trouble in supporting that position by abundant citations from the Scriptures.

Peace officers frequently arrested them for working on what the law counted as Sunday, and one of these cases Stevens took to the highest court. This he did with the full knowledge that that very court had already adjudicated the matter adversely to his position some thirty years before.

The Old Commoner's argument was an ingenious one and is set forth in the reports at greater length than the opinion of the Court itself. Stevens contended that the law was unconstitutional in that it attempted to control or interfere with the rights of conscience. It required no argument other than the reading of the Act to prove that the legislation "looks to enforcing the religious observance of the day." If the Legislature could do that then there was no limit to its power over religious subjects. If it could direct the people to stay at home quietly, it could direct them to go to church, and if it could direct them to attend church, it could direct the church to be attended.

In short, if it had any power over religious subjects, it had all power. Such authority would be a perfect union of church and state, so much abhorred by the people of this republic, and would inevitably lead to religious prosecution and finally to civil and religious tyranny.

The old doctrine that the "Christian Religion is a part of the common law" was no doubt the foundation and justification for the law. But that doctrine was promulgated in the worst times and by the worst men of a government that avowedly united church and state; in times when men were sent to the block or the stake on any frivolous charge of heresy. To deny transubstantiation or the supremacy of the Church was a capital offense under one reign; and to admit them was a capital offense under another. Men were punished as blasphemers for denying the divinity of our Saviour because "the Christian religion was a part of the common law."

At one time men were executed in great numbers by the civil power for denying the Real Presence because that was "a part of the Christian religion and the Christian religion was a part of the municipal law." But when the Protestants gained the ascendency, to believe in the Real Presence was contrary to the Christian religion and therefore a violation of the law and punished by the secular arm.

If the Christian religion was part of the common law, then all who disbelieved that religion were habitual breakers of the law. The Jew, the Hindu, the Pagan, were perpetual malefactors.

Those consequences, of course, were entirely satisfactory to the English government at its origin. They enabled tyrants of the fifteenth and sixteenth centuries to find a convenient excuse for sending to the block anyone who became obnoxious to them. "If such tyrant were a Roman Catholic, the heresy of the Reformation was sufficient. If he were a Protestant, adherence to the Church of Rome was equally good excuse."

He continued at length in this line of argument to support a principle that was dear to him. He was making no attack upon the Christian religion, but was pleading manfully for religious tolerance.

The Court treated his argument respectfully, but, of course, could do nothing but sustain the judgment of the Court below.[11]

Not all of his practice was based on matters of high principle. Some of his cases involved the picayune unpleasantries of heated contacts in smaller cases. When a man broke faith with Stevens, he showed no restraint of tongue in bringing it to the attention of the offender. On one occasion, a lawyer whom he had always respected as a friend, and for whom he had done many favors, betrayed him. The next time Stevens met him, he hobbled up to him, rested upon his cane, and looking the fellow squarely in the face, struck him with the grim pronouncement: "You must be a bas-

tard, for I knew your mother's husband and he was a
gentleman and an honest man." [12]

It was during these years that he rose in his profession to a point where people referred to him as one
of the great lawyers in his State. An eminent jurist
who never liked him but who, because of constant contact, was well qualified to give an opinion, rendered
this critique upon him. "When he died, he was un-
equaled in this country as a lawyer. He said the smart-
est things ever said." [13]

Though immersed deeply in his practice, extending
his good legal reputation and rebuilding his fortune,
Stevens was not unaware of the political currents that
were moving in the country. He had been strong
enough to name a staunch follower of his, representative from the district in 1854.[14] In that year, those
who had supported the compromise enactments, not
satisfied to let well enough alone, had precipitated
through a piece of legislation, a sectional strife which
culminated in the War of the Rebellion.

The Kansas-Nebraska Act which repealed the Missouri Compromise, provided in effect that the territories themselves should decide the question of slavery
within their borders. This could have no other result
than a rush of fanatics from both sides into the territories that were ripe for statehood, in an effort to control opinion there.

Kansas was an outstanding example. Certainly the
supporters of the law had no thought of such evil results, but were merely attempting to remove artificial
boundaries and provide for self-determination. However, the repeal of the Missouri Compromise united

Democratic opposition in the North in 1854, into a new party calling itself Republican. To it the old Whigs moved, almost in a body. Southern Whigs, adrift of their moorings, retreated to the Democratic Party and the stage was set for War between the sections.

Abraham Lincoln out in Illinois, profoundly interested, was closely watching the reformation. His shrewd, political eye had marked Stevens as a strong man long before. He had apparently investigated the Lancastrian's feelings on the slavery matter, and concluded that the Pennsylvanian had much in common with him. As early as 1848, he had written Stevens:

"You may possibly remember seeing me at the Philadelphia Convention—introduced to you as the lone Whig star of Illinois—Since the adjournment, I have remained here, so long, in the Whig document room—I am now about to start for home and I desire the undisguised opinion of some experienced person and sagacious Pennsylvania politician, as to how the vote for that state, for governor, and president, is likely to go—In casting about for such a man, I have settled upon you, and I shall be much obliged if you will write me at Springfield, Illinois.

"The news we are receiving here now by letters from all quarters is steadily on the rise, we have none lately of a discouraging character—This is the sum without giving particulars." [15]

But Stevens, perhaps remembering his early championship of Anti-Masonic principles and its unhappy ending, was slow to come out for the new party.

The Republican movement reached Lancaster in

1855, when a small group met in Fulton Hall to organize. Leading Whigs did not appear and only seventeen persons assembled. Among them was Stevens who delivered a perfunctory address. He was feeling his way and what was done in the way of organization received little publicity. Inconspicuous newspaper accounts furnished the sole reports. No mass meetings were held and no speaker's committees appointed. But late in that year, Stevens was elected to represent the new party in Lancaster County and attended the Philadelphia Convention in 1856, when a president and vice-president were nominated.

In a short time the Republican movement was gathering momentum in the North with the vari-complexioned groups moving in mass to its standard. Almost the entire South, watching the rapidly growing new party with a half fear and a half bravado, began unconsciously to dissolve their local political differences and amalgamate geographically.

The years 1857 and 1858 crystallized the movement that welded together the North in opposition to slavery. The Dred-Scott decision declaring in effect that the black man had no rights which the white man was bound to respect, was merely grist in the mill that was grinding out disaffection.

Having early placed himself at the head of the new party in Lancaster County, its virile sweep over the entire North made it easy for Stevens to regain his seat in Congress in the election of 1858.

His law practice now became of secondary importance. When human rights were to be considered, especially where an entire race was involved, the Equalitarian felt his high duty must not be interfered with. Surely the issue was made. The contest, probably the final one, was beginning. The Lancastrian would be heard in the forum that held the destiny of the blacks of the country, and what he stood for would be irrevocably written into the fundamental laws of the land.

BOOK FOUR
DEFENDER

BOOK FOUR—DEFENDER

I

EVE OF THE CRISIS

THE Thirty-Sixth Congress which convened in December of 1859, embraced in its membership the men who formulated Slave State strategy in a final struggle to preserve the institution. Those great leaders of the South had brought with them to Washington the alarm of their people at what, they were convinced, was Northern aggression.

The dim but massive shadow of the new Republican Party growing with startling rapidity, hovered a menacing threat in the background. Less than five years old, it already claimed more representatives in the House than any other party. The South knew it must expect the worse if that group reached control. Its fears were in no way lessened when they found Thaddeus Stevens returned.

Just a decade before, he had come to Congress and stunned the South by his boldness. Undaunted by the threats that they had used to advantage for years, he had calmly challenged them to proceed. His audacity caused less concern than his shrewd tactics. They recognized his ability from the very outset and appraised him as by far their most dangerous adversary. But through the appeal that Clay, Webster and others had made to the country, they had been able to shade him into the background.

Successful in obtaining a compromise adjustment, Southern leaders themselves had breached it by repealing the Missouri Compromise and attempting to force slavery on Kansas.

The national situation in 1859 was, on the surface, not nearly as serious as ten years before, but Slave State men who lacked nothing in intelligence understood that an ever expanding feeling of spontaneous resentment surged in the North. The year before, Seward had delivered his "Irrepressible Conflict" speech at Rochester; John Brown had made his fanatical "raid" on Harper's Ferry and such straws were enough to indicate to the South how the winds in the North were blowing.

The Republicans counted one hundred nine in the House, which gave them a plurality, but not a majority. The Democrats numbered about one hundred, and there was a scattering of other minor parties.[1] When the House was called to order, the Republicans nominated John Sherman of Ohio for Speaker, and Stevens submitted the name of his fellow Pennsylvanian, Galusha A. Grow. The Democrats concentrated on Bocock, of Virginia. There were several other candidates and on the first ballot, no one received a majority. Then the wrangling started. Mississippian Clark precipitated it.

A North Carolinian, by the name of Helper, had written a book which he called, "The Impending Crisis of the South and How to Meet It." It was an inoffensive little volume in which the author discoursed on a range of subjects from the "Old Testament" to "Book Making in America" and the time occupied by Goldsmith in preparation of "The Traveller." With pages of tables and figures, it professed to be an argument to show that slavery was unsound economically.

For solution of the "crisis," Helper advocated non-intercourse with, and boycott of, slave owners and slave sympathizers.

Saying little, if anything, that was new, without literary merit, and lacking forceful argument and stirring appeal, the book probably would have passed with slight notice as a period writing. But some Abolitionists in the North thought it had value as a propaganda item and circulated it widely. The Governor of New York contributed one hundred dollars for its distribution, and the New York *Tribune*[2] recorded that "a number of earnest and active Republicans of this city, united in an appeal to their fellow Republicans for aid in an effort to print and circulate one hundred thousand copies of Mr. H. R. Helper's admirable 'Impending Crisis of the South.'"

In the early part of the year, an endorsement was circulated among the Republican Congressmen, and both of that Party's nominees for the Speakership had signed it. Clark brought this to the attention of the House, placed it in the record and read long paragraphs from the volume. He made much ado of Sherman's and Grow's endorsements and insisted that their recommendation of the book allocated them to the group which would disrupt the Union in order to destroy slavery. He resolved that no endorser of the volume was fit to be Speaker of the House, and many Southerners rose to support him.

Millson, of Virginia, held that anyone who had deliberately "lent his name and influence to the propagation of such writings, is not only not fit to be Speaker, but is not fit to live."[3] Gilmer, a member of the South

American Party, who attempted to offer a moderate substitute for Clark's resolution was brushed aside.

Southerner Keitt ridiculed Sherman's explanation that he had signed the approval but had not read the book. "The South here asks nothing but its rights. As one of its representatives, and as God is my Judge, I would shatter this Republic from turret to foundation stone before I would take one tittle less." He dared the North to elect its candidate and stand upon its platform. "Proceed," said he, "and then let each party fight out its own cause."

But Stevens had heard such challenges before, and as he had so many times told them, understood Southern strategy. When Keitt finished, he arose and reiterated what he had pointed out the day before; namely, that "until this House is organized, it is not competent for the Clerk to entertain any question except that of proceeding to the election of a Speaker or on a motion to adjourn." He could not sit down without saying that he did not "blame the gentlemen from the South for taking the course they do, although I deem it untimely and irregular . . . nor do I blame them for the language of intimidation, and using this threat of rending God's creation from turret to foundation. (Laughter). All this is right in them, for they have tried it fifty times and fifty times they have found weak and recreant tremblers in the North who have been affected by it, and who have acted from those intimidations." (Applause).

With piercing irony, he jibed, "they are right, therefore, and I give them credit for repeating with grave countenances that which they have so often found to be

effective when operating upon timid men." His remark
sunk deep, for the Southerners understood what he
meant when he referred to their words which had been
effective upon "timid" men.

They hated him with all the fullness of their fiery
passions, and could tolerate no more of his telling barbs.
Unable to restrain themselves longer, several Southerners leaped to their feet and raced toward him. Representative Barksdale of Mississippi, drew his knife.
But other members quickly intervened and the fracas
was soon over. Just what Stevens said to so enrage his
opponents is not clear, for the words that appear in
the record seem no worse than many that he had at other
times uttered with impunity. Of course it well may
be that he said more than is reported.

The official report of what happened states, "during
the above colloquy, members from the benches upon
both sides, crowded down into the area, and there was
for a time great confusion and excitement in the Hall."[4]
It was the occasion that Stevens frequently referred to
thereafter "when bowie knives were drawn."[5] A
Democrat warned the next day, "a few more such
scenes and we will hear the crack of the revolver and
see the gleam of the brandished blade." When quiet
had been restored, Stevens laughed it off 'as a "mere
momentary breeze" and renewed his point of order.

Southerners delayed organization, insisting upon delivering their fiery but irrelevant speeches. Some would
openly "raise the banner of secession and fight under it
as long as blood flowed in their veins."[6] Of course the
attack centered on Stevens. Some attempted to answer
him in lighter vein. Lamar, of Mississippi, almost

trembled "for the South, when I recollect that the opposing forces will be led by the distinguished hero of the Buckshot War." (Great laughter.) "However gloomy the catastrophe, his saltatory accomplishments will enable him to leap out of any difficulties in which he may be involved. I understand that he gave in an ingenious way, a practical illustration of peacable secession." [7]

But it was not long that Stevens could be treated lightly. Within a year, he had become the feared master of the House. If any Southerner thought of joking him thereafter upon the slavery question, it is not recorded.

He was the more puzzling to his adversaries because they never knew exactly what he would do. On one of the ballots for Speaker, he had voted for Gilmer of North Carolina, reputed to be one of the largest slave owners in Congress.[8] When taken to task for his action, he rose "to a personal matter. It is well known," said he, "that I departed from the general rule of obeying party decrees and voted for an honorable gentleman from North Carolina." Making a joke of the matter, he said it might "require some explanation" as was indicated from a newspaper he held in his hand. He sent the paper to the Clerk's desk to be read. The Clerk looked at it and announced that the paper was printed in German, and he, therefore, could not read it. "Well," said Stevens, amid laughter, "then I postpone my remarks until the Clerk can read it," [9] and the reason for his strange vote was never made known.

Anderson, of Missouri, claiming to be above partisan bias, suggested that the Democratic Party, the South

American Party, and the Anti-LeCompton Party
"meet at this Capitol tonight . . . to agree upon a full
organization of this House, from Speaker down to
Doorkeeper."

Such combination could outvote the Republicans, and
for that reason Stevens gave the suggestion his attention. "The gentleman has realized what I thought was
a myth before; that is, he has proposed—and I hope
that they may have a good time of it—he has proposed
that happy family described in "The Prairie," where
the wolf, the owl and the rattlesnake live in one hole.
(Great laughter.) When they get together in this hole
to-night, I trust that there will be no biting." [10]

Montgomery suggested a temporary chairman so
that important matters could be taken up immediately.
But Stevens stood fast for a regular organization of
the House before any business was acted upon. Tenaciously, he held that no business could be transacted
until a Speaker was elected.

For eight long weeks the House dilly-dallied along
unorganized. Stevens restrained himself admirably,
rarely deviating from his pertinent insistence for proceeding in order. The Republicans could not organize the House; the Democrats showed no desire to help,
unless they could force their minority Speaker.

Late in January,[11] when the pressure of the country
for organization of the House was making itself felt,
Stevens, though ill, delivered probably the most important speech of the session. What he said was in good
parliamentary order, because it was on the question of
the election of Speaker. But the speech itself from a
political viewpoint, was quite unusual. From the stand-

point of plain honesty and fair dealing, it is superb.

At the outset, he mentioned the "Democratic Party —which means, of course, the Democrats of the South; the others are mere parasites." Vallandigham objected to the word "parasites" and Stevens in mock courtesy, said he would utter no other language than the gentleman from Ohio desired, but he could not anticipate in advance precisely what would suit him. Nevertheless, if the word parasite were offensive, he would "withdraw it and use satellites—revolving, of course, around the larger body as according to the laws of gravitation they must." That, certainly, could not be "offensive."

In his ingenious argument, with the time near, as he appreciated, for a vote on the all-important Speakership, his aim was to divide the opposition. "The South American Party," he complimented, "is a highly respectable body . . . representing a large constituency known as the Southern opposition. Had they the aid of a single Democrat in their election? Were they not elected in conflict with that organization and with that party? There is one principle perhaps in which they agree with them, while in all others, I venture to say, they differ."

Was there but one principle in this government which this administration has to look to? And were all the other great interests of the people to be overlooked by these twenty-three gentlemen and by the country at large, so that they would throw into the gulf which the administration has provided for them, the whole power of the government? When such demands were made, they should remember that no Republicans opposed them and that with one single exception, Republican principles and their principles were almost homogeneous.

"With what face," then, could those gentlemen be appealed to, not simply to stand by their own organization, but to go over to the other? "Sir, I find no reason to reproach them for not voting for a Republican. I know that at home, such is the condition of things that it would not be fair to ask that of them, and I do not ask it. But it would be doubly unfair for the party in hostility to which they were elected to expect their aid." So he disposed of the "South Americans."

To the group of "eight respectable gentlemen"[12] who would not agree to thrust slavery upon Kansas against her will, he would say that "they were all elected in hostility to the Democratic Administration Party" and solemnly inquired "in the name of God, what mercenary motives could be expected to induce them to act in concert with that party?" Although many Republicans voted for them, Stevens did not ask them to vote for a Republican, nor did he upbraid them because they had not seen proper to do so.

He pointed out that the Republican Party, the South American Party, and the Anti-LeCompton Party, had one hundred fifty members in the House. "They are opposed by a single party of ninety; and all are opposed to the ninety." Now, on what theory was it that a portion is expected to go to a minority party instead of coming to the larger one? "These men, if they take either side, and if the principle of representation in this government is to have any effect, must honestly take ours. But," he said judiciously, "there is no principle on which they can be expected to come to us, nor no honest one on which they can be blamed for not going with the Democrats."

He charged the delay of organization on President Buchanan. He "has long believed, and, I doubt not, still believes, that the true way to aid the increase of the Democratic Party North, is for the South to frighten them into the belief that if they venture to elect a northern man with northern principles, this Union is to be dissolved, and all their industrial and pecuniary interests sacrificed.

"I have just as firm a belief as that I live that this whole programme was drawn up at the White House, and is carried out in pursuance of the idea that the old women and the men in petticoats and the misers at the North are to be frightened." The moment the Democratic party was sufficiently strengthened in the North, "by the cry of disunion, and these epithets of traitor that have been launched against this side, a word from the White House will organize this House by the withdrawal of a few Democratic gentlemen." He would not be surprised if a few of the Covenanters (laughter) were to do it.

Then "we will proceed to do what we should have done long ago—provide for the wants of the country, instead of heaping abuse on the Representatives of freemen, and threatening a dissolution of the Union."

When a Democrat asked him how he knew so much about the man in the White House, he, in mock seriousness, answered that "the gentleman must remember that the President is one of my constituents." "Well," said his questioner, very much to the point, "if the gentleman represents his other constituents no better than he does the President, there is little hope for him." [13]

"We are told," Stevens continued, "that unless we yield, this House shall be disorganized until 1861, and discord shall reign perpetual." He did not know that his friends would follow his views but he was convinced that "having fixed on an honorable and worthy standard bearer for our candidate, we should stand by him if this House were not organized until the crack of Doom." The Republicans had listened to the Democratic threats "without fear, for whatever effect they might once have had, some of us always and all of us now, have come to regard them as idle menaces and barren thunder."

Then came the more important part of what he had to say. He wished to "give an answer plain, temperate, and true to all of those allegations," by stating in the briefest possible manner, what he considered the principles of the Republican Party. He would have no man vote under false pretenses. "In my judgment, Republicanism is founded in love of universal liberty and in hostility to slavery and oppression through the world." Had it the legal right and physical power, it undoubtedly would aim to abolish human servitude, and overthrow despotism "everywhere."

But it could claim "no such high privilege or mission. The law of nations gives us no authority to redress foreign grievances and the Constitution of the United States gives us no power to interfere with the institutions of our sister states."

He placed himself and his party on record when he said, "we do deny now as we have ever denied, that there is any desire or intention on the part of the Republican Party to interfere with those institutions. It is a stern and inflexible, a well-recognized principle of the Republican Party that every law must be obeyed, until it is either repealed or become so intolerable as to justify rebellion."

In those words, Stevens stated the problem to which he devoted his remaining years. How to eradicate forever slavery from America had been and continued to be a life concentration. It was by far the largest and most stubborn task of the Equalitarian. As he spoke that January afternoon, he knew of no solution. War, red War that flamed within the year, furnished his answer.

"But," said he, "while we claim no power to interfere with any institution in the states, yet where the law of no state operates, and where the responsibility of the Government is thrown on Congress, we do claim the power to regulate and the right to abolish slavery. No other power on earth exists that can do it, for there is no other legislative body, and it would be an intolerable shame and reproach upon this Republic if there was any spot within its wide expanse where no such power existed." This authority extended to the territories and the District of Columbia, the navy yards and the arsenals, but he would not and did not bound his work for slavery exclusion by climate, or latitude, or soil.

His hostility was of higher character. If it were not, there would be no necessity for the existence of the Republican Party. "If I believed that slavery was right in itself, and it might be permitted in places where certain labor was or was not satisfactory, I cannot see what principle the Republican Party could stand upon. The whole ground is yielded and this Republican Party is a nuisance and this agitation a crime in my judgment."

Agreeing with Clay and Webster that Congress had the power to abolish slavery in the District of Columbia, he felt that the time had not yet arrived, "nor," said he, "do I see the period, for the present, when it will." But sometime, somehow, it could be justly and safely abolished, he believed, and it was the purpose of Republicanism so to do.

These, as he understood them, were the principles of the Republican Party. "Let those who condemn them oppose us. For ourselves, we have resolved to stand by them until they shall become triumphant and we cheerfully submit them to the judgment of our fellow countrymen, to the civilized nations of the earth, and to posterity."

The striking feature of this brief speech is its outspokenness. No leader of the time dared speak so plainly of the new Party. At the risk of being expelled from it, Stevens had practically usurped its leadership in Congress. Only a strong man dared so act. It is of more than passing interest to notice that to him it stood for one proposition and one proposition alone. That was the abolition of slavery where it could be legally done. No wonder he was a zealot in its cause. It promised not only slave liberation where it could then be consummated lawfully, but no one could foretell what great opportunity might come to remove the institution, perhaps even from the entire Nation. Surely it was the party for the Equalitarian.

The House finally organized on the first of February, by electing Pennington, of New Jersey, Speaker on its forty-fourth ballot. Stevens supported him. He had been an old Whig but was not strongly opposed to slavery. The South felt kindly toward him, because he had, while Governor of his State, insisted upon a stringent enforcement of the Fugitive Slave Law. There was little of importance transacted through the balance of the session.

Stevens knew that in the contested elections which came before the House, the contestant from the majority party was generally seated, right or wrong. He recognized the British system of laying the entire matter judicially before a Committee with power to hear and try a case fully, and make a final decision, as far more just and he recommended its adoption. But his suggestion never got further in the House than the talking stage.

Being in Rome, he was not loath to accept the custom of the Romans. Stumping in one day just as the vote was about to be taken on a contested seat, he inquired what was under consideration. "Oh," said a follower, "we are just about to vote on the question of two damned rascals fighting for a seat." "Well," inquired Stevens, reaching for a ballot, "which is our damned rascal?" [14]

In a desultory fashion, he had something to say in support of a high protective tariff and made a few other suggestions. He condemned the warehouse system then in use in the United States, whereby foreign merchants could fill American storehouses with goods and let them lie here as long as three years, without paying

duty. To him it was "a great atrocity." Foreigners
were allowed to send in their goods with duty postponed. When the freight was lowest, and when there
was no demand for the goods they had at home, they
sent them here and put them in storage. They held
them there until the demand came, and then were able to
put the articles in the market, and even glut it, before
our people could get their goods there.

"Take, for instance, iron. A couple of years ago,
there was a line of packets plying between Glasgow
and Philadelphia, which brought in emigrants. I one
day asked a person interested in the Line, what freight
he got on pig iron. 'We get nothing on it,' said he;
'we are bringing it in free of freight as ballast and are
glad to get it. All we ask is for the owners to pay for
the loading and unloading.' Thus they sent in an enormous quantity of iron, filling the warehouses in Philadelphia; and when a little spurt of a rise came in the
iron market, the English iron was taken out of the warehouses and thrown upon the market, which was sur-
feited before our iron masters on the Susquehanna and
Lehigh" could make deliveries. Such had ever been
the deleterious operation of the warehousing system in
regard to other articles.[15] The House accepted his
suggestion and passed a bill supporting it, but the
Senate voted it down.[16]

If Stevens had any idea that War was near, he concealed it most carefully. On the Bill to enlarge the
army in order to better protect the Texas frontier,
he said, "In the first place, it proposes to increase
the military forces of the country which I think
is unnecessary. I believe that our army is quite as

large as necessary for the defense of the country." [17]

However, it should be noticed that the request would move the new troops to the frontier of Texas, and Stevens probably felt that if War were precipitated, it were better to have no troops than to have them in an environment sympathetic to the South.

II

SECESSION

Congress adjourned late in June of 1860, with the country in a nervous suspense, partially masked in an attitude of sullen waiting. Everything depended on the Presidential election in the Fall, and thereupon the Nation's eager attention was focused.

Lincoln was generally looked upon as the sectional candidate of the Anti-slave North, and there were ominous forebodings of what might happen if he were elected.

The fated day came; the result which the South and the Democratic North dreaded most was soon announced. Lincoln, although he had received less than a majority of popular votes, would be the next President of the United States.

To the South it meant that its challenge had been accepted. For thirty years its leaders had threatened what they would do if slavery were interfered with. The mere election of a President could, by no stretch of the imagination, be construed as interference. But throughout the entire South, the determined action of the North that put the Man from Illinois in the White House, was pregnant with meaning.

Early the next month, Congress met in an atmosphere of daze and despondency. Nearly everyone seemed tensely poised, awaiting some dreadful thing to happen. No one knew just what to expect, but an explosion seemed near. President Buchanan was bewildered. Characteristically, he thought the best thing to do was in some way to appease the bristling South.

This he tried to accomplish by condemning the North. For some reason or other, he appeared to agree with the South that it had been wronged by the Presidential choice.

Speaking as judge more than Executive, he believed "the long continued and intemperate interference of Northern people with the question of slavery in the Southern States," had at length "produced its natural effects." His whole argument was pointed to an indictment of the North for its "incessant agitation against slavery for five and twenty years," with which those people had "no more right to interfere than with similar institutions in Russia or in Brazil."

South Carolina, threatening secession at the moment, opened the way for his discussing state withdrawal from the Union. In that State, "all the Federal officers, through whose agency alone laws can be carried into execution, have already resigned." And then he proceeded to announce an amazing dictum.

On the opinion of his Attorney General Black, he was convinced that the Executive had "no authority to decide what shall be the relationship between the Federal Government and South Carolina." Furthermore, he startlingly asserted, "after much serious reflection, I have arrived at the conclusion that no power to coerce a seceding state into submission has been delegated to Congress or to any other department of the Federal Government."

Although he thought no State had a right to withdraw from the Union, he committed himself to the position that the Federal Government could not prevent secession through any or all of its departments,

nor force the return of a seceded State to the Union.
He would solve the stupendous problem of the Nation
by an "explanatory amendment" to the Constitution,
guaranteeing protection to slave property and slave
owners' rights.

"It ought not be doubted," said he, "that such an
appeal to the arbitrament established by the Constitution itself would be received with favor by all of the
States of the Confederacy." In any event, it should
"be tried in a spirit of conciliation before any of these
States shall separate themselves from the Union." [1]

That fourth annual message of President Buchanan
is a conspicuous example of exactly what a Presidential
message should not be at a time when strain is felt
upon the ties that bind the States together. In his
famous comment, Seward summed it up as holding "a
State had no right to secede unless it wished to, and
that the Government must save the Union, unless some-
body opposes it."

In the thirteen printed pages that the important part
of the Presidential communication occupied, not only
did it fail, because of weakness, to help the situation;
it was positively injurious to the cause of the Union.
The fact is, that had Buchanan wished to encourage retirement of the States from the National Confederacy,
he probably could not have written a more efficacious
paper.

He was an honest, intelligent gentleman, and in his
own way, thoroughly patriotic. How he possibly could
have brought himself to such a writing at that crucial
time has puzzled those who have studied his life. Even
if his close friend, neighbor, and Attorney-General

Black did advise him of the legal aspects of secession to the effect set forth, surely he need not have broadcast such an enheartening pronouncement for secessionists.

There is no doubt that to the Southern States already contemplating withdrawal, it gave the greatest encouragement. If it were true that the Nation dared use no force toward a State, South Carolina and her neighbors could feel very justifiably that there was nothing to be lost and perhaps much to be gained by retiring. While in the Union, they were helplessly exposed to Anti-slavery assaults. Independent, they might force concessions.

One reasonably could have expected that there would be no secession until there had been some real show of agression against slavery. During that session of the Congress, there was no actual change in Federal attitude. True, a new President had been elected, but the same government obtained as had for the past three and one-half years. No single act of encroachment or threat could be pointed out by the representatives of the slave states.

But that didn't seem to matter. With utter lack of calm, and with no show of the judicial attitude that should characterize state dealing and the interrelationship of Government, the slave states proceeded headlong into chaos. Time was not given even to learn if the new party actually intended to molest slavery unlawfully and in violation of the Constitution.

Surely Buchanan's message had afforded all stimulation necessary. Seventeen days after its delivery, South Carolina, by unanimous vote of her Convention, withdrew from the Union of the States. The "Empire of the West" which had promised so much; which had furnished greatest hope for an ideal governmental set-up, was facing disintegration and destruction.

That distressful day in December of 1860, and the afternoon in which the Senate of the United States voted acquittal of President Johnson in May of 1868, accurately bracket the most dangerous crisis this country has passed through since the adoption of the Federal Constitution.

Had a stern, quick-acting executive been in office at its beginning, American history would very probably have been different. If South Carolina's secession effort had been nipped in the bud, there need have been no War at the time. Certainly a reasonable, compensated adjustment of the slavery question could have been worked out as was done in other countries where slavery was eradicated without bloodshed. There is absolutely no justification for a belief that war was the only means through which the institution could have been abolished in the United States.

But in those fateful days of 1860, the Federal Government had to face the alarming fact of a State, so far as it was concerned, already out of the Union, and the Nation, under Buchanan's dictum, utterly without power to do anything in the matter.

Stunned by the precipitate action of the Palmetto State, the two Houses of Congress hurriedly appointed special committees to study what could be done. The Senate, with a sentimental touch, had a Committee of Thirteen, and the House, an assembly of thirty-three, one selected from each state. The groups were given no instructions, but had it vaguely indicated to them that some compromise or adjustment should be looked for to retrieve the seceded State and bar other secessions then threatened.

One of the surprising developments was that the Senate seemed less able to compromise than the House. Before the month ended, the Committee of the former reported back that it was unable to agree upon any satisfactory proposal for submission. But oddly enough, the House Committee, whose members had come more lately from the people and should have reflected the sentiment which elected Lincoln in greater degree than the Senate Committee, disclosed a more tolerant and compromising attitude and worked on steadily.

The slave states seemed only to have been waiting South Carolina's lead, for shortly thereafter, they proceeded with intemperate haste to pass their secession ordinances.

Through all these strenuous days, Stevens sat almost dramatically silent in the House. Whatever he thought or felt, he kept within himself. Not even Buchanan's tragic message which must have rankled him sorely could stir him to speech. Time vindicated the wisdom of his silence.

With no great surface disturbance, matters of great importance were happening underneath. There were few men in the Congress who failed to recognize that the long evaded crisis was upon them and they made what they fully believed were sincere efforts to again avoid it. While the Senate and House Committees on conciliation were fretfully trying to devise a compromise, leaders of both sides labored without rest.

Toombs of Georgia suggested an irrevocable amendment to the Constitution which would protect slavery in the Territories; enlarge Federal protection of property in slaves; provide for delivery up of fugitives who committed crime against slave property by the State into which the criminal fled to the one where the act was perpetrated and make the laws of the latter the test of what was a crime; require summary surrender of escaped slaves without the right of Habeas Corpus or trial by jury, and provide efficient laws to protect the Southern States against interference with slavery by Northern States.

Crittenden of Kentucky submitted nearly similar proposals.

Seward, then Senator from New York, was willing on the part of the North to support an irrepealable, "unamendable amendment" to the Constitution which would forever secure slavery in the States where it already existed, and effectively prohibit non-slave State interference with the institution.

Meantime in the House, some Southerners showed impatient desire for radical action. Reuben Davis of Mississippi, with two dozen of his Southern colleagues, addressed a manifesto to their constituents setting forth that "all hopes for relief in the Union" were gone, and that the aim of each slaveholding state "ought to be its speedy and absolute separation from an unnatural and hostile Union." [2]

On January 5, 1861, Senators from seven Southern States [3] held a caucus in which they recommended secession and the organization of a Confederate Government.

Stevens watched and listened to it all. He was not

adapted to the role of peacemaker. But even the com-
promisers were painfully impotent. The South seemed
bent on a secession plunge which nothing could avert,
and the grim procession continued. No one was closer
bound to the Union of the States than the Old Commoner, and to him the act of any state that attempted
to break it down, was highest treason. For a slave state
to do it, deliberately and for the purpose of protecting
that hated institution, was to him an offense beyond
name.

The House Committee on conciliation reported on
January 13. Briefly, it proposed a constitutional
amendment prohibiting further modification of the Constitution in the matter of slavery, except at the instance
of a slave state, and further, that no such amendment
should become valid until ratified by every state of the
Union. The Committee also recommended another
amendment for the rendition of fugitives from justice,
giving jurisdiction to the state from which the escape
had been made, and thirdly, immediate admission of
New Mexico as a slave state.

By late January, Stevens was apparently convinced
that the time had come for him to break his disturbing
silence. On the twenty-ninth, while the House was
considering the Conciliation Committee's Report, he
obtained the Floor. Immediately he became the center
of rapt attention, for his colleagues were vitally interested in what he had to say.

Most of them recognized him as the man who, a
decade before on that very Floor, had boldly dared the
Southern States to carry out their threat of secession.
He, as much as anyone, was held responsible for an un-

yielding opposition to slavery, whose policy was to know no compromise.

Now that six States had already left the Union in a movement whose seriousness no human brain could then adjudge, would he, in the interest of the Nation's preservation, hearken to or even advise adjustment? Or would he, in stubborn defiance, stand fast in a position that well might mean the end of the Nation?

At the time he was physically ill, and he admitted it. Mentally, he was never more alert. He felt that the occasion had arrived when some things should be made clear.

The day before, Pryor of Virginia, had said that no compromise could be made which would have any effect in averting the present difficulty. Stevens concurred in that belief; "for when I see these States in open and declared rebellion against the Union, seizing upon her public forts and arsenals, and robbing her of millions of the public property; when I see the batteries of seceding States blockading the highways of the Nation and their armies in battle array against the Flag of the Union; when I see our Flag insulted and that insult submitted to, I have no hope that concession, humiliation and compromise can have any effect whatever. This I deeply regret, as I should be willing to go to to the verge of principle to avert this catastrophe."

The morning papers had carried a report of Ambassadors sent by Virginia to South Carolina for the purpose of having the seceded State, through commissioners, propose amendments to the Constitution of the United States for the securement of her rights.

The Palmetto State had peremptorily refused to

move in the matter, and her General Assembly, after such official refusal, "resolved unanimously" that the separation of South Carolina from the Federal Union is final and she has no further interest in the Constitution of the United States; and that the only appropriate negotiations between her and the Federal Government are as to their mutual relations as foreign states. "Thus," said Stevens, "ends negotiations; thus ends concession; thus ends compromise, by the solemn declaration of the seceding party that it will not listen to concession or compromise."

The slaveholding states had the day before, he believed, shown just how much contribution toward compromise they were willing to make. Immediately after Pryor's speech "a bill came up to admit Kansas into the Union; and I am sorry to say that almost every Southern man—men who have just been appealing to us to furnish them ground to stand upon—almost in a solid body, the Southern men voted against even the consideration of the question of admitting Kansas, that source of all our woes." He left the inference to the country.

There was no hope that anything which Congress could say or do "would have the least effect in retarding or accelerating the onward career of the secession movement." He did not believe that words would have any weight. Yet the effort should be made. "It is right that . . . from this hall, sacred to freedom and free debates, we should inform our constituents of the condition of things that they may well consider them; so that if we are wrong, they may correct us, and if we are right, they may strengthen our hands."

The grave question of dissolution of the Union "should be approached without excitement or passion or fear. The virtue most needed in times of peril is courage; calm, unwavering courage which no danger can appall and which will not be excited to action by indignation or revenge. Homilies upon the Union and jeremiads over its destruction can be of no use, except to display fine rhetoric and pathetic eloquence." The long, tiresome days of aimless speech-making had passed. "The Southern States will not be turned from their deliberate and stern purpose by soft words and touching lamentations."

He appraised accurately the position of the Southern leaders. They could not retreat. "After the extent to which they have gone it would do them no credit; condemnation which is now felt for their conduct would degenerate into contempt."

He took sharp issue with Buchanan's statement of "intemperate interference of the Northern people with the question of slavery. Search the proceedings of their Legislatures, their conventions, and their party creeds, and you will find them always disclaiming the right or the intention to touch slavery in the States where it existed."

That part of the message of the President, who "has been the slave of slavery," was not "worth a moment's consideration." But Stevens did not perceive when any better occasion could present itself "to decide whether this Nation exists by the sufferance of individual States or whether it requires a constitutional majority to absolve them from their allegiance." If it should be determined that secession was a rightful act or that there

[281]

was no power to prevent it, then the Union was "not worth preserving for a single day; for whatever disposition shall be made of the present difficulty, fancied wrongs will constantly arise, and induce state after state to withdraw from the Confederacy."

But "if, on the other hand, it should be decided that we are one people, and that the Government possesses sufficient power to coerce obedience, the public mind will be quieted, plotters of disunion will be regarded as traitors, and we shall long remain a united and happy people."

At this early date, Stevens championed the right of the Nation to maintain its integrity with force and went at length into a supporting argument. The President was vested with power to take care that all the laws were faithfully executed, and Congress was armed with authority to make all laws necessary and proper for carrying that power into execution. If such were not done or even tried, then "posterity will wonder whether the statesmen of this age were fools or traitors."

He did not rest on the defensive. Southerners were free to visit the North and "her orators deliver lectures and speeches in which they propagate the doctrines of slavery, not only with impunity, but they are listened to with respect and silence. They exercise entire liberty of speech, without being molested either by officer or mob." The reverse was not true. For twenty years past it had been unsafe for Northern men to travel or settle in the South, unless they avowed "their belief that slavery was a good institution. Every day brings news of unoffending citizens being seized, mobbed, tarred and feathered, and hanged by scores without semblance of trial by legal tribunal, or evidence of guilt."

The real aggression, which "one of the States frankly assigns as the reason for secession, was that the North had taken from them the power of Government, which the South had so long held." Such a charge to him was astounding. According to the strictest forms and principles of the Constitution, they have elected the man of their choice President of the United States. "No violence was used; no malpractice charged; but the American people dared to disobey the commands of slavery; and this is proclaimed as just cause of secession and civil war. Sir," he inquired, "has it come to this? Cannot the people of the United States choose whom they please President, without stirring up a rebellion and requiring humiliations, concessions, and compromises to appease the insurgents?"

For himself, he would take "no steps to propitiate such a feeling. Rather than show repentance for the election of Mr. Lincoln, with all its consequences I would see this Government crumble into a thousand atoms. If I cannot be a freeman, let me cease to exist."

He thought that the Committee of Thirty-three had shown their estimate of the magnitude of southern grievances by a most delicate piece of satire. As a cure for their wrongs, and to seduce back rebellious States. they offered to admit as a State ⁴ about two hundred and fifty thousand square miles of volcanic desert, with less than a thousand white Anglo-Saxon inhabitants and some forty or fifty thousand Indians, Mustees, and Mexicans, who did not ask admission, and who had shown their capacity for self-government by the infamous slave code which they "have passed, estab-

lishing the most cruel kind of black and white slavery.
To be sure, the distinguished chairman of that committee [5] seems to have become enamored of peonage. He
looks upon it as a benevolent institution, which saves
the poor man's cow to furnish milk for his children,
by selling the father instead of the cow."

He would see to it that the Federal Government
collected its revenue in the seceded states. Had the
present administration done its duty, "there would have
been no necessity for shedding blood." Within the collection district of South Carolina, the Government had
several formidable forts. Had they been properly gar-
risoned and supplied when it became evident that the
State would secede and seize them, they could have
been impregnable. No ships could have entered the
harbor of Charleston without the consent of those who
held the forts. The revenues might have been collected
anywhere in the harbor or district. But due to the
Government's negligence, only one fort still remained
"to us there, with less than one-eighth of the proper
garrison, provisions, and munitions of War."

He could not believe that the President had inten-
tionally left those forts in a defenseless condition so
that South Carolina might seize them before his successor had time to take means for their safety. If that
were true, "it would make Mr. Buchanan a more odious
traitor than Benedict Arnold." Yet it must be a "tame,
spiritless administration" which permitted the "Star of
the West" episode to pass unnoticed.

Nevertheless, he had a fully sustained confidence
that the gallant officer in command of Fort Sumpter
would "successfully defend the Stars and Stripes or

gloriously descend with his last soldier to his gory bed."

Here he made his important suggestion which had very pertinent bearing on the entire War policy. He proposed that if the revenue could not be collected, and smuggling prevented, the government should abolish the laws establishing ports of entry and collection districts within the seceding states, and thus prevent all vessels, foreign or domestic, from entering or leaving any of our ports. With "no national officers to give her a clearance, the vessel would be without papers, without nationality, and a prize to the first captors."

Had the Government acted to that end, it might have postponed violence and given time for a calmer consideration. Stevens made much of this point all through the War and the Reconstruction, insisting that it was a mistake to attempt to blockade Southern ports. His sound, legal argument was that Southern ships could not clear because they bore no clearance papers of a recognized Nation, and foreign ships could have no contact without breaching the rights of the United States. Thus all lawful commerce with the seceded states would be effectively prohibited.[6]

Chiding the states which had withdrawn, he inquired, "if they will have War, who is to protect them against their own domestic foes? They now tremble when a madman[7] and a score of followers invade them. If a citizen declares his opposition to slavery, they hang him and declare as a justification that it is necessary for their personal safety, because they say they are standing on the thin crust of a raging volcano which the least jar will crack open and plunge them in. How, then," he wondered, "would they withstand the booming of cannons and the clash of arms?"

He was convinced that in order to retain slavery, the South would go to any extent, even that of War. At times other causes had appeared on the surface as their basis of complaint, but slavery was always at the bottom of it. "The secession and rebellion of the South have been inculcated as a doctrine for twenty years past among slaveholding communities. At one time tariff was deemed a sufficient cause. Then the exclusion of slavery from free territories; then some violations of the Fugitive Slave Law. Now the culminating cause is the election of a President who does not believe in the benefits of slavery or approve of that greatest missionary enterprise, the slave trade."[8] The truth was, all those things were mere pretenses. The "restless spirits of the South desire to have a slave empire and to use these things as excuses. Some of them want a more brilliant and stronger government than a Republic. The domestic institution and the social inequality of their people naturally prepare them for a monarchy surrounded by a lordly nobility—having a throne founded on the neck of labor."

But they were disappointed, he explained, to see the regular march of civilization, wealth and population fast wresting power from them and giving it to the North. Then it was "that they diligently began to prepare themselves for rebellion against the Constitution when the time came that they could no longer rule under it." He credited the South with farsightedness in its planning, and then accused it of not only adjusting its state of mind to rebellion, but making actual physical preparation.

"It became evident that Mr. Buchanan was to be the last of Southern Presidents, and his Cabinet, being almost wholly devoted to the interests of slavery, set themselves boldly at work to weaken the North and strengthen the South. They transferred most of the best weapons of war from the North where they were manufactured, to the South where they could be readily seized. They plunged the Nation into heavy debt in time of peace. When the Treasury was bare of cash, they robbed it of millions of bonds and whatever moneys they could lay hands on. They fastened upon us an incipient free trade system which impaired our revenue, paralyzed our national industry, and compelled the exportation of our immense production of gold. They had reduced our Navy to an unserviceable condition, or dispersed it to the furthest oceans. Our little army was on the Pacific Coast, sequestered in Utah or defending the southern states from their own Indians."

After the South had thus made ready, it was easy to understand that Lincoln's election had "precipitated the explosion." But "it was well that it did," for "had Mr. Breckenridge been elected, they would have had four years more to strengthen the South and weaken the North." And so the rebellion had "not come an hour too soon." Altogether, the late events convinced him the "South was dealing in a high-handed manner and actually forcing war." [9]

There were some facts on which the conviction might rest. It was notorious that many Southern leaders were anything but conciliatory in their attitude after

South Carolina's retirement. On the second day that
the Senate Committee of Thirteen sat for the purpose
of finding some peaceful adjustment, Senator Toombs
of Georgia, telegraphed an address to his people reporting that his demands had been received with de-
rision by his fellow Republicans on the Committee,
and that nothing could be done by, or hoped for from,
either of the Congressional Committees. Allowing no
time to really find out if anything could be done, he
advised Georgia to secede before Lincoln's inauguration.[10]

South Carolina showed a haughty attitude, seemingly aimed to provoke war, from the very beginning
when her Congressmen called upon President Buchanan
on the eighth of December. In spite of the fact that
he was their best friend, and sought to deal with them
kindly, they tried by garbled reports of the conference,
to embarrass him.

The contemptuous way in which the State treated
the Ambassadors from Virginia, who petitioned her to
negotiate with the Government, could be construed
only as undiplomatic and antagonizing.

Could South Carolina deny that she was inviting
War when she officially stated that she had no further
interest in the Constitution of the United States, and
that the only way that she would treat with the Government was as one foreign state to another? Stevens'
belief that the slave states insisted on physical strife, he
felt, was corroborated by the headlong manner in which
they passed their Ordinances of Secession. Was it not
a deliberate and concerted plan of action?

The Republican Party always stood and would con-

Stevens' Home in Lancaster as it was at the Time of His Death. The Office
Entrance is on the Right

tinue to stand by and "religiously observe the present compact." [11] Although there might have been reason to complain against the attitude of some of the States on the Fugitive Slave Law enforcement, there was not a single actual grievance that could be charged against the Government of the United States. The refusal of seceding states to await real aggression showed their determined purpose.

Moreover, Southern leaders utterly ignored Seward's offer to support an unamendable, irrepealable amendment to the Constitution, guaranteeing forever slavery protection where it already existed. It is beyond the point that such might have been unacceptable to Seward's party. If there had been any earnest desire to compromise, it offered a real opportunity to begin negotiations. The South merely scoffed at it.

Exactly how far Stevens would go to avert war, is not clear. If there was a time, late in 1860, when he would have been willing to negotiate and compromise, he was never given, he believed, any opportunity to set forth his position. South Carolina's defiance and the refusal to vote on the Kansas Bill, he felt closed the door to all adjustment. If the South itself refused to deal with the Government except as an independent Nation, then nothing could be done, for acceptance of that position would admit that the States were already out of the Union absolutely and therefore, there would be nothing to compromise.

Practical equalitarian that he was, the rooting out of slavery from the Nation was probably the greatest ambition of his life. But time after time, he admitted the conclusiveness of the Constitutional limitation which precluded interference by non-slave states with slavery. So there remained but two ways in which it could be done.

The first one—emancipation by the slaveholding states of their own motion, no reasonable man could hope for. As long as those States were States, therefore, there was no legal way on earth to that end. If he were to remain consistent, then the only other method was through War which, having broken down the status of Statehood, would give the Federal Government a sufficient authority.

He fully respected the ability and courage of the South and knew there was no assurance that the North would be successful in an appeal to arms. But certainly he was not appalled as Senator Iverson of Georgia, seemed to think Northerners should be, when he declared that War would cost the North one hundred thousand men and one hundred million dollars. He "would not advise the shedding of American blood except as a last resort," but could not go as far as his fellow representative, Charles Francis Adams, who, rather than permit a break-up of the Union, believed that "every other cause should be sacrificed."

In all of the nerve-racking distress, he was careful, collected, and intelligent. His first appeal after secession was to the peaceful process of the law. He would "send no armies to wage Civil War," meaningly pointing out that there was "legal redress against treason, misprision of treason, murder and sedition." It would be better that "the general Government should annul the postal laws and stop the mails at the lines of seceded states . . ." Commerce regulation and revenue collec-

tion by the Federal Government were strong arms
"which would hold the Union together and punish re-
fractory members without bloodshed."

By no single act or word did he in any way encourage or invite War, unless it can be said that he did so
by his stolid attitude of waiting. He was cautious in
his expression and would not provoke the issue. During his period of enforced silence, the South herself
deliberately and irrevocably fixed the course. At the
time the secession movement was being decided upon
and through its early execution, Stevens obscured himself in the deep background. After secession he spoke,
but not until then.

"The attempt of one or more of these cotton states
to force this Government to dissolve the Union," was
to him "absurd." Greeley might be willing to let the
"erring sisters depart in peace," but Stevens felt those
who counselled the "Government to let them go and
destroy the National Union, are preaching moral
treason."

Surely the Government had the right and it was
its highest duty to defend itself. He would deal with
the situation with calm mind but iron hand. "Let us
be patient, faithful to all constitutional engagements,
and await the time of the Disposer of events. Let
there be no blood shed until the last moment; but let
no cowardly counsels unnerve the people, and then, at
last, if need be, let every one be ready to gird on his
armor, and do his duty." [12]

The time for Conciliation and Compromise had gone
irretrievably. The Nation shuddered with War not on
its doorstep, but within its very house.

III

LINCOLN AND WAR

Before the end of the first month of 1861, five states had left the Union. No one could foretell where and when the secession stampede would end.

In February a Union Peace Conference, representing fourteen non-slaveholding States and seven slave States met in Washington to seek some basis for peaceful adjustment. Less than a week before Buchanan's administration would end, it referred a long series of proposals to the Congress, which it recommended should be incorporated into Constitutional amendments.

Before the Senate could act upon its suggestions, Virginia Senators indicated that the proposals would be unacceptable to that State, even if they were adopted. Their statement withered all promise that the Conference had inspired. But the Senate finally did adopt, just before its close, House Resolutions providing for an amendment which, in effect, would guarantee and protect slavery as long as the slave States desired to have it.

In the meantime, the country at large had lapsed into an ominous quiet, with all eyes turned to Lincoln. Tight-lipped, he indicated nothing as to his position, biding the time until he could speak officially to the Nation as its President.

The new President's inaugural address is a tribute to the statesmanship of the man and shows a shrewd insight into the temper of the people, both North and South. Aiming his remarks at the departed and departing states, he reassured them that he had "no purpose, directly or indirectly to interfere with the institution of slavery in the States where it existed." He believed he had no lawful right to do so, nor was he so inclined. States Rights should be maintained inviolate, especially as to control of their own domestic institutions.

Lawless invasion by armed forces of any State or Territory, no matter under what pretext, was denounced as among the gravest of crimes. But he held that the Union was perpetual, and that no State, upon its own mere motion, could lawfully retire. Resolutions and ordinances to that end were legally void. Therefore, he deemed it his simple duty to see that the laws of the Nation were faithfully executed in all the States. He hoped that what he said would not be regarded as a menace but only as the declared purpose of the Union that it would defend and maintain itself.

The only real dispute was between one section of the country which believed that slavery was right and ought to be extended, and another section which believed it wrong and should be restricted. His argument was directed toward a "peaceful solution" and was convincing and well-grounded.

"Physically speaking," the Nation could not separate. The sections must remain face to face, and intercourse, either amicable or hostile, must continue. "Is it possible," he inquired, "to make that intercourse more advantageous and more satisfactory after the separation than before? Can aliens make treaties easier than friends can make laws?" Or could treaties be more faithfully enforced between aliens than laws could be among friends?

"Suppose you go to War. You cannot fight always; and when, after much loss on both sides and no gain on either, you cease fighting, the identical old questions as to terms of intercourse are again upon you. In your hands," he said to his dissatisfied countrymen, "and not in mine, is the momentous issue of Civil War."

He admonished them to "think calmly and well upon this whole subject." Characteristically, he counselled them "nothing valuable can be lost by taking time." He promised the seceding states that the Government would not assail them and that there could be no conflict unless they themselves were the aggressors.

The tender-hearted patriot was impelled to close his message with a sentimental and hopeful prophecy. "The mystic chords of memory stretching from every battlefield and patriot grave to every living hearth and hearthstone, all over this broad land will yet swell the chorus of the Union when again touched as surely they will be by the better angels of our nature."

Elected upon the platform of slavery restriction, he had said nothing about it. Sagaciously, he had made the keynote of his message the integrity of the Union. That appeal, he knew, would have a sympathetic reception, not only in the North, but in many sections of the South. It was the logical, and in fact, the only one commonly inviting. Had he attempted to stand upon the platform on which he had been elected, there is little doubt that he would have precipitated another torrent of secession and immediate War.

For a few weeks, the surface indicated a tense waiting, but under it there was much movement. Commissioners from the seceded states were in Washington, attempting to notify Lincoln of the withdrawal of their States and the formation of the Confederacy. They wanted to meet him, in order, as they said, to adjust the questions growing out of the political separation.

Supreme Court Justices (Nelson and Campbell) were intermeddling and although their motives were perhaps sincere, their actions gave nothing but embarrassment to the administration.

Fort Sumpter, undermanned and with supplies exhausted, was the immediate crux of concern. Indisputably Federal property and in Federal control, Southern guns, nevertheless, controlled approach to it. Did the Nation dare to compromise its self-respect by withdrawing from its own property or show equal weakness in permitting its own soldiers to starve?

Oddly enough, the commanding officer, so direfully in need of relief, had been the President's commanding officer when he mustered Lincoln, a private, out of the service in the summer of 1832.

Surely Lincoln had to act and he properly ordered relief. Before it could arrive, but after mature deliberation, the Confederate Government had ordered capture of the Fort. Shell-fire upon the Nation's flag in execution of that order precipitated the War of the Rebellion.

The long threatened conflict had come. The precise manner in which it came was an incident most fortunate for the Union cause. Southern aggression upon Sumpter furnished the Nation with a real basis for its claim that it was fighting a War of defense. The most grevious error committed by the Confederacy once the States had seceded, was to fire deliberately upon the

flag of the Nation, and by violence, take possession of
Federal property.

Restriction of slavery would have been a weak position on which to wage a war. Shell-fire upon Fort
Sumpter aroused the most terrible anger in the North.
Secession sympathy melted away; half-hearted Union-
ists became staunchly Union and strong Union men
became almost fanatics. No single act could have so
hurt secession's cause.

There were those who were certain that there could
be no real war and that the South would be conquered
in rapid manner. The Philadelphia Press and the New
York Times allowed thirty days. The New York
Tribune thought it might take a little longer. It notified the Nations of Europe that they could "rest assured that Jefferson Davis and Company will be
swinging from the battlements at Washington at least
by the fourth of July." It would "spit upon a later
and longer deferred justice."

The Chicago Tribune thought that the West alone
could fight the battle and win "within two or three
months, at the furthest." The fact was "Illinois can
whip the South by herself."

Lincoln probably was of similar though milder opinion as his call for seventy-five thousand militia for a
three months' enlistment would indicate. However, he
might have well understood just how serious the War
would be and feared that larger and longer call might
alarm the people and be more difficult to obtain. Be
that as it may, his next call a month later was for three-
year volunteers.

With his first call, the President had followed the

regular procedure of summoning Congress into special session. A striking thing about that notice to convene was that it set July 4, more than two and one-half months later. Lincoln believed that, in great crises, when there seemed to be no possible solution, mere waiting, frequently cleared the atmosphere and disclosed the path. His hope was that those two and one-half months might yield some event or movement which would indicate the way, or which could be turned advantageously to the cause of the Union.

Master strategist, even at that time, he saw his course lay in an appeal to the border States. If they were swept away by the surge of secession, the task of preserving the Union would be stupendous, if not almost hopeless. But if they could be persuaded to remain loyal, the moral effect, as well as their physical weight, would be of greatest help. To bring them to the support of the Union was his immediate objective and to this end he bent all of his political craftsmanship.

That, however, made necessary an attitude on his part which would give least offense to those States. It prevented a bold declaration of War purposes. When he said in his first message that he would defend the Union, that was as strong as he could put it and as far as he could go.

But his hope that time would ease his path was laid in barren disappointment. The passing of the days yielded no better basis on which to ground his cause and the disappointing reports from the battle fields raised gravest uncertainties of the War outcome.

In the meantime, the Congress was meeting in Special Session to deal with the emergency.

IV

LEADER

When the "Star of the West" carrying reinforcements to Fort Sumpter was fired upon on January 9, Buchanan ignored the insult. Three months later when Southerners shelled the Fort itself, Lincoln, helpless to do otherwise, termed it war and called for volunteers. There had been much thought and talk of war but the suddenness with which it came, stunned both North and South. That was on the fifteenth of April.

The crisis in which the new President found himself, was the most appalling in the country's history. There was no precedent to act upon, and no one to point the way. The capacity of the President-elect to assume an active leadership was, at the time, gravely doubtful. A middle west lawyer, who had achieved no great eminence in his chosen field, he had shown himself shrewd and able in debates, but the only official records on which he then could be weighed, were three terms as an Illinois Legislator and a single term as Congressman wherein he reached no especial prominence.

Lincoln was seldom a leader in thought. He is best described as the high minded patriot who, as master politician, geared his official conduct to a policy epitomized by the motto, "I follow the people." During his entire term as President, much as might be said to the contrary, he was never the director of public opinion. In every single stand he took, which superficially might appear to be an original attitude, either substantial or important groups had passed that point before him, and it was only the support that they had gathered and their potential strength that enticed Lincoln to the position.

And so, in those early days of crisis before Congress met, the country floundered without leadership. No one appeared on those great scenes of tragic action to unite the different theories of the War or effectively coordinate the energies of the North.

The prognosis was most uncertain. It was impossible for even the most intelligent of the Nation to penetrate the fogs and uncertainties and see ahead for even a short period. Varied schools of war theory vigorously and sometimes vehemently expressed by a type of orator able to stir deeply the masses; the complicated cross-currents and under-currents; the utter inability to detect any substantial underlying trend, and the controlling influence of unforeseen happenings, were nearly if not wholly, sufficient justification to Abraham Lincoln for the waiting policy that ruled him.

Failure of the Northern armies at the beginning added more uncertainties. Feelings ran high. There were conflicting policies and methods of procedure proposed and multitudinous opinions and suggestions. But what the country needed most direfully was a leader.

From the private citizenry of the country, there arose no volunteer great enough. Horace Greeley, commanding the tremendous influence of a widely circulated and highly respected newspaper, had failed miserably. Secretary of State Seward embarrassed the President before he even got started with his plans to defend the Union by practically promising commissioners from the South evacuation of Fort Sumpter.

Could there be found in Congress, one staunch and intelligent enough to devise a plan and under it set in motion a program that would save the Union?

In vivid contrast to the wrangling and delays that marked the organization of the House at the prior session, the one which convened at Lincoln's call organized in record time. In the former, Stevens was just a member; of the latter he took command.

The grim determination with which he reached out his iron hand to grip the control reins of the Body did not show on the surface. He had nominated Galusha Grow for Speaker. Appointed teller, he declined, saying, "I cannot write." That was a half joke. He made writings but only experts could decipher them. The House laughed.

Grow received ninety-nine votes on the first ballot and Blair, of Missouri, forty. When this was announced, Blair asked that his name be withdrawn and requested his friends who voted for him to change their votes to Grow. Stevens, who had received a single vote, arose to say, "I have the same remark to make. I will not be a candidate any longer and request my friend who voted for me to withdraw his vote." The remark gave rise to "great laughter," and on the next ballot, Stevens' candidate, Grow, was elected.[1]

But the fact that he could provoke laughter at such a time was proof that he was calm, self-possessed and in mood in which he worked most efficiently.

Superficially it might appear that there was at the time, no great question but that Congress would support Lincoln to the limit. This was by no means a then apparent certainty, as the enthusiastic Philadelphia and New York City meetings protesting War evidenced.[2]

Congress was decidedly Republican and the burst of

flaming resentment that swept the North when the flag
was fired on at Sumpter, was general, but no one could
be sure that such outburst was not a hasty show of
temper which might rapidly cool. Emulating the great
Lincoln, many of the Federal Legislators had their ears
to the ground to sense the real attitude of the country
toward the South, and had there been at the moment
hesitancy on the part of Congress in supporting Lincoln
and furnishing him with the sinews of War, the outcome
might have been greatly different.

The situation demanded immediate, unequivocal, and
strenuous action. No one in all the House of Representatives was as well suited to play that part as was
the Lancastrian. And Stevens did act.

When the House convened at one of the next day,
that is, within twenty-four hours from the time of Committee assignments, Stevens as chairman of the all-
powerful Ways and Means group, asked leave to report
a bill from it, authorizing a national loan. It was
granted. The bill was read twice, ordered printed, and
made special business for the next day.

He also reported from the same Committee a bill appropriating six million dollars to pay the soldiers whom
Lincoln had called into Federal service under his April
proclamation. They had received not a dollar up to
that time. Immediate payment was important if their
morale were not to be further impaired. His bill was
read three times and passed within an hour of the time
the House convened. The record stands in less than
three hundred words; a rare monument to Congressional
expedition.[3]

The same day, in stern, business-like method and with

no ceremony, Stevens bludgeoned through a bill authorizing the Secretary of the Treasury to borrow up to two hundred fifty million dollars for War purposes. The funds were necessary—why waste time with speeches?

Here he used for the first time a procedure which became renowned. When opposition was raised by those whom he knew to be unalterably opposed to everything that would assist the North in carrying on the War, he made no attempt to answer. They were permitted to have their say and when they had finished, he quietly and simply moved the previous question. That ended the speeches; a quietly disciplined House majority did the rest.

A few days later, trouble arose in Baltimore. Strategically located on a main artery of traffic, her disloyalty gave Lincoln and his administration no little concern. It was rumored that plans were being made to destroy railroad communications between Washington and the North, and so expose the Capitol to Confederate capture. In great fear, Lincoln hastily placed Baltimore under military law.

But no appropriation existed to take care of the President's order. With ever vigilant eye on the situation generally, Stevens, on July 24, brought from his Committee a bill appropriating one hundred thousand dollars for maintenance of police organized by the United States in Baltimore.

Some Southerners objected. Stevens patiently permitted discussion and this in face of the fact that his very important tax bill was awaiting consideration. When Burnett of Kentucky, assailed the measure as

highhanded, Stevens struck him to defenselessness and
silence by openly stating that the local police chief there
was a "traitor," and that the Police Board, "plotting
treason and acting a large part of it," had been arrested,
having been "found surrounded by arms, hidden, buried
and ready to be used against their fellow citizens who
were loyal to the government . . ." He peremptorily
refused further request to be heard, moved the previous
question and carried the bill, 97 to 6.

Before the session was a week old, Stevens' committee
had already framed a bill providing for a national loan.
He knew that all Southern sympathizers and many
neutral Democrats would, if given opportunity, make
long speeches and take much time in debate. He introduced a novel technique to prevent it. He moved
a suspension of the rules so that the House could go into
Committee of the Whole on the state of the Union to
consider the bill. Before that was voted upon, he moved
that "general debate on the bill be closed in one hour
after its consideration shall be commenced." That
brought forth a torrent of attack from Vallandigham
but the House supported its Ways and Means Committee Chairman.

So successful was this device that Stevens began to
use it as a matter of course. He even reduced the time
of discussion to five minutes,[4] then to one minute,[5] and
on one occasion, went so far as to move that all debate
on part of a bill "be terminated in one-half minute after
the Committee again resumes its consideration."[6]

Lovejoy watched him intently for several days.
When Stevens presented his tariff bill, the former arose
to ask him if he expected "to drive this thing through

with a tandem team." If so, he warned the Lancastrian he would find some obstacles in the way. Stevens answered that he did not expect to drive the bill through with " 'tandem team' for there are too many mules here." Lovejoy rejoined that "mules are very obstinate when they have long-eared drivers."[7]

On this bill, Stevens had, with the concurrence of the House, made allowance for only one hour of debate, but showed himself tolerant when it ran far beyond that limit.

He was not too insistent with his own party. Some matters coming before his committee required a positive stand and frequently an unpopular one. When he offered a second tariff bill, levying a heavy tax on tea and coffee, it met the quick opposition of his own followers. As soon as Stevens sensed this he immediately withdrew the Bill with leave to present an amended one the next day.[8]

He would permit no resolutions of any kind to be acted upon, whether they supported his policy or opposed it. When Crittenden offered some that the prior Congress had passed, Stevens objected and no more was heard of them at that time.[9]

Holman resolved, among other things, that no adjustment of pending difficulties be ever sanctioned by the Government that did not acknowledge the integrity of the Union. Vandever wished to place the House on record as pledging to the country and the world the employment of every resource, national and individual, for the suppression, overthrow and punishment of rebels in arms.

These latter two were much in harmony with Stevens'

Washington, Sept 3. 1848

Hon: Thaddeus Stevens
            Dear Sir:
                        You may possibly remember see
ing me at the Philadelphia Convention — introduced
to you as the lone whig star of Illinois — Since the
adjournment, I have remained here, so long, in the whig
document room — I am now about to start for home;
and I desire the undisguised opinion of some experienced and sagacious Pennsylvania politician, as to how
the vote of that State, for governor, and president, is
likely to go — In casting about for such a man, I
have settled upon you; and I shall be much obliged if you will write me at Springfield, Illinois.
        The news we are, receiving here now, by letters from
all quarters is steadily on the rise; we have none
lately of a discouraging character — This is the sum, with
out giving particulars —
                                        Yours truly,
                                        A. Lincoln

Abraham Lincoln, Shrewdly Calculating the National Situation, Writes Stevens
for Information of the Political Outlook in Pennsylvania

own position, but he said, "I must object. I do not believe that any resolution of this kind from any committee is calculated to do any good or to strengthen our hands." [10]

He was intelligent enough to understand that the future was very difficult of appraisement, and committing the Congress to any policy at the time was unwise.

Late in July, he pressed through an appropriation of ten million dollars to be placed in the hands of the President for the purchase of arms. Another two hundred thousand dollars he had set aside for the defense of the Capital City and on the same day, placed at Lincoln's command an additional ten million dollars for the purchase of ordnance.

The manner in which he was able to do this, is nothing less than astounding. Much of it was done by unanimous consent. Certainly there were many dissenters but they realized the futility of objecting. If they did, Stevens merely moved for a suspension of the rules, and under it, by majority support, got what he asked. The record of these three separate bills and their passage is set forth most laconically. The entire reports for all use less than five hundred words.

By early August, the House was ready to adjourn. Already in July, Stevens reported that the House, the place of origin of all the then important legislation, had swamped the Senate and because of that Body's delay, could do no further work. He suggested adjournment until the next Monday. VanWyck thought that if the House did adjourn, the Senate might defeat the purpose of it by following its example. "No," answered

Stevens. "I never knew the Senate to follow a good example." The House laughed and agreed to his motion.

In less than a month, the Congress of the United States, bereft of its Southern members, had shown a waiting world that what was left of the United States would vigorously defend its tradition, its Government and its President. Lincoln needed this whole-hearted support. It made its impression on many doubters in the North and furnished an all-important warning that the Nation would fight to extremity to protect itself against dissolution and that withdrawal from the Union of the States could not be attained merely by passing Ordinances of Secession.

Stevens' bold step to the front not only placed in the President's hands at a crucial time, the material means to prosecute the War, but his vigorous program and flaming speeches rallied his colleagues and gave body to indefinite, and in some localities, indifferent War sentiment.

Whatever adverse criticism is made of him, whatever errors of policy may be charged to him in his Chairmanship, whatever may be said of him as a roughshod commoner, if we accept the Union victory as the proper one, it must be recorded to his everlasting credit that he furnished the absolutely necessitous support in the House of Representatives, without which in those early days of general bewilderment, Lincoln and the North could never have carried on the War.

When the Special Session of the Congress convened early in July, the country was frantically searching for a leader. When it adjourned, little more than a month later, it had found one.

FINANCIER

Buchanan's administration bequeathed a $100,000,000 deficit to Lincoln.[1] Worse, finances of the United States had been so loosely managed that the Nation's credit was badly impaired. The Government was paying as high as twelve per cent for borrowed money and running behind at the rate of $20,000,000 per year.[2] Still worse, seven of the states had left the Union and this, of course, diminished federal income proportionately.

These conditions alone made the Nation's financing extremely difficult, but when to them was added the hazard of a war threatening its very existence, the problem of obtaining additional credit became enormous.

Practical-minded Salmon P. Chase, reelected to the Senate from Ohio, realizing the size of the task, was most reluctant to take the Portfolio of the Treasury when it was tendered him by Lincoln. At first he flatly declined, because, as he said, he was not suited for it, either by education or habits and because he was better fitted for work in the Senate.[3]

Upon reconsideration, however, he accepted the office, feeling a refusal might place him in the position of shrinking "from cares and labors for the common good which cannot be honorably shunned." [4]

When Congress met in Special Session on July 4, 1861, the Senate took its time getting started. The House, under Stevens' whip, organized in record time. The Pennsylvanian, who priorly had been a member of the Ways and Means Committee, was made Chairman of that group in the Thirty-seventh Congress.

In that day, the Committee was charged not only with the work of originating revenue measures, as is its function today, but also with the duty of what now is the work of the Committee on Appropriations. In peace times, the combined duties of these two Committees are onerous; in time of War, laboring under a weakened national credit, the job is stupendous.

In his message of July 4, 1861, Lincoln had asked Congress to place at his disposal $400,000,000 and 400,-000 men.[5] The burden of raising this then tremendous amount of money fell largely upon Stevens, for not only was he Chairman of the Ways and Means Committee, but even at this early time he was the "unquestioned leader of the House of Representatives."[6] He bore the full responsibility at the outset and he knew it. In the sudden emergency, whatever he suggested would undoubtedly be approved.

The Lancastrian had had no great training in matters of large finance, but he had been active for a number of decades as a student of financial and economic problems and had experience along these lines, which, although limited to smaller matters, gave him solid foundations for his great task.

Beginning as counsel for a county town bank in Gettysburg, he had been closely affiliated with the legislation of Pennsylvania affecting banks and money. Also, he had been a leader in the movement which brought the Bank of the United States under Pennsylvania Charter after President Jackson had forced the closing of the Federal institution. His task might appall a weaker man. Amounts to be dealt in had never been approached by any government in our history, but the duty had devolved upon him, and with the equipment at hand, he would act.

At the time he stood four-square behind Lincoln and earnestly desired to place at the President's disposal all that was needed to crush the rebellion. War was upon the country. Its continued life or destruction was to be decided upon battlefields. But battles could not be won without armies properly equipped.

Stevens as Chairman of the Ways and Means Committee was in the key position. He could hamper and delay, drift in uncertainty and doubt, or force vigorous action. From the time Lincoln had called for volunteers until the assembly of Congress, he had remained practically silent. There might have been some who were not sure just what course he would take. He made his answer in works rather than words. The quiet, masterful way in which he took command of the House and noiselessly proceeded through emergency legislation, is told in another chapter.

Over at the Treasury, Chase was slow in getting his stride. For some reason or other, he felt it necessary to call attention officially to how imperfectly he was qualified "by experience, by talents, and by special acquirements" for his work.[7] Of uncommon ability and highest integrity, he commanded widespread confidence in the North, having been a contender with Lincoln for Presidential nomination. He owed his position in the Cabinet to Lincoln's policy of appointing those who had been his formidable competitors for the office. Stevens thought "Lincoln's Cabinet was made up of an assortment of rivals whom the President appointed from courtesy; one stump speaker from Indiana, and two representatives of the Blair family."[8]

Though poorly fitted at the outset,[9] for the great War task of the Treasury Portfolio, Chase by earnest application soon showed a substantial grasp of financial matters. In his first message, he had correctly said that the financial problem consisted of apportioning loans and taxes in proper manner.

When he submitted his first plan to Congress, setting forth his solution, he laid the basis for a policy on which is blamed many of the evils of financing the War. He estimated that $320,000,000 would be required for the fiscal year then ensuing. Of this amount, he proposed only $80,000,000 should be raised by taxes and the remaining $240,000,000 obtained on a secured loan. The $80,000,000 barely covered the estimated expenses of the government outside of War requirements.

In other words, Chase proposed that the expenditures of the government made necessary by the War, should be obtained in toto from borrowings and that there should be no attempt to raise even the interest on those obligations from new taxes.

Since that time, students and critics of the matter have very largely agreed that this was error on the part of the Secretary. In their opinion, a policy should have been laid down at the very outset of the War, substantially increasing taxes so as to take care of, in some measure, the indebtedness created.

Distasteful as that might have been to the North and even though it might have cooled in some degree the War ardor, it nevertheless was the only sound method. To raise the War costs in their entirety by borrowings, not even providing for interest in current taxes, was certainly a nearsighted way of dealing with the problem. Whether Chase, sensing Lincoln's opinion that the War would soon be over, adopted this procedure to permit all States, including those in rebellion, to share in the cost of the War instead of forcing payment only from loyal states, is not clear.

In July of 1861, there was less than $65,000,000 of specie in the country. Today one wonders how those in control of the Government could have imagined that this comparatively small amount of coin was sufficient to bear the weight of the money work ahead and function for any length of time. The theory of having it revolve fast enough to maintain a specie basis soon showed itself no more than a theory.

Chase seemed to think that when the first $50,000,000 of the authorized loan of $250,000,000 was offered for sale, the Government would receive specie in return. By paying it out immediately for War materials, he would place it in the hands of those who would be logical purchasers of the next loan installment. This would create an endlessly revolving specie.

The first $50,000,000 of Treasury Notes, bearing seven and three-tenths per cent interest were disposed of to banks without delay. The second $50,000,000 were similarly sold by the Government in October. But when the time came for the third installment in December, the Government had to accept approximately eleven per cent discount, and so received only about $44,500,-000.

This was clear and certain notice that Chase's theory would not work. The hard money just would not cir-

culate. The Government borrowed that year $150,000,-
000 in gold, and with little foresight, paid it out in War
expenditures. Then, too late, it learned that it was up
against the problem of hoarding. Not only did individuals hoard, but banks joined them.[10]

The inevitable happened. On December 28, 1861,
banks suspended specie payments and the Government
was forced immediately to follow. The country faced
a financial crisis. National bankruptcy was feared here
and abroad.[11]

Chase continued to follow the policy laid down in his
first Treasury Statement.[12] Expenditures proved more
than $200,000,000 above his July estimate, and he re-
ported that nearly a half billion dollars would be required for the next year.

Adrift on befogged financial seas, those in control of
the money matters of the Nation were suddenly con-
fronted with uncharted places over which no government had ever moved in that kind of ship, and where,
if some definite course were not quickly engaged upon,
the Ship of State must founder. No one knew what to
do. The Chairman of the Senate Finance Committee
said, "I declare here today that in the whole number of
learned financial men that I have consulted, I never
have found any two men who agree."[13]

Some method other than Chase's must be found to
finance the War or the Government must capitulate to
the enemy. Stevens stepped into the breach. At least
he was courageous enough to try something. He never
claimed great knowledge in financial theory or
methods, but this was an actuality which had
to be met. Everyone except him seemed paralyzed.

The War waited; the Nation watched; Stevens acted.

Early in 1862, he reported out his Bill to authorize the issue by the Government of legal tender notes. This, of course, was a bold departure from what was then looked upon as sound finance, but as has been pointed out, circumstances were such that all premises upon which arguments could be based to support conservative financing, had been swept away. It was utterly impossible to continue under hitherto accepted methods.

Even he had not come easily to the proposals.[14] He submitted the "measure, of necessity, not of choice. No one would willingly issue paper currency not redeemable on demand and make it legal tender." He agreed that it was "never desirable to depart from the circulating medium which by the common consent of civilized nations forms the standard of value."

Outlining the situation, he began with the debt of $100,000,000 that faced the Lincoln administration at the very outset. Congress had been counselled to authorize a $250,000,000 loan and had been able to dispose of only $200,000,000 of it, and some of that at fearful discount.

Before the banks had paid in full for the last installment of the loan, "they broke down under it and suspended specie payments. They have continued to pay that loan not in coin but by demand notes of the Government . . . That has kept them at par, but the last of that loan was paid yesterday and on the same day the banks refused to receive them." Even Government demand notes "must now sink to depreciated currency."

There was a floating debt of $180,000,000 with a

daily expense of approximately $2,000,000 and an estimated $700,000,000 more required before the next Congress, in addition to the $350,000,000 already appropriated. Under conservative procedure, the only way to raise this tremendous amount of money was to sell Government bonds in the open market to the highest bidder.

But, said Stevens, the amount was so huge that judging by experience the Government had already had, the obligation would sell "no doubt for as low as sixty per cent of its par value." This would require a bond issue of a billion and a half dollars to carry over to the end of the next fiscal year. It was "too frightful to be even considered."

Some leaders suggested the issuance of seven and three-tenths per cent interest bonds payable in one year. But that would mean that the Government would be forced to receive in payment, from the banks who bought them and none of which were then on a specie paying basis, the depreciated notes of those banks. These would be all the Government would then have to pay creditors.

Moreover no one who appreciated the financial problem believed that the Government could redeem its pledges at the end of the year, and so the Government's bonds would be thrown into the market and sold for whatever purchasers chose to pay for them. The folly of the scheme, Stevens thought, needed no illustration.

For the same reason he opposed Chase's plan to furnish banks with their circulations to the amount of Government bonds which each would purchase and pledge with the Treasury for security. In order to purchase the Government bonds the banks would necessarily use their own devalued circulation. "How," Stevens pertinently asked, "would that be any better than the Government's own notes?" Certainly the security of the Government was equal to that of the banks. Another objection was that the banks would have their circulations without interest and at the same time draw interest on their Government bonds.

So far Stevens was on solid footing, but all his remarks had been directed at fallacies in the schemes of others. Now he advanced his and his Committee's plan.

At the time, gold and silver were not money. They were rarely, if ever, seen in the ordinary passing of what was used for money, and had become more or less of commodities which were bought and sold. Substantial part of what was used was notes of the various State Banks. Having gone off specie payment, none of these were worth their face in hard money and, of course, they varied in value as widely as did the reputation for security of the banks issuing them. It was a mere guess to say just what each bank's notes were worth, and even that had to be adjusted from day to day.

The country had arrived at a condition where it, in fact, had no uniform or stable currency. Stevens' proposal was to create one with a direct issue by the United States of its own notes.

Novel and radical, it might be viewed as illegal. He admitted that nowhere in the Constitution was specific permission granted, but "the right to emit bills of credit which the Constitution expressly refused to grant as a substantive power, has for fifty years, by the common consent of the Nation been practiced and is now openly conceded by every opponent of this bill."

If then, it were permissible to emit bills of credit, it would require a "sharp and unreasonable doubter" to deny the power of the Government to make them legal tender.

When Vallandigham, who was already acting as a drag upon War legislation the House was attempting to enact, objected that the legal tender clause would depreciate the notes, Stevens made intelligent answer that it was "not easy to perceive how notes issued without being made payable in specie could be made any worse by making them legal tender."

To those who challenged the right of the Government to make the proposed notes legal tender, Stevens correctly pointed out that the Constitution contained no prohibition on Congress against passing laws impairing contracts. But even if this were the fact his proposal could not be so condemned, for contracts "are made not only with a view to present law, but subject to the further legislation of the country."

He reminded them that the Government in 1853 had "changed the value of coin, regulated its weight, even rebated it seven per cent and made it legal tender."

It is no flattering commentary on the intelligence of his colleagues in the House to find in the record that two of them who were lawyers [15] viewed Stevens' bill as an ex post facto measure. Cutting the one and excusing the other, he set them aright, saying, "It is not wonderful that my distinguished colleague [16] not being a professional lawyer, should be unaware that the ex post facto laws of the Constitution refer only to crimes and misdemeanors and not civil contracts. The gentleman from Ohio [17] no doubt knew it but forgot it."

Stevens showed he really understood the function of this kind of money and the limits within which it may properly be used. He said, "the value of legal tender notes depends on the amount issued compared with the business of the country." He probably strained the point a bit by adding that "if a less quantity were issued than the huge and needed circulation, they would be more valuable than gold."

Having in mind all important limitation, he "expected the $150,000,000 asked for to be all that would be needed." It was his idea that if these notes could be kept circulating, they would do the work of $500,-000,000 of bonds.

The Government would issue the notes, and use them to pay contractors for War purchases. They, by reason of the nature of their business, would again pay out a large part of them and so the notes would be kept circulating until they arrived in the hands of those who could afford to retain them. Now, instead of retaining the notes which were convertible into United States Bonds, they would, in order to obtain interest, buy bonds from the Government which would thereby retrieve the notes into the Treasury, which would again start them through the same course of useful work. [18]

Certainly the Lancastrian was not wrong when he argued that these notes would be better currency than the notes of State Banks, which were "merely local issues sadly depreciated and many so badly that they had little or no value at all."

He did not "much sympathize with the money-lenders who feared that debtors should more easily pay

their debts." While some "men have agonized bowels
for the rich man's cash, they have no pity for the poor
widow, suffering soldier, and wounded martyr to his
country's good, who must receive these notes without
legal tender, or nothing, and then give one-half of their
value to the Shylocks to get the necessaries of life. Sir,
I wish no injury to any, nor with our bill could any
happen, but if any must lose, let it not be the soldier,
the mechanic, the laborer and the farmer."

It was not correct, as had been said, that the legal
tender clause would tend to depreciate the notes, for
Stevens asked pertinently how notes that "any man
must take" would be "worth less than the same notes
that no man need take."

Roscoe Conkling had proposed to issue a quarter of
a billion dollars of seven per cent bonds to be sold or
exchanged for the currency of the Boston, New York
and Philadelphia Banks. This procedure, Stevens
thought, was wanting in "every element of wise legislation," for it would permit those banks to issue without restraint unlimited amounts of their own mere
paper and with it buy "good hard money bonds of the
Nation." The notes which the Government would receive for its bonds soon "would become trash. Was
there ever such a temptation to swindle? If we are to
use suspended notes to pay our expenses, why not use
our own?"

The minority group of the Committee had filed a
report recommending a circulation bearing interest.
This idea the Lancastrian viewed as a curiosity. He
said it would be rather inconvenient on a frosty day
for a tailor or shoemaker to calculate the interest on

one of them before he used it in the market or store. It would force "every man to carry an arithmetic and interest table with him to gauge the value of his money."

The question was whether to place interest bonds on the markets between that date [19] and December, sufficient to raise the next $600,000,000 required, or issue notes as he suggested, not redeemable in coin, but fundable in specie paying bonds maturable in twenty years. His opinion was that if bonds were to be sold, they could not be sold at over seventy-five per cent of par, and even then would be paid for in a currency which was itself at a discount. That would produce a loss which no nation or individual, doing business, could stand even a year.

Cautioning the House against abuse of the type of financing he saw as the only possible way out, he solemnly warned them that such legal tender notes as were contemplated should not "be issued in excess of demand."

If his bill were rejected, the financial credit of all the great interests of the country as well as the Government itself, "will be prostrated." Its passage was essential to the very "existence of the Government." But if the House should see fit to defeat it, he would gladly resign from the Ways and Means Committee and leave his opponents to suggest other measures.[20]

Stevens' proposition to meet the financial emergency, therefore, was a very clear one. It provided simply for the issuance by the Government of $500,000,000 of twenty-year six per cent gold bonds and $150,000,000 of notes. The notes would enjoy a full legal tender status; be fortified by every right to circulate as currency on a parity with coin, and be convertible at the holder's option into the bonds.

Learned ones and frequently those not so learned, have written reams pointing out the errors and mistakes of the War financing, and condemning the theories on which it was laid. In the main, they may be right, but even so, none of their criticism can touch Stevens.

The error into which his critics have fallen is their assumption that the Old Commoner was responsible for the legislation finally enacted, and on that they base their observations.

Nothing could be further from the facts. True, he voted for the final bill with its "many uncouth (he would not call them absurd because the House had already adopted it) [21] features," as it came from the Committee on Conference, but he did so only because of the pressing emergency.

If he is to be indicted for his money theories, every iota of the charge must rest on supposition and not facts. The sweeping truth generally overlooked is that the Old Commoner's theories were never put into effect. What he suggested was never tried.

He was always opposed to the policy adopted and consistently said so. When the bill came back from the Senate with amendments, he approached it "with more depression of spirits than I ever before approached any question." He had a "melancholy foreboding" that they were "about to consummate a cunningly devised scheme which will carry great injury and great loss to all classes of people throughout this Union, except one."

He told the story tersely. When his bill, as it

passed the House, was reported to the country, congratulations from all classes poured in from all quarters. The Boards of Trade of Boston, New York, Philadelphia, Cincinnati, Louisville, St. Louis, Chicago and Milwaukee approved its provisions, and urged its passage as it was. But a doleful sound came up from the caverns of bullion brokers, and from the salons of the associated banks. Their cashiers and agents were soon on the ground, and persuaded the Senate, with but little deliberation, to mangle and destroy what it had cost the House months to digest, consider and pass.

The Senate had "so disfigured and deformed it that its very father would not know it." He denounced it with the amendments as "positively mischievous," charging that it "now creates money and by its very terms declares it a depreciated currency." Furthermore, it made two classes of money, one for the banks and brokers and another for the people, and so, discriminated between the rights of different classes of creditors, permitting the capitalist to demand gold and compelling others to "receive notes which the Government had purposely discredited."

Agents of the great capitalists had been heard in the Senate of the United States with a much more sympathetic ear than they had in the House.[22] Of the several amendments added to Stevens' bill by the Senate, two struck at its very vitals.

Stevens' idea was to have the $150,000,000 of Treasury notes circulate as full legal tender. Inasmuch as they could be used to purchase six per cent Government gold bonds, it was only reasonable to suppose that there would be a desire on the part of those into whose hands they came, to convert them into these long term interest bearing bonds. As he said, one of the great objects of the bill was to induce capitalists to invest in these bonds or lose their interest, and thus to furnish a continually recurring currency.

A Senate amendment would permit anyone having $100 or more of these notes to deposit them with the United States and receive in return therefor five per cent interest or if they were exchangeable for the July 17th issue, as the Senate would allow, a still higher rate could be obtained. This provision, as the Lancastrian pointed out, would "effectually prevent the funding of a single dollar in those bonds." Moreover, a little fellow who could not accumulate $100 or more of these notes, could get no interest. Certainly it is hard to conceive of a more effective way than the Senate proposed, to defeat Stevens' plan of having the $150,000,000 circulate back to the hands of the Government in payment for the purchase of the twenty-year bonds.

In his bill, the Old Commoner had planned that the notes authorized should be receivable "for all salaries, debts and demands owed by the United States to individuals, corporations, and associations within the United States," but the Senate struck that out and in its place inserted that the notes should be receivable for "all claims and demands against the United States of whatever kind *except for interest on bonds and notes, which shall be paid in coin.*"

To test the mettle of the House, Stevens moved to amend the Senate amendment by making not only the interest on bonds and notes payable in coin, but also the pay of officers, soldiers, sailors and all supplies purchased for the Government. This, of course, would nullify not only the Senate amendment, but the effective part of his own bill.

He offered it "only to illustrate absurdity." He said he knew if adopted the whole bill would be "pernicious," but he hoped that soldiers and sailors and those who supplied them with provisions would "not be thought less meritorious than the money-changers." Even if the original bill is to be "entirely impaired, those who are fighting our battles and their widows and children" should not be placed upon a "worse footing than those who hold the bonds of the Government and the coin of the country."

Holders of gold would sell it, limited by no other rule than what their consciences would allow. The Nation would be absolutely at their mercy. The first purchase of gold by the Government would fix the value of the notes. At whatever discount the bonds would have to be sold, and they certainly could not be sold for par, by just so much would the notes which they were then attempting to call legal tender, be depreciated. And the notes at "seventy-five or eighty-five per cent" would still be "legal tender to those who held the coin of the country." [23]

Stevens was one of the managers of the House on the Committee of Conference, and on February 24 reported the bill back. He mentioned the changes the Senate had made in the House bill, saying he thought it had been done "erroneously."

The Committee had to take the bill as they found it, for it could "see no way to raise coin but by selling the Government's paper." This would inevitably bring "our currency below par with the Government still declaring that it was at par." He recognized the "absurdity," and its attendant effect of making one currency for the coinholders and another for the people.

But unsound as the bill then was and disheartened as he was about it, Stevens would be done with it and called the previous question. The conference report was agreed to and the amended bill passed by a vote of ninety-seven to twenty-two. In spite of his positive knowledge that it was bad, he supported it as the best possible compromise.[24]

The Senate had been so adamant that in the emergency there was nothing to do but accept its amendment although it mutilated his bill and precluded his theory. Otherwise, the Nation would suffer financial breakdown. Broadmindedly, he was willing to submit the measures to the stern test of trial. If he were wrong, the country would soon be out of its financial difficulties. If his prophecies were correct, other measures would be enacted.

By the end of the year every single forecast he had made for the February law, had become an actuality. Instead of the $150,000,000 note issue being used by the holders to purchase six per cent Government bonds, only $20,000,000 had been so invested, while $80,000,-000 of the issue had been deposited on call and was drawing interest from the Nation.

The Government was reaching a point where it would require $60,000,000 of gold annually to pay interest under the provisions of the February measure and Stevens said the requirements would "soon double that amount." This in spite of the fact that the "banks and brokers have scarcely that amount on hand." It was a simple matter for the holders of gold to make their half-yearly sales to the Government, take in return Government bonds at a great discount, and so "clear by a single operation thirty per cent on their capital, and have all the profits of interest on deposits and currency circulation besides."

Then, as he pointed out, the gold would return to the vaults of the sellers, partly through payment of interest by the Government on the very bonds the sellers themselves held, and so supply them for the same operation at the next semi-annual payment time. In this way, large capitalists and gold jobbers could double their capital in three years. "If a financial system which produces such results be wise, then I am laboring under a great mistake."

The February law had been given fair trial and failed, as he had feared. He had not changed his opinion that it was fundamentally bad, and still believed his own plan the only sensible way out of the financial bogs. By December, he was sure his country had had enough of the Senate scheme.

Full of hope, he introduced a bill solely on his own responsibility. "Neither the Secretary of the Treasury nor the Ways and Means Committee has been consulted with regard to it, nor has it ever been considered by them." It was, in substance, a timely adjustment of the House Committee bill of the prior January, with emphasis placed upon the necessity for a national currency. That the January bill had been "mangled and destroyed as it passed through the Senate" did not deter him. Experience since then, proving the mistake of the law enacted, should have convinced the Nation that a new scheme was advisable.

The first thing he proposed was to repeal in the main, obnoxious provisions of the February law. He would call the 5-20 bonds and all others whose interest was payable in gold, "exchanging them for new bonds on such terms as might be agreed upon, or pay them in legal tender." He would liquidate all legal tender interest bearing deposits and annul the law authorizing them. He would repeal the law requiring payment of duties in coin, except one-fifth, as well as interest on future bond issues.

"Thus the whole currency needed in this country would be legal tender United States notes. The bullion mongers would lose, the merchants and Government would gain."

Having restored the law to original order, he would pay off all pressing debts through an issue of these notes, not to exceed $200,000,000 beyond those already authorized and issue a billion dollars of six per cent bonds which in twenty years, would be redeemed in coin. But of greatest significance to him, interest upon these bonds would be paid in any kind of lawful money and not necessarily specie. He was convinced more strongly than ever that with the $500,000,000 legal tender notes in circulation, holders would be glad to turn them to profit by "purchasing bonds." And he doubted not that "before the year would expire, the whole billion dollars would be called for at par."

State Banks had wrought havoc by issuing, without regulation or even limitation, their own notes which passed as currency. Uncontrolled, many of them kept printing and circulating their notes not only beyond reason, but beyond the bounds of conscience and decency.

Stevens would cure the evil by imposing a fifty per cent tax on all their circulations beyond half or three-quarters of their capitals. This he frankly said, was intended for prohibition and not for revenue. Its purpose was two-fold—to give wider circulation to United States notes and thus induce their conversion into bonds; and to prevent undue inflation of the currency.

It would, no doubt, drive from circulation at least $100,000,000 of State Bank notes, but would leave about that amount afloat. With the $500,000,000 of United States notes, the country would be furnished with a $600,000,000 circulation. That, Stevens thought, was sufficient, for before the War, there was only one-third of that amount. He added what is generally accepted today, that checks which pass as "currency in our large states are as much a paper circulation as bank notes."

His system "would not reduce bank profits below a fair gain," for while suspension continued, they might hold, as they were doing, their whole capital in Government securities bearing at least six per cent interest; have the benefit of a circulation equal to three-fourths of their capital and obtain return on whatever deposits they had. This, he figured would net them at least ten per cent to pay their expenses and dividends to stockholders and he believed that "was enough."

But he had not much hope of the Congress adopting his plan for there was "no great prospect" that the country "would return to the system" he indicated, "nor do much to protect the people from their own eager speculation." What he had proposed he did, not with the thought of its being adopted, but so that a "few years hence, when a general bankruptcy had come through unregulated enterprise, he would have the satisfaction of knowing that he had attempted to prevent it." [25]

He didn't live to see it but the post-war panic years bear record of the correctness of his prediction.

The bill, however, alarmed financial editors and their clients. One referred to it as the "wild recommendations of the extravagant-headed Republican from Pennsylvania." But it "affected the money market only as a 'flying fowl affects a herd of cattle, making a huge flutter but doing no damage.'" Stevens "would call in one loan and issue another to benefit banknote engravers." [26]

The New York *Tribune* said, "the general features of the bill have caused much discussion in the street. The section suspending payment of interest on the public debt in specie, and the section imposing a large tax on bank circulations have been universally condemned." However, an examination of the proposal showed "it to be essentially a currency measure, which is what the Street wants." [27]

The *Daily Express* Editor, at Lancaster, who claimed to know Stevens well, saw no reason why any alarm should be occasioned by the Commoner's bill. He thought Stevens had introduced it merely as a strategic move to throw determined opponents in the House off the track and "divert their attention while, in the meantime, he quietly completes his real preparations." [28]

If the Editor was correct at all, he was only limitedly so, for the bill was merely an up-to-date restatement of Stevens' original plan for financing the War cost, and one to which he adhered vigorously and consistently from the time he first proposed it until his death.

The reason he seemed half-hearted in his speech upon it, was because he already knew from the February vote that the Senate would hear nothing of it, and even his own House would not support him in it.

By early 1863, he had lost support of the majority of the Ways and Means Committee on his proposition to pay interest on the Government debts in money, instead of specie. Unscrupulous ones, who owned and controlled gold, had by one means or another, convinced the Lower Body that interest payments on national borrowings necessarily had to be made in gold. Unusual as it seems, they were little concerned how the principal amount was paid; that they would attend to when the time came, but current payments they insisted must be made in the shining metal. [29]

Government expenses were mounting at a terrific rate, running now to between two and three million dollars per day. New financing was again necessary.

On January 12, 1863, Stevens introduced a bill upon which his Committee had spent a great deal of time. In outline, it provided for issuance of $900,000,000 of twenty-year bonds, payable in money with interest payable in coin, and $300,000,000 of interest bearing Government notes. Such would increase the national debt to $2,120,000,000.

But that was the Committee's bill, not his. He of-

fered a substitute. In aggregate amounts, the two proposals were alike, but there all similarity ended. The
Committee would pay interest on the bonds in gold and
redeem them in lawful money; Stevens would pay the
interest in money and redeem the bonds with gold.

The Committee would issue interest bearing notes.
Stevens would issue an equal amount of non-interest
bearing legal tender. The Old Commoner was more
conservative and infinitely more farsighted than the
Committee.

He would prevent the issue of more of the five-
twenty bonds, whose interest was payable in gold. He
would, furthermore, repeal the law authorizing the de-
posit of legal tender notes, which under the then program, were drawing interest at five per cent.

But the obligations of the Government, already contracted to pay in gold, he would not disturb. His substitute would make "all our interest payable in just
such money as other people pay theirs in, except where
our faith is already pledged to pay gold." At the time
the Government was actually paying over ten per cent
interest on monies borrowed.

Again he rebuked the Government for using two
kinds of money. What justice was "there in compelling
the people to receive their interest in a currency of forty
per cent less value than is paid to the banks and capitalists who invest in Government bonds?" It was "rank
injustice."

If the Government were to build up a financial structure that would pay all interest on its borrowings in
gold, it would soon reach a point where performance
was impossible.

Under the Committee proposal, interest would amount to $180,000,000 per annum. More than $50,-000,000 of this was premium the Nation would pay for gold. All the banks in the country had but $87,000,000 in that currency. "Where will you find the balance? Sixty per cent premium may bring it out from its vaults or from foreign parts. I do not believe a lower price will."

The policy already in effect and that proposed, showed every lack of intelligence as to time of payment. Stevens seemed to be the only one who noticed this. For instance, $150,000,000 of the seven and three-tenths per cent bonds fell due within two years. They, of course, must be refinanced. With the five-twenties, the Government would be called upon to pay off at one time from two to four billion dollars of its paper. The Old Commoner correctly believed that to be a "financial impossibility."

His plan would take care of practically the same amount of financing. By paying interest in money, he showed how the principal debt could be made more than $100,000,000 less than the Committee's bill would make it. Combined, his improvements on the bill would save the Government more than $50,000,000 a year in interest payments, which, during the life of the bonds, of course, would be more than a billion dollars.

Who can say that the gold bonds which he proposed would not sell more quickly and at a higher price than the lawful money bonds of the Committee? No commentator or critic has proven him wrong when he said, "how much better to receive the interest in legal tender, which will answer all the purposes of business now, and get the principal in gold when you come to realize your capital, than to take and dissipate the driblets of interest in coin, and get the substantive capital in legal tender, or whatever else the Government makes money, possibly the notes of a Treasury bank." [30]

Irrevocably opposed to the devastating policy of paying interest on Government obligations in gold, but all the time knowing the Senate did not and would not agree with him, he tried to reach a compromise. While the new finance measures were still before the Congress, he introduced a bill "suggested by a very eminent financier." [31] The proposal would permit the Treasury to issue its notes or bonds "to whatever amount the public necessities require," with interest at three and sixty-five one hundredths per cent per annum. The measure partook of the qualities both of a funded debt and a currency and would, of course, very materially lessen the Government's interest charges. It struck the House as a "very important measure, indeed," but after some perfunctory discussion, was discarded. [32]

When the proposal to sell Treasury gold came up in March of '64, Stevens took a firm position in favor of it. Contending that Congress, by its legislation two years before, had enacted a policy which made gold no longer money in the actual and "practical sense of the word," he could see no objection to selling it. Gold might be a standard of value abroad, but in this country it was not, for here the lawful money of the United States was "practically the standard of value." When articles were quoted for sale, the price was quoted in the money of the United States and not in gold.

"This commodity called gold . . . has risen in price

just as every other metal has risen. Iron is rising in price, brass is rising in price." When someone suggested copper also, Stevens turned aside to say that was true but it was "owing more to the amount used in making Copperheads than anything else."

Of course his position was motivated by his desire to prevent, or at least retard, advance in the cost of gold which struck the Government so severely each time it had to go into the market to purchase it to pay interest. Gold hoarders and great capitalists had taken advantage of the shortage of the metal in America and had cornered it, forcing the Government to pay a ridiculously high price for it.

The Nation now had opportunity to realize some profit by selling gold and why should it not be done? "Is there any shame, for the Government to sell \$12,-000,000 of it for \$20,000,000?" It is merely "selling an article and converting \$12,000,000 of gold into \$20,000,-000 of greenbacks to pay off our debts." It was indeed a "tender conscience" that could not do this.[33] However he was but slightly interested in the profit to be made; his real purpose was to force down the price of gold.

Even then he understood the financial problem well enough to make a forecast that proved conservative. He said, "I trust I may be a false prophet, but if gold does not go up to two hundred per cent, my judgment is entirely at fault." He was entirely right for within a few months, gold was selling well above two hundred.[34]

Those who had or could obtain gold did what was to be expected, and what has been done under similar conditions throughout all history. They manipulated

the market to get most for their holdings. In his annual
report, the Secretary of the Treasury had called the
attention of Congress to combinations of men who
sought to "raise the price of coin and depreciate the
value of lawful money" of the United States, and had
asked for "some remedy of the evil."

Stevens, always conscious of these machinations, had
studied a long time for some prohibition or restriction.
As soon as the Treasury complained, he introduced a
bill attempting to declare "lawful money and legal
tender of equal value for all purposes to gold and silver
of like denomination." The measure was a radical one
and is generally referred to by economists and finan-
ciers as unsound. At the time, it was criticized as an
attempt to fix the value of gold and silver by legislation with no regard whatsoever to the labor required
to produce it, or the relation of supply and demand of
the substance.[35]

The bill created a furor not only in the House, but
in the financial circles of New York, being variously
referred to as "unheard of," "absurd," and "unsound."
One member said it was like trying "to make the mer-
cury in a thermometer regulate the weather."

The bill was smothered, but in January, Stevens
called attention of the House to similar measures enacted by Great Britain in the latter part of the eighteenth and the early part of the nineteenth, century.
At the time she was engaged in her European Wars
and under "all similar circumstances." The English
measures which were attempts, resulting successfully, to
curb the gold gamblers in England, had the support
of "Lord Stanhope, the great Lord Chancellor Eldon,

and the eminent English financier, Vansittart." [36]

With the War ended the Government's financial problem was immediately transformed. At the time hostilities ceased, the Nation was experiencing a prosperity never approached in its history. Commerce and industry were flourishing, and agriculture was at unprecedented peak. Then expenditures for war material ceased abruptly, and the army of soldiers rapidly retired from the Federal payroll to peace time pursuits. Because of these conditions with heavy wartime tax levies still functioning, money accumulated rapidly in the National Treasury. The Government need borrow money no longer. Its task now was to pay off the huge obligations it had contracted.

Stevens had taken large and conspicuous part in wartime financing. When peace came, there was little to legislate about in money matters, and consequently, he could do but little in that field.

But there was other work of paramount importance to engage his failing energies. Seventy-three years of age in the month of Lee's surrender, he was physically worn out. Night and day he had labored continuously for four years. Disease had crept upon him, broken his health, and left but a shadow of the man.

Ahead lay the great problem of the reconstruction of States in Rebellion. To him this was as important as the War itself and unless a firm course were pursued, he feared that all the suffering and expenditure that had gone into the conflict would be wasted. But he found himself so spent physically that he just could not carry on in the prodigously active way he had during the War. Some lines of his work he must yield to other hands. He was not long in making up his mind. What little energy he had left he would give to consolidating and making permanent the victory of the Union. Those opposed to his financial methods had the field to do as they would.

This opposition which had cloaked itself as long as possible, was soon forced into the open. Its identity was as might have been expected. Stevens' enemies, who had fought his money policies in various disguises, were now isolated into the creditor class which held the obligations of the Government. The War of the Rebellion had given the Nation its first substantial group of war profiteers. While soldiers carried on upon the battlefields, these people had sold war supplies to the Government at tremendous profits. Payment was made by, or converted into, Government securities. Those, of course, who loaned their money to the Nation, received Federal obligations. These two groups found themselves in April of 1865, in possession of $2,800,000,000 of the bonds, securities, and promises to pay, of the United States.

In addition, there was a total circulating currency of approximately $704,000,000.[37] Application of a conservative financial policy would now require currency contraction and a return to specie. With this, Stevens was in full accord. In all his speeches and writings, he showed from the inception of Greenback Legislation to his death, that he thought of paper money only as an emergency makeshift, which the country should abandon for specie as soon as was safely possible after the emergency had passed. Therein, of course, he was fully practical and eminently sound. He was well aware that abrupt contraction could bring nothing but devastating deflation with accompanying panic and bankruptcy. Gradual and reasonable contraction, providing a gentle absorption, was not at all inconsistent with a continuing national prosperity.

McCulloch, Secretary of the Treasury, showed no hesitancy in adopting a contraction policy. In that he was right. But in the shocking suddenness with which he did it, he was entirely wrong. Because well over a billion dollars of the debt of the United States was payable soon after the close of the War, and some of it payable at the option of the Treasury, McCulloch's position had great weight.

To him the greenbacks were not real money and he would precipitately call them in and cancel them.[38] Not only this, but he went the whole distance, insisting that all obligations of the Government, greenbacks, notes and bonds, should be, without question immediately redeemed in gold. The creditor class heard him and smacked their lips. Some of the Government securities they held they had bought as low as forty cents on the dollar.[39] They had received interest in gold all the time they held the obligations and now what could be more splendid than for them to receive one hundred dollars in gold for what they had paid but forty.

Would anyone dare say the securities should be paid in other than gold? They were horrified at the thought.

Most of the metropolitan newspapers, as well as many smaller ones, rushed to their support. Moreover, they saw to it that their cause was heard, not only throughout the country, but even on the Floors of Congress. The non-creditor class, the poorer people of the Nation, the

average American, was but slightly represented and
faintly heard. Their great champion was almost impotent; for the Old Commoner's physical strength was
fast ebbing. However, he could not stand by in silence
and see such tremendous fraud perpetrated upon the
people without some resistance. When the occasional
opportunity came in the midst of reconstruction
struggles, he did what he could.

No discussion will be made here of the policy engaged
upon by the Government which led to the post-war panic
that ravaged the country. Stevens was with the subdued minority, had little opportunity to object, and
all the time realized the utter hopelessness of contest.
Post-war money policies were exclusively within the
control of the Treasury Department and beyond Stevens' reach.

Years before the panic came, his work had ended, and
he was spared witnessing the calamity he prophesied.[40]

He engaged in but one altercation and that arose
through a question of how the five-twenties should be
paid. McCulloch said, "the bonds were negotiated with
the definite understanding at the time that they were
payable in coin."[41] Stevens took sharp issue. He insisted the bonds were payable in lawful money. Nowhere on their face nor in the enabling legislation was
there mention of kind of payment.

Stevens was charged with understanding at the time
of the debates in February of '62, that the bonds were
to be paid in coin. In a Floor discussion, he had said
he pitied no one "who has money invested in United
States Bonds payable in gold in twenty years, with
interest semi-annually." At another time, he had said

that even a miser would invest his money in "United States loans at 6 per cent, redeemable in gold in twenty years; the best and most valuable permanent investment that could be desired." [42]

Representative Garfield called the attention of the House to these words of Stevens as showing conclusively that he intended payment of the bonds in gold, and not in lawful money. Old, broken and in pain, the Lancastrian was "too feeble to explain this whole matter," but would "take occasion hereafter to expose the villainy of those who charge me with having said on the passing of the five-twenty bill, that its bonds were payable in coin." It was "a total perversion of the truth," and even "an absolute falsehood."

He pointed out that the whole debate from which his remarks were quoted, was on an entirely different bill, and before any discussion whatsoever of the medium of bond payment. That was correct, and if Garfield were not utterly partisan, he would have so announced. But had he done so, he would not only have weakened, but destroyed, his argument. Furthermore, Stevens answered that he "spoke only of payment in gold after twenty years, as no one doubted the resumption of specie payment." [43]

He was quite perturbed. It was a matter of many millions of dollars to the Government. Too weak to make a frontal attack, and near death, (within the next month he was in his grave) he did a striking thing. It was the year for presidential election. The Democrats had nominated Seymour and with him for the Vice-Presidency, Francis Blair, Jr., Stevens' oldtime enemy. Stevens had consistently condemned the Blairs and everything they stood for. He blamed them for Lincoln's War policy, which he did not consider aggressive enough; he blamed them for the Hampton Roads Conference; he blamed them for a weak-kneed reconstruction policy, and above all, they were Democrats.

But Seymour and his Democratic party had taken no stand to pay the bondholders in gold.[44] Stevens felt his party leaned toward gold payment. Amusing the Nation and shocking the House, when a member insisted that the obligations must be paid in gold, he said, "If I knew that any party in this country would go for paying in coin that which is payable in money, thus enhancing it one-half; if I knew there was such determination this day on the part of my party, I would vote for the other side, Frank Blair and all."

He would aid no such swindle upon the tax payers of the country; "I would vote for no such speculation in favor of the large bondholders, the millionaires who took advantage of our folly in granting them coin payment of interest, and I declare—well, it is hard to say it—but if even Frank Blair stood upon the platform of paying the bonds according to the contract and the Republican candidates stood upon the platform of paying bloated speculators twice the amount which we agreed to pay them, then I would vote for Frank Blair, even if a worse man than Seymour headed the ticket." [45]

To the Republican New York *Tribune*, Stevens, in standing for payment of the bonds in lawful money, was a "swindler." Typical city newspaper, it showed the intensity of its fervor for the bondholders by remarking upon the Commoner's challenge, "if he wishes to

swindle efficiently, let him join the party to which
swindling is natural—that one which will gratify by
repudiation its partisan malignity as well as its innate
rascality." [46]

Horace Greeley said of Stevens that "no swindler
that the world has known ever perpetrated a fraud so
gigantic as that he meditates." [47] The Republican party
leaders were unmoved. They did "not intend to accept
the Old Commoner's interpretation. Everyone of
their papers assails him." [48]

Back home, his remarks created such a resentment
that many thought his "chances for renomination to be
wholly worthless." [49] Writing from Washington on
July 23, he insisted he had "not declared for Seymour
and Blair and never expected to. I have only declared
against fools and swindlers who have fabricated the most
atrocious falsehoods as to my position upon the currency question." [50]

In a long letter to his banker friend, Gyger, of Lancaster, on July 28, he reviewed his financial policy, insisting that he never had any thought but that the five-
twenty bonds were payable in lawful money. [51]

It remained for his bitter enemy, the Democratic
New York *World*, to point out the truth. After his
death, that newspaper said he was "the author of more
evil than any other human being on the globe," but in
fairness, it would give "the devil his due . . . by correcting misrepresentations . . . put forth in yesterday's *Tribune*. We had marked pages enough in the
Congressional *Globe* to overwhelm his adversaries, but
his own vindication renders it unnecessary that we produce them. It is perfectly absurd to quote Mr. Stevens'

explanation of the House Bill as his opinion of the actual law. He said nothing about the five-twenty bonds, for no five-twenty bonds were contemplated by the original bill. He believed that twenty-year bonds would be paid in coin only because he thought specie payments would be resumed before they fell due." [52]

And before the session ended, the matter was cleared to Stevens' satisfaction. The five-twenty bonds were exchanged, par for par in new bonds payable in gold in thirty and forty years. The Old Commoner quickly put his finger on the point. "If the five-twenties had already been payable, principal and interest in gold, nothing need have been said except as to time, which the Government had the right to extend, but they did provide that the bonds to be substituted," be payable in gold and bear interest at only four, instead of six per cent. The interest reduction was the equivalent of the difference between lawful money payment and gold payment. "If the principal were already payable in gold, there could have been no occasion to repeat it nor to reduce the coin interest by one-third. This proposition, containing so just and convenient an arrangement . . . was a happy thought, settling an irritating question."

To Stevens, it was vindication in full of his position. Closing the incident, he said, "It does not do to exult but it must be gratifying to those who held that there was a difference in value between the five-twenties and what they would be worth if they were payable in coin." [53]

Stevens at no time posed as an authority on the theoretical side of money matters. The task of suggesting ways and means to finance the country in a great emergency was thrust upon him in an official capacity. Most of the adverse criticism levelled at him is based upon the legal tender enactments. As he so often reiterated, he would have issued only $150,000,000 of the money, and had his plan been adopted, no one has shown that more would have been required. But Congress would not accept his proposal. A policy was adopted in utter contravention of the very plans Stevens had for limiting greenback issues. If the War could have been financed with the modest issue of legal notes he suggested no one can fairly say that it would have been unintelligent financing.

In the aimless course adopted by the Congress, it was found necessary to create more than a half billion dollars of them. This proved expensive and even prodigal. In dollars and cents these issues cost the United States Government the difference between their aggregate parity and the real value of that for which they were exchanged. Exactly how much this is cannot be found. Estimates are as varied as the estimators.

Spalding, a member of Stevens' committee, claimed to have been the author of the original greenback idea and no one has ever challenged his statement.[54] It is recorded that Stevens at first thought the fiat unconstitutional, believing in Webster's definition of money.[55] If this be fact, he never indicated it, for whatever argument he had in the Committee, once it had agreed, it was his policy to stand firm.

When the bill came to the Floor of the House, he made the ablest Constitutional argument in favor of it, holding that under the implied powers of the Government it had authority to issue legal tender notes.

From the moment Congress adopted a policy which opened the door to unlimited issues of these notes, Stevens was in opposition. In 1862, he said, "I do not approve of the present financial system of the Government." [56] In 1864, he said the same thing.[57] Less than a month before he died, he wrote, "I have not approved and do not now approve of the financial policy pursued by our government for the last six years. I think we have thrown away our billions and are still throwing away our millions by mismanagement." [58]

His greatest objection was to the payment in gold of interest on the national debt when the country was off the gold standard. To him such action was reprehensible and deliberately unjust. He estimated that insistance upon it cost the Government $737,000,000 more than his plan would have cost [59] and he never lost an opportunity to condemn the methods adopted.

Why should the country have two forms of currency; one which it used to pay the soldier and his widow, and the other the capitalist and bondholder? [60] These are not the words of a demagogue. Fair critics must find them honestly uttered, with no desire other than to see justice done. As is generally the case, in time of War, the money powers were looking out for themselves.

In the Civil War, they saw to it that they got at least all they deserved for lending their money to the country. Stevens frequently referred to the "conclusive arguments of the bankers and brokers of New York," who, through their influence in the Senate, inserted a provision which made interest on bonds payable in gold.[61] In describing them, he said the "New York money-changers made their appearance, Jew and Gentile mingling in sweet communion to discover some cunning invention to make in a day what it would take weeks for honest men to earn." [62]

There has been much hocus-pocus written about the lofty patriotism of the bankers during the War of the Rebellion, but it takes no intense study to reach the conclusion that the lobbyists of the money interests got results for their employers. Stevens was practically the only man in Congress, who from the beginning of the wasteful financing of the War, openly and boldly told the truth about it. All he asked was fair and equal treatment for all.

He would have financed the War with long term bonds payable in gold at maturity with interest payable in lawful money, while the country was off specie. For currency he would have used a strictly limited amount of legal tender notes. To those who would argue that the trouble with the greenback theory is that it cannot be limited, answer is made that in Stevens' proposal of February, 1862, there was a logical plan for limitation which probably would have worked. Whether or not it would, is unanswerable. Certainly it cannot be said that it would not work, for it was never tried.

In normal times, by virtue of the very fact that they are normal, governments find no great money problems. When War or panic disturbs the financial equilibrium, those problems spring to the forefront of importance. No one in all history has ever been able to devise an all embracing solution.

Stevens' theory was sensible, apparently sound and geared to the emergency. Certainly it was more farsighted and constructive than the plan set forth in his Committee's Bill, and was in every way more business-like than the expensive and haphazard schemes finally adopted. No fair minded person could object because it would pay the rich man with the same kind of money used to pay the poor worker and the nation's soldiers. Stevens stood adamant to prevent deliberate discrimination against the masses in favor of the capitalists.

His labors in these matters alone vindicate his title of "Old Commoner."

BOOK FIVE
HELMSMAN

BOOK FIVE — HELMSMAN

I

THE CONSTITUTION

At the very outset of the War, a great Constitutional problem presented itself. The question that shaded all others into insignificance was the legal status of the seceded states. Men of intelligence quickly saw that some theory that would permit an aggressive war was necessary, or the whole conflict would end in stalemate. Moreover, that theory must have sufficient appeal to the people to arouse their sympathetic war support, and in the event of victory, permit a rational reconstruction.

In 1861, there were but few who did not hold that whatever action the Government took, it must be in accord with the Constitution. The Crittenden resolutions of July 22, 1861, almost unanimously adopted by both Houses of the Congress evidenced this. Lincoln himself had announced that the War was to be fought solely to defend the integrity of the Union.

It was insisted that the Constitution was the very basis on which that Union rested. Therefore, if the Government went outside Constitutional limits, it breached the very compact that the War was being fought to preserve. Surely if the Nation's policy were consistent, then its first duty was to hold that instrument inviolate and proceed under it. In fact, it was generally felt that the Constitution was the very epitome of everything for which the North was fighting.

If that were true, the Nation could wage war only through Constitutional means. All rights, and equality of the States must be respected. There could be no interference with State governments or their domestic laws. Pendleton reiterated this position in his resolutions of July 31, 1861. "The Federal Government dared not," he submitted, "destroy any of the States or reduce them. All of their Constitutional relations must at all times be recognized and held inviolate, and even if the Union arms were successful, peace must be established on a basis of full integrity of the States." The Government was bound to treat a State that warred against it exactly the same way as a loyal state.

If that were the rightful and accurate interpretation, then it was plain that the Nation could never conquer the Confederacy. If that doctrine were correct, then even the mild Lincoln was wrong in the War measures he had already taken. If that theory were followed, the Government had no right to blockade Southern ports, and no right to send soldiers to retake its property.

It was wrong for Lincoln to suspend the Writ of Habeas Corpus. Confiscation of slave property could not be countenanced. Emancipation, military arrest, and practically every major War measure from the calling of the first troops to the recognition of the last slave state under reconstruction was utterly illegal and wholly unconstitutional. Invasion of Southern territory without permission of the States themselves could not be justified and about all the Nation could do would be to mass its troops on the borders of the loyal states and defend itself from attack.

The practical result of this would be to admit the absolute efficacy of a secession and the Government's utter inability to prevent it. It was, in effect, merely a reiteration of the helpless doctrine laid down by President Buchanan in his last annual message. Certainly no one who believed that the Government had the right to preserve itself could subscribe to such views.

Stevens had seen the point before it was raised, and had prepared the only reasonable answer to it that could be justified on legal grounds. On the second day of August, 1861, the House was discussing a bill to confiscate slave property. This, of course, would result in a freeing of all slaves captured and a great objection was raised in the House on the ground that the Constitution would not permit such action on the part of the Government.

"Who is it," Stevens inquired, "that pleads the Constitution? Who says it must come in bar of our action?" Only the "advocates of rebels who fight to overthrow the Constitution and trample it in the dust."

The seceded states had not only breached the Constitution, they had wholly repudiated it. "These rebels who have destroyed and set at defiance that instrument are, by every rule of municipal and international law, estopped from pleading it against us." That was sound. If it is conceded that the Constitution should have been otherwise binding, by what line of legal reasoning could one party to it breach the compact and still insist that the other party be bound by its terms?

But Stevens went further. "I thought the time had come," said he, "when the laws of War were to govern our actions; when Constitutions, if they stood in the way of the laws of War in dealing with the enemy, had no right to intervene."

The Law of Nations was plain and had been "from the days of Cicero. 'In the midst of War, laws are silent'—is a rule that has been enforced down to the present time and any nation which disregards that rule is a poor, pusillanimous nation which submits its neck to be struck off by the enemy."

Stevens did not hedge on the measure. He spoke plainly. It was the first time his theory had been advanced on the Floor of the Congress, and he was severely questioned from many angles. One Congressman understood him "to admit that this bill is unconstitutional but to press his defense by urging its passage upon the ground that during the existence of the Rebellion and while the War continues in operation, this Congress has the right to do an unconstitutional act."

Stevens replied that what he asked was "Constitutional and according to the laws of the nations in time of War. (Laughter). I admit that if you were in a state of peace, you could not confiscate the property of any citizen. You have no right to do it in time of peace, but in time of War, you have the right to confiscate the property of every rebel." Then, questioned another, why legislate "to do what the country already has the right to do? Will the laws of War be rendered any more rigorous in consequence of any civil act this Legislative body may pass?"

Stevens' answer was "that the sovereign power must execute the Law of Nations. I deny the right of the executive in certain exigencies to carry into effect the Law of Nations unless the sovereign power gives him authority."[1]

At the outset, therefore, the Old Commoner held

that so far as the Confederate States were concerned, they could not insist that the War be levied on a Constitutional basis. His position at that time seemed to horrify the opposition.

Today, he is credited with advancing not only a correct theory, but the only one on which the Union cause could be prosecuted to victory. Certainly he was right when he said that no stretch of any legal principle forces one party to observe restrictions of a contract made with another when the second party has repudiated the agreement in its entirety. It is neither sense nor law to hold that the obligations of an instrument are binding on one party when that instrument has been renounced by the other.

But over and above all that, Stevens pointed out that the Constitution of the United States never contemplated a War between the States; made no provision for it and, therefore, could not be controlling if ever such emergency arose. The Government must proceed under the Laws of War. The Constitution would be wholly respected and lived up to as far as relationships with the loyal States were concerned. Further than that, it was in no sense binding.

Not only did he speak for that policy; he acted under it in a straight-forward manner that was refreshing. When the Virginia Legislature at Richmond passed a secret secession ordinance in April of 1861 the representatives of its western counties, which were largely loyal, met under the protection of Federal soldiers at Wheeling and presumed to restore a loyal Government to the State. Putting themselves on record as representing the State of Virginia, they proceeded in Constitutional order to divide the State and seek admission of the dismembered part to the Union. The bill to admit West Virginia came up in the House in December of 1862.

Expert Constitutionalists were hard-pressed to hold the proceeding legal. Everyone knew that the majority of the people of Virginia were sympathetic with the secession policy that the State had regularly adopted. It was plain that the minority, combined in Western Virginia, were the only ones who agreed to a division of the parent State. The truth was that Virginia itself had given no consent to its division and a majority of the citizens never would.

Congress, however, was largely in favor of admitting the new division and needed only a reasonable theory to stand upon. Still following the idea that the Federal Government could act only under the Constitution, many were attempting to justify their votes on the ground that the procedure by which West Virginia was seeking admission had been entirely in accord with the compact.

Stevens was honest enough to think and speak the truth about it. He did "not desire to be understood as being deluded with the idea that we are admitting this State in pursuance of any provisions of the Constitution." He found nothing there that could justify it. "The argument in favor of the Constitutionality of it is one got up by those who either honestly entertain an erroneous opinion or who desire to justify by a forced reconstruction, an act which they have predetermined to do."

It was "but mockery to say that the Legislature of

Virginia has ever consented to this division." Only two hundred thousand out of a million and a quarter people participated in the proceeding. Pursuant to a decree of that Convention, delegates met and formed a government. But at the time of that meeting, the State itself had a "legal organization and a Constitution under which that corporation must act."

The large majority of the people of Virginia had directed secession. That, of course, he said was treason. "But so far as the Commonwealth or corporation was concerned, it was a valid act and governed the State." To say that the Legislature which called the seceding Convention was not the Legislature of Virginia, was asserting that the Legislature chosen by a vast majority of the people of the State was not the Legislature of that State. To this doctrine, he would never subscribe.

He would admit that that body was disloyal, but it was still the disloyal and traitorous Legislature of the State of Virginia; and the State as a mere State, was bound by its acts. Afterward, a "highly respectable and very small number of the citizens of Virginia—the people of West Virginia—assembled together, disapproved of the Acts of the State of Virginia, and with the utmost complacency, called themselves 'Virginia.' Now," he asked, "is it not ridiculous? Is not the very statement of the facts a ludicrous thing to look upon?" But for all that, he would vote for its admission. He would not stultify himself "by supposing that we have any warrant in the Constitution for our proceeding." He would do it "not by virtue of any provision of the Constitution, but under the absolute power which the laws of War give us in the circumstances in which we are placed." On that theory would he vote and upon that alone.[2]

Stevens' position on the Constitutional relationship of the seceded states was clear and consistent from the very beginning. It was that the Ordinances of Secession, plus the declaration of War and active waging of it against the Nation, took the States out from under the Constitution.

Eminent authority has held that this meant "that secession had been temporarily successful." Such is not at all the fact, for the Old Commoner never admitted the legal accomplishment of the withdrawal so far as the Nation itself was concerned, and his argument contrariwise is conclusive.

No one who studies the Lancastrian's life can fail to see that he would never consent to a reconstruction plan that permitted even the last vestiges of slavery. If the Federal Government had no right to interfere with that institution where it existed within the States, then it was necessary to reduce the areas where it did exist to something less than a state status. Stevens' first step was to convince the country that the seceding states had, by their deliberate acts, irretrievably repudiated the Constitution, and therefore taken themselves out from under it. From that it must closely follow that they were no longer States within the Union.

When the Government conquered them, it was under no obligation to recognize the old state boundaries nor the areas as anything except so much conquered territory. If the sections were ever again to attain statehood, it must be by an erection of new states and a formal admission into the Union.

That suited precisely, for it gave the Congress the all-important power to everlastingly purge the Nation of slavery.

Shellabarger of Ohio in the House, and Sumner in the Senate, realizing the soundness of this doctrine, seized it immediately after Stevens pronounced it, and with the nice adornments of their language, presumed to make some refinement in it. If the trouble is taken to boil down their many pages of eloquent verbosity, one finds the residue is nothing other than Stevens' rugged plan. It was the theory finally adopted by the Congress, and the one which Constitutional experts of to-day commend as the only consistently legal one.

Stevens proposed it a few months after hostilities began. At the time, it was shocking to the conservative Nation. But he stuck to it while it was tried in the flaming crucible of War. It met all tests and emerged as the fundamental framework on which the great Reconstruction was laid.

II

EMANCIPATION

Lincoln was elected on a platform that would prevent slavery extension. At the outset of the War, he
defined his purpose as one solely to defend and protect
the Union. That was an all-embracing appeal and rallied more support to the Government than any other
that could have been used.

Stevens approved Lincoln's strategy as far as it went,
but that was not far enough for him. He was resolutely
and unqualifiedly for the Union, but with the Nation
in arms, would not rest there. The old Union with
slavery in it must pass. He would have a new United
States with slavery irrevocably eradicated. In fact, he
early saw a possibility that a reunited country might
go even to the entire fulfillment of his Utopian dreams
in establishing a status where all men would be equal
before the law.

Up to the very moment that War came he had stood
in a good Constitutional position. Speaking in Congress early in 1860, he stated that his purpose was not
to disturb slavery where the Constitution protected it,
but to prevent its further extension and abolish it where
Congress had the power.[1]

War among the States, as Stevens saw it, removed
all Constitutional barriers. He was convinced and repeatedly stated that the South had deliberately brought
about the conflict. With that view, he now could ask
boldly for everything he desired.

He did not move abruptly. Known as the most outspoken man in Congress, in this matter he showed him-

self strangely cautious. Expert diagnostician of the public mind, he apparently felt that his approach should
be a careful one, and so when Lincoln in the early
months, reiterated his original War purpose as one
solely of defense, Stevens was silent. He was prudent
enough not to endanger his hopes by thrusting them
upon the country while the fury which arose from Confederate capture of the Nation's fort in South Carolina
was raging.

On the other hand, he was astute enough not to let
the sentiment of the country crystallize around that
single war purpose, as Lincoln stated it. From the
outset, he understood that his strategy was to switch
the country from its original purpose, as the President
framed it to a dual purpose of Union preservation and
slavery abolition. Of course, if the second could be injected as a means to the former, it would be equally
satisfying. How to proceed to that end was the problem.

The slavery issue, which had vexed both North and
South for decades, was subdued in the early days of the
War in the spontaneous rally to defend the Union.
The country had been torn by it for so many years that
simple mention of it was obnoxious to both sides.
Eminent proof of this lay in the cold reception the
people gave the proponents of a stronger Fugitive
Slave Law on the one hand, and the Abolition advo-
cates on the other.

Now the Nation was at war. From the standpoint
of Stevens, the Equalitarian, the important thing about
that war was that slavery sympathizers were aligned
on one side against slavery opponents on the other. Out
of the conflict great changes might come. No one in

public life could foresee, not even Stevens himself dreamed that it would bring about such fundamental changes as were made by the Thirteenth, Fourteenth, and Fifteenth Amendments.

He had always championed equal rights for all. Here was an opportunity to obtain it. Far ahead of the people, he knew that the limit of their advance would be determined only by the lengths to which he could lead them. Tact, intelligence and skillful maneuvering were necessary. Encounter on the battlefields would be in other hands—his problem was to bring the thought of the country up behind him.

His strategy is a study in technique. As a leading supporter of the War, he was asked in Congress, three months after it started, to state its purpose. Scrupulously avoiding what might be dangerous consequences, as far as he then would go on record, the Nation had no positive purpose. The fact was, he parried, the conflict had been thrust upon the Nation. "Why say we make it for certain purposes when we do not make it at all? Ask those who have made it what is its object." Of only one thing was he certain; the Nation was fighting "to subdue the rebels." [2]

In that speech, however, which was closely attended, Stevens indicated the line of his attack. "If this War is continued long and is bloody," he prophesied, "I do not believe that the free people of the North will stand by and see their sons and brothers and neighbors slaughtered, by tens of thousands, by rebels with arms in their hands and forbear to call upon their enemies to be our friends and to help us in subduing them." [3]

For Stevens, this was mild language. It was probably the gentlest approach he ever made to a great issue. Strikingly guarded, but eager to prepare the people, he risked the statement that it would be the "doctrine of the whole free people of the North before two years roll round." [4]

From then on, "arming the black" became his minor objective. This was his wedge and it was an ingenious one. If he could bring the negro under Federal sponsorship, Stevens' battle was well begun. The negro's status as a soldier would bring the first glimmerings of some rights which he might claim.

Although Lincoln, prior to the presidency, had stated his Anti-slavery position in no uncertain terms, Stevens soon saw that the Executive would take no lead for emancipation. His historian advisor, George Bancroft, had written him that one of the results that the war should bring about, was an increase in the number of Free States. But Lincoln's ultra-conservative reply was that he would deal with the matter "with all due caution." He did not intimate the least assurance or promise even to his close friend.

It did not take long for the Lancaster Congressman to see that the only way Lincoln could be brought to emancipation was by pressure. Congress was largely conservative. The President, sometimes impressing his intimates as being actually opposed to emancipation, would at best lag. [5] Stevens' appeal must be to the people.

He knew that no legislation to that end could be passed at the time, and he therefore proposed no law. His first step was a resolution submitted to the House in December of 1861. It set forth that inasmuch as slavery had caused the present rebellion and that there could be no permanent peace and union in the republic so long as the institution existed; and inasmuch as slaves were being used by the rebels as an essential means of supporting and protracting the War and that by the Law of Nations it was right to liberate the slaves of an enemy to weaken his power—therefore, he would have the Congress request the President to declare free all slaves who would leave their masters or who would aid in quelling the rebellion.

Laying the groundwork for subsequent action of the abolition Generals in the field, he would also have the President direct army officers in command to order the freedom of all such slaves. But he would protect loyal citizens by pledging the faith of the Union to make full and fair compensation for all losses that they might sustain through such act.[6]

Emboldened by Stevens' proposal, Lovejoy, a week later, introduced a bill to protect fugitive slaves, which, of course, the Old Commoner supported.

Stevens' resolution came before the House in Committee of the Whole for discussion and debate in January of 1862. Upon it he delivered probably the greatest emancipation speech in all the history of Congress. He struck out boldly and directly. "The Declaration of Independence and the Constitution of the United States were a constant reproach to the slaveholding South."

In palpable contradiction to their domestic institutions, Southerners were conscious of the impropriety of being "governed by a Constitution which was an evident condemnation of their actual principles and of their institutions founded on individual despotism."

They feared that the proposition of "freedom and the equality of man before the law might be gradually breathed from the North into Southern ears and Southern minds and establish there the doctrine of the rights of man." They determined to arrest that "evil by building up a barrier between freedom and slavery."

He submitted facts showing how the South had very deliberately prepared itself for "rebellion" and took Lincoln's election as the cue to act.

Now grim War was upon the Nation and it was the "appropriate time to solve the greatest problem ever submitted to civilized man." He spoke of the divine right of kings and the hereditary right of lords and nobles to govern the people without their consent. Always those rulers had insisted that the "people were incapable of self-government and that free republics could not exist except in small communities where all could assemble for deliberation."

They denied utterly the possibility of maintaining a widely extended representative republic controlled by universal suffrage and predicted "with utmost confidence the overthrow of this Union from internal dissensions." But eighty years of unexampled prosperity and loyal support seemed to belie their predictions.

"We were fast establishing on a firm basis the great truths proclaimed by our fathers and which formed a memorable epoch in the science of Government. But the unhallowed ambition of the most infamous traitors that ever disgraced the earth is now concurring with the wish of the prophets of despotism to accomplish their prediction."

The Nation must refute "this argument of tyrants;

this attempt of unholy rebels." If the Government were victorious it would enjoy benefits that would compensate for all costs, and success in this dreadful issue would give to the Nation centuries of peace and constitutional freedom. Of equal importance to Stevens, a successful termination of the War would "give the civilized world assurance that the maintenance of perfect liberty, as well as regular Government is compatible with republican institutions."

But to conquer the South was no light task. He proposed his key question, which was, "how can this great rebellion be suppressed?" Beginning with the very simple and wholly apparent proposition, he cited Vattel to show that self-preservation was the duty of the Nation. The War had gone on for nearly a year with but indifferent success. He warned the country that Southern soldiers "are as brave as yours, nor have we abler generals than they," and if the War were to be prosecuted "on its present principles, the South could never be reduced."

Some new mode of attack must be found; some more effective means adopted. So long as Southerners were left the means of cultivating their fields through forced labor, "you may expend the blood of tens of thousands of free men and billions of money, without being any nearer the end, unless you reach it by your own submission, the ruin of the Nation and the destruction of constitutional freedom." Their domestic institutions gave them great advantages over the Free States in time of War. They need not and they did not withdraw a single hand from the cultivation of the soil. Their free men never labored. "Every able-bodied white man can be spared for the army. Although the black man never lifts a weapon, he is really the main stay of the War."

On the other hand, the North, with twenty millions of free men, "cannot spare much over one-fourth of its able-bodied men for War." The agricultural, mechanical and manufacturing businesses required the rest. It could not be denied that the "weakness of the South is her great strength in time of War, if her enemy is willing to permit it. What, then, must be done to save the Union and constitutional liberty?"

With attention of the House focused upon him, he announced his answer: "Prejudice will be shocked, weak minds startled, weak nerves may tremble; but they must hear and adopt it. Those who now furnish the means of War, but who are the natural enemies of slaveholders, must be made our allies." Plowman for Lincoln, he told the country, "universal emancipation must be proclaimed to all."

That assertion was the first championship of a general liberation and by far the boldest statement of it that had been made on the Floors of Congress up to that time. The Congress heard it; the country heard it; and so did the President. Truly, as Stevens said, weak minds might be startled and weak nerves might tremble, but from then on he would concentrate all his energies upon it. The country must understand that it was the only possible way to victory.

If slaves no longer raised cotton and rice, tobacco and grain for the rebels, the War would cease abruptly. Even if the liberated slaves should not lift a hand against their masters, Southern fields would produce not nearly

enough to sustain the Confederate States and uncon-
ditional submission would be the immediate and necessary result.

Sympathizers with treason might raise an outcry
about the horrors of a resulting servile insurrection.
But, "which is more to be abhorred—a rebellion of
slaves challenging their masters, or a rebellion of free
men fighting to murder the Nation? Which seems to
you the more cruel—calling on bondsmen to quell the
insurrection or shooting down their masters to effect
the same object? You send forth your sons and brothers
to shoot and sabre and bayonet the insurgents, but you
hesitate to break the bonds of their slaves to reach the
same end. What puerile inconsistency!"

There were some who would "prate learnedly about
the Constitution and object to the measure because it
would authorize Congress to interfere with slavery in
the States." He passed the point with the all embracing answer he found occasion to use frequently after
War had begun: the "Constitution now is silent and
only the Laws of War obtain."

He admitted there was no authority by express provision in the Constitution to emancipate the slaves.
But "whence," he asked, "do you derive authority to
kill the rebels? That is given by no express power in
the instrument. You do it as a means of granted power
to suppress insurrection." Hence, also, the power of
emancipation.

But even if nothing express or implied were there
given "and it became inevitably necessary for the safety
of the people, the first law of Nature would give it."
The people's safety was the supreme law.

All had to admit that slavery was the cause of the
War "and without it we would have a united and happy
people." But so long as it existed anywhere there could
be no solid Union. No limited emancipation, therefore,
was sufficient. A sweeping liberation of all slaves was
the only possible answer. Doing the thing partly would
hold no lasting good. "Patch up a compromise now,
leaving this germ of evil and it will soon again over-run
the whole South, even if you free three-fourths of the
slaves. Your peace would be a curse. You would have
expended countless treasures and untold lives in vain.
The principles of our Republic are wholly incompatible
with slavery. They cannot live together. While you
are quelling this insurrection at such fearful costs, remove the cause, that future generations may live in
peace."

But he would do no injustice to loyal men. While
he never admitted "the rightful ownership of any human
being in any human soul," he would, "in deference to
chronic error and prejudice, treat them as if such a
thing were possible." He offered a plan for compensated emancipation of the slaves of loyal owners, esti-
mating that the liberation would cost the government some $440,000,000. Such was wholly justifiable,
for "manumit the slaves" and the War would end in
six months. "Leave them to the rebels, and I doubt if
six years will end it. Six years with slavery and a debt
of two billion dollars; manumition with peace in six
months, slavery extinguished, and a debt of five hundred million. These are the alternatives. Let the tax-
payers and patriots choose between them."

Manumition might be merciful, but it also was "the

most terrible weapon in our armory." But that should be no argument against its use, for "instruments of war are not selected on account of their harmlessness. You choose the cannon that has the longest range; you throw the shell that will kill the most men by its explosion; you grind to its sharpest edge the bayonet sabre."

Of Lincoln's rebuke to Freemont for liberating captured slaves, he said, "we have put a sword into one hand of our generals and shackles into the other. Freemen are not inspirited by such mingled music."

With subtle approach to expanding the War purpose as Lincoln framed it, he said, "Let the people know that this government is fighting, not only to enforce a sacred compact, but to carry out to final perfection, the principles of the Declaration of Independence, which its founders expected would long since have been fulfilled on this Continent, and the blood of every free man will boil with enthusiasm and his nerves be stirred in this unholy warfare."

Over in the White House, the President was watching and waiting. Stevens knew Lincoln well enough to appreciate how much prodding it would require to move him, and lost no time beginning. He mentioned the awful "responsibility" which rested "on those in authority. Their mistakes may bring mourning upon the land and lasting sorrow to many a fireside. Let them not say 'it may come at last, but not yet!' Remember that every day's delay costs the Nation one million five hundred thousand dollars and hundreds of lives."

He was disappointed by the President's quiescent

From the Lancaster County Historical Society Collection.

The Only Known Authentic Portrait of Lydia Smith, Stevens' Mulatto Housekeeper. Made After the Old Commoner's Death

attitude, even though the loyalty of the middle states might be at stake. "If an effectual course is not to be pursued for fear of offending border state friends, better submit at once, and if we cannot save our honor, save at least the lives and treasure of our Nation."

Aiming directly at Lincoln, he said, "if those in authority will not awake to their responsibility and use the stern energy necessary for the public safety, let the people speak and teach them that this is a responsible government in which the rulers are the servants of the people."

What an opportunity was presented to the Republic to vindicate her consistency and become immortal! The occasion "is forced upon us and the invitation presented to strike the chains of four millions of human beings and create them men; to extinguish slavery on this whole continent; to wipe out so far as we are concerned, the most hateful and infernal blot that ever disgraced the escutcheon of men; to write a page in the history of the world, whose brightness shall eclipse all the records of heroes and sages." [7]

This speech of the Old Commoner was the first step in the country's march to the Thirteenth Amendment. Before it, the Anti-Slavery movement had rested solely on a moral basis. Stevens took the issue from that narrow bottom and set it on a broad and practical foundation. He held forth emancipation as the only sure means of war success.

His argument was convincing and efficient. It enticed to the emancipation cause all loyal Northern men. Abolitionists found hard-hearted practical men and political leaders who had previously little tolerance for them rapidly moving to their support. The North must conquer the Confederacy. If that could be brought about only through emancipation, then emancipation must be invoked.

Stevens had definitely opened the way to enlarge the War purpose. Slave liberation became a means as well as an end. Before his speech, the North believed it was fighting solely to preserve the Union, and gave little thought to whether or not slavery would remain. After the speech, the War purpose of Stevens was made the purpose of the country—the old Union, of course, but with slavery gone from it forever.

Before he spoke, Congress seemed reluctant to even discuss emancipation, fearing that such might divide the North. But Stevens' argument was irrefutable. Slave liberation no longer appeared a vexing problem to divide the Nation; it was elevated to the dignity of a patriotic necessity.

The Old Commoner's address was an intelligent and daring appeal, over Lincoln's head, to the country.

Biding his time, the President seemed reluctant to even discuss the wiping out of slavery. But from this time on, he found himself between the House leader, Stevens, and the people. Pressed on both sides, he later wrote his name as the Great Emancipator, but actually he was forced to that position.

Had the War ended then, emancipation propaganda would have been smothered in a desire to forget the War and everything about it, and slavery would no doubt, have been retained. Stevens would not have gained the prominence he did and the new Union might have been much like the old. But the South was to be con-

quered neither easily nor quickly. Her very strength
in the early War gave Stevens opportunity to bring the
country to him and so made way for the three great
amendments, which stand out as milestones to Democracy.

By March, Lincoln felt that the country was calling
for some kind of emancipation. He recommended to
Congress a proposal that the Government cooperate
with states which would adopt a gradual abolition by
extending financial aid to them to compensate their
citizens for losses so sustained. The President based
his recommendations on the very grounds that Stevens
invented. The Lancastrian introduced Lincoln's message and had it, without discussion, referred to Committee of the Whole on the state of the Union.[8]

A few days later, when debate arose as to when
it should be considered, he showed what he thought of
it. He was forced to confess that he was unable "to
see what made one side so anxious to pass it and the
other so anxious to defeat it." To him, it was "the most
diluted milk- and water-gruel proposition" that was
ever given to the American Nation. The only reason
he could find why "any gentlemen should wish to postpone the measure is for the purpose of having a chem-
ical analysis to see whether there was any poison in it." [9]
When it first came before the House for discussion,
there was an apparent approval which seemed to indicate its passage. But Stevens led a determined opposition to it.

He would go so far as to pay for the slaves of loyal
men, but he would hear nothing of any offer to compensate rebel owners for the loss of slaves which might

be freed. Wadsworth took him to task for refusing to yield, even when "the President called upon him to do so." Stevens' terse reply was that "whenever the President of the United States or any one else convinces me that I am wrong, then I will give up. Until then, the gentleman will find me pursuing the course I have commenced." [10]

Missing no opportunity, the Lancastrian agitated constantly for slavery abolition in the District of Columbia.[11] That area was Stevens' most advantageous battle ground, because it was under the direct supervision of the Congress, and even cautious men might be led to use it as a laboratory for emancipation experiments.

In May, two of Lincoln's Generals attempted some emancipation of their own. Hunter proclaimed that the persons in the three States of Georgia, Florida, and South Carolina, "heretofore held as slaves, are declared forever free." Humphreys followed with a similar action for a part of Virginia eight days later.

Lincoln lost no time in voiding the two proclamations. In a part of that order, he showed that he had adopted Stevens' argument and was preparing the way for some kind of emancipation in the event he had to come to it. In characteristic, guarded language, he said, "I further make known that whether it be competent for me as Commander-in-Chief of the Army and Navy to declare the slaves of any state or states free, and whether at any time, in any case, it shall become a necessity indispensable to the maintenance of the Government to exercise such suppressed powers, are questions which under my responsibility, I reserve to myself."

He had now come far enough to indicate that if emancipation were an indispensable necessity, he might use it. But as his later statements showed, he was by no means convinced that it was a necessity. He injected into his order an extraneous reference to his gradual abolition proposal and made another "earnest appeal for it."

There can be no doubt that at this time Lincoln favored some kind of manumission, but if he were to have his way, it would be a long dragged out program of compensated liberation. Of course, he was, in spite of everything, clinging tenaciously to what he believed to be a good Constitutional position.

Congress was preponderantly behind the President in May of this year. In that month, his March 6th proposal to give the states pecuniary aid for gradual slavery abolition was voted upon by both bodies. The House adopted the resolution by a vote of eighty-nine to thirty-one, and the Senate joined in approval by vote of thirty-two to ten. When one notices the overwhelming votes by which this assertion of policy was made, it is difficult to understand just why nothing ever came of it. It seems that either the Congressmen recorded their votes as they did merely to show constituents that they were supporting the President, or Stevens and his group were making such rapid headway that the resolutions could not be made effective by enactment into law.

At any rate, it is significant that the combined forces of the Executive and two-thirds of the Congress did not even attempt to consummate their policy, which was opposed by Stevens and his scant few followers.

During the summer, the Old Commoner was encouraged by two specific victories. Congress, at the instance of himself and his co-workers, had advanced far enough to prohibit military and naval officers "from employing any of the forces under their respective commands for the purpose of returning fugitive slaves." And late in July, military commanders were directed "to employ as laborers, so many persons of African descent as can be advantageously used for military and naval purposes." Moreover they were to be paid "wages for their labor."

At about that time, Lincoln in strict confidence, submitted to his Cabinet a draft of a proclamation in which he stated that it was his purpose "upon the next meeting of Congress, to again recommend the adoption of a practical measure for tendering pecuniary aid to the free choice or rejection of any and all states which may then, by recognizing and practically sustaining the United States and which then may have voluntarily adopted, or thereafter may voluntarily adopt, gradual abolishment of slavery within such state or states; that the object is to practically restore, thenceforward to be maintained, the Constitutional relation between the general government and each and all the states wherein that relation is now suspended or disturbed; and that for this object War, as it has been, will be prosecuted, and as a fit and necessary result for effecting this object, I, as Commander-in-Chief of the Army and Navy of the United States, do order and declare that on the first day of January, in the year of our Lord one thousand eight hundred and sixty-three, all persons held as slaves within any state or states wherein the Con-

stitutional authority of the United States shall not then
be recognized, submitted to and maintained, shall then,
thenceforward and forever be free."

This contemplated pronouncement, of course, was
never issued. It was the first inkling of the sounder one
than was proclaimed in September. Lincoln was still
emphasizing his position inside the Constitution and
endeavoring as best he could to make all his acts consistent with the position he took in his inaugural address. When Greeley, in his New York *Tribune* of
August 19, submitted to Lincoln his "prayer of thirty
millions" urging emancipation, the President felt the
necessity of a reply. It was in usual Lincoln form,
and, although many words were used, threw little if
any light on his real attitude toward emancipation.

In part, he said, "as to the policy I seem to be pursuing, as you see, I have not meant to leave anyone in
doubt. I would save the Union. I would save it in
the shortest way under the Constitution.

"The sooner the national authority can be restored,
the nearer the Union will be to the Union that it was.

"If there be those who would not save the Union
unless at the same time save slavery, I do not agree with
them.

"If there be those who would not save the Union
unless at the same time destroy slavery, I do not agree
with them.

"My paramount object is to save the Union and
not to save or destroy slavery. If I could save
the Union without freeing any slaves, I would do
it—and if I could save it by freeing all the slaves,
I would do it—and if I could do it by freeing some

and leaving others alone, I would also do that." [12]

The pertinent parts of that so-called answer seem to indicate that Lincoln was still thinking of the Union as it was, and that slavery was a more or less irrelevant and immaterial question. Certainly no one from that writing could think of Lincoln as "The Emancipator."

But Stevens was waging his own fight in Congress, and it seems that he called on Lincoln occasionally to urge his emancipation program. At any rate, the President is reported as complaining to Senator John B. Henderson of Missouri of the Old Commoner and his collaborators constantly pressing him. "Stevens, Sumner and Wilson simply haunt me," said he, "with their importunities for a Proclamation of Emancipation. Wherever I go and whatever way I turn, they are on my trail, and still in my heart, I have the deep conviction that the hour has not yet come."

He said they reminded him of an incident in a little log school-house he had attended "when reading books and grammars were unknown. All our reading was done from the Scriptures, and we stood up in a long line and read in turn from the Bible. Our lesson one day was the story of the Israelites who were thrown into the fiery furnace and delivered by the hand of the Lord without so much as the smell of fire upon their garments.

"It fell to one little fellow to read the verse in which occurred for the first time in the chapter the names of Shadrach, Meshack, and Abednego. Little Bud stumbled on Shadrach, floundered on Meshach, and went all to pieces on Abednego. Instantly the hand of the master dealt him a cuff on the side of the head and left him wailing and blubbering, as the next boy in line took up the reading.

"But before the girl at the end of the line had done reading, he had subsided into sniffles and finally became quiet. His blunders and disgrace were forgotten by the others of the class until his turn was approaching to read again. Then like a thunderclap out of a clear sky, he set up a wail which alarmed even the master, who with rather unusual gentleness, asked what was the matter now. Pointing with a shaking finger at the verse which a few moments later would fall to him to read, Bud managed to quaver out, 'Look there, marster, there comes them same damn three fellers again!'" [13]

Two days after he had issued his preliminary proclamation in September, wavering Lincoln showed no joy in his act. He said, " I can only trust in God I have made no mistake." [14] He seemed to view emancipation merely as a matter of expediency, for in writing to Hannibal Hamlin shortly after he had announced it, he said that although the time for its impression southward had not come, "northward the effect should be instantaneous. It is six days old, and while commendation by newspapers and distinguished individuals is all that a vain man could wish, the stocks have declined and troops come forward more slowly than ever. This, looked soberly in the face, is not very satisfactory. We have fewer troops in the field at the end of the six days than we had at the beginning—the attrition among the old outnumbering the addition by the new. The North regards the Proclamation sufficiently in breath; but breath alone kills no rebels." [15]

In his second annual message, striving to be wholly

consistent, Lincoln quoted a part of his inaugural address that bore on slavery. Now, however, he would recommend the adoption of a resolution to amend the Constitution, so that slavery should be abolished "at any time or times before the first day of January, A. D. 1900" with compensation from the United States. One thing stands out in that message and that is the fact that he had by this time become convinced that "without slavery it, (the rebellion) could not continue."

He discussed at some length his compensated emancipation proposal with particular emphasis upon the thirty-seven years of time involved to perfect it. He used some estimates to argue its comparatively small costs. That, however, would have been more per person than he estimated, for his figures were based on a percentage increase that would make the population of the country in 1930 more than two hundred fifty-one millions of people. This, of course, is more than double what proved to be the fact.

A study of the message seems to indicate that at the time Lincoln wrote it, he was in grave doubt of the outcome of the War. He believed that his plan would "secure peace more speedily and maintain it more permanently than can be done by force alone; while all it would cost, considering amounts and manner of payment, and times of payment, would be easier paid than the additional cost of the War, if we rely solely on force. It is much—very much—that it would cost no blood at all."

Significantly, he said, "the plan is recommended not but that a restoration of national authority would be accepted without its adoption."

Hammering away through the summer, Stevens advocated "sending the army throughout the whole slave population of the South, asking them to go from their masters, take the weapons which we furnish and join us in this War of freedom against traitors and rebels. Until that policy is adopted, I have no hope of success." [16]

He was brave in assuming such an advanced position. That fall he must face his constituents for reelection. But back in Lancaster, he spoke just as openly as he had in Congress. The Government must separate the slaves from their owners and rally them to Union support. "Yet," he complained "we are, at the point of the bayonet, keeping them loyal to their masters instead of to the Union."

Southeastern Pennsylvania had paid heavy toll in casualties and deaths and it registered when he asked if it "would not be better that fifteen thousand armed slaves should lie wounded around the battlefields near Manassas than that your friends and mine should be there?"

In his many speeches, he rarely missed putting some pressure on the President. He told his constituents that he had protested against the Government's policy of refusing to accept negro soldiers "not only to the people, but to the face of the President and his Cabinet, as well as on the Floor of the Congress." He warned them that they were exercising too much levity at the request of border statesmen, "not one of whom, in my judgment, has loyalty in his heart."

Lincoln was still slowly feeling his way. When Stevens called upon him personally to press his demands, the President heard him, considered a moment, and cautiously replied, "it may come to this." [17] The exact date of this conversation is not known, but it must have occurred late in the summer. It indicates that Stevens and Lincoln were dealing with each other at arm's length, for the President could have made no intimation to Stevens of the emancipation draft which he read before his Cabinet on July 22. He appears to have permitted Stevens to go his way, satisfied to observe the drift of the country. But all the time he kept a watchful eye on the Lancastrian and his co-workers, prepared to follow them if expedient. /

Relying upon the correctness of his diagnosis of public opinion, Stevens was not afraid to differ with Lincoln, even at the risk of losing his Congressional office. It required some daring, to announce, "I will not go with the President in paying for all the slaves—I did not vote for his resolution—I will not vote to pay for any slave of a rebel." Already he sensed the country's trend toward him in his policy to free and arm the black. Naively and so that the President might notice, he said, "I have spoken so in Congress in the last week, and after a few remarks of mine, the vote was eighty-four to forty-two—eighty-four agreeing with me where a year ago, not fifty could have been found."/

Stevens would not stop half way. Any talk of separation or of a country divided was treason. He would "free every slave, slay every traitor, and burn every rebel mansion if these things were necessary to preserve this Temple of Freedom." The time called for action and not waiting. "He who falters now is a traitor, not only to his country, but to himself, and to his God." [18]

[380]

On that blunt platform he placed his candidacy in the hands of his people. He had a Democratic opponent who referred to him as a "pestilent abolitionist." [19] But the Old Commoner disdainfully ignored him.

Less than a week after Stevens delivered his campaign speech, Lincoln suddenly issued his first Proclamation setting forth that on January 1 of 1863, he would declare free the slaves in all rebel territory. The Lancastrian had sensed the temper of the people before Lincoln and as his guide and prod had done a good job of preparing the way. Busy in Washington, he wrote an open letter to his constituents in Lancaster County in which he said, "Lincoln's proclamation contained precisely the same principles which I had advocated." He referred to him as "the patriotic President" and promised that if elected, he would give him full support. [20]

All was well now. The President had abandoned his fully compensated emancipation plan and his idea of a constitutional amendment to have slavery eradicated by the year 1900. He had come to Stevens' demand for an unequivocal and immediate freeing of the blacks. On January 1 of 1863 he issued, as an Executive Order, his famous "Emancipation Proclamation."

And, so, Lincoln had finally been brought to emancipation. [21] Throughout the year 1861, he would hear nothing of it and some of those close to him, believed that he was actually opposed to it. [22] Certain it is that as he assumed the Presidency, he was willing to go to the very limit of Constitutionally guaranteeing perpetual slavery in the United States.

In his first annual message after both Houses of

Congress had passed an abortive Thirteenth Amendment, and before further action was taken, Lincoln said "I understand a proposed amendment to the Constitution . . . has passed Congress to the effect that the Federal Government shall never interfere with the domestic institutions of the States, including that of persons held to service. . . . I have no objection to its being made express and irrevocable."

In a letter to Seward in February of 1861, he advocated better enforcement of the Fugitive Slave Law.

Surely his journey from those positions in 1861 to his Proclamation of September 22, 1862, was a long one. The fact that the proclamations freed not a single slave is of relative unimportance.[23] As they were proclamations of Lincoln, it can be assumed that it was his conservative conclusion after intensive study that the country then demanded that much if not more. The Nation, or what was left of it, was surely for emancipation.

Stevens by the ingenuity and forcefulness of his speeches had led the people to that position. He it was who first pointed out that slave liberation was not only essential but the quickest and surest way of winning the War. Of course he had an extensive support both within and outside of Congress but he took the lead; he prepared the arguments and published them. He and his followers were in pitiful minority when they began their campaign, but in less than eighteen months their intensive work had drawn a majority of the country behind them. The President had been forced to follow.

There can be no question about this and Lincoln freely admitted it. His early reluctance and even objec-

tion he explained by saying that he first believed that
emancipation was wholly unconstitutional and such act
on his part would be in violation of his oath. He found
a consistent and logical argument for modifying his
stand by adopting literally the theory first proposed by
Stevens in his August 2 speech of 1861.

Said Lincoln, "I felt that measures otherwise unconstitutional might become lawful by becoming indispensable to the preservation of the Nation. Right
or wrong, I assumed this ground and now avow it. I
could not feel that, to the best of my ability, I had even
tried to preserve the Constitution if to save slavery or
any minor matter I should permit the wreck of Government, country and Constitution all together.

"When early in the War, General Freemont attempted military emancipation, I forbade it, because
I did not then think it an indispensable necessity. When
a little later, General Cameron, then Secretary of War,
suggested the arming of the blacks, I objected because
I did not think it an indispensable necessity. When still
later, General Hunter attempted military emancipation,
I again forbade it because I did not think the indispensable necessity had come.

"When in March and May and July of 1862, I made
earnest and successive appeals to the border States to
favor compensated emancipation, I believed the indispensable necessity for military emancipation and arming the blacks would come, unless averted by that measure. They declined the proposition, and I was, in my
best judgment. driven to the alternative of either sur-
rendering the Union and with it the Constitution, or of
laying strong hands upon the colored element. I chose

the latter. In choosing it, I hoped for greater gain than loss, but of this I was not entirely confident." [24]

Again in his own account, he said very frankly, "in telling this tale (of the Emancipation Proclamations) I attempt no compliment to my own sagacity. I claim not to have controlled events, but confess plainly that events have controlled me." [25]

Abraham Lincoln is known to history as the Great Emancipator, and, of course, it never can be disputed that it was his act and his act alone by which the Proclamations issued.

Preparing the way, leading the country to insist upon it, and finally actually forcing Lincoln to it, was the work of a small group, most of whom were in Congress, and of whom Thaddeus Stevens was one of the most prominent, if not the leading actor. Although the Lancastrian never aspired to any such great name as "Emancipator" the incontrovertible record certainly gives him some claim to that title.

Even in that day, the fact was recognized by those who had knowledge of what was going on. Probably the most authentic record of it is set out fairly, honestly and accurately by a man who frequently and sometimes bitterly challenged Stevens in his positions and in his procedures.

Representative Mallory of Kentucky, was no particular friend of the Commoner, as their many clashes indicate, but he left a memorial to Stevens inscribed upon the official records of the Congress. His report was made while the facts were fresh, on the Floor of the House and in the presence of those who would have reason to know if what he spoke were truth. Of great-

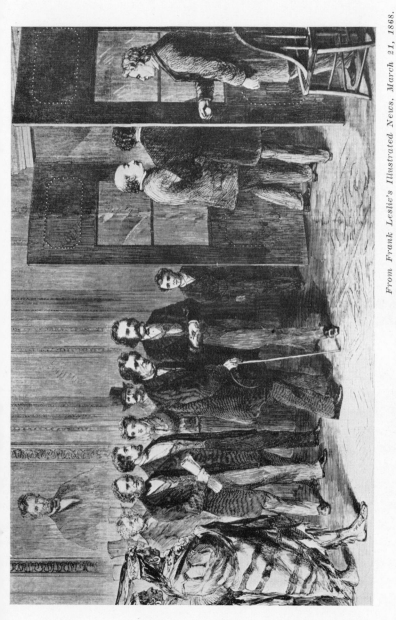

From Frank Leslie's Illustrated News, March 21, 1868.

Stevens Being Assisted to the Senate Chamber to Report Officially the Impeachment by the House of President Johnson

est significance is the fact that although so declared and so published, it was never challenged.

Said Mallory, summing up the emancipation movement, "soon after the War broke out, the gentleman from Pennsylvania (Stevens) and his great allies, Horace Greeley and Wendell Phillips, and all his little allies in the House, began their pressure on the President and the Republican Party. In vain the President from time to time besought his friends, and those who had not been his friends, to relieve him from this pressure.

"The gentleman from Pennsylvania and his allies persevered. They demanded of the President his proclamation of emancipation. He refused. Again they demanded it; he refused again, but more faintly, and exhibited himself in his letter to his 'dear friend Greeley' in the most pitiable and humiliating attitude in which an American President was ever exhibited to the American people. . . . But the gentleman from Pennsylvania still pressed him and educated him and the Republicans."

The Committee of Divines from Chicago, "armed with authority from the other but not the better world, was brought to aid in the pressure; but apparently in vain. Sir, do you remember the reply of the President to that committee? It was conclusive, unanswerable. The reasons given for refusing to proclaim the freedom of slaves in the rebel states are perfectly irrefutable. 'I have not the power to do it,' said the President, 'and if I had, the proclamation would be impotent; it would be like the Pope uttering his Bull against the comet.'

"We then supposed that the matter had been settled.

But scarcely had this confidence entered the great conservative heart of the Nation, when feeble or false, or both, or yielding to the teachings of the gentleman from Pennsylvania, he suddenly, without notice, issued his celebrated Emancipation Proclamation." [26]

In his writings and the reports of what he said, Stevens makes no reference to his part in emancipation. As was his custom, he was satisfied to rest upon the official record. At any rate, liberating the black from the shackles of slavery was but an incident in his program. It was merely the first step in obtaining for him equal rights before the law.

Abraham Lincoln is known as the Great Emancipator. As the whole truth becomes known, Thaddeus Stevens will ever more clearly appear as one who seemingly against the great President's will, gained for him that name.

III

RESTORATION UNDER LINCOLN

WITH Gettysburg and Vicksburg behind, it was clear that the War must end successfully for the Union. The appeal to arms had irrevocably concluded that the sovereignty of Statehood must be subservient to the sovereignty of the Nation. That dread court of War, from whose decision there lay no appeal on earth, had inscribed with its bloody pen that all which was the old South should pass. An aristocracy which rested on a slave support had shown itself offensive, and the empire which it had built in the short century and a half of its fruitfulness, lay crushed. It did not matter that in that empire there was much of beauty and romance, more of culture and larger living than in the North. All that must go so that a Nation might live at peace with itself.

The earnest South believed from its uttermost depths that its cause was right, but could find no forum for further hearing. Southerners might feel that in the destruction of their social institutions, civilization itself was the grievous loser, but in the bitterness of that feeling, they must weep alone. As they stood at the end of the War upon the threshold of a most uncertain prospect, they had cause aplenty to mourn their defeat, and it was best that they then could not know of the heartbreaking years just ahead.

Had a kindly, indulgent master been in control to weave them back into the Union, their fare, even then, would have been hard enough. Had someone sympathetic to their Constitutional interpretations and their culture, loomed into power to ease their way, still history would find their toll for daring to differ, heavily exacting. If the times had given a Union leader who, having the support of the North, could command the real ungrudging cooperation of the whole South in a yielding desire to get back into the Sisterhood of States, the ugly scars of the Reconstruction that mar American history might be absent. But the record bears a sadly different story.

The problem of restoring or reconstructing the areas in rebellion did not await the determination of the War. It precipitated itself upon the Government in slightly more than a year after the fighting began. The first rebel stronghold to fall before the Union arms was New Orleans, and its environs, which were captured by Federal forces late in April of 1862. With this large section of enemy territory suddenly thrust into the lap of the Nation, the all-important question arose. What was its status? Had it and its citizens merely strayed temporarily from the Union, in such manner that a speedy restoration should be granted, or was the recaptured area conquered territory and its people conquered enemies? The Government at the time gave no answer.

The President of the United States had been, through his military officers, in command of the operations in the War zones, and so it was but proper if his jurisdiction continued unchallenged, that he remain in control until the States were brought back into the Union. Accordingly, in August of that year, Lincoln appointed General George F. Shepley, formerly Mayor of New Orleans, Military Governor of Louisiana.

He, under Presidential instruction, called an election to designate Congressional representatives for Louisiana. The election was held but less than eight thousand votes were cast. In due course, the two Representatives presented themselves at Washington and were, without substantial objection, seated by the House on February 9 of 1863.

The quiet way in which these Louisiana Congressmen were permitted to take their seats, while of little importance in itself, is of highest significance to the student of Reconstruction. It indisputably proclaims that the House of Representatives at the time was in most tolerant frame of mind, and willing to go along with Lincoln on an easy restoration plan. Not only that, it would accept even an executive restoration.

As yet, the House had not been alarmed into mounting a guard to protect it from invasion of its jurisdiction. The fact of the matter is, the question of jurisdiction was hardly thought of. True it is that the wary and penetrating eye of Stevens already saw far enough ahead to perceive the consequences of this act of the House with the result that he refused to assent to the move. But the whole procedure was treated as of no more than passing importance. The Congress seemed satisfied when rebel territory was once conquered to join in most any reasonable plan permitting early reestablishment. No jealousies between it and the Executive showed themselves.

This was the critical period of the Reconstruction. One of the reasons that all seemed well was that slavery was unmentioned. There was, however, a deep-rooted feeling that no restoration policy would be acceptable that did not permanently eliminate slavery. Stevens was foremost in this attitude. He was merely watching and saying nothing. The smoldering embers that could ignite a nation into an all-consuming fire, burned on in his brain, kept alive only by a determination to battle to the death a restoration that permitted slavery and a far-called fear that such proposal might come. Had the conquered South been willing to yield when it laid down its arms, those flames would have been quenched by a deluge of overwhelming public disapproval, or would have burned themselves out through lack of fuel when Stevens realized that a gentle restoration was called for in the calendar of the Fates.

But this cooperative relationship of 1863 between the President and Congress which gave false promise of an easy and rapid restoration, soon moved through the varying shades of doubt, suspicion, distrust, concealed antagonism, and open conflict until it culminated on that fateful anniversary of Washington's birth in 1868 in a decisive vote by the House of Representatives, impeaching the President of the United States.

During the former year, the War went on, each engagement giving added hope of victory to the Union. The time drew near for Lincoln's annual message to Congress and he understood that sooner or later the Government must meet the problem of how to treat the conquered rebel states. Political strategist that he was, he assumed the lead position for his executive office by proposing a plan. This he did through no desire to intrude his department upon the jurisdiction of another branch of the Government, but mainly, it now appears, through a desire to be in a strong position to dictate a conservative restoration policy.

Accordingly, therefore, on December 8, 1863, in proclamation form, he presented to the Congress and the country, the first plan for dealing with the rebel states. It had received no great amount of study and was soon dubbed "Lincoln's Ten-Per-Cent Plan." However, it should be remembered that little opportunity had been given to develop a scheme, and furthermore, for our form of Government, history knew no precedent.

The proclamation was terse but in theory comprehensive, and was offered to all of the ten states then in rebellion.[1] The problem, of course, was to erect a loyal government in a territory that had shown itself disloyal.

At the outset, Lincoln recognized that "an attempt to guarantee and protect a revived State government, constructed in whole or in preponderating part from the very element against whose hostility and violence it is to be protected," was "simply absurd."

Some method must be invoked to distinguish the loyal from the disloyal, so that the foundations of a new State government could be laid on solid bottom. Lincoln thought that a sufficiently liberal test was one which would accept "as sound, whoever will make a sworn recantation of his former unsoundness." With this premise, he would exercise his executive authority to pardon the masses who had "directly or by implication participated in the Rebellion," upon their subscribing to a fixed oath which he set forth in his Proclamation.

The oath was brief. It required the subscriber to swear support of the Constitution and the Union, and

abide by the laws of Congress passed during "the existing Rebellion with reference to slaves," so long as the
Supreme Court had not changed them, and also to abide
by and support the Presidential proclamations referring to slaves.

Certain classes, however, were excepted from the
benefits of his offer. In fixing those groups, Lincoln
attempted to purge the new State governments of the
leaders of the Rebellion, and specifically excluded the
civil and diplomatic officers or agents of the Confederacy; those who had left judicial positions under the
United States to aid in the Rebellion; military officers
above the rank of colonel and naval officers above the
rank of lieutenant; those who had given up their seats
in the Congress to assist in the Rebellion; those who
had resigned commissions in the army or navy of the
United States and afterwards aided in the Rebellion,
and those who had treated colored persons or white
persons in charge of them, otherwise than lawfully as
prisoners of war.

As soon as groups in the ten rebel states, or any of
them, not less than one-tenth in number of the votes
cast in such state in the presidential election of 1860,
had taken such oath and if qualified to vote by the
state law, should reestablish Republican State Government, such, Lincoln promised, "shall be recognized
as the true government of the State" and would receive
full Constitutional protection.

The Proclamation itself was a bare plan but in the
President's message which accompanied it, he presented
his supporting brief. The message conclusively shows
that Lincoln's desire was to offer the states in Rebel-

lion an easy and gentle return. He referred to their
coming back as "resumption" and explained that he
presented his plan mainly as a rallying point for the
loyal elements.

Although he was careful to acknowledge that the
admission to Congress of members sent from any state,
rested "exclusively with the respective Houses, and not
to any extent with the executive," he, nevertheless, said
to the states in rebellion, that his plan could be accepted
as one "which they are assured in advance, will not be
rejected here."

Subsequently in his message, he wrote, "saying that
Reconstruction will be accepted if presented in a specified way, is not saying that it will never be accepted in
any other way." The inference is that the President
had no doubt of the executive authority to plan a restoration procedure and assure the rebel states of its acceptance. He felt no duty to confer with Congress in
the matter and treated it as subservient in the premises.
At the time the Legislative branch occupied no large
space in the picture, and he would "trust that Congress
will omit no fair opportunity of aiding these important
steps to a great consummation."

Partly because there was a fertile soil in and about
New Orleans for the implanting and growth of Union
sympathy, and partly because Lincoln was anxious to
promulgate his plan as quickly as possible,[2] Southern
Louisiana was thrust under the spotlight of history as
the laboratory where early reconstruction ideas under-
went experiment. With an entire freedom of movement permitted by Union bayonets, which discouraged
all interference, the necessary political steps of con-

[393]

formance to Lincoln's proclamation, came in rapid succession. By the evening of March 4, 1864, that part of the State which had been captured by the Federal armies, had, with the assistance of Lincoln's military Governor, held what was complacently recorded a Free State Convention, elected state officers and installed what was called a duly elected Governor of Louisiana; all this in spite of the fact that only about one-fifth as many votes were cast as in 1860.

Under a surface reserve, but with shrewd political eye and fervid interest, Lincoln watched closely the experiment in his Southern laboratory. On March 13, he wrote the newly installed Governor Hahn a "strictly private" letter congratulating him on having fixed his "name in history as the first Free State Governor of Louisiana," [3] and in order that he might proceed with the experiment, the President invested him "with the powers exercised hitherto by the military Governor of Louisiana." With no loss of time, a convention met and framed a new State Constitution, which was adopted by a five to one vote of the people in an election where about sixteen per cent of the 1860 vote was cast.

Meanwhile, the Thirty-eighth Congress had convened on December 7, 1863, and quietly and unobtrusively, but none the less irresistibly, Stevens glided into domination of the important policies that guided reconstruction. On the opening day, under his resolution, three so-called representatives from West Virginia were admitted. Immediately thereafter, he presented a resolution to strike from the roll of the House the names of the members from Louisiana who had been admitted to the prior session over his objection. He knew that this was tantamount to expulsion and furthermore, was out of order in point of time, for the House had not yet organized. The Clerk so ruled and Stevens did not press the point, for he had obtained all that he wished, which was merely, as he said, to place "on record my protest against the appearance of the names of these gentlemen on the rolls of the House." [4]

The Body was organized in accordance with his wishes. As soon as this was accomplished, he renewed his attack on the Louisiana representatives by objecting to their being sworn in. In reply to Stevens' objections, Brooks reminded him that his procedure was at least unusual, and begged his indulgence, saying that the Lancastrian was "sure of the Clerk, sure of all other officers of the House, and sure of the Committee of Elections, to whom all credentials of those seeking seats will be referred. . . ." Why not wait until the Committee was appointed to pass upon the credentials of the men from Louisiana? [5]

Moving gently, Stevens said he did not "wish to be discourteous," and was satisfied to have the Louisiana question referred to the Committee on Privileges and Elections. [6]

On December 14, he served notice that he wanted to debate a resolution which would restore the seceded states to the Union as soon as they were subdued or voluntarily submitted to the authority of the Constitution. Alertly on watch, he prevented an expression by the House on other resolutions that would commit the House to a restoration policy. [7]

In a speech on the subject of confiscation, on the

twenty-second of January, he showed that his mind was already concentrated on the single question, the answer to which alone must determine all reconstruction procedure, and that was the status of the rebel States. He spoke of the great confusion of ideas and diversity of opinion on the subject, wherein some thought that they were still in the Union and entitled to protection of the Constitution and the laws of the United States, and others held that having waged war and been vanquished, they should be treated as "conquered provinces."

With terse but powerful argument, he supported the latter position, quoting copious authorities on the subject. Not only did he show that he had assumed an irrevocable position, but already he was prepared to sustain his stand with sound reason and irrefutable authority.

On January 29th, he pointed out that of the members of the prior House who had voted to seat the Louisiana representatives, there were but very few then present in the new House. The inference he left to the wavering ones.

On the same date, he indicated his opposition to Lincoln's restoration plan by questioning the authority by which the military Governor of Louisiana had been appointed. In February, aware that he was far ahead of the House, his strategy was to permit the President's asserted policy toward the seceded states to acquire dull edges and clouded boundaries. He said, "I do not wish that we shall inadvertantly, by any record of ours, so entangle ourselves that hereafter we may be estopped from denying the particular condition of those states."

His stark honesty showed when he was taken to task
for his opposition to seating the Louisiana delegates, in
spite of the fact that he had moved to seat the West
Virginia representatives. Cox had charged that the
latter "was a violation of the Constitution." Abhorring
dissimilation, and using no words which would insulate
his thought or meaning, he said he did not regret having
voted that way. He had never held that the action was
in accordance with the Constitution administered in
time of peace, but he did know that the "constitution
and martial law were not at war with each other." [8]

Master of the House, but with many Representatives
in concealed antagonism to him, he worked with no
subtleties and little finesse. His method was the hard
blow, straight from the shoulder, delivered in the open
and only after warning.

When Blair, of Missouri, his inveterate opponent,
attacked one of Stevens' supporters and pressed him
hard on a personal matter, Stevens intervened and
called Blair to order, under the rule requiring a Representative to speak on the pending question. Blair
turned upon the Lancastrian saying, "the gentleman
takes very good care of his bantling," but Stevens broke
in with, "I take care of nobody," pointedly adding "and
I do not care much for anybody." [9] I "call the gentleman to order." [10]

Confident of majority support, and skilled in parliamentary tactics, he wielded tremendous power in the
manner in which he could press through legislation.
On a revenue measure which he wished to present out
of order, and which would therefore require unanimous
consent, an objection was made. Scorning the objector,

Stevens immediately moved for a suspension of the rules and resolution of the House into the Committee of the Whole on the state of the Union, in order to take up the measure. Through this device, the objector knew that Stevens could accomplish his purpose and so withdrew his objection. This was a weapon frequently resorted to by the Old Commoner. With it, of course, he could at will crush the minority opposition to silence in debate and resulting helplessness.

In the early months of 1864, a decided sentiment against Lincoln's plan took form in Congress. There were several reasons for it. Among them was the underlying one of doubt of the permanence of the antislavery legislation which the President's plan provided. Determined insistence that slavery eradication must be effected in some lasting manner was beginning to show itself.

Furthermore, influenced by Stevens' relentless arguments, Congress was beginning to think of Reconstruction as a matter peculiarly within its own province. The more the members thought of it, the more it appeared that the Old Commoner was right when he said the task was a legislative, rather than an executive one. Realizing that any plan would defeat no plan, the two Houses rapidly constructed a Congressional scheme which was set forth in the so-called Wade-Davis Bill. It was offered by its sponsors in their respective bodies and briefly provided:

That as soon as military resistance in the rebellious communities had ceased, the President was authorized to appoint provisional governors.

For enrollment of white male citizens.

For election of delegates to Constitutional Conventions after a majority of the voters enrolled should take a specified oath of allegiance.

For adoption of Constitutions providing for suffrage disability and disqualification from office of particular holders of military and civil office under the Confederacy.

For perpetual prohibition of slavery and repudiation of Confederate debts.

The bill also abolished slavery in all rebel territory.

After these requisites had been met and properly reported, the President, with the assent of Congress, could recognize the State government and Congress might admit Representatives.

Although the measure was much more severe than Lincoln's plan, and conformed more nearly to Stevens' ideas, it did not receive his approbation. He viewed with suspicion the clauses in it which he thought might be interpreted to give the rebel states certain rights under the Constitution. Furthermore, when he spoke on the bill, Davis had referred to the Confederacy as "states whose governments had been overrun." The use of that word "states" raised grave questions in Stevens' mind.

Endeavoring to straddle the division in Congress, Davis had insisted that his bill should receive the support of both the group that held the rebel states beyond the protection of the Constitution and therefore a conquered territory, as well as the other which considered the seceded area as still in the Union, though unable to exercise political privileges.

Altogether, the Wade-Davis Bill was not a clear

enough expression of the status of Secessia for Stevens. To test the feeling of the House, he attempted to insert the words "so-called" before the designation "Confederate States." The defeat of his motion was notice that he was too advanced in that point for a majority of the House. He had little more to say about it, and refused to vote either for or against the bill.[11]

However, the Old Commoner let himself out pleasantly. The opportunity was given when Grinell attempted to explain his vote. He was refused permission and then stated that he voted "Aye" on the measure, but "under protest." Another representative said he voted "Aye" under "very strong protest," which gave Stevens the cue to record, "I ought to say that I refused to vote, under protest."[12] The Bill passed by a vote of seventy-four to fifty-nine, and two months later, within a few hours of the close of the session, the Senate added its sanction.

Lincoln had no relish for this upshot of Congressional opposition. It was plainly a thrust aimed directly at him and challenging executive authority to reconstruct rebel states. Instead of awaiting the ten day expiration which would have effected a pocket veto of the bill, he adopted an unique procedure of issuing a proclamation upon it four days after it had been submitted for his action. He was quick to understand the political significance of the issue raised, and decided to go directly to the people.

With several whereases, he called the country's attention to the fact that the bill was presented to him "less than one hour before the sine die adjournment" of the Congress, and furthermore, that it had not been

From Frank Leslie's Illustrated News, March 14, 1868.

Stevens Discussing Reconstruction with His All-Powerful Committee

signed by the presiding officer of the Senate. "While I am unprepared," he wrote, "by a formal approval of this bill to be inflexibly committed to any single plan of restoration, and while I am also unprepared to declare that the free state constitutions and governments already adopted and installed in Arkansas and Louisiana, shall be set aside and held for naught, . . . or to declare a constitutional competency in Congress to abolish slavery in the United States, nevertheless, I am fully satisfied with the system for restoration contained in the bill as one very proper plan for the loyal people of any state choosing to adopt it. I am and at all times shall be, prepared to give the executive aid and assistance to any such people, as soon as the military resistance to the United States shall have been suppressed in any such state, and the people thereof shall have sufficiently returned to their obedience to the Constitution and the laws of the United States, in which cases military governors will be appointed with directions to proceed according to the bill."

He closed by vetoing the bill.

Lincoln's action, coupled with his unusual appeal in defense of his restoration plan was offensive to Stevens,[13] and so enraged Wade and Davis that in the heat of temper, they published an angry attack on the President. In ill-chosen language, they denounced the proclamation as a "studied outrage on the legislative authority of the people." They notified the President that the Congressional authority was paramount, and had to be respected, and if he wished radical support, he should confine himself to executing the laws and not interfere with the making of them. His business was "to suppress by arms, armed rebellion and leave political reorganization to Congress." [14]

At the time, Lincoln's political strength was at its ebb. With a Presidential election due in the autumn, he was not a popular candidate. Chase, Sumner, Chandler, Wade, and other leaders made no effort to conceal their opinion that he should not be returned to the White House. [15] But before October, Lincoln managed to retrieve his popularity while radical influence waned. He was reelected with but a scattered opposition while Davis, due mainly to his attack upon the President, was defeated.

But the return of Lincoln to the White House, which in all fairness had to be interpreted as a swing to the right, did not discourage his Congressional opponents. When that Body convened early in December, recognition of the President's new Louisiana government was barred and it refused even to count the electoral votes that had been cast for him in that State and in Arkansas.

With these two blows, Congress irreparably shattered Lincoln's scheme for restoration of the rebel states. The advantage which he had gained through submission of the first plan was wiped out and from then on, the Congressional group showed itself strong enough to wage a real contest.

The duel was on between the legislative and executive branches of the Government to determine which should have the right to reconstruct Secessia.

IV

RESTORATION OR RECONSTRUCTION

The bud-bursting April that came to Washington
in 1865, brought with it two events of transcendent importance in the history of the States. One was the
breakdown of the tragic War of the Rebellion; the
other, the snuffing out of the life of one whose career,
though forever an enigma, requires in the record of the
Nation, a space second in size to but one.

It was not given that the Great Emancipator should
take up the challenge hurled at the executive by Congress. Had Lincoln survived, to match his tact, skill,
and political strategy against the so-called radical Congressional block, the terrors of reconstruction would
undoubtedly have been largely palliated if not wholly
absent. Master of the gentle approach, he was more
ideally qualified to meet the stupendous after-war problems than any other president in all our history.

When forced to assert his position at the outset, he
did it in firm words demanding the limit of what he
deemed proper. If creditable opposition showed itself,
he was unfailingly inclined to yield until a practical
compromise was reached.

But Stevens, probably from his experience on the
emancipation issue, seemed to think that Lincoln was
not always ready to yield. The Commoner had found
the Emancipator made of sterner stuff. He thought
the President had been quite firm in insisting on the
right of executive restoration, and felt that he had
shown his disposition in demanding Congressional
recognition of Louisiana.

"That," Stevens said, "gave uneasiness to the country. The people had begun to fear that Lincoln was misled and was about to fall into error." Were such to be the outcome, then it was "well for his reputation that he did not live to execute it. From being the most popular, he would have left office the most unpopular man that ever occupied the executive chair."

The Lancastrian anticipated the critics by fifty years when he said "but that overruling Providence that so well guided him, did not permit such a calamity to befall him. It allowed him to acquire a most enviable reputation and then, before there was a single spot upon it, he 'sailed into the fiery sunset and left sweet music in Cathay.'"

The Old Commoner paid tribute to "that good man who never willingly infringed upon the rights of any other department of the Government," saying "so solid was the material of which his whole character was formed that the more it is rubbed the more it will shine."

There was "no danger that the highest praise that the most devoted friends could bestow on him would ever be reversed by posterity." Oddly enough, Stevens added in the same paragraph, "what we say at the graves of admired friends or statesmen or heroes is not biography. The stern pen of history will strip such eulogies of their meretricious ornaments." [1] Just what the Old Commoner had in mind, and just what his latter sentences meant, was as irrevocably sealed as were the lips of the man about whom he spoke.

While Lincoln was in the White House, he and Stevens saw little of each other. Their divergent characteristics could tolerate no intimate contact. Stevens, far ahead of the party, was a voice crying in the wilderness. Lincoln, in the rear, moved up only when the way was well prepared. Each regarded the other as a powerful and honest character, and from these appraisals, bore mutual respect.

Occasionally they enjoyed a joke between themselves. When Stevens complained to the President about the exorbitancy of some war contracts reflecting adversely on Cameron, Lincoln said, "why, Mr. Stevens, you don't think the Secretary would steal, do you?" The Old Commoner answered, "well, Mr. President, I don't think he would steal a red-hot stove." Lincoln enjoyed the reply so much that he related it to Cameron. The Secretary of War became furious and insisted that Stevens retract. Stevens went immediately to Lincoln and told him that Cameron in his wrath had made him promise to withdraw the remark. "That I have come to do," announced the Lancastrian. "I said that I did not think Mr. Cameron would steal a red-hot stove. I am now forced to withdraw that statement." [2]

But there was little sympathy between them. When a Pennsylvania editor, warm supporter of Lincoln, early in 1864 asked Stevens to introduce him to some member of Congress who desired Lincoln's renomination, Stevens took him over to the desk of Arnold, a Congressman from Illinois and close personal friend of the President saying, "here is a man who wants to find a Lincoln member of Congress. You are the only one I know and I have come over to introduce my friend to you." [3]

At Lincoln's death, Stevens if he felt a genuine grief,

kept it to himself. When Johnson took the office, most
of the radicals rejoiced in the hope that the new President, by his prior utterances, had committed himself to
a more stringent policy toward the South.[4] The Tennessean's remarks, upon taking the oath, gave little indication of a future course. He had asked Chase to
write an address for him, but unable to await the Secretary's return, he was forced upon his own resources.
His speech, liberally punctuated with "I's" and "me's"
referred mostly to his personal career.

But Ben Wade was wholly confident. He said to the
new President, "Johnson, we have faith in you. By
the gods, there will be no trouble now in running the
Government!"[5]

Sumner was enthused by a personal interview with
the former tailor, and felt that Johnson, even at that
early date, was in favor of negro suffrage.[6] Stevens
was not so sanguine. Again he said nothing and waited.
He had watched Lincoln grow definitely conservative
overnight when he ascended to the Presidency, and this,
no doubt, warned him of what might be expected from
the new President.

Johnson, probably under Seward's influence, had already done a political somersault. In bold contrast to
Lincoln's method, he did not wait to acclimate himself,
but swung quickly into action.

On May 9, by executive order, he recognized the
shadowy Pierpont Government of Virginia. This gave
the radicals their first shock. Stevens, interpreting it
as indicative of the new President's policy, was greatly
disturbed. Twenty days later, Johnson precipitately
took his first major step in carrying out, as he believed,

the restoration policies of his predecessor. Two proclamations were issued.

The first was "to the end that the authority of the Government of the United States may be restored, and that peace, order and freedom may be established." It provided for a general "amnesty and pardon, with restoration of all rights of property except as to slaves," to all who had "directly or indirectly participated in the rebellion." Fourteen classes of persons were excepted, but all others, upon subscribing to a simple oath, could receive the benefits of the proclamation. The apparent purpose was to serve as a dragnet for all eligibles who had not taken advantage of Lincoln's proclamations of December 8, 1863, and March 26, 1864.

In the second edict, Johnson appointed a provisional Governor for the State of North Carolina, with directions to him to arrange for a Convention of delegates to amend the State Constitution in a way "to restore said State to its Constitutional relations to the Federal Government." In the election of delegates to that Convention, those persons only should vote who were qualified by the laws of North Carolina in force immediately before the twentieth day of May, 1861, "the date of the so-called Ordinance of Secession."

Some authorities believe that the two proclamations of May 29 were but a continuation of Lincoln's policies [7] and that the martyred President, sooner or later, would have acted in a somewhat similar manner. Of course, no one can say definitely whether or not that is correct, but even if so, it would not have been the Lincoln known to history to move as hastily as did his successor.

Instead of allowing a sufficient time to elapse in order to study the experiment in North Carolina, and the country's reaction to it, which would have left open the door to a satisfactory adjustment, if opposition arose, Johnson on the thirteenth of June, issued a third proclamation which applied the North Carolina plan of restoration to Mississippi. On the seventeenth, it was extended to Georgia; on the twenty-first, to Alabama; on the thirtieth, to South Carolina; and on July thirteenth, to Florida. Contemporaneously, many other executive orders and proclamations corollary to the above-mentioned, were issued. Johnson was moving with stunning rapidity, and by mid-summer, restoration throughout the entire South was in lively progress.

The country at first did not appear to be perturbed at the new President's sweeping action. Rather it seemed to be satisfied to give the plans an opportunity to prove themselves.

Stevens was the first to show alarm. In May he wrote Sumner saying he feared that "before Congress meets, Johnson will so have be-deviled matters as to make them incurable." And he "almost despaired of resisting executive influence." [8] In early June, he was so concerned that he again wrote the Senator, asking if it were possible to "collect bold men enough to lay the foundations of a party to take the helm of this Government and keep it off the rocks." [9]

Two weeks later, unusually disturbed over Johnson's barrage of proclamations, he wrote, "is there no way to avert the insane course of the President in reorganization?" He suggested that Sumner get up such a "movement in Massachusetts" as he had thought of "trying" at the Pennsylvania State Convention.

In forlorn desperation, he endeavored to spur action by warning that "if something is not done, the President will be crowned king before Congress meets." He could not, for the life of him, understand how Johnson interfered "with the internal regulations of the States, and yet considered them as States in the Union." [10]

Through the midsummer heat of August, the sick Old Commoner made his club-footed way to Washington to see if anything could be done on the scene of action, but for some reason, failed even to see the President. Perhaps he concluded it useless, or was so enervated by the trip as to make the task physically impossible. He explained that he had been called away from the Capitol before he had "an opportunity to talk with Johnson on reconstruction, as he had intended."

In some things, he was pleased with the President's attitude. He sensed the approaching duel but judiciously suggested to Sumner that while "we can hardly approve of all of the acts of the Government, we must try to keep out of the ranks of the opposition." The danger was that the President's stubborn course might drive "the people to almost anything." [11]

Unable to advise personally with Johnson, he wrote to him twice, urging that he "stay his hand until Congress meets." But the President gave him not even the courtesy of a reply. [12] Ben Wade was gravely concerned lest the "great Union or Republican Party would be bound hand and foot to the tender mercies of the rebels, we have so lately conquered in the field, and their copperhead allies of the North." [13] Strangely enough, Sumner first showed little if any objection to Johnson's course. But the alarm of his radical colleagues soon had its effect and he began to share their feelings.[14]

Complain as they might at Johnson's all-embracing program, the Senators and Congressmen were wholly ineffective while Congress was in recess. Stevens urged a special session [15] but no thinking person believed that Johnson was foolish enough to convene a body that was already showing itself hostile. So no move could be made until the Congress came into regular session late in the year. The body was to convene on Monday, December 3, at noon.

In the preceding days, Stevens was busily engaged with the Pennsylvania Union State Central Committee meeting at Harrisburg, endeavoring to shape the policies of that group. Its resolutions would be of weighty effect as indicating the latest expression of the people of a great State, and it was of highest importance to the Commoner to have the Convention support. It might reflect on his program if the opposition could point out that the assembly of his own State had gone on record contrariwise. But important as the record of that meeting might be, matters of greater consequence must be attended to in Washington.

Leaving the Convention to shift for itself, on the last day of November, the Lancastrian hobbled into his home in the Capital.[16] He had not been in good health since the summer adjournment. In his seventy-fourth year, time and a vigorous life had taken its toll. But his indisposition gave him plenty of time for deliberation.

Before the War was a year old, he had developed and announced the theory upon which he believed reconstruction should be made. Now that victory had come for the Union, Secessia was no longer made up of a number of states. They were merely conquered provinces held at the disposition of the conqueror, and subject only to the rules of humanity. They could have no status as States in the Union until readmitted by Congress. This had been his clear doctrine and he had never faltered in proclaiming it, nor swerved in supporting it.

It was laid down at a time when no one could know how the War would terminate, and was propounded at that early date so that in the event of Federal victory, it would not fall harshly upon the ears of the people as a newly found theory.

Through those late summer and autumn days, the Old Commoner had followed with avid and consuming interest, the acts of the new President, looking toward a hasty restoration. With all the burning passion that flamed in that broken body, he resented Johnson's assumption of the role of Restorator. At the time he bore no enmity toward Johnson, nor was he opposed to quick reentry of the rebel states. To him there was but one matter of importance and its accomplishment alone motivated his conduct. The Union should not be rebuilt until slavery theoretically and actually, had been irrevocably eradicated. If those who controlled the Government did not definitely secure that result, then all the devastation of the War went for nothing.

Johnson's procedure gave the Lancastrian no assurance. Under the policy the President had invoked,

[411]

Southern States would have their representatives back
in the next Congress, fully constituted to take part in
the Government. Northern Democrats who, during the
War, had been inert, would spring suddenly to life and
action, and with their aid, the old slave owners of
Secessia would begin the battle all over again. They
might be able even to resurrect slavery.

Not only that, debts contracted to make War upon
the Union would be paid. Those who made the War
would be rewarded; the Union debt might be repudiated; the policy of rebuilding the Nation would be dictated by those who had attempted to destroy it and altogether the Government would be in the hands of the
rebels. Stevens thought one might as well have called
in Confederate Generals to sit in the War Councils of
the North as to accept such procedure.[17]

Most of his colleagues were perplexed and utterly bewildered. But Stevens, as was characteristic of him,
met the situation ingeniously.

In his invalid days in Lancaster, the sick man had
evolved a plan of action. When he got to Washington,
not a moment was lost in gathering together a few of
the faithful. On the Friday night before Congress
met, an informal gathering was held preliminary to a
Republican caucus.[18]

Stevens quickly presented his idea, and although the
records of the meeting are meager in the extreme, there
is nothing to indicate that he had any trouble in obtaining support. When the full Republican caucus met the
next evening, Conservatives and Johnson supporters
were present, as well as Stevens' colleagues. Apparently
no reference was made to the gathering of the night

before, wherein the preliminary work had been done.

For some odd reason, which no student of the incident has discovered, even Johnson's friends who certainly must have understood the effect of Stevens' intended procedure, were strangely acquiescent. The record shows, for instance, that Representative Henry J. Raymond, of New York, staunch supporter of the President, was at the meeting, but there is nothing to indicate that he or his friends scented any danger.[19] At any rate, Raymond was notified of what was going on, though he probably might not have grasped the full portent of the Lancastrian's proposal. In the caucus, he was among those who voted for its unanimous approval.[20]

The true explanation might be that at that very critical time, the Southern States themselves were piling ammunition in Stevens' hands. Almost daily there came reports from the several seceded States of some legislation purposing in spite of the Thirteenth Amendment, to practically restore slavery in those states. These so-called "black codes" have been treated so thoroughly that no discussion of them is made here. But the efficacious way in which Stevens could use them as illustrating the real attitude of the South must not be lost sight of. No more weighty reason for supporting his resolution could be found and it certainly cannot be assumed that Stevens overlooked it.

Johnson was informed of Stevens' scheme, but he did not appear uneasy. He was satisfied to rest the matter in the hands of his fellow Tennessean, Maynard, whom it was generally known, was fully prepared to answer if any objection was made to his being seated.

The President felt certain that even the fertile and resourceful brain of Stevens could find no sound reason to bar Maynard, and in that absence, would not dare refuse him his seat.

All eyes were turned on the convening of Congress. Oddly enough, the center of interest was not the Senate, which had shown itself more radical than the House in its treatment of the Thirteenth Amendment. A quick-spreading rumor had it that some subtle strategy was to be attempted and the Lower Body would be the scene of it. By the hour for convening, the galleries were overflowing and the corridors packed. Gradually the interested ones understood that Stevens would be the General of the attempted procedure.

Most of the spectators had come, cursorily to view what promised to be merely a verbal battle with some wordy fireworks. Few, if any, were aware they were to see the opening of a War between the Legislative and Executive arms of the Government, which would shake to its foundation our entire political structure, and come within a hairsbreadth of upsetting the tripartite balance set up in the Constitution.

The Clerk rapped for order. Slowly the uproar subsided and the voice of the man at the desk could be heard. He was calling the roll of Representatives to ascertain if a quorum were present. Stevens sat comfortably in his center aisle chair, well toward the front, confidently watching.

He must have felt as a Captain, who, having carefully trained and prepared his soldiers, is about to enter a battle wherein numbers will be the deciding factor, knowing all the while that such advantage is on his side.

Preparation had been made for the important moves. Before organization, the Clerk occupies the chair. Clerk McPherson, was not only a faithful friend of the Commoner, he was his devout disciple. Born in Gettysburg while Stevens was a promising young lawyer there, he himself had sat in the House of Representatives for two terms. Defeated for the office when he ran the third time, Stevens had made him Clerk of the House, and the placing of that favor was for many years one of the sources of Stevens' strength and an incident in Stevens' legislative career that has never been given its proper share of importance.

McPherson was a man of highest character and pleasing personality. For a brief part of his early life he devoted himself to law, but gave it up for a journalistic career. Tactful, suave, and reticent, he filled his office as Clerk of the House admirably. He was of the studious and scholarly mental make-up and with the facts and figures which he loved to accumulate, was a veritable well of information for Stevens. Honest and honorable, he never differed with the Old Commoner. He had known Stevens from his early years and nothing could shake his confidence in him. Convinced utterly of the clubfooted old man's integrity, he followed him implicity and faithfully. Whatever Stevens proposed, he was satisfied to assist in as far as he could, for he knew the old man, and he couldn't be wrong.

Some men in that hall knew that the roll from which the Clerk was reading had been passed upon by Stevens, but everyone was waiting until he reached Tennessee. Those who did not know expected the name to be called, but did not doubt that the right to receive the oath would be challenged. The Clerk came to the point where Maynard's name should have been called if in the list. It was not there and the Clerk read on.

Springing to his feet, the Tennessean attempted to address the officer, but was waved aside with the comment "that the Clerk could not be interrupted while ascertaining whether a quorum is present." Maynard sat down. The roll call was finished. The Tennessean observing the rules, gave the battle over to Democratic leader, James Brooks, of New York. He protested the omission of Maynard's name and demanded authority for the act. The Clerk gave none and Brooks, slowly comprehending the situation, turned to Stevens to ask "when the matter of admitting Southern members will be taken up." With utter serenity, Stevens said quietly, "I have no objections to answering the gentleman. I will press the matter at the proper time." The work of organizing the House went merrily on.

There was neither trouble nor delay in reelecting Stevens' supporter, Colfax, Speaker. He was fully cognizant of the Lancastrian's proposed measures, and would give him all the help that his office could command.[21] But to Stevens, who sat with his masterfully drawn resolution in his pocket, all of this was preliminary to the main event. He calmly permitted several perfunctory items to be acted upon, among which was Washburn's resolution for the appointment of a committee to join a similar Senate committee to wait upon the President and inform him "that Congress is ready to receive any communication he may make."

Late in the afternoon, Stevens obtained the Floor. He had no oratory for the packed galleries; he had no

The Old Commoner while Engaged in Providing Ways and Means in the War of the Rebellion

lecture for the opposition, nor had he any words to exhort or encourage his followers. In sparing, simple language, he said "I offer the following resolution and call the previous question upon it:

'Resolved by the Senate and House of Representatives in Congress assembled, That a joint committee of fifteen members shall be appointed, nine of whom shall be members of the House and six members of the Senate, who shall inquire into the condition of the States which formed the so-called Confederate States of America, and report whether they or any of them are entitled to be represented in either House of Congress, with leave to report at any time by bill or otherwise; and until such report shall have been made and finally acted upon by the Congress, no member shall be received into either House from any of the said so-called Confederate States; and all papers relating to the representation of the said States shall be referred to the said committee without debate.' "

His disciple, General Ashley of Ohio, had an amendment which was recorded but never voted upon. Eldridge asked if unanimous consent had been given for the introduction of the resolution out of order, and the Speaker answered that it had not. Whereupon Eldridge objected to it. But Stevens was unperturbed. He merely moved "to suspend the rules so as to enable me to introduce the resolution." The vote was taken immediately and permission was given with one hundred twenty-nine "yeas" and thirty-five "nays." The Lancastrian moved the previous question.

Dawson made a point that Stevens' resolution was not in order until after the President's message had been received. But the House was prepared for action, and by a vote of one hundred thirty-three to thirty-seven, overrode the point of order. In a very few minutes, the Old Commoner's proposition was adopted by the House, by a vote of one hundred thirty-three to thirty-six, with thirteen not voting.

The Resolution and the manner in which Stevens engineered it through the House, is a fine example of the way he worked. Had any other member drawn it, it very probably would have been much more lengthy and prefaced with many whereases. Moreover there were few who would presume to precipitate such an important measure upon the House without at least one speech upon it.

That was not Stevens' way. In his caucus and the preliminary meeting, he had felt out the membership and obtained their promise of support. Certainly he could rely upon that. With so much granted, then, why waste words and time? The majority knew what it was and understood at least part of its purpose. He would proceed with business.

That brief resolution, brain-child of the Lancastrian, is one of the outstanding resolutions of all the Congresses. It sprang up suddenly before President Johnson as an impenetrable wall to block his way, and veritably stopped him in his tracks. It was astoundingly efficacious. It not only barred representatives of the Southern States; it actually denied them even a hearing.

It opened a war between executive and legislative branches, which came near revolutionizing our system

of Government. It marked the end of restoration and
the beginning of reconstruction. It made Thaddeus
Stevens absolute dictator of the early years of that
movement, and put in his hands, a devastating power,
the equal of which no Federal Legislator has ever
wielded before or since. With it, he doomed a civilization and built anew a great Government.

The Senate was in sympathy with Stevens' resolution, but it touched the Senatorial pride to be asked to
swallow it whole. The Body, however, was able to
maintain its dignity by refusing to approve the measure as a joint resolution, but passed it verbatim as a
concurrent one.

Stevens was made House Chairman of the Committee. Where so much depended upon the action of this
group of fifteen, it is surprising to find that only seven
others who thought as he did were appointed to it,
while the Conservatives could count upon the remainder.
With the dictatorial power Stevens had at the time and
his certain knowledge of the importance of the committee, one wonders why he did not secure a larger representation. There is little doubt but that he named the
House contingent and certainly was consulted about
the Senate members. He could have filled the entire
Committee with his followers. But where great issues
were concerned, he generally gave opponents an opportunity. It even became customary for him after he
had introduced a radical measure, to permit the opposition first to speak against it before anything was
said in its favor. At any rate, the other side was given
full representation on the Committee of Fifteen.

The newspapers of the country made various comments upon the Congressional action. Of course all of the Radical element approved, while the Conservative and Democratic sides, condemned. Tilton, Editor of the New York *Independent,* praised Stevens for the manner in which he had "thrown down the gauntlet to the President's policy." It "pleased our Radical friends hereabouts so thoroughly that we are all hearty, merry, and tumultuous with gratitude." [22]

The New York *World* thought that by the resolution, Stevens "strangled the infant restoration, stamped upon it with his brutal heel, and proclaimed his plan for keeping the Union disunited." [23]

The National *Intelligencer* gave the best outline of the sweeping purpose of the measure, even before it was adopted by the Congress. Ironically, it stated, "we cannot for a moment imagine that this hasty resolution means to imply that debate be stifled on Constitutional questions arising from attempts to admit Southern members, nor to check the President in his program, nor to put Congress on record as asserting its jurisdiction in matters relating to the rebel states." Oddly enough, this appears to be an accurate summary of just what Stevens did intend.[24]

The New York *Independent* called it a most important measure in its immediate practical effect, and spoke of it as expressing "a wise, brave and satisfactory policy. On learning of its passage, the whole country draws a long, free, and joyous breath. The first danger of a precipitated reconstruction has passed, and ample time is secured for a deliberate review of the President's policy and a minute scrutiny into all the elements of the problem of reuniting the fractured states. The first day of Congress was a victory of liberty." [25]

When the President's message was read in the House, it was proper for Stevens to assume charge of it, break it down and have the constituent parts referred to the respective committees. After introducing twenty-four resolutions of reference, he sat down, but before any other person got the Floor, suddenly arose again. He had forgotten the most important of them all. His amendment was to have "so much of the President's message and accompanying documents as relates to the subject of reconstruction referred" to his Committee.

Perfunctorily all was "agreed to" and Stevens took the Floor to deliver the greatest speech on reconstruction that had been made up to that time. Congress had boldly declared its policy under his resolution of December 4, 1865. Nothing had been said about it formally. The time had now arrived when an explanation should be given of the proposed plan and an argument put forth to support it. In keeping with his regular procedure, it was the Old Commoner's duty to furnish intelligent and reasonable justification and lay the foundations on which to build.

Reconstruction was no doubt the most vital subject before the people of the time. A candid examination of the principles of the program could "be offensive to no one and might possibly be profitable by exciting inquiry."

He began at the beginning. "The President assumes what no one doubts—that the late rebel states have lost their Constitutional relations to the Union and are incapable of representation in Congress, except by permission of the Government." With so much admitted, he concluded that it mattered "but little whether you call them States out of the Union, and now conquered territories, or assert that because the Constitution forbids them to do what they did do, that they are therefore only dead as to all national and political action, and will remain so until the Government shall breathe into them the breath of life anew and permit them to occupy their former position. In other words, that they are not out of the Union, but are only dead carcasses lying within the Union."

This latter was rebuke to the state suicide theory of Sumner, which Stevens later called absurd. But he was not precipitating that argument yet. In either case, it was very plain that it required the "action of Congress to enable them to form a State Government, and send representatives" to Washington. That was his great major premise and on it he built the whole policy of the reconstruction.

Certainly "nobody pretends that with their old Constitution and frames of Government they can be permitted to claim their old rights under the Constitution." The Constitutional States had torn themselves into atoms "and built on their foundations fabrics of totally different character." Suppose they had died; "dead men cannot raise themselves" nor could dead states restore "their existence 'as it was.'" Whose duty, was it, then, to raise those states again? "In whom does the Constitution place the power? Not in the judicial branch of the Government, for it only adjudicates and does not prescribe laws. Not in the executive, for he only executes and cannot make laws. Not in the commander-

in-chief of the armies, for he can only hold them under
military rule until the sovereign legislative power of
the conqueror shall give them law."

Stevens found no difficulty in answering the question.
In the Constitution there were two provisions, under
either one of which the case must fall. The first was,

"New States may be admitted by the Congress
into this Union."

To him, that was the full and sufficient answer. "In
my judgment, this is the controlling provision in this
case." Unless the Law of Nations was a dead letter, the
late War between the two acknowledged belligerents
had severed their original compacts, and broken all the
ties that bound them together.

Here he said what he continued to reiterate to the
day he died. "The future condition of the conquered
power depends on the will of the conqueror. They must
come in as new States or remain as conquered provinces.
Congress—the Senate and House of Representatives
with the concurrence of the President—is the only
power that can act in the matter." There was summed
up Stevens' theory and the one which the Nation finally
adopted.

Pausing a moment to answer another school of
thought and pay his respects to Sumner and his "State
suicide" theory he said, "Suppose, as some dreaming
theorists imagine, that these States have never been
out of the Union, but have only destroyed their State
Governments so as to be incapable of political action."
Then the second provision of the Constitution must
apply:

" 'The United States shall guarantee to every

[423]

State in this Union, a Republican form of Government.'"

But who is the United States? "Not the judiciary, not the President, but the sovereign power of the people exercised through their representatives in Congress with the concurrence of the Executive." The separate action of each "amounts to nothing, either in admitting new states, or guaranteeing responsible governments to lapsed or outlawed states."

Aiming directly at Johnson's restoration attempts, he queried, "whence springs the preposterous idea that either the President, or the Senate, or the House of Representatives, acting separately, can determine the rights of States to send their representatives to the Congress of the Union?"

Well-grounded in the theory of Government, he felt he could conclusively prove that the rebel states "are and for four years have been out of the Union for all legal purposes, and being now conquered, are subject to the absolute disposal of Congress." If they were an independent belligerent, and were so acknowledged by the United States and by Europe, or had assumed and maintained an attitude, which entitled them to be considered and treated as a belligerent, then during such time they "were precisely in the condition of a foreign nation with whom we were at war." Nor need their independence as a nation be acknowledged by us to produce that effect.

He cited opinions of the Supreme Court which held the Confederate States in the same position as an independent belligerent. They gave a very solid and dignified foundation on which to rest his argument and he used them skillfully. "After such clear and repeated decisions, it is something worse than ridiculous to hear men of respectable standing attempting to nullify the Law of Nations, and declare the Supreme Court of the United States in error, because, as the Constitution forbids it, the States could not go out of the Union in fact."

Such argument was in the same category as the one that "no murder could be committed for the reason that the law forbade it." The theory that the rebel states, for four years a separate power and without representation in Congress, were all the time here in the Union, "was a good deal less ingenious and respectable than the metaphysics of Berkeley, which proved that neither the world nor any human being was in existence." If it were simply ridiculous it could be forgiven, but its effect was deeply injurious to the stability of the nation. "I cannot doubt that the late Confederate States are out of the Union to all intents and purpose for which the conquerer may choose so to consider them."

He referred to one of the first resolutions passed by South Carolina in January of 1861, when its Legislature resolved unanimously that South Carolina's separation from the Federal Union was final, that she had no further interest in the Constitution of the United States, and that the only appropriate negotiations between her and the Federal Government could be as to their mutual relations as foreign states. The other seceding states had passed similar resolutions. The speeches in their Congress, their official papers, and their executive orders, together with "the answers of their Government to our shameful suings for peace, went upon the defiant ground that no terms would be offered or received except upon the prior acknowledgment of the entire and permanent independence of the Confederate States."

In the face of all this, "to deny that we have a right to treat them as a conquered belligerent, severed from the Union in fact, is not argument but mockery. Whether it be in the interest of the Nation to do so is the only question hereafter and more deliberately to be considered."

If the states were not out of the Union, but had been merely destroyed, and were "now lying about, a dead corpse, or with animation so suspended as to be incapable of action, and wholly unable to heal themselves by any unaided movements of their own," the Congress alone could resuscitate them.

He quoted the Supreme Court again in holding that if such were the case, "Congress must necessarily decide what Government is established in the State before it can determine whether it is Republican or not." And Congress did not mean the Senate or the House of Representatives or the President, acting severally. "Their joint action constitutes Congress."

He came to his next great point. "Hence, a law of Congress must be passed before any new State can be admitted or any dead ones revived," and until that time, no member could be lawfully admitted into either House. "So, it appears with how little knowledge of Constitutional law each branch is urged to admit members separately from these destroyed states. The provision that 'each House shall be the judge of the elections, returns, and qualifications of its own members,' had not the most distant bearing on the question.

"Congress itself and Congress alone must create states and declare when they are entitled to be represented. Then, but not until then, each House must judge whether the members presenting themselves from a recognized State possess the requisite qualifications and whether the election and returns are according to law." Separately, the Houses could judge of nothing else. To him, it was "amazing that any man of legal education could give it any larger meaning." This was his gentle slap at those Senators who had refused to pass his resolution as a concurrent one and insisted on it being made a joint measure.

To Stevens, military rule then obtaining in the South was wholly objectionable. "Necessarily despotic, it ought not to exist longer than is absolutely necessary." It was a first duty of Congress "to pass a law declaring the condition of these outside or defunct States and provide proper Civil Governments for them." There were, at the time, no symptoms that "the people of these provinces will be prepared to participate in Constitutional Government for some years," and he knew of no arrangement so proper for them as territorial governments. "There they can learn the principles of freedom and eat the fruit of foul rebellion." In territories, "Congress fixes the qualifications of electors and I know no better place or better occasion for the conquered rebels and the conqueror to practice justice to all men" and accustom themselves to make and obey equal laws.

Inasmuch as the fallen rebels could not, at their option, reenter the Union it became "important to the welfare of the Nation to inquire when the doors shall be reopened for their admission." He was convinced that they should not be recognized as states until their Constitutions had been properly amended.

It was high time "that Congress should assert its sovereignty in these questions of reconstruction and prepare to do its duty." Fortunately, the President had invited "Congress to take this manly attitude." He credited Johnson with "great frankness in his able message," but believed that his theory of restoration had been found to be impracticable.

The rest of his speech he devoted to a withering attack upon those who were urging the propaganda that "this was a white man's Government." [26] His pregnant address was another call for support by a leader far in advance of his followers.

Altogether, it was a potent brief in support of his position. In part it had been advanced by him previously. As early as 1862, he had laid down the proposition that if and when the rebel states were overcome, they could have no status other than that of conquered provinces. But at that time, there were not many in the country who would listen to him, and of those who did hear what he said, few regarded it seriously. Now, late in 1865, his audience and supporters were substantial enough to demand at least a respectable consideration. That was the reason he took occasion to consolidate his arguments.

Carefully timed, his speech served as a keynote address to rally his followers about him and supply them with a logical and legal argument. But even though he

had a respectable following, he felt it necessary to state
before he sat down that he trusted "the Republican
Party will not be alarmed at what I am saying." Fully
aware of the risk he was taking he announced, "I do
not profess to speak their sentiments, nor must they
be held responsible for them. I speak for myself and
take the responsibility and will settle with my intelligent constituents."

Blaine thought that when Stevens opened "the great
debate on reconstruction with this speech," he had taken
"the most radical and pronounced grounds." [27] It "gave
great offense to the administration" and although
Stevens had not directly assailed the President, Johnson nevertheless fully understood what it meant.[28] The
fact was Stevens had gone so far as to assume that
Johnson had willingly referred the matter of reconstruction to the Congress.

It is rather stretching Johnson's message to infer
this from it, and might have been an attempt on Stevens'
part for conciliation.[29] The Lancastrian's pleasant
interpretation furnished a ground on which Johnson
could converse with Stevens on the subject without
impairing his standing or dignity in the least.

The administration thought it better strategy to have
a Republican answer Stevens than that a Democrat
attempt the first reply. Raymond was chosen for the
task. But as might be expected, he failed miserably.
With all his art he was unable to raise even a weak refutation of the Old Commoner's logic and argument.

Johnson was bitterly aroused by Stevens' resolution
and his speech upon it, but held himself until Washington's birthday. His friends told him that a group of

admirers might call upon him that evening to congratulate him upon his veto of the Freedman's Bureau Bill, but warned him not to risk making an extempore speech.[30] Johnson answered, "I have not thought of making a speech and I shan't make one." [31]

Strangely enough, when his friends got there, he lost no time in reading to them "his speech, by the light of a guttering candle." [32] There is some doubt whether the address was completely written or merely outlined. In a corrected copy of what he said, Johnson refers to it as "my extemporaneous remarks." [33]

The President took occasion to vent his ire upon Stevens' committee, calling it "an irresponsible Central Directory, assuming nearly all the powers of Congress without even consulting the legislative and executive departments of the Government."

Somehow Johnson could never learn that the flamboyant, barnstorming, rough and tumble politics which he had practiced in Tennessee, were wholly out of place for a President of the United States. He seemed to enjoy being heckled and invariably got the worst of his bargain. After he had gotten well along in his speech, he came to a point where he referred without naming them, to some men whose policies he condemned. A heckler called upon him to name them, and with his usual indiscretion, the President plunged into personalities.

"Suppose," he said, "I should name to you those whom I look upon as being opposed to the fundamental principles of this Government, and as now laboring to destroy them. I say Thaddeus Stevens of Pennsylvania; I say Charles Sumner of Massachusetts; I say

Wendell Phillips, of Massachusetts." Someone suggested Forney, and the President responded, "I do not waste my fire on dead ducks."

Continuing, he said, "I have occupied many positions in the Government, going through both branches of the legislature." Someone in the crowd added, "you were also a tailor." Instead of ignoring the remark, Johnson unseemly replied, "when I was a tailor, I always made a close fit and was always punctual to my customers and did good work."

Although there were other interruptions, he restrained himself to devote the rest of his speech to what he considered the most important matters at hand, namely, Andrew Johnson and the Constitution—but mostly Andrew Johnson.[34]

A few days prior to this, Stevens had taken Johnson to task for his premature comment that even if the Fourteenth Amendment were passed, he would be compelled to veto it. To the Commoner, the uncalled for remark was a defiant snub to the legislative arm of the Government and he minced no words. Such a statement, said Stevens, issued "at a time when this Congress was legislating on the question, was made in violation of the privileges of this House and had it been made to Parliament by a British King, it would have cost him his head." [35]

Johnson himself was using ugly language. Late in February, in a public speech he demanded, "are those who want to destroy our institutions and change the character of the Government not satisfied with the blood that has been shed? Is their thirst still unslaked? Do they want more blood? Have they not honor and courage enough to effect the removal of the 'Presidential obstacle' otherwise than through the hands of the assassin?" Working himself up to a near frenzy, he shrieked, "if my blood is to be shed . . . let it be so." [36]

The first open break between the President and Congress had come with his veto of the Freedman's Bureau Bill. Johnson threw down the gauntlet and indicated a desire to fight it out. The House promptly overrode the veto by repassing the bill by more than a two-third's majority, but the Senate, reluctant to come to an open breach with the executive, sustained the veto. However, with slight modifications, a second measure was shortly thereafter passed, which Johnson also rejected. The House repassed it by more than a three to one vote, and the Senate fell in line giving the measure more than the necessary two-third's vote.

On January 10, illustration was made of one of the practical effects of Stevens' resolution. When Eldridge attempted to offer a reconstruction resolution not in harmony with Stevens' program, the Speaker ruled that it could not be brought before the House until first referred to the Reconstruction Committee and then by it, reported out. That fixed a policy and smothered completely all measures on the subject not approved by the Committee of Fifteen. The resolution would work not only positively but could be used efficiently to stifle opposition.

In the meantime, Stevens and his colleagues were by piece-meal, making their policy known. The House resolved that the military force of the Government should not be withdrawn from the rebel states until both Houses of Congress declared their further pres-

From Harper's Weekly, March 14, 1868.

A View of the House when Stevens was at the Height of his Power. He is Seen in the Left Foreground

ence there no longer necessary.[37] When a communication arrived, purporting to be from the Governor
of North Carolina, Stevens immediately objected to
reception of the paper on the ground that the House
recognized no Government nor Governor of the State
of North Carolina. He was sustained by a three to
one vote.

The Lancastrian had apparently intended to make
some answer to Raymond, but yielded the Floor to a
younger member. He waited more than a month and
a half, and then felt it necessary to "apologize to the
House for the tameness of" his remarks. As to Raymond's attempted refutation, he had only to recall that
the facts and authorities which he (Stevens) had submitted seemed more than ample to support his position.

Raymond had mentioned not a single legal authority
to either modify, contradict, or overrule those the Lancastrian cited. To the Old Commoner, the whole question was a legal one "to be decided by authority, by
judicial decisions or by the works of distinguished
elementary writers." The gentleman from New York
did not except to the facts as Stevens stated them, but
denied "the correctness of Vattel's doctrine." This he
did, "giving no authority but his own."

Stevens admitted the gravity of the gentleman's
opinion, and with but the slightest corroborating authority, would yield the case. "But without some such
aid, I am not willing that the sages of the law whom I
have been accustomed to revere, Grotius, Rutherford,
Vattel, and a long line of compeers, sustained by the
verdict of the civilized world, and armed with the pan-
oply of ages, should be overthrown and demolished by

the single arm of the gentleman from New York."

A part of Stevens' speech is an enigma, as it bears upon his personal relations with Johnson. Soon after he had arisen, he referred to the newspaper reports of the President's February speech, which he said were attempts "to disturb the harmony which existed between the President and myself."

He would say, "once and for all, that instead of feeling personal enmity to the President, I feel great respect for him. I honor his integrity, patriotism, courage and good intentions. He stood too firmly for the Union in the midst of dangers and sacrifices to allow me to doubt the purity of his wishes. But all this does not make me fear to doubt his judgment and criticize his policy. When I deem his views erroneous, I shall say so; when I deem them dangerous, I shall denounce them. While I can have no hostility to the President, I may have, and do have grave objections to the course he is pursuing. I should have forgot the obloquy which I have calmly borne for thirty years in the war for liberty if I should turn craven now." This seems to be a sincere and honest tribute to Johnson.

But at that point, a Representative interrupted to ask whether or not the Speaker was the same Thaddeus Stevens that the President had referred to in his Washington Birthday speech. Stevens turned to him saying, "does the learned gentleman suppose for a single moment that that speech to which he refers as having been made in front of the White House was a fact?" (Laughter.) He would put the gentleman right. But what he was about to say was in confidence and he hoped it would be so regarded.

The whole thing was an imposition and was one of the "grandest hoaxes ever perpetrated." He was glad to have the opportunity to "exonerate the President from ever having made the speech." (Renewed laughter.) It was a part of a cunning contrivance of the copperheads to embarrass the President. They had constantly denounced the President since the inauguration and as an example of their "vile slander," he sent the Clerk a copy of the New York *World* of March 7, 1865, to be read.

The article referred to Johnson on that occasion as an "insolent, drunken brute, in comparison with whom even Caligula's horse was respectable." That, Stevens said, was a serious slander, but the Republican Party never believed it and never would. "Being therefore unable to fix some odium upon our President by evidence which the lawyers would call *aliunde,* they resort with the skill of a practiced advocate to another expedient.

"My friend before me (Mr. Bingham), if he were trying in Court a case *de lunatico inquerendo,* and if outside evidence were introduced, leaving it questionable whether the jury would adopt the view that insanity existed, would cautiously lead the alleged lunatic to speak upon the subject of the hallucination. If he could be induced to gabble nonsense, the intrinsic evidence of the case would make out the allegation of insanity." So, said Stevens, if those slanderers could make the people believe that the President ever uttered that speech, then they had made out their case. All of it had been worked up very shrewdly. "But we who know the President, knew it was a lie from the start." (Renewed laughter.)

A reading of the whole speech indicates that this was a diversion not intended by Stevens. It does not fit harmoniously into the address and was perpetrated probably merely for the effect of creating the laughter which it interspersed. The paper sent to the Clerk to be read was perhaps one of a number which Stevens had in his desk.

He soon returned to the issue. He contested the authority of Johnson to appoint a military Governor of Tennessee, if that State was, as Johnson contended, a State in the Union. Virginia had assembled the free representatives of fragments of about eleven townships out of one hundred forty-two counties, and elected under Federal bayonets, twelve men, who met within the Union lines. They called that meeting a Convention, formed a Constitution, and ordered elections for the whole state. Pierpont was elected with about thirty-three hundred votes and proclaimed "Governor of Imperial Virginia, the Mother of Statesmen."

The President recognized him as Governor and those twelve men as Representatives of a million and a quarter people, and counted Virginia as one of the twenty-seven states that adopted the Constitutional amendment. "I am fond of genteel comedy," said Stevens, but "this low farce is too vulgar to be acted on the stage of Nations. Are these free republics, such as the United States is bound to guarantee to all the states in the Union? Should these swindlers, these imposters, bred in the midst of martial law without authority from Congress, be acknowledged here?" The thing that aggravated him most was the absurdity of calling such a small minority, the people of the State.

He wished devoutly "that there should be no collision between the different branches of the Government, no controversy as to the rightful jurisdiction of either," and for that reason, he had made the reference to the President's message that he did in his prior speech.[38]

At about the time Stevens made this former speech, a Civil Rights Bill had been passed by the two Houses, vetoed by Johnson, and promptly repassed by the required votes of the two Bodies. Johnson seemed fixed in his purpose to veto all pertinent action of Congress, regardless of merit in an apparent hope to hold the Congress in check until an appeal could be made to the people in the fall election. At any rate, from then on to the end of the session, the executive veto seemed the regular procedure.

In the remainder of the First Session of the Thirty-Ninth Congress, Stevens devoted most of his attention to obtaining Congressional support for his Fourteenth Amendment.

A single other matter of importance was the Reconstruction Committee's report which was filed on June 18, just before adjournment. Both sides were seeking the country's support, and before the Congress would again come into session that final court of arbitrament, the voters, would have passed upon the case and given their unappealable decision. Bearing the imprint of Stevens in every paragraph, the Committee report was framed not only to set forth clearly the Congressional plan of Reconstruction, but by fact and argument to support it in an appeal to the reason of the people. It was the brief of the Congressional block that had obtained and wielded control of the Thirty-Ninth Congress up to that point and on it they rested their case.

The document is impressive and important. Like all of Stevens' writings and speeches, it is most difficult to paraphrase, and it is practically impossible of condensing with retention of accurate meaning. It is, however, too long to repeat in full, although it gives the best and most authoritative statement of the position of Stevens and his followers. Those interested in the period should study it minutely. It was submitted in the Senate by Fessenden, and by Stevens in the House.

Holding that the rebel states had protracted their struggle against Federal authority until all hope of successful resistance had ceased and laid down their arms only because they had no longer any power to use them, the people of those states had found themselves bankrupt in their public finances, and shorn of the private wealth which had before given them power and influence.

Necessarily, they were in a state of complete anarchy without governments and without the authority to frame governments except by permission of those who had been successful in the War. The President had recognized this. Plainly it was his duty in enforcing the national laws to establish, as far as he could, some such system as might be provided for by the Federal laws. As commander-in-chief of the victorious army, it was his duty to restore order, preserve property, and protect the people against violence.

This he could do in two ways. As President, he might assemble the Congress and submit the matter to the

law-making power, or he might continue military supervision until Congress acted. He chose the latter course.

That the authority in those states was a military one
could not be questioned, for those in command were
military officers acting in military capacity and paid
by the Secretary of War from military funds. The
President could decide how far he would exercise his
military authority or how far he would relax it, or
even on what terms he would withdraw it, but it was
not for him to determine upon the nature or effect of
any system of Government which the people of those
states might see fit to adopt. That power was lodged
by the Constitution in the Congress.

What the President had done, therefore, was an intimation to the people of the rebellious states that as
commander-in-chief of the army, he would consent to
withdrawing military rule, if they would, by their acts,
manifest a disposition to preserve order among themselves, establish governments denoting loyalty to the
Union, and exhibit a settled determination to return to
their allegiance. He would permit the law-making
power to fix the terms of their final restoration. This,
the report held, was certainly the view of his power
that the President had taken, as evidenced by his acts
and communications. Any other supposition would im-
pute to the President designs of encroachment upon a
coordinate branch of the Government.

When Congress assembled in December of 1865, the
people of most of the rebellious states under the President's advice, had organized local governments and
some had even acceded to terms proposed by him. In
his message, Johnson had stated in general terms what

had been done, but he "did not see fit to communicate the details for the information of Congress."

The report reviewed the call upon Johnson for the pertinent facts and papers and how, after some six weeks of delay, they were finally delivered. But even this gave no fully definite or sufficient information, and the committee was forced to call its own witnesses in order to obtain any real knowledge of the situations in the late Confederate States.

It was contended that representatives of the rebel states should be admitted immediately to seats in Congress. To support this position, it was argued that "inasmuch as the states had no legal right to separate themselves from the Union, they still retained their position as states, and consequently the people thereof had a right to immediate representation without imposition of any conditions whatever."

It had even been charged that until such admission, all legislation affecting their interests was, if not unconstitutional, at least unjustifiable and oppressive. But that proposition, the committee held, was wholly untenable, and if admitted, would tend to the destruction of the Government.

Those states, without justification or excuse had risen in insurrection against the United States, deliberately abolished their State Governments, so far as the United States was concerned, renounced their allegiance and proceeded to establish an independent Government for themselves. They had seized the Nation's forts, arsenals, and dockyards, driven out those who remained true to the Union, and heaped every imaginable insult and injury upon the United States and its citizens.

Finally, they had opened hostilities and levied war.

The report continued in Stevens' familiar phrases that "one of the consequences of that War was that the conquered rebels were at the mercy of the conquerors, limited only by the laws of humanity," and that the Government, thus outraged, had a most perfect right to exact indemnity for injuries done and security against recurrences.

What the nature of those amends should be was a question for the law-making power to decide. Some had insisted with great gravity that due to the nature of our Government, no such right on the part of the conqueror could exist; that from the moment the rebellion ceased, all rights of the rebel communities were at once restored, and because the people of a state of the Union were once an organized community within the Union, they necessarily so remained and their right to be represented in Congress and to participate in the Government, admitted neither question nor dispute.

But if that were true, then the United States was powerless for its own protection, and flagrant rebellion carried even to a Civil War, was a pastime for any State to play with, knowing that it could lose nothing in any event, but might even be the gainer by defeat. If rebellion succeeded, it accomplished its purpose and destroyed the Government; if it failed, the War was barren of results and the battle might still be fought out in the Legislative halls of the Nation. "Treason defeated in the field had only to take possession of Congress and the Cabinet."

The Committee would not discuss the question as to whether the late Confederate States were still States of the Union. Such was but a profitless abstraction about which too many words had already been wasted. It was more than idle—it was mockery, to contend that the disloyal people still retained the perfect and entire right to resume at their own will and pleasure, all the privileges within the Union, and especially to participate in its Government. "To admit such a principle for one moment would be to declare that treason is always master and loyalty a blunder."

Constructively, the Committee held "it most desirable that the Union of all of the States should become perfect at the earliest moment, consistent with the peace and welfare of the Nation; that all these States shall become fully represented in national councils and take their part in legislation of the country."

But the War had brought slavery abolition, and a large part of the population had been converted from mere chattels into free men. The country dared not abandon them without securing some rights to them. Most of them had been loyal and were entitled to some consideration. Unless security was given to them, the whole civilized world would cry out against such base ingratitude, for the bare idea of it was offensive to all right thinking men. After much study and deliberation, the Committee was convinced that Constitutional provisions were the only means.

To complicate the problem, the question of representation must be adjudicated. The practical effect of the law as it was would have increased the voice of the rebel states in the Government. This would have the inevitable effect of rewarding secession.

Next followed a review of the action of the conventions and legislatures in the rebel states under the provisional governors appointed by President Johnson.

"The language of all the provisions and ordinances of those states on the slavery subject amounted to nothing more than an unwilling admission of an unwelcome truth." Although the secession ordinances had in some cases been declared null and void, and in others repealed, there was no instance where Constitutional refutation was made of that deadly heresy.

Ordinarily the authority for reframing the State Governments emanated from Congress, but "under the peculiar circumstances," the committee was not disposed to "criticize the President's action in assuming the power exercised by him in this regard." Irregularities of the Conventions were pointed out, and especially those in South Carolina, "where the Convention, although disbanded by the provisional Governor, on the ground that it was a revolutionary body, assumed to redistrict the State."

Hardly had the War closed, when the "insurrectionary States haughtily claimed as a right, the privilege of participating at once in the Government which they had fought to destroy." Encouraged by the President to organize State Governments, they had at once placed in power leading rebels, unrepentant and unpardoned, and contemptuously excluded those who had been loyal to the Union. As an example of this, the report pointed to the election of A. H. Stephens, late Vice-President of the Confederacy, to the Senate.

The Southern press, with few exceptions, abounded with abuse of institutions and people of the loyal states, defended the leaders of the rebellion, reviled Southern loyalists, and strove constantly and unscrupulously to keep alive the fires of hate and discord between the sections.

The National Banner was openly insulted, and the National Air scoffed at, not only by an ignorant populace at public meetings, but by notables. The Freedman's Bureau was permitted to function only under military protection, and a deep-seated prejudice against color was assiduously cultivated by the public journals. All this led to acts of cruelty, oppression, and even murder, which the local authorities were at no pains to prevent or punish.

True it was that some of the large planters and men of the better class were honestly striving to bring about a better order of things and were employing freed-men at fair wage, and treating them kindly, but that was the exception and not the rule.

The conciliatory measures of the Government did not seem to have been met halfway. The bitterness and defiance exhibited toward the United States was without parallel in the history of the world. In return for leniency, it was getting only an insulting denial of Federal authority.

Even the President had not deemed it safe to restore the Writ of Habeas Corpus, nor to withdraw the troops from any localities, and Federal resentment was so heated that the commanding generals felt an increase of the army indispensable to the preservation of order and protection of the loyal people in the South.

The Committee was therefore of the opinion that the rebel states, at the close of the War, were disorganized communities without civil Government, and without

Constitution or other forms by virtue of which political relations could legally exist between them and the Federal Government; that Congress could not be expected to recognize as valid, elections of representatives from disorganized communities, who were unable to present their claim under the established and recognized rules, hitherto required; that Congress would not be justified in admitting such communities to participation in the Government of the country, without first providing Constitutional or other guarantee that would tend to secure civil rights for all citizens, a just equality of representation, protection against claims founded in rebellion and crime, temporary restoration of the right of suffrage to loyal persons, and the exclusion from positions of public trust of at least a portion of those whose crimes had proved them to be enemies of the Union, and unworthy of public confidence.[39]

The report is conspicuous for its lack of strong language. Compared with most of the speeches and writings of the time, both in and out of Congress, it is exceedingly mild. The President was dealt with gently and impersonally. Up to that time, it was the best presentation of the Congressional idea of reconstruction.

Congress adjourned in July with the country embroiled in a far-reaching and all-important duel between the executive and legislative arms of its Government. The differences were not so great as to be irreconcilable, but there were stubborn men on both sides. That many were convinced they were fighting for principle, made the contest all the more bitter.

More and more the members of Congress showed a distrust and antipathy against Johnson and he reciprocated their feelings. He repeatedly said that he feared assassination at the hands of radical leaders and went so far as to speak of it publicly.[40]

On the other hand, Congressional leaders were just as suspicious that Johnson might recognize their opponents as the Congress, and they perhaps had some basis for their fear. In a Senate speech, Davis, of Kentucky, threatened them, saying it was the "President's prerogative to decide what body of men constituted Congress, since it was a part of his duties to communicate with it. Whenever Johnson chose to say to Southern leaders, 'get together with the Democrats and Conservatives of the Senate, and if constituting a majority, I will recognize you as the Senate of the United States,' what then, shall become of you gentlemen?" [41]

With ten states locked outside the gates of the Union, a second clash of stupendous proportions, affecting all of what was left, augured most terrible consequences for the Nation. Both sides understood this full well, but neither would make the slightest overture toward conciliation. Each was determined to fight it out to the end.

The issue was clearly framed. The people must judge between restoration and reconstruction. The case went to the country.

V

THE DECISION

In the fall of 1866, citizens of the United States went to the polls to decide one of the most far-reaching questions that had ever been submitted to the electorate. They were to choose between the Executive and Congressional plans for reconstruction. The issue was not wholly an impersonal one. Proponent of the former was Andrew Johnson, President of the United States. Thaddeus Stevens led advocates of the latter. Vindication of one meant repudiation of the other.

The fact that no less than four national conventions assembled, indicates that the importance of the matter was recognized at the time.

Those who had borne arms in the War made up a large and influential part of the public opinion of the country, and each side made an appeal to them through a "Soldiers' and Sailors' Convention."

One of these, under the name of National Union Convention, met at Philadelphia in August, and claimed to have represented within it every state North and South. Its leaders were followers of Johnson and his policy, who attempted to consolidate support by a program that called for a quick restoration and extension to the seceded states of an immediate and full representation in the Congress.

One of the interesting sidelights was a carefully planned entrance by General Couch of Massachusetts, and Governor Orr, of South Carolina, who entered the Convention hall with their arms intertwined. The incident was made so much of that it gave name to the assembly, which was thereafter known as the "Arm in Arm" Convention. The whole tenor of the meeting was a sentimental one, wherein old grievances would be forgot and "joyous harmony" composed.

Congressional leaders were quick to make fun of it. They dubbed the Convention Hall a "Noah's Ark" into which "the animals entered two by two, the elephant and the kangaroo; of clean beasts and of beasts that are not clean, and of fowls and of everything that creepeth upon the earth." There is, however, no record that Stevens either inspired or used any of these references.[1]

Johnson's opponents, that is, the men who were dictating the Congressional policy and their followers, held their Republican Convention in early September. Ex-Attorney General Speed, who had resigned from the Johnson Cabinet when the President took a firm stand against the Fourteenth Amendment, presided. Johnson and his quick restoration plans were strongly denounced and the pending amendment was set up as the real issue.

When a report of the Convention was made to Johnson, he was bitter and resentful, referring to Congress as "a body called or which assumes to be called the Congress of the United States, while in fact it is a Congress of only a part of the States, hanging, as it were, upon the verge of the Government."[2]

As was to be expected, the Congressional block had been successful in their ingenious appeal to the country for support of the program embodied in Stevens' proposed amendment. Johnson was politician enough to understand that the situation for him was serious

Stevens at the Age of Seventy, Just Before His Physical Decline Began

and that his "policy" had been maneuvered into a
very precarious position. He determined on a last
minute personal appeal to the voters and used as a
pretext a visit to the dedication of the tomb of Douglas
in Chicago.

In that famous "swing around the circle," he did
himself and his cause more harm than any President
had or has ever done in all our history. Angry, perplexed, upset, but militant, he took the stump on every
proferred occasion to vindicate his program, and entered pellmell into the hurly-burly of the heated political dissension.

In his speeches, instead of making an effort to hold
himself to a dignity in keeping with his high office, he
seemed desirous and even anxious to place himself on
the level of an ordinary stump speaker. Apparently
he relied on the resourcefulness and repartee that he had
developed as a campaigner, in the mountain districts
of Tennessee. He seemed eager to prove his ability at
meeting and conquering the hecklers.

On the trip, he took with him General Grant, who
went under protest,[3] Admiral Farragut, and three
members of his Cabinet; Seward, Welles and Randall.
At every place where the train stopped and a group appeared, he made his characteristic and extempore
speeches, practically all of which were in bad taste.

At the beginning of the journey, the adventure held
some promise. In the East, especially in New York,
he seemed favorably received, but as he moved West,
the success of the tour became greatly tempered, until
in Cleveland and in St. Louis, the President's impetu-
osity in his public remarks made him no end of trouble.

It not only repelled all good he might have done his cause, but went to the extent of placing in the hands of his enemies ammunition from his own lips which caused, in large measure, his repudiation.

In Cleveland, although he stated at the outset that he did not appear "for the purpose of making a speech," he did exactly that. Instead of ignoring the hecklers who constantly interrupted him, he seemed to enjoy their low grade banter, and entered into it enthusiastically. Early in the speech, when someone called to him, "hang Jeff Davis!", Johnson answered, "why don't *you* hang him?"

Someone else had shouted, "hang Jeff Davis and Wendell Phillips!" At the time, Johnson ignored that remark, but later in his address, without any suggestion from the outside, as the reported speech shows, he returned to the subject with, "then I would ask you why not hang Thad Stevens and Wendell Phillips? I tell you, my countrymen, I have been fighting the South and they have been whipped and crushed, and they acknowledge their defeat and accept the terms of the Constitution, and now, as I go around the circle, having fought traitors in the South, I am prepared to fight traitors in the North." [4]

Five days later, in St. Louis, he again opened his address by saying that he had been introduced but "not for the purpose of making a speech." After repeating that remark, characteristically, he then proceeded to make one.

With much haranguing and language that could have no effect other than to alienate his listeners, he reached his familiar but wholly inexcusable words, "I might ask you a question. Why don't you hang Thad Stevens and Wendell Phillips?"

When Congress adjourned in the summer, Stevens was a physically sick and broken man. He had given what he thought was the last of his energies to human welfare and his closing speech intimated his fear that he might never again appear on the Floor. Resting on his famous Reconstruction Committee Report,[5] he did but little in the campaign, confining himself to a few addresses in his home town of Lancaster. But in spite of his illness, he followed with amusement the reports of Johnson's tour, early appreciating the drift of support from the President's policy to the Congressional one.

In the single important speech that he made at home before the election, he said, "when I left Washington, I was somewhat worn down by labors and diseases, and was directed by my physician neither to think, speak, nor read until the next session of Congress, or I should not regain my strength. I have followed the first injunction most religiously, for I believe I have not let an idea pass through my mind since. The second one, not to speak, I was seduced from keeping by some noble friends in the mountain districts of Pennsylvania . . . The third one, not to read, I have followed almost literally."

But it was true that he had entertained himself with a little frivolous reading. He had taken up the daily publications and read things which would not exhaust him. "For instance, there was a serious account from day to day of a very remarkable circus that traveled through the country." He had followed the reports expecting "great wit from the celebrated character of its clowns. They were well provided, for instead of one, there were two, as the circus was covering a large circulation.

"One of these clowns was high in office and somewhat advanced in age. The other was a little less advanced in office, but older in years. They started out with a very respectable stock company. In order to attract attention, they took with them a celebrated general, and an eminent naval officer whom they had to chain to the rigging so that he could not escape, as he tried once or twice to do.

"Though announced as a most respectable stock company, they even went forth with a manager that had no very good man for the spring boards, but they did take with them for a short distance, a fellow well accustomed to the ground and lofty tumbling, called Montgomery Blair."

Stevens looked upon the performance as rather silly, especially when the older clown (Seward) said the younger one (Johnson) had it in his power, if he chose, to be dictator. The elder "pointed to the other one, and said to the people, 'will you have him for President, or will you take him for King?'⁶ He left you but one alternative. You were obliged to take him for one or the other.

"Sometimes they cut outside the circle and entered into street brawls with common blackguards. One of them said he had been everything; a tailor, city alderman, legislator, congressman, senator, and was then President. In fact, he had been everything but a hangman and now he asked leave to hang Thad Stevens."

But in serious vein, he said plainly, "the great question between the President and the Congress is not how we shall reconstruct the states, but whom shall have that power?" That, of course, was the crux of the whole issue presented to the people. He argued at some length to justify Congressional jurisdiction and Congress as the sovereign power because the people spoke through it. "Andrew Johnson must learn that he is your servant and that as Congress shall order, he must obey."[7]

The tremendous energies consumed by the Nation's leaders in devising issues and appeals that would sway the people to them in that crucial year; the political cross currents, group movements, and economic incidents that functioned, are a study in themselves. No attempt has been made here even to mention them, for Stevens, invalided at his Lancaster home, took little part after filing his comprehensive Committee Report.[8] The radical Congressional group had it widely published as the basis of their appeal to the Nation.

When election day came, the people gave no uncertain verdict. Johnson's policy was condemned beyond recall and the voters delivered to the Congressional group a mandate to proceed. One hundred forty-three Republican members were elected to Congress, against forty-nine Democrats. To carry out the designated plan, there was a safe margin beyond the necessary two-thirds in each of the Houses. The Presidential veto, even if exercised, could be of no avail.

The people had spoken—restoration was rejected; reconstruction ordered.

BOOK SIX
DICTATOR

BOOK SIX—DICTATOR

I

BEGINNINGS OF RECONSTRUCTION

IN the decisive elections of 1866, the country spoke
with a clear and firm voice. No intelligent person
could have misunderstood that the people had flatly
repudiated the President and his policy and shown a
decided preference for the Congressional plan of reconstruction.

In the face of that verdict, Johnson had three logical
courses open. He could have submitted completely
and supported any method Congress might adopt, all
the while disclaiming responsibility for whatever might
happen. He could have attempted an adjustment and
compromise, or, if he felt that principle precluded his
yielding to any extent, he could have resigned. He did
none of these.

In his second annual message, he showed unmistak-
ably his unveering determination to fight it out with
Congress to the bitter end, the people's verdict against
him notwithstanding. His communication was a bold
and defiant, although able reiteration in even stronger
language of his original program. It offered not a
single opportunity for conciliatory adjustment. More
than ignoring what the people had ordered, it openly
flouted their will and challenged their command.

But Stevens did not take the message seriously
enough to prevent his joking about it. Johnson, in-
tentionally or otherwise, had permitted his communication to be printed in a newspaper circulated before the
original reached the House. Stevens moved the Clerk

proceed to read the President's message. When that officer reported that it had not yet been officially communicated, Stevens sent down a copy of the newspaper containing it. But he didn't press the matter. His gibe at the irregularity had registered and amidst laughter, he withdrew the motion.

For several months, Johnson had been using his power to remove hostile Federal officers and replace them with his friends. In this, he certainly showed no attempt to appease rising Congressional opposition, and had he deliberately sought a way to irritate it, he could have found no better. When some flare of temper was suddenly shown by a Congressman against the President, the jocular question his colleagues always turned to ask, was, "did he remove *your* collector, too?" [1]

Congressmen soon discovered that the patronage as Johnson was using it, was a most effective weapon against them. With it, he could reach directly into the district of each and there build up an assertive opposition. The feeling was general that unless something were done to curb him, he would make trouble for any and every member whom he felt was not supporting him.

For some time the Committee on Retrenchment had been endeavoring half-heartedly to agree upon some sort of measure to strike down the President's power of removal. Of course the problem was a new one and its solution required boldness of thought.

Stevens gave the Committee what he thought was reasonable time to act and then, because they had submitted nothing, presented his own measure. Spalding asked him if he were aware that the subject was then

before a designated Committee, but he brushed aside
the question with the remark, "all I know is that I
offer this bill. If the gentleman does not like it, he
can vote against it." [2]

In substance, it provided that the President could
not remove from office, appointees nominated by him
and confirmed by the Senate unless that body concurred
in the removal. The bill became the Tenure-of-Office
Act, alleged violation of which precipitated the Impeachment.

On the second day of the session, the Commoner had
passed without even a record vote, a joint resolution
reappointing the Committee of Fifteen on Reconstruction, the forerunner of which had expired with the close
of the prior session. That group went to work immediately, and its meeting place was Stevens' workshop.

While the Committee was laboring, there was much
talk on the Floor looking toward some hasty method of
getting the rebel states back into the Union. With one
eye on his reconstruction group and the other on the
House, Stevens showed his remarkable will in the way
he drove his sick body to the dual work.

On January 3, 1867, he offered a bill, the importance
of which has never been duly credited. In it was set
forth a plan under which the States would be regarded in
a status nearer statehood by a far greater margin than
under the legislation finally adopted. The fact is, the
Old Commoner would even accept, to an extent, the
governments which President Johnson had set up.

He was careful at the very beginning of his bill to
designate those governments as "illegally formed in the
midst of martial law, with Constitutions in many in-

stances adopted under duress and not submitted to the people for ratification." But he would go at least half-way toward a compromise, by having Congress recognize those governments "as valid for municipal purposes."

His plan would require each state to hold an election prior to May of 1867 for the purpose of choosing delegates for a Constitutional Convention. Significantly, all male citizens resident there one year were to be permitted to vote. Rebels who had served in the civil or military government of the Confederacy were precluded from voting or holding office for five years but might cast their ballot in the preliminary elections upon subscribing to a specified oath.

The States were warned that "no Constitution should be submitted to the Congress which denied to any citizen any rights, privileges or immunities which are granted to any other citizen in the state." All laws had to be impartial without regard to "language, race, or former condition."

Stevens' dexterous mind showed itself in his attempt to make these provisions binding beyond the limits of the ordinary statute. He inserted in his bill the qualification that if any of the requirements set forth should "ever be altered, repealed, expunged, or in any way abrogated by the state" that such state thereupon would "lose its right to be represented in Congress."

His speech upon the bill was delivered immediately and was in the main, a reiteration of his reconstruction theories. He seemed satisfied that by this time the country had accepted generally his original proposition that the rebel states were irrevocably out of the Union, and could be raised to statehood only by act of Congress.

One cannot study the incident, however, without noticing that Stevens did not show his usual vigor in following up his proposal. It was introduced and submitted with his characteristic forcefulness. But having fully explained it, he appeared to leave it to its fate. The House in those days had become accustomed to follow in a general way the lead of the Lancastrian, and as might be expected, when he was indifferent, there was no one who cared to move in matters so important as the one his proposal covered.

Neglected, his bill drifted into the discard. He never intimated that it was submitted as a test of compromise between the Executive and Congressional plans. But in substance, that is what it was. The Old Commoner, who secretly admired consistency and orderly movement, no doubt offered it for the purposes of the record. If it were accepted, he would be satisfied to support it. If not, he could honestly feel that his compromise had been refused.

As he saw it shunted to the background, he showed more and more insistence that Congress refuse to recognize as valid, the Johnson state governments then existing. To him, they were the products of a "bastard reconstruction." [3] Of course, that did not apply to Tennessee, for he said "I feel kindly toward her." Maynard answered that his state "reciprocates the sentiment of the gentleman from Pennsylvania" and invited him to spend a day or two there to recuperate. But the tottering dictator, fainting frequently in the cloak rooms, with death grappling for him, could still joke. He had to respectfully decline the offer because he "had made no preparation for a burial down there." [4]

With his compromise plan disregarded, Stevens returned to his Reconstruction Committee room. There, after many wearied hours of labor, he finally whipped together enough support to emit as a Committee measure, another and infinitely harsher program of reconstruction.

On February 6, he reported out his bill "to provide for the more efficient Government of the insurrectionary States." Revolutionary though it was, it bore Stevens' characteristic stamp of brevity. The whereases which premised the proposed enactments were condensed to one paragraph. Following the theory that he had advocated since the beginning of the Rebellion, his plan would ignore state boundaries. He disdainfully omitted using the word "states" in even a limited sense.

The areas that had been ten States, that is, all of the Confederacy except Tennessee, were divided into five military districts, each under the supreme command of a regular army officer not below the rank of Brigadier General. He would have detailed to him "a sufficient force to enable him to perform his duty and enforce his authority within the District."

Ignoring the President utterly, the commanding officers were to be selected and assigned by the General of the Army. Their duties would be to protect the personal and property rights of everyone, and punish disturbers of the public peace, and criminals. Several tribunals were provided to take jurisdiction, or if in the judgment of the commanding officer it were necessary, military tribunals could be constituted and resorted to.

The Writ of Habeas Corpus was withheld in behalf of persons in military custody, unless the petition bore the approval of a military officer. But prompt trial was ordered and no cruel or unusual punishment would be inflicted. Furthermore, no sentence could be executed except with the approval of the officer commanding the district.

Again, as on so many previous occasions the Old Commoner found himself pressed for time. The Congress would adjourn within the month, and if his measure were to pass, it must move with unusual speed. Few men of all the Congresses could have forced through such a radical measure in the brief time remaining, but such was the forte of the dying Lancastrian.

Representative Finck said it was, in his judgment, "the most important measure that has ever been presented to an American Congress," and demanded time for a deliberate discussion. Stevens knew how revolutionary it was, and therefore desired to allow all time possible for debate.

But none knew better than he that because the time was so limited, it required no filibuster to defeat it. Even the meagerest of debate would use up so much of the few remaining days that there could be no hope of making it law before March 4.

The opposition were very much alarmed as to when Stevens would call for the vote upon it, some fearing that he might do so even before the bill was printed. But he had no such rash intent. As he pointed out, much had been priorly said on some sort of program. LeBlonde reiterated a demand for a full discussion. Stevens responded that he was "very willing that the

debate which has been going on here for three weeks
and which the gentleman will find in the Globe, shall
be read over. . . ." But he saw no necessity for argument upon it "beyond tomorrow."

He would give the opposition every possible moment
and even went so far as to offer a "gentleman on the
other side" half of the time allotted to himself. He
trusted that there was no disposition on the part of the
majority "to occupy much time in debate upon the bill,
but to yield the time to a great extent" to its adversaries.[5]

He took but a few minutes of the allotted hour to
speak in support of his proposal. Nearly two years had
passed since the War ended. In all that time, said
he, the rebel areas had been in a "condition of anarchy"
and "the loyal people of those ten States have endured
all the horrors of the worst chaos of any country. Per-
secution, exile, murder, have been the order of the day
within all these territories" so far as loyal men were
concerned, either white or black, and more especially
if they happened to be black.

"We have seen the best men—those who stood by the
flag of the Union, driven from their homes and compelled to live on the cold charity of a cold North. We
have seen loyal men flitting about everywhere, through
your cities, around your doors, melancholy, depressed,
haggard, like the ghosts of the unburied dead on this
side of the River Styx, and yet we have borne it with
exemplary patience.

"We have been enjoying 'our ease in our inns'; and
while we were praising the rebel South and asking in
pitious terms for mercy for that people, we have been

From Frank Leslie's Illustrated News, March 28, 1868.

Stevens, too Weak to Walk, is Carried to a Meeting of the Impeachment Committee

deaf to the agonies, and groans which have been borne to us by every Southern breeze from the dying and murdered victims."

The nervous minority, fearing Stevens' steam roller, again sought delay. Rogers begged him to "consent to let the debate go on today and tomorrow and take the vote on Monday." But the Lancastrian was adamant, saying "I have already, I think, three times refused that proposition." The days were moving too speedily and he realized that if Johnson held the bill ten days before vetoing it, there would be but the narrowest margin of time remaining.

Blaine, by amendments, attempted to modify Stevens' plan, but condemning the changes as only another step "toward universal amnesty and universal Andy-Johnsonism," Stevens forced his measure through exactly one week after he had introduced it. The vote was one hundred nine for the bill, fifty-five against it, and twenty-six not voting.[6]

The Old Commoner's eyes, with the fog of death in them, brightened for the moment as he exulted "in the language of good old Laertes, 'Heaven rules as yet and there are Gods above!'"[7]

The measure probably never would have been resorted to by Stevens, had the Southern States taken a less offensive position. After all the devious means they had tried to avoid the Thirteenth Amendment, their stubborn resistance and insolence was brought to a climax by the startling record of their attitude toward the proposed Fourteenth Amendment.

On the day that Stevens brought his bill from Committee, the eleven States which had constituted the Confederacy had voted upon that amendment. Tennessee had quietly adopted it, but every other State had defiantly rejected it, and some had gone so far as to repudiate it by unanimous vote of their conventions.

The measure as Stevens conceived and wrote it, was, above all, a merely temporary one. And therein lay his objection to the Blaine Amendments which raised the whole Reconstruction question by setting forth conditions on which the rebel states should be readmitted. To the Old Commoner, it was impolitic for the Government to bind itself when no one would attempt to foretell what unusual conditions even the near future might bring. Furthermore, as a Parliamentarian, he took the position that it was not fair "to pledge future Congresses."

His bill was not intended as a Reconstruction measure but "simply as a police bill to protect loyal men from anarchy and murder until this Congress, taking a little more time, can suit gentlemen in a bill for the readmission of all those rebel states upon the basis of civil government."

The Senate, under the leadership of Sumner, showed a distinct leaning toward Blaine's idea and passed the House bill with some features of those amendments in it.

Stevens was again embarrassed. Lack of time made quick action imperative and the Upper Body, either out of sympathy with the measure completely, or not appreciating the situation, was adopting a course that would defeat it. Stevens denounced the modification, saying "the Senate has sent back to us an amendment which contains everything else but protection. It returned a bill which raises the whole question in dispute as to the best mode of reconstructing the states and embodying future pledges which this Congress has no authority to make and no power to execute." [8]

The Committee on Conference reasserted some of the House proposals and the bill was finally passed on the twentieth day of February. Only twelve days were left before the session expired, and ten of those Johnson might permit to pass with nothing more done. That is exactly what he did.

On the last day of the ten allotted to him to take action on the bill, he returned it with his veto. That was on Saturday afternoon. The new Congress came into being at noon of the following Monday. In spite of the way Stevens had curtailed debate, not a moment was to be lost, and even then there was grave doubt that minority filibustering could be overcome in so short a time. One of the members had challenged that the bill would not pass unless he "was overpowered by physical exhaustion or restrained by the rules of the House."

But the Dictator knew how to handle such opposition. In mock seriousness, he said he was "aware of the melancholy feeling with which opponents are approaching this 'funeral of the Nation!'" Blaine had been satisfied and was now working with the Lancastrian. After permitting a short discussion, Stevens called upon his colleague to offer the resolution for the vote. The House, "amidst great applause on the Floor and in the galleries," overrode the veto by a vote of one hundred thirty-six to forty-three, with twelve not voting. The Senate followed and the first great military reconstruction measure became law. [9]

Stevens has been consistently damned since that March day in 1867 for bringing about the terrible conditions and hardships that came to the South in the next decade.

That is wholly unfair for the measures which he contemplated were never tried. When Stevens introduced his bill, the South was in an almost unbelievable condition of chaos. Government had broken down completely. Secret groups and mobs were in control and neither property nor life was in any measure secure.

The Congress knew all this and so did the North, for horrid examples frequently exaggerated, had been used widely in the election campaign of the previous autumn. The Commoner's proposal was simply a police measure aimed solely to safeguard life and property. Everyone understood that some such effective national protection was utterly imperative, if in no other name, then, in that of humanity.

The Senate's untimely and ill-considered insistence in expanding the bill into a permanent policy of reconstruction is largely responsible for much of the trouble that resulted. Not only did Senators force what was for all practical purposes an irrevocable ultimatum to the rebel states, but they did it at a moment that marked the climax of severity of the Congressional attitude against the South.

The Old Commoner's idea of a temporary measure, because it would provide merely for an emergency could have been modified easily in one direction or the other, depending on the manner in which reconstruction proceeded. The hard and fast plan set forth in the legislation as it finally passed could not be retracted or alleviated without Congress appearing to admit error.

Certainly it was not only irregular, as Stevens pointed out, to bind future Congresses, but it was, as events proved, wholly unsound. The conditions imposed were so harsh that few believed they could ever be met, and their mere announcement further enraged the South. All in all, it was excellent evidence to support the Southern contention that Congress had no sincere desire to fix terms upon which the rebel states could return to the Union.

There was nothing vindictive or punitive in Stevens' mind. This was very forcibly shown while a simultaneous measure was under discussion. Lawrence of Ohio, had introduced a bill to repeal a limitation statute so as to permit the prosecution of rebels for treason. The Commoner heard some discussion upon it, and then took the Floor.

Showing, under the circumstances, an admirable sense of justice and fair play, he said, "I approach with great distrust all bills of this kind, which are evidently brought forward for the purpose of ascertaining how we can convict men whom we cannot convict under laws existing when the crimes were committed." Such action to him was fundamentally unsound and unsafe and the Government "must be careful how it tampers with the crime or the remedy." He was fully aware that there were traitors in the South, but added, "I should never attempt to try them for treason," for there were so many engaged in the crime that such procedure would be impracticable and unjust.

The bill itself indicates that there were revengeful men in the House at the time. Stevens' stern rebuke of them is a striking bit of evidence, showing with what lack of fairness the critics who had called him revengeful have judged him. He disdainfully repudiated the measure, insisting that "there must be some quieting law."

When he finished his two minute speech against it, its sponsors, thoroughly chastized, quickly dropped it and it was heard of no more.[10] It remained for him who has been called the greatest hater of the South, to annihilate at the beginning, the plans and program of those who really did the hating.

Congress, working under great stress and violent pressure, applied by both sides, had seen fit to reject Stevens' mild bill of January, wherein the Old Commoner was open to compromise. His February bill as a temporary measure was not only reasonable, but necessary for the welfare of the South itself.

Through either inability or lack of desire to understand the Lancastrian's idea of a calm and steady, step by step, approach to reconstruction, the Senate precipitated an untimely plan, harsher than Stevens would have invoked at the time, and rashly and blindly jumped in a single leap to a goal which an intelligent feeling of the way might have reached with infinitely less hardship.

The March legislation became effective immediately, and under it, the South began to murmur and then to groan. There was but a year of life left for the hoary Dictator. Had he lived, the South very probably would have found its travails alleviated. Military reconstruction was distasteful to him as he showed when he vehemently objected to the report of the Committee on Conference.[11] Its ravishment of the South came after Stevens was dead.

II

CONFISCATION

Boldest advocate of a confiscation policy, Stevens was, at the time and even today is, roundly condemned for his proposal. He had abundant legal authority and precedent to support him, and his opponents, unable to answer his arguments, turned their attack upon him. Critics without exception have attributed his confiscation demand to an insatiable personal hatred of Southerners, coupled with a selfish desire to be reimbursed for his own losses.

Even a brief study of the facts shows the shallowness of such conclusions.

As Chairman of the House Committee charged with those duties, Stevens had been largely responsible for raising and appropriating the monies needed for the War. Opinion today credits him and his collaborators with having done their work well.

Few men of the Nation realized at the outset how stupendous would be the ordeal of subduing the Confederacy. The Lancaster Congressman was among the few. He was the first man to publicly state his opinion that the task was no small one and would require greater expenditure of life and money than any leaders, including Lincoln, believed it would. The long, drawn-out War proved only too convincingly how right he was.

When it was over, the Government found itself owing between three and four billions of dollars. The Old Commoner estimated that when the miscellaneous debts and pensions were capitalized and funded, the national debt would substantially exceed the latter figure.

Annual interest on that amount, even if its average could be reduced to six per cent, would exceed two hundred forty millions of dollars. The ordinary yearly expenses of government were one hundred twenty millions and the extraordinary expenses of the army and navy, one hundred ten million. This total of more than four hundred seventy millions of dollars per year for current expenses and carrying charges appeared overwhelming, even to Stevens.

The four billion dollar national debt was the largest that any nation ever found itself burdened with. Great Britain's debt at the time, of approximately that amount, was in reality not nearly as large as ours, for she was paying but three per cent interest, which made her annual charges considerably less than half of ours.

While the conflict lasted, governmental financing meant only the improvising of means to borrow, or tax, sufficiently to satisfy the voracious maw of War. The end of the struggle marked the arrival of the day of financial reckoning. Stevens, who by that time had far greater experience in the raising of revenues than any other man in the Congress, had grave doubts that the appalling sum could be liquidated solely through taxation.

For more than a year before the War ended, he had been talking of a confiscation and the figures of his specific plan, when he announced it, are eloquent of its purpose. He never "pretended that the doctrine of universal or general confiscation or of general capital punishment should be inflicted upon the conquered belligerent."[1] He asked merely for a "mild confiscation." [2] With such the Nation could "pay at least three-fourths of its debt and the balance could be managed with" the then "present taxation." [3]

He had gathered many statistics and done much figuring. [4] Near the end of 1865, he estimated that there were about six million freed people in the South. The land acreage there was about four hundred sixty-five million. Of this amount, land owned by the former States and about seventy thousand persons made up three hundred ninety-four million acres. The remaining seventy-one million acres were owned by people, each of whom held less than two hundred acres. These he would not disturb. [5]

He figured that "by forfeiting the estates of the leading rebels, the Government would have three hundred ninety-four millions of acres besides their town properties, and yet nine-tenths of the people would remain untouched." This land he would divide into convenient farms of forty acres for each adult freeman. He estimated that there were about a million of these and that would leave more than three hundred fifty million acres for sale. At ten dollars per acre, it would produce at least three and one-half billion dollars. This he would use as follows:

(1) Invest three hundred million dollars in six per cent Government Bonds and use the interest semi-annually for soldiers' pensions.

(2) Appropriate two hundred million dollars to pay the damage done to loyal men of the North and the South by the Rebellion.

(3) Apply the residue of three billion forty million dollars toward payment of the national debt. [6]

At least the financial problems of the country would be solved.

No one can read Stevens' remarks on the subject without concluding that his confiscation ideas were very closely affiliated with a more comprehensive plan to care for the freed negro. Slavery was gone. The Government had turned "into the open world five or six millions of men, women and children, not one of whom has a hut to shelter him, an article of property, or a cent of money. By the accursed policy" of their masters, they were totally uneducated, forbidden to learn their religious and moral duties, and the simplest principles of Government. Wholly unversed in contracts and the means of sustaining their families, they were unfit to contend with the world unless guided by wiser heads "until they shall have acquired practical knowledge. To trust to the tender mercies of their former masters and to the protection of State legislation, without giving them any voice in making the laws, is simply to turn them over to the torture of their enemies. To turn them loose unaided and unprotected is wholesale murder."

The Humanitarian was speaking. "Far better," said he, "to have left them in slavery which gave them a support, although it annihilated their manhood." He scoffed at the idea of colonizing the freed negroes, as some eminent men then advocated. "They must be provided for on the soil where they worked and furnished with homes, however small." This matter he placed "above all others" for "justice, humanity, policy and public faith" required the Government to "settle" it "without the intervention of Southern slaveholders." [7]

But with the public debt so overwhelming, it was

useless to think of the Nation purchasing land and erecting homes for the freed blacks. Confiscation offered a simple solution.

Still, he never feared to say that one of the purposes of his confiscation proposal was to punish the leaders of the Rebellion. When he formally introduced his final measure in March of 1867, he did it not as the thought of the Republican Party. "No committee or party is responsible for this bill." Ironically he said, "it is chargeable solely to the President and myself."

By that time, Andrew Johnson was vigorously opposing all confiscation and it must have piqued him to have Stevens read, as a part of his supporting address, an extract from a speech that Johnson had delivered in the summer of 1864. Then Johnson had said "treason must be made odious and traitors must be punished and impoverished; their great properties must be seized and divided into small portions and sold to honest, industrious men." [8]

Stevens said he was in hearty accord with that thought. "Andrew Johnson was the Apostle whose preachings I followed." He called upon the President's friends to stand by him in "this, his favorite policy. If you now desert him, who can you expect to defend the 'much enduring man' at the other end of the avenue?"

For all of the tragedy and sorrow they had brought upon the Nation, the rebels should be punished. However, he would be gentle about it. He "had early in life adopted the view of Boccario and his school of mild punishments" but he nevertheless "insisted that some kind of punishment, fine, banishment, or confiscation should be inflicted upon the conquered belligerent so far as the responsible, rich and culpable leaders were concerned."

He had "uniformly said that the poorer classes, those even in moderate circumstances, who have been compelled by the law of their Government when it became the Confederate States of America, to take a hostile part against the United States . . . ought to be excused from the penalties which guilt inflicted."

Stevens' thought was that "the Lords of Manors, the owners of Dukedoms, the intelligent owners of slaves, and the unembarrassed holders of from fifteen to twenty thousand acres of land" should be "punished by inflicting a fine which should cover the costs and damages which they created." He admitted "their guilt was not always in proportion to wealth, and the ability to respond in damages should be taken into account." [9]

And who could argue that such was not the rule and tradition? "That a vanquished belligerent in an unjust war shall be compelled to pay the expenses and damages thereof is a principle as old as history and as firm as justice. As early as the seige of Troy, one of the indisputable conditions of peace insisted upon by the enlightened Greeks was not only that Hellene should be restored together with the goods which were abstracted, but that Troy should make 'compensation' for the expenses of the War. From that day to this, no publicist or poet has ever disputed the principle."

The Law of Nations was unusually clear on the subject. Stevens went at length into the authorities and quoted in support of his argument, Halleck, Wheaton, Kent, Phillimore and others.

But the opponents of his theory raised the matter of the Constitution. Certainly the Confederate States, even though they had attempted to withdraw from the Union, were indisputably a part of that Union immediately before the War began. The Conservatives, under the slogan, "the Union as it was and the Constitution as it is," represented at the time a substantial part of the people, and appeared to be slowly growing stronger.

President Johnson and his supporters contended "that the War had made no changes in the conditions of our institutions under the Constitution" and insisted that "the rights and liabilities of our fellow citizens, rebels as well as loyal, remain untouched." [10]

Representative Raymond had said in his speech at the Democratic Convention a short time before, and the Convention had adopted his view that the Constitution of the United States was precisely the same after the War as it was before. "It is the supreme law of the land, and inasmuch as there is no Constitutional power to invoke a penalty against the South, the United States was precluded from so doing."

As is pointed out in the chapter on the Constitution, the pertinent question was the exact legal status of the Confederate States. Were they, as States, a part of a de facto belligerent, only temporarily out of the Union? If one accepted the theory of the indestructibility of the State, that conclusion might be plausible and the absent member might be privileged to return as a matter of right. Or, as an independent government which waged active War against the United States, had they lost their status as States and upon defeat become under the

Law of Nations mere conquered territory, subject to the will of the conqueror? Stevens met the point at the outset.

Referring to Raymond's doctrine, which the Democratic Party approved, the Lancastrian exclaimed, "What! Six millions of rebels who had renounced the Constitution, murdered five hundred thousand of our citizens, loaded the Nation with debt and drenched it with blood, when conquered had forfeited no right, lost no jurisdiction, or civil authority?"

And had the conquerors acquired none, solely because of a Constitution which, while the seceded States obeyed, protected them, but which "they had deliberately discarded and torn to pieces by War? No principle in national law is clearer," he announced, "that when belligerents inaugurated War which was acknowledged to be a public War, all former obligations and compacts between the parties become null and void, and after the War are to be renewed or repudiated as the parties agree or as the conqueror decrees." [11]

Stevens held that the Confederate States were out of the Union not by consent of the National Government "but by operation of law." As States, they had formed a government, raised large armies, did what no State in the Union could consistently do, that is, issue letters of marque which were recognized by the United States and foreign nations. There could be no doubt, he said, "that for three years we acknowledged that rebel government as a belligerent as did the whole civilized world."

He quoted Vattel, an authority on the Law of Nations, who held that "when a nation becomes divided into two parties, absolutely independent and no longer acknowledged a common superior, the State is dissolved, and war between the two parties stands on the same ground in every respect as a public war between two different countries." Again "the conventions and treaties made with a nation are broken and annulled by a war arising between the contracting parties. This Stevens said, was "the doctrine of Grotius as well as Vattel and Rutherford and Puffendorf."¹²

And our own Supreme Court was authority eminent enough for the statement that by their rebellion and subsequent acts, the Confederate States had taken themselves out from under the Constitution and raised a public war. In referring to the separation between the colonies and Great Britain, Justice Chase had said, "before these solemn acts of separation from the Crown of Great Britain, the War between Great Britain and the united colonies was a civil war. But instantly on that great event, the Declaration of Independence, the War changed its nature and became a public war, and thereupon all the rights of public war attached and all the former political connection between Great Britain and Virginia and between their respective subjects were totally dissolved. And not only the two nations but all the subjects of each were in a state of war."¹³

The Confederate States were in a position exactly similar to that of Virginia, with the secession ordinances corresponding to the Independence Declaration.

In July of 1862, Congress had enacted the first real confiscation measure, one section of which made it the duty of the President to seize "all the estates and property, money, stocks, credits and effects" of all those "engaged in or aiding the War of the Confederate States." The law was never vigorously enforced and Stevens referred to it only as indicating that a limited confiscation was early approved.[14]

This was his last and greatest speech upon the subject. Sick unto death for many months past, it is a monument to the driving will of the man. The abundance of authorities cited and the range they cover, indicate the great time and patience he spent upon it. The preparatory notes are all in his own scribbled handwriting, showing, as was characteristic of him, that he relied upon no other person's help or counsel.

His effort created a "profound impression throughout the country." [15] Because of the haughty attitude that the South had shown after the War, one editor thought that there were "hundreds of thousands of those who had been ready to carry out the liberal terms which Grant offered Lee, who would now hail with joy the enactment of precisely such a statute as that recommended by Mr. Stevens." [16]

Harper's Weekly took his proposal quite seriously, saying it was "very foolish to speak of Mr. Stevens' confiscation measure as a frantic act of vengeance." His position "is very far from ridiculous, and to suppose that it has no definite reason, is absurd." [17]

The Old Commoner was so deeply interested in the matter that he did what he was never known to do on any other occasion. He had his private agents circulating through the South doing what they could to gain support for his measure.

From Virginia, one of them who signed himself in cipher, wrote that he had been through the lower part

From Frank Leslie's Illustrated News, March 7, 1868.

A Family Quarrel

Andy—"Well, if I can't get in myself, I'll get this stick in."

of the State, and had "done a splendid business, having organized seven camps of the Grand Army which are recruiting rapidly. The objects, as I explain them (privately, of course) take amazingly, and I believe, sir, if all our agents would follow my plan, we would be safe in allowing reconstruction immediately. I tell them that our plan of confiscation is only to affect the large landholders, to compel them to divide their large bodies of land, say, into fifty or a hundred fifty acre farms; these farms to be sold to all classes of persons in the South only." Other agents in South Carolina and Georgia were also "doing a good business." [18]

Stevens has been accused of pressing his confiscation plans with the idea of obtaining recompense for his personal losses. The New York *World* said that "mad with longing to get back from the government at least twice the value of his iron mills, destroyed by the rebels" . . . he had "brought into the House a Bill for confiscating all sorts of property in the South for the benefit of loyal sufferers." [19]

When War began, Stevens was the owner of large iron ore mines and smelting plants at Caledonia, in South Central Pennsylvania. The Confederates were not unaware of this, and surely would miss no occasion to pay their respects to him through a visit to the establishment if circumstances permitted.

Their long awaited opportunity came in July of 1863, when the Southern armies invaded the Keystone State and, of course, destroyed everything they could find that was available for war purposes. The destruction of Stevens' property and equipment proved a luscious morsel and if the thoroughness with which they did it is an index to their pleasure, they enjoyed themselves to the full.

When a messenger took the news to Stevens, he said he told Stevens the Confederates had destroyed the whole plant at Caledonia and burned everything he had. Stevens, who apparently had expected some such act after he knew the Confederates were near his properties, jokingly inquired, "did they burn the debts, too?" [20]

At the time it was commonly reported that his loss was between $150,000 and $200,000 but writing to his junior law partner at Lancaster shortly after the raid, he said the figures had "been exaggerated." The facts were, he wrote, that the Confederates on Tuesday had taken "seven or eight thousand dollars worth of horses, carriages, and mules with their gear." When they returned, "on the following Friday or Saturday, they burned down a furnace, two forges and a rolling mill, nearly new." The building had cost $65,000 and Stevens estimated the total loss to be about $90,000.

A few days after his first letter he again wrote, saying that on their first visit the Confederates "seized my bacon (about four thousand pounds) and other goods of the store, took about $1,000 worth of corn in the mills and a large quantity of other grain." When they set fire to the works on Friday and Saturday, they burnt the store room and the office with all the books, and even hauled "off my bar iron; being, as they said, convenient for wagons and shoeing horses."

They destroyed all fences and about eighty tons of hay, and "broke in the windows of the dwelling houses where the workmen lived." Wiping out the livelihood of his employees grieved him most, and he wrote, "I know not what the poor families shall do. I must provide for their present relief." And altogether, he concluded, "the rebels could not have done the job much cleaner."

In the first letter Stevens significantly says in reference to these great losses, ". . . all this gives me no concern, although it was just about the savings of my life, not the earnings . . . We must all expect to suffer by this wicked War. I have not felt a moment's trouble for my share of it. If, finally, the Government shall be reestablished over our whole territory, and not a vestige of slavery left, I shall deem it a cheap purchase." [21]

The accusation that Stevens was endeavoring to get some personal benefit from his confiscation plan, like so many charges against him, is entirely without foundation. Had his critics at the time and those who have attempted to berate him since been willing to give only a superficial study to the easily acquired facts, they would have learned that Stevens early put himself on record disclaiming absolutely even a single dollar of damages for the losses he had suffered through destruction of his property.

About the time he made his vigorous House speech in 1867, he was gathering data on the amount of damage caused the border states by the Confederate invaders. In writing to one whom he asked to make such appraisement for him in Southern Pennsylvania, he made it clear that none of his holdings should be even looked at and no appraisal made of his losses. He had never asked to be reimbursed, he did not then and had no thought of ever doing so. In that letter, in his own hand, he instructed the recipient how appraisal should be made, but specifically directed him to ignore all of his properties in and about the Caledonia works "as no remuneration is claimed for it."

This letter in full was published by the *Lancaster Intelligencer* on June 4, 1867. It has not been found in any other print and its omission certainly indicates a lack of desire on the part of other newspapers who frequently copied from the Lancaster publication to notice it. At any rate, the great cry that was made over the country that Stevens was pressing his confiscation measure in order to receive personal benefit, had no basis in fact and anyone who wanted the truth could easily have gotten it.

Altogether, confiscation to the Lancastrian meant more than the seizure of part of the rebel property in the South as punishment of those who to him were traitors. He was looking far enough ahead to see the problem of the then emancipated negro. Not only the black but the country itself, was vitally concerned. In the interest of its own welfare, the Nation could not desert the liberated blacks, precariously suspended as they were, in that indefinite position between serfdom and citizenship. Their continued existence as such would be an ever menacing danger. Sooner or later they must become citizens, and assume the responsibilities of free men. If that were to come, the freed slave should be given a careful preparation. So much from the Nation's standpoint.

As to the negro, however right it might have been in the great scheme of things to emancipate him, it would be a most impractical and heartless procedure to abandon him as he gained freedom. Stevens knew that some real assistance and protection had to be extended while he was finding himself and being trained for citizenship. His March bill would not only give each head of a family or widow forty acres of land, but would also appropriate $50 to each for a "homestead."

The lands given could neither be encumbered nor sold for ten years, and in that time, if ever, the negro should have learned how to take care of himself. But "homesteads to them now are far more valuable than the immediate right of suffrage, though both are their due. Nothing is so likely to make a man a good citizen as to make him a freeholder. Nothing will make them so industrious and loyal as to let them feel that they are above want and the owners of the soil which they till." [22] In his humble home, on his modest farm, the negro might prepare himself for citizenship and the enjoyment of equal rights.

Fairly judged the confiscation which Stevens advocated was neither selfish, vindictive, ruthless, nor contrary to precedent. It was but an integral part of his comprehensive plan to deal with conditions of the time. It would punish Southerners by having them help pay for a War which he felt they had made, and at the same time act as a great deterrent to any later contemplated secession. It would happily solve the national debt problem and insure pensions for those who had suffered in the Northern armies. And of outstanding importance to the Equalitarian, it gave a sensible means of discharging the obligations which the Nation owed to a race it had precipitated to freedom.

III

THE THIRTEENTH AMENDMENT

When the Twelfth Amendment to the Constitution was adopted in 1804, it seemed that the fundamental fabric of Government had been made comprehensive enough to serve the Nation for many years. And so it proved for more than a half century.

When anti-slavery agitation took new life, in the early 1830's, a shrewd prognostician could have guessed that the next amendment would concern slavery. Having reached that conclusion, he would have found as each decade passed more evidence to support him. By 1860 the forecast would appear almost a certainty.

But just what form it would take was another question. James Buchanan, President of the United States, in his last annual message, "earnestly recommended" an explanatory amendment of the Constitution on the subject of slavery. Briefly, he would have added a thirteenth article that would recognize the right of property in slaves, with protection of that right in the territories and an easier repossession by the owner of an escaped slave.

Early in 1861, a proposal was submitted in the Congress setting forth that "no amendment of this Constitution having for its object any interference within the states with the relations between their citizens and those described in Section Second of the First Article of the Constitution as 'all other persons' shall originate with any state that does not recognize that relation within its own limits or shall be valid without the assent of everyone of the states composing the Union."

For this, however, a substitute was accepted as follows: "no amendment shall be made to the Constitution which will authorize or give to Congress the power to abolish or interfere within any State with the domestic institutions thereof, including that of persons held to labor or service by the laws of said State."

In the House, the latter received one hundred twenty votes in its favor to seventy-one opposed, but lacking the necessary two-thirds, was defeated. Upon reconsideration, on February 28, 1861 the measure was passed by a vote of one hundred thirty-three to sixty-five. Stevens was among the objectors.

The Senate approved it on March 2 and it was regularly recommended to the States for adoption as the Thirteenth Amendment to the Constitution. The Legislatures of Ohio and Maryland promptly ratified it.

Two days after it was referred to the people, the Republican Party came into control of the Government. Lincoln's election had created a steeled tension. Now was added the terror of the secession stampede.

Though the proposed amendment seemed to embrace everything that the South had asked for in the matter of slavery, they would wait for no compromise. After State withdrawal from the Union had already started it could accomplish no good and so was discarded.

It is important as marking the extreme rightward movement of the country in its attempt to compromise with slavery.

Had it been adopted, slavery would have remained unmolested in the United States as long as the States which permitted it wished. Of course, it should be noted that the Southern States perhaps had no hope that the compromise would ever be finally adopted, and under that conviction, were moved to secession.

Nevertheless, the proposal stands in history as a conclusive answer to any charge against the North that it was unwilling to go the full limit to avert War. Even Lincoln who personified the rapidly growing Northern sentiment had said in his inaugural address that he would have no objection to its adoption.

Secession came with stunning swiftness and War was its inevitable sequel. Sowing the abolition seeds over the bloody fields of battle, laboring incessantly in the care of their growth, proponents soon looked to the harvest. Legislation was first thought of to make their work effective, but the real objection to this was quickly apparent.

If emancipation were brought about merely by Congressional statute, whenever the complexion of that body changed, it would take but a bare majority to repeal it. It was, therefore, soon understood by all parties interested in the movement that a Constitutional amendment must be obtained to satisfactorily fix the victory.

In January of 1864, Henderson of Missouri, submitted in the Senate a proposal for an amendment providing that "slavery or involuntary servitude, except as a punishment for crime, shall not exist in the United States." Sumner would have the amendment read "everywhere within the limits of the United States and of each State or Territory thereof, all persons are equal before the law and no person can hold another as a slave."

Both were referred to the Judiciary Committee, which lost no time in reporting out a joint resolution in the following terminology: "neither slavery nor involuntary servitude, except as punishment for crime whereof the party shall have been duly convicted, shall exist within the United States or any place subject to their jurisdiction." The Senate passed the measure on April 8 by a vote of thirty-eight to six.

The matter was not presented to the House until February 15 when Arnold proposed that the Constitution should be amended so "as to abolish slavery in the United States wherever it now exists and prohibit its existence in every part thereof forever." After refusing to table, that Body adopted it by a vote of only seventy-eight to sixty-two, presaging its later unfavorable action.

On the same day, Windom of Minnesota, offered in the House an amendment resolution in the exact words of the Senate Judiciary Committee measure. Although the House at the time contained men who seemed even more anxious than the Senator sympathizers to put through an Anti-slavery amendment, the proposition was not pushed there.

Stevens in control, was fully apprised of the situation in his Body. Congressmen who had been elected in 1862 were still members of the House. In that year, the reaction had swept into the Lower Body a weighty opposition. Because there had been elected to the Senate but one-third of its membership, the Upper House reflected in a larger degree the advanced sentiment that had carried Lincoln into office. The reason, therefore, that Stevens delayed action was because he knew it had no chance of passage. Defeat would injure its prestige and there was nothing to do save wait and hope for more strength in the next Congress.

But the agitators were pushing and Stevens, partly because he was not satisfied with the Senate terminology, and partly because it would absorb time, offered a substitute. He would divide the amendment into two articles, the first providing that "slavery and involuntary servitude, except for the punishment of crime whereof the party shall have been duly convicted, is forever prohibited in the United States and all its territories."

His second article stipulated that "so much of Article Four, Section Two, as refers to the delivery-up of persons held to service or labor, escaping to another State is annulled." The latter referred to that part of the Constitution which preserved slavery without mentioning the word. It is as follows:

"The citizens of each State shall be entitled to all privileges and immunities of citizens in the several States.

"A person charged in any State with treason, felony or other crime, who shall flee from justice and be found in another State, shall, on demand of the executive authority of the State from which he fled, be delivered up to be removed to the State having jurisdiction of the crime.

"No person held to service or labor in one State under the laws thereof, escaping to another, shall, in consequence of any law or regulation therein, be discharged from such service or labor, but shall be delivered up on claim of the party to whom such service or labor may be due."

The above-quoted part of the Constitution stands

today. Of course, it is in conflict with the Thirteenth
Amendment and although the latter section of
Stevens' proposal might have been inferred, it certainly would not have detracted from effectiveness or
clarity. However, within a few minutes after he introduced his proposals, he asked leave to strike out the
second article. This was at first refused, but was
later permitted by a vote of sixty to five.[1]

Stevens' substitute is enlightening because of the use
of the words "and all its territories." They indicate
that he and his followers had already concluded that if
it became necessary their aim would be to reduce the
States in rebellion to a territorial status.

In the debate the House displayed a preference for
the Senate form of statement. When the measure came
up on June 15, it received ninety-five votes in its favor
and sixty-six in opposition. Substantially short of the
necessary two-thirds, the vote shows how correctly
Stevens had appraised the attitude of the House and
explains his reluctance in pressing the matter concur-
rently with the Senate.

When the next Congress met, it was among the first
business considered after reorganization. Reinforced by
the 1864 elections, the Old Commoner now felt certain
of his position. He engineered the matter through
some nine pages of closely printed debate, but said not
a single word directly upon it after he had cleared the
way for its passage.

A large part of the discussion was taken up by Her-
rick who opposed it and offered a substitute which
would abolish slavery on January 1 of 1880. But that
was merely using time. The final vote on the amend-

ment showed one hundred nineteen in favor, fifty-six opposed, and eight not voting. The House was in transition stage and the War sentiment was no stronger than actually needed for passage. Three more members voting "nay" would have defeated again the joint resolution.

Announcement of the vote was received by the House, as well as the spectators "with an outburst of enthusiasm." It is unusual to find recorded in the *Congressional Globe* such report as is made of this vote. Members on the Republican side of the House, it states, "instantly sprung to their feet, and regardless of parliamentary rules, applauded with cheers and clapping of hands. The example was followed by the male spectators in the galleries, which were crowded to excess, who waved and cheered loud and long, while the ladies, hundreds of whom were present, rose in their seats and waved their handkerchiefs, participating in and adding to the general excitement and intense interest of the scene." Ingersol moved that "in honor of this immortal and sublime event, the House do now adjourn." His motion was carried five to one.[2]

Upon passage, the measure was sent irregularly to the President, who strangely enough, signed it on February 1. The error of submitting a proposed Constitutional Amendment to the Executive for signature was soon discovered and the Senate noted in a resolution that it had been done through "inadvertency." The States lost little time in ratifying it and the Secretary of State proclaimed it part of the Constitution on December 18, 1865.

Probably the most far-reaching Amendment of all, its

incorporation into the parent document was noted with little excitement or celebration. When Stevens and his supporters brought Lincoln to the Emancipation Proclamation, it was ample evidence to those who knew, that the country demanded the abolition of slavery. Otherwise, that shrewd appraiser of the public mind would not have taken the step.

Pitiably emaciated by disease and age, the seventy-three-year old Commoner had lived to see slavery eradicated from the Nation. It had been one of his fondest dreams and its consummation, of course, thrilled him. But practical fellow that he was, he looked at the situation squarely. The leap from slavery to freedom was a tremendous one and brought a tremendous responsibility to those who had agitated for it.

Stevens, keenly sensitive of the fact that the emancipated now needed protection more than ever, summoned his waning energies to the task.

IV

THE FOURTEENTH AMENDMENT

The Constitution of the United States, as it was originally written, provided that Representatives to Congress should be apportioned among the several states according to their respective numbers. At that point, the framers were faced squarely with the problem whether all persons should be counted or only free persons. As might be expected, the difficulty was solved by compromise.

It was agreed that Indians who were not taxed should not be included, but that "three-fifths of all other persons" should be counted.[1] Under this method of calculation, therefore, slaves were actually represented in the Congress to three-fifths of the extent that free persons were. Inasmuch as the blacks were permitted no part whatever in the elections, the practical effect of the arrangement was to give the voter of the South a larger voice in the House of Representatives than the voter of the North.

This status was tolerated with sporadic complaints until 1865. Then came the adoption of the Thirteenth Amendment, which prohibited slavery and therefore raised the blacks to the status of free persons. Unless the Constitution were changed, the slaveholding states which had so long enjoyed this irritating advantage, would be granted a substantial enlargement of it.

Stevens was the first to point out in detail the resulting injustice and the actual dangers involved.[2] In 1860, the states which later rebelled had "nineteen Representatives of colored slaves." With the new Amendment in effect, nearly a score more would be added, and the total representation of non-voting negroes would be "about thirty-seven."

The Lancastrian visualized what would happen. Southern States when readmitted would be entitled to eighty-three Representatives, which, "with the Democrats that in the best times will be elected from the North, will always give them a majority in Congress and in the Electoral College. They will, at the very first election, take possession of the White House and the Halls of Congress."

The Old Commoner said, "I need not depict the ruin that would result," and then naively proceeded to do so. Assumption of the rebel debt and repudiation of the Federal debt were "bound to follow." Freedmen would be oppressed, Southern State Constitutions would be reamended, and slavery reestablished.

The black codes then being enacted in the South and especially in Mississippi, were forceful evidence in support of his contention. "That they would scorn and disregard their present Constitutions inflicted upon them in the midst of martial law would be both natural and just." The feet of the aged Lancastrian were still on the ground when he remarked, "No one who has any regard for freedom of elections can look upon those governments forced upon them in duress with any favor."

If all that had been gained from the War were not to be sacrificed, the Constitution must be modified and then was the time to do it. It was plain that if the correction were to be made it must be done "before the defunct states are admitted to be capable of state action, or it never can be." [3] And Stevens, when Congress met in December of 1865, had already made up his mind how it should be done.

On December 5, he introduced three propositions embodying his ideas. First, the United States or any State in the Union should never assume or pay any part of the debt of the so-called Confederate States of America, or of any State, contracted to carry on War with the United States.

Secondly, Representatives should be apportioned among the states according to their respective legal voters, and none would be counted as such who were not either native born citizens or naturalized foreigners.

Up to that point, the Lancastrian had said little about the freed negro. But that did not mean that he had forgotten. Freeing him was only the first step. He was now the ward of the Nation, and it was to the interest of the country as well as the negro himself that he be properly cared for.

He had a third proposal; namely, that all National and State laws should be equally applicable to every citizen, and no discrimination should be made on account of race or color.

This was the original framework of the Fourteenth Amendment.

The Old Commoner's resolutions were referred to the Judiciary Committee and ordered printed. Inasmuch as it was clearly within the jurisdiction of that group, Stevens was satisfied to leave its control there.

But, reconstruction plans were crystallizing and he would countenance no delay. He expected prompt consideration and report back within a reasonable time.

Harper's Weekly, May 2, 1868.

"Old Thad" Commanding Impeachment

He waited until the twenty-second of January. No report was forthcoming, and he thought he had been sufficiently patient. Sick, tottering and emaciated, he was in earnest concerning the Amendments. Would the Judiciary Committee postpone action until he was too weak to even attend the sessions of the House? That must not happen.

Ignoring the rules, he reported from the Joint Select Committee, a resolution covering Congressional representation and direct taxes. Still the Judiciary Committee failed to act.

Nine days later, he reported from the Committee on Reconstruction a substitute for his original section providing for the apportionment of Representatives. This was his own Committee, and he had seen to it that it was "authorized to report at any time." [4]

He made no apology for usurping the duties of the Judiciary Committee, who then were considering his original resolution. He who by now was the acknowledged Dictator of the body, need not observe the proprieties. And in a matter which the Old Commoner held so important as he did this one, there was not a single member who dared even mention the irregularity of his procedure.

But what he then presented was not nearly as sweeping as his original proposal. Upon investigation he learned from his Committee of Fifteen that it was too radical for working purposes, and he was told that even if it were passed by the Congress, the States were still too conservative to ratify it. [5]

More than anything else, he wanted to carry through the changes to the Constitution which he believed would perfect it to the broad extent its framers had intended. One way of doing that was to minimize the power of the late Confederate States in the Congress.

He therefore had originally provided that Representatives should be apportioned among the States on the basis of their respective legal voters, and for that purpose, none could be named who were not either native born citizens or naturalized foreigners. This, of course, would prevent even the slightest representation of freed slaves. His Committee's information that the States would not ratify it seemed to satisfy him as correct.

Convinced that such would be beyond attainment, he showed his practical-mindedness. Some men would have insisted stubbornly upon fighting it out on the lines drawn, especially if they held a position as powerful as the one Stevens then held. But he did not. With as much cheer as he could muster, he said, "It was dear to my heart, for I had been gestating it for three months. (Laughter.) But when I came to consult the others and found that the States would not adopt it, I surrendered it."

A compromise which he had reached with his Committee, and which they had informed him was as much as the States could be counted on to ratify, provided for apportionment of Representatives on the basis of the whole number of persons taxed, providing that whenever the elective franchise was denied or abridged in any State on account of race or color, all persons therein of such race or color, should be excluded from the basis of representation.[6]

Notwithstanding the fact that Stevens' Committee viewed this as a compromise, the Old Commoner had not yielded much. And although he made much of giving up his original proposition, the substitute was only slightly less severe in minimizing the Congressional power of the Southern states when readmitted.

Stevens was much perturbed about the pressure of time. He apparently hoped that his proposal could be gotten through so quickly that State Legislatures which would adjourn in "two or three weeks," could act upon it before their sessions ended.[7] He therefore said that he intended "if the House is ready, to have this joint resolution passed before the sun goes down." [8] That was putting it strongly, but he was determined not to lose a minute in having the body which he controlled, act upon it. He gave the House what seemed to him a reasonable time to debate it, and then, nine days after its introduction, decided the time had come for vote upon it. He moved its consideration.

The Judiciary Committee did not seem to be offended by his usurping their duties, and Wilson, of Iowa, a member of that group, stated that "after careful consideration, his Committee had reached the same conclusion on this subject as the Joint Committee on Reconstruction." [9] Schenck attempted to modify the Lancastrian's substitute by permitting to the rebel states, a limited representation in Congress. Stevens opposed it firmly, saying "I do not want them to have representation—I say it plainly. I do not want them to have the right to appear before this Congress has done the great work of regenerating the Constitution and laws of the country according to the principles of the Declaration of Independence." [10]

That might appear somewhat brutal, but under the

circumstances, was the only practical way of proceeding if the Constitution were to be modified. It could be accomplished only in the absence of rebel state representation in Congress. Admission even to a limited extent would permit a combination with Northern Democrats that would block effectively all such amendments. The House arose spontaneously to support Stevens and brushed aside Schenck's substitute by a vote of one hundred thirty-one to twenty-nine.[11]

When those who desired to speak seemed to have said what they wished, Stevens took the Floor and delivered one of his characteristically short speeches. He explained how he had come to modify his original resolution and showed his disposition where objection presented itself, to obtain the best compromise possible. He was willing to yield on the apportionment matter, but still treasured the hope that his provision for equal application of all State and National laws to every citizen would be carried. That to him was "a genuine proposition and one which," he trusted, "before we separate, we shall have educated ourselves up to the idea of adopting, and our people up to the point of ratifying."

Johnson had taken the position that no further changes were necessary, saying that "propositions to amend the Constitution were becoming as numerous as preambles and resolutions at town meetings."[12] The interview in which he made this remark had been published and Stevens could not pass it without comment. He considered it in extreme bad taste for the President to make such a statement at the very time Congress was legislating on the subject.

[500]

But dejectedly, the Commoner would notice it no further, feeling that Congress was very "tolerant of usurpation in this tolerant government of ours." Of course, the President had nothing to do with proposed amendments and the Constitution required no action of his upon them.[13]

With a calm complacency, eloquent of his assurance of mastership of the House, Stevens pressed to the vote. Debate was not precluded, nor was anyone prevented from objecting. But opposition speeches could accomplish nothing. The House voted and Stevens' substitute was adopted by a vote of one hundred twenty to forty-six, with sixteen not voting.[14]

The striking manner in which the Old Commoner drove it through is indicative of the tremendous power wielded by him. That he would get his proposition through sometime could be reasonably expected. But that he was able to get it through in such a surprisingly short time, is truly remarkable. The *Chicago Tribune* viewed it as a great personal triumph for him, proving "most strikingly, the strong influence of his native shrewdness, boldness and power over the House, for the majority divided but yesterday by a diversity of opinions, apparently puzzled, restive and at a loss whither to turn—seemed to yield to him as does a mettlesome charger to the hand of the practiced rider." [15]

The measure went to the Senate. That body had its own idea of the form the Amendment should take and rewrote it completely, joining together the three propositions that Stevens had originally submitted in December of the former year, and another one which he presented on April 30, to disqualify insurrectionists and those who assisted them, from voting for Federal representatives, president and vice-president.

Although the Lancastrian felt he had the laboring oar when the Senate's revision was returned to the House, he nevertheless proposed that no speech upon it should exceed thirty minutes. When the other side became alarmed at what he might attempt to do, he answered that it was his intention to "allow the largest and fairest debate desired by any member."

On the same page where these words are printed, it is intriguing to contrast his act of unhesitatingly invoking his power to suspend the rules and so override those who would object to his irregular procedure, in order to get the matter considered that evening. As usual, the House sustained him by more than a two-thirds vote.

When he called up the measure for discussion on May 8, he made the opening speech upon it. With some show of sadness, he admitted that the Senate draft was not all the Committee desired, but although it "fell far short of his wishes, it fulfilled some of his hopes."

He analyzed the composite measure the Upper Body sent back. The first section conferred citizenship upon all persons born or naturalized in the United States. It prohibited abridgment of privileges or immunities to citizens, contained "the due process of law" clause, and gave equal protection of the laws to all.

Stevens felt that no one could deny "that everyone of these provisions is just." They were all asserted in some form or other in the Declaration of Independence or the organic law.

But the Constitution, up to that time, was a limitation in those respects only upon the action of Congress and not upon the States. "This amendment supplies the defects and allows Congress to correct the unjust legislation of the States, so far that the law which operates upon one man shall operate equally upon all."

The second section which fixed the basis for Congressional representation, he properly considered of greatest importance at the time. His method, he felt, would have secured the enfranchisement of every citizen at no distant time. That, together with the "amendment repudiating the rebel debt which we also passed, would have gone far to curb the rebellious spirit of secession and to have given to the oppressed race its rights."

But that proposition had been "mortally wounded in the house of its friends." He chastized the Senate for the denunciatory language it had used in discussion of his plan, and aiming directly at Sumner who had led the fight, said, "It was slaughtered by a puerile and pedantic criticism, by a perversion of philological definition which if, when I taught school, a lad who studied Lindley Murray had assumed, I would have expelled him from the institution as unfit to waste education upon." [16]

The change the Senate had made was just this. Stevens had proposed that if any State refused to count in its list of legal voters any of a particular class, all in that whole class should be denied representation. That was clearly punitive. The Senate had been fairer in denying representation only in proportion to those not counted. Stevens' principal objection to the Senate substitute was that it allowed States "to discriminate among the same class and receive proportionate credit in representation. That," said the Lancastrian, "I dis-

like. But it is a short step forward. A large stride
which I in vain proposed is dead; the murderers must
answer to the suffering race. I would not have been
the perpetrator. A load of misery must sit heavy on
their souls."

The provision that Stevens had added on April 30
disqualified from voting for Congressional Representatives and Presidential electors, until July 4, 1870, "all
persons who voluntarily adhered to the late insurrection." That came back from the Senate as the third
section of the proposed amendment, and Stevens, knowing that it was as stringent as anything that could be
passed, was forced, of course, to accept it. His only
objection was that "It is too lenient." In fact, if it
were within his power, he would prohibit every rebel
who had shed the blood of a loyal man from having voice
in the Government, "not only to 1870, but to 18,070."

Section four, which validated the United States debt
and invalidated the Confederate debt, he felt he need
say nothing about, for "none dared to object to it who
is not himself a rebel."

On May 10 on Stevens' motion, the House adopted
the articles of the joint resolution as the Senate had
modified them, by a vote of one hundred twenty-eight
to thirty-seven. But the Senate was not satisfied with
the phraseology of the first section, nor with the plan
set forth in section three, and appeared overly cautious
about the fourth section.

Through its Conference Committee, the Upper Body
seemed to be quite assertive and determined to insist
upon its statement of the reforms contemplated. On
June 8, it passed the Fourteenth Amendment in its

final form and the measure was sent to the House.
Stevens, in command, was forced to make the best of
what to him was a compromise. He took a moment to
explain the changes made by the Senate.

That Body had defined in the first section just who
were citizens of the United States. This the Lancastrian thought, was an excellent improvement. The second section he was still dissatisfied with, for it had "not
half the vigor of the amendment which was lost in the
Senate." The third section had been wholly changed
by substituting the ineligibility of certain high offenders
for the disfranchisement of all rebels until 1870.
To him, this certainly was not an improvement. It
opened the "elective franchise to such as the states chose
to admit" and therefore endangered the Government
of the country, both state and national.

In fact, he thought that it might even "give the next
Congress and President to the reconstructed rebels."
With their enlarged basis of representation and exclusion of the loyal men of color from voting, "I see no
hope of safety unless in the prescription of proper
enabling acts, which shall do justice to the freedmen
and enjoin enfranchisement as a condition precedent."

Section four was enlarged by a declaration of validity
of the public debt of the United States. Section five,
which was the enabling section in the usual words, was,
of course, unchanged.

Sometimes there was a touching pathos in the old
man's lament.

"In my youth, in my manhood, in my old age,
I had fondly dreamed that when any fortunate
chance should have broken up for awhile the

foundation of our institutions, and released us from obligations the most tyrannical that ever man imposed in the name of freedom, that the intelligent, pure and just men of this Republic, true to their professions and consciences, would have so remodeled all our institutions as to have freed them from every vestige of human oppression, of inequality of rights, of the recognized degradation of the poor, and the superior caste of the rich. In short, that no distinction would be tolerated in this purified Republic but what arose from merit and conduct. This bright dream has vanished 'like the baseless fabric of a vision.' I find that we shall be obliged to be content with patching up the worst portions of the ancient edifice, and leaving it, in many of its parts, to be swept through by the tempests, the frosts, and the storms of despotism." [17]

But whatever sentiment the Commoner showed, he never strayed far from a very practical handling of the matter. Again, as was happening so frequently in his later years, he found time to be of the essence of all his labors. The situation demanded a speedy adoption of as much as could be agreed upon then, for Stevens feared that before any Constitutional guards could be invoked, "Congress would be flooded with rebels and rebel sympathizers." Making the best of it, he counselled, "let us no longer delay. Take what we can get now and hope for better things in future legislation." [18]

The Senate had passed the amendment resolution by a vote of thirty-three to eleven. Stevens pressed for a quick vote, and five days later, the House concurred in the measure by a vote of one hundred thirty-eight to thirty-six, with ten not voting.[19]

Congress had passed a proposed Fourteenth Amendment granting civil rights to the negro, and Secretary of State Seward moved to submit it to the States for ratification.

THE FOURTEENTH AMENDMENT

AS STEVENS PROPOSED IT:

Section I. All national and State laws shall be equally applicable to every citizen, and no discrimination shall be made on account of race and color.

AS IT WAS FINALLY ADOPTED:

Section I. All persons born or naturalized in the United States, and subject to the jurisdiction thereof, are citizens of the United States and of the State wherein they reside. No State shall make or enforce any law which shall abridge the privileges or immunities of citizens of the United States; nor shall any State deprive any person of life, liberty, or property, without due process of law; nor deny to any person within its jurisdiction the equal protection of the laws.

Section II. Representatives shall be apportioned among the States which may be within the Union according to their respective legal voters; and for this purpose none shall be named as legal voters who are not either natural-born citizens or naturalized foreigners. Congress shall provide for ascertaining the number of said voters. A true census of the legal voters shall be taken at the same time with the regular census.

Section II. Representatives shall be apportioned among the several States according to their respective numbers, counting the whole number of persons in each State, excluding Indians not taxed. But when the right to vote at any election for the choice of electors for President and Vice-President of the United States, Representatives in Congress, the executive and judicial officers of the State, or the members of the legislature thereof, is denied to any of the male inhabitants of such State, being twenty-one years of age, and citizens of the United States, or in any way abridged, except for participation in rebellion, or other crime, the basis of representation therein shall be reduced in the proportion which the number of such male citizens shall bear to the whole number of male citizens twenty-one years of age in such State.

Section III. Until the 4th day of July in the year 1870, all persons who voluntarily adhered to the late insurrection, giving it aid and comfort, shall be excluded from the right to vote for Representatives in Congress and for electors for President and Vice-President of the United States.

Section III. No person shall be a Senator or Representative in Congress or elector of President and Vice-President, or hold any office, civil or military, under the United States, or under any State, who, having previously taken an oath, as a member of Congress, or as an officer of the United States, or as a member of any State legislature, or as an executive or judicial officer of any State, to support the Constitution of the United States, shall have engaged in insurrection or rebellion against the same, or given aid or comfort to the enemies thereof. But Congress may, by a vote of two-thirds of each House, remove such disability.

Section IV. Neither the United States, nor any State in the Union shall ever assume or pay any part of the debt of the so-called Confederate States of America, or of any State, contracted to carry on War with the United States.

Section IV. The validity of the public debt of the United States, authorized by law, including debts incurred for payment of pensions and bounties for services in suppressing insurrection or rebellion, shall not be questioned. But neither the United States nor any State shall assume or pay any debt or obligation incurred in aid of insurrection or rebellion against the United States, or any claim for the loss or emancipation of any slave; but all such debts, obligations and claims shall be held illegal and void.

Section V. The Congress shall have power to enforce, by appropriate legislation, the provisions of this article.[20]

Section V. The Congress shall have power to enforce, by appropriate legislation, the provisions of this article.

The Congress improved Stevens' first section by specifically defining citizenship. In the second section, it accepted Stevens' plan for the apportionment of Representatives, but tempered the penalty where groups or parts of groups were not counted.

The third section also was improved by disqualifying from office the leaders of the rebellion in lieu of denying suffrage to the whole group. The Old Commoner seemed satisfied in section four merely to repudiate the Confederate debt, but Congress, more distrustful than he of what the reconstructed states might attempt, added a clause validating the War debts of the Government.

When the joint resolution on the amendment was referred to the Secretary of State, Seward, on some unintelligible theory, submitted it to the legislatures of all the States. He drew no line between the loyal States and those which had been proclaimed States under Johnson's plan of restoration.

Stevens held the correct theory on the point,[21] insisting that there could be found no reason whatever to consider as a State any State except a loyal one. All that was necessary was to have three-fourths of them ratify the amendment in order to incorporate it into the Constitution. It would then have the same force and effect over the Confederate States when they were readmitted as if it had been specifically ratified by them.

Seward's action not only was irregular and inconsistent,[22] but opened the way for Johnson's reconstructed States to show their contempt by repudiating the submitted article.[23]

It required more than two years to obtain a ratification conforming to Seward's method of counting. That left but two weeks of life to Stevens, in which he could rest assured that all people in the Nation were guaranteed civil rights.

Sections one and two of the amendment, as it was finally adopted are, of course, the important ones today. The first one was close to the heart of the Lancastrian and the second was important to him only in so far as it would make the first applicable and enforcible. With the former the freedman was granted civil rights and elevated to the second step of the three which gave him full rights of citizenship.

The amendment stands today as a Constitutional monument on which is deeply carved the name of the Old Commoner.

V

FIFTEENTH AMENDMENT

The Thirteenth Amendment freed the negro and the Fourteenth elevated him to a status where he could enjoy civil rights. Full citizenship entailed only the conferment of suffrage. If the first two steps were right and proper, the third should follow in logical sequence. If the first two steps were wrong, the accepted maxims of the Independence Declaration were meaningless.

The so-called radical group in Congress was easily strong enough to carry through a suffrage amendment, and the country undoubtedly would support it. Sometime it must certainly come. But the question was, when? The problem was not only difficult—it might be even dangerous. Putting the ballot in the hands of the newly emancipated was much like giving a child a high powered rifle.

At the time there were many sentimental and extravagant humanitarians agitating individually and through organizations for immediate suffrage for the freedman. Stevens, however, could not be counted among them. No one was more earnestly desirous to obtain for the black man and all others, for that matter, equal rights and privileges. The doctrine of a white man's Government, with its resulting restriction of the suffrage, had always been anathema to him. In one of his speeches he had said:

"How shameful that men of influence should mislead and miseducate the public mind! They proclaim, 'this is the white man's government'; the whole coil of copperheads echo the same sentiment, and jealous upstart Republicans join the cry. Is it any wonder that ignorant foreigners and illiterate natives should learn this doctrine and be led to despise and maltreat a whole race of their fellowmen?

"Sir, this doctrine of a white man's government is as atrocious as the infamous sentiment [1] that damned the late Chief Justice [2] to everlasting fame; and I fear, to everlasting fire." [3]

However, the Lancastrian always gave due weight to the factual situation. He knew how utterly ignorant the average freedman was and how thoroughly incompetent his exercise of the franchise necessarily would be. Consistently he held to his early position that suffrage should come to the negro, but only when he was properly prepared for it.

In 1866, the Commoner said that "forty acres of land and a hut would be more valuable to the freedman than the immediate right to vote." [4] There must be a period of training and education. "I want our Christian men to go among them,—the philosophers of the North, the honest Methodists, my friends the Hard-shell Baptists, and all others; and then, four or five years hence, when these freedmen shall have become intelligent enough," they should be extended the right of suffrage. [5]

But satisfied as he seemed to permit a reasonable time to elapse before suffrage should be granted the black, he was forced from that position.

The Southern States had given no real recognition even to the Thirteenth Amendment and were generally flaunting their contempt of Congressional legislation. The so-called black codes were becoming universal

Washington Aug 7 18 68

Dear Thad

your uncle has bin
quit law I had almos
given up but he is bitte
he has diarhea which
you know would at
has on him he was so
well I will writ to you
Every day and lett you
know hoe he is

yours

Lydia Smith

From the Frank P. McKibben collection.

The Only Known Writing of Stevens' Housekeeper, Lydia Smith. A Letter to
Thaddeus, Jr., Reporting the Condition of the Old Commoner

throughout the South. Many of the rebel states had taken advantage of the provision in the Thirteenth Amendment which abolished slavery except for crime, by punishing convicted blacks in a way that amounted to reenslaving them.

As an example, the Commissioner of Freedmen had notified Stevens of a case in Florida, in which six negroes had been sold into slavery for twenty years for minor crime. The Lancastrian's explanation of how this was done was simple.

"They pass a law that any man guilty of assault and battery shall be sold into slavery for twenty years. It is the law now. They go into the street and a white man jostles a black one or a black man jostles a white man. He is taken right to the courthouse, is convicted of assault and battery, and is sold for twenty years into slavery. There are hundreds this day in the Southern States who are serving as slaves on just such contrivances. They have so altered the law that they have introduced a system of peonage, even worse than in Mexico and the middle southern provinces." [6]

He received a continuous stream of correspondence from the South, alleging atrocious happenings there. Typical was a letter reporting that his correspondent had actually witnessed the burning of a negro church, and when he passed the spot next morning, saw twenty-four dead blacks hanging from the trees.[7] Such action the Commoner viewed as bad faith on the part of Southerners.

Moreover, by this time, every single one of the States which had seceded had rejected the proposed Four-

teenth Amendment. Some had done it by unanimous
votes of their Conventions, and practically all the others
by overwhelming majorities.[8] Their decisive and unanimous repudiations were to Stevens, merely cumulative
evidence that the South was determined not to yield.
With regret, he was led to doubt whether "after we
shall have admitted them into the Union and after the
morrow's sun shall have set upon them, they will not
be ready to call a new Convention and reestablish slavery in some shape or form." [9]

The white leaders would not admit their defeat. They
seemed determined still to fight for the very propositions that everyone believed the War had concluded
against them. The only weapon left for the Congress
to use was the ballot in the hands of the freedmen.

That might be an extremely radical move, for surely
the negro was not at all prepared for it. It might be
harsh and cause innumerable hardships, but it seemed
no other device could be found. Certainly it should
prove effective. That was the primary reason for the
Old Commoner switching his position from a slow approach to negro suffrage to a precipitate leap to it.

Another fact that influenced him was his certain
knowledge that but a short time remained for him to
complete his life's work. Although he never referred
to it, he was fully aware of his almost absolute power,
not only in the House, but probably in the Congress.
Sometimes the Senate would snarl or temper his demands, but in the end, it supported him.

Negro suffrage was the only remaining step to be
taken for consummation of his life's ambition to establish by law equal rights for all. If left to other hands,

no one could venture how long it might be postponed. He determined to move, and unripe though the time might be, he would nevertheless demand it immediately. Whatever harm might result from its sudden grant, he believed, would be more than counter-balanced in the end by the righteous goal achieved.

During the summer of 1866, he was at most a moderate on the proposition. By September he had become its ardent champion. In a speech to his constituents he said, "I am for it, first, because it is right. Second, because it protects our brethren there. Thirdly, because it prevents the states from going into the hands of the rebels, giving them the President and Congress for the next forty years. When Congress meets, I will support it with all my might." [10] And so he did.

In January, he introduced his first great reconstruction measure.[11] Under it the Southern States would be given an opportunity to vote for delegates to a State Constitutional Convention. Of course, it was necessary to fix the qualifications of the voters. Stevens significantly provided that the blacks should be permitted to vote in those elections.

In his supporting speech, he put himself flatly on record in favor of "negro suffrage in every rebel state." Scorning those who opposed him on the ground that it was negro equality, he explained that what he desired was to have "the same law which condemns or acquits an African, condemn or acquit a white man, and the same law which gives a verdict in a white man's favor, give a verdict in the black man's favor, on the same statement of facts. That," said he, was "the law of God and ought to be the law of man."

His doctrine did not mean that a negro "should sit on the same seat or eat at the same table with a white man;" that, he insisted, was a matter of taste which every man should decide for himself, and with which the law had nothing to do.[12]

In 1867, the Congress showed its determination to assert a stern control of reconstruction by passage of Stevens' military reconstruction measures. The country was awaiting adoption of the Fourteenth Amendment, and feeling its way toward the Fifteenth. Late that year, alarmed by the Southern States' rejection of the former, and convinced that the latter was immediately necessary, the Lancastrian decided upon a little campaigning of his own.

He opened a correspondence with an old German Professor friend in Lancaster, knowing, of course, that what he wrote would be eagerly and widely published. In the exchange of letters, he set forth his argument that suffrage was necessarily included in the rights referred to in the Declaration of Independence. Life, liberty and the pursuit of happiness had been there enumerated as universal and inalienable.

On that premise, the Old Commoner insisted, it follows "that everything necessary for their establishment and defense is within those rights. If, as our fathers declared, 'all just government is derived from the assent of the governed'; if in Federal Republics that assent can be ascertained and established only through the ballot, it follows that to take away the means of communication is to take away from the citizen his great weapon of defense and reduce him to helpless bondage. It deprives him of an inalienable right."

Therefore, he concluded, the elective franchise ranked with "life and liberty in its sacred, inalienable character."

But while the Declaration clearly states what the intention then was, the action of the Convention in framing the Constitution of the United States, it seemed to him, "bartered away for the time being, some of those rights, and instigated by the hellish institution of slavery, suspended one of the muniments of liberty."

Before the Fourteenth Amendment, nothing could be done about it. But after its adoption, every American citizen was on a perfect equality, as far as national rights were concerned. If, then, by the amendment of the Constitution, every American citizen was entitled to equal privileges with every other; and if every American citizen in any one of the states should be found entitled to impartial suffrage with every other American citizen in any state, then it followed, as an inevitable conclusion, that suffrage throughout this nation is impartial and universal as far as every human being is concerned, without regard to race or color, in so far as it affects the whole Nation.[13]

Back in Congress in the last year of his life, Stevens made a characteristically forceful speech on the subject while the bill to admit Alabama was under discussion. Reconstruction was the vital question and now the Old Commoner had gotten to the point where he believed nothing would expedite reunion as quickly as the ballot in the hands of the negro. They could and would use it to beat down the disloyal sentiment in the South that was blocking readmission of the States.

He was, therefore, fighting for it now not only as

a part of the ideality of his political philosophy, but as an effective means of reuniting the Union into an indiseverable whole. Congress was then "not merely expounding a Government," but was actually "making a Nation." He proposed "to go to universal and impartial suffrage as the only foundation on which the Government could stand." There was no other by which men could protect themselves against the injustice, inhumanity and wrong that otherwise would be inflicted. The time had come when the Nation had opportunity to adopt a "great and glorious principle."

Moreover, that opportunity had been reached by means of the Constitution, and "not by violating it." The forefathers, who proclaimed that principle and would have adopted it, could not do so without violating the compact which they themselves had made. Such action would have destroyed the great Government they were then building, and bound to defend.

"But," the Lancastrian proclaimed, Federal Legislators had "now reached the point which our fathers did not reach and could not reach." The Declaration of Independence had "laid the foundation of the Government on which this Nation was built." Its authors "had been inspired with such a light from on High as never man was inspired with before, in the great work of providing freedom for the human race through a Government in which no oppression could find a resting place."

However, the Constitution of 1789 did not carry out the principles of Government laid in the Declaration. The compromise with slavery, which had been forced in the meantime, was the root of the dissension which led to the War of the Rebellion. The opportunity was before them, and they could consummate their Fathers' desires in a thoroughly Constitutional manner.

He offered a resolution which was one of the forerunners of the finally adopted Fifteenth Amendment, as follows:

"And be it further enacted, That every male citizen of the United States above the age of twenty-one years, who was born or naturalized in the United States, or who has declared his intention to become naturalized, shall be entitled to vote on all national questions which may arise in any State in the Union where he shall have resided for the term of thirty days; and no distinction shall be made between any such citizens on any account, except for treason, felony, or other infamous crimes, not below the grade of felony at common law." [14]

The Lancastrian was now committed to the proposition that no rebel state should be readmitted until it had constitutionally provided for universal suffrage. Acting in his role of Dictator, he wrote his friend Forney, publisher of the Philadelphia *Press,* a letter, which because of its importance, received wide notice. It was an ultimatum to the South in which he bluntly stated that his Committee had finally "resolved that no State should be readmitted into the Union except under that condition." [15]

Congress passed the resolution embodying the Fifteenth Amendment late in February of 1869, and the proclamation of adoption was made by the Secretary of State on March 30 of 1870. That was nearly two years after Stevens' death. He was not living to take part in the Congressional action, but the momentum which the sentiment that forced it had gained under his driving sponsorship, made its passage inevitable even though before its accomplishment, the Old Commoner had lain many months in his grave.

VI

IMPEACHMENT

It was but natural that the ever enlarging areas of friction that were generating heat in post war days would sooner or later burst into flames.

With ten States lying prostrate outside the gates of the Union, an embittered and sweeping controversy arose inside over the precise terms on which readmission would be permitted. When Lincoln and Johnson inaugurated their restoration policy, it seemed that a quick, quiet and gentle return of the States was assured. But before Executive restoration had gotten under way, Stevens and his followers became convinced that it held no assurance of permanent slavery abolition. And that to them was not only an important item in the national program, it was *the* program.

Unable to accept Johnson's method because it did not provide for an absolute slavery eradication, they therefore submitted their more stringent Congressional plan of reconstruction. And in the autumn elections of 1866, the voters of the Nation decided that the country should have Congressional reconstruction and not Executive restoration. That direction inevitably forced the contest.

President Johnson, exponent of the restoration theory, refused to acknowledge the clearly given mandate, and stolidly and almost sullenly, carried on his fight against the Congressional policy. Not only did he wage his battle in Washington, but he reached out over the country to remove office holders in sympathy with the Congressional bloc, and supplant them with his own followers. This went on to an extent further than generally appreciated, and without doubt, was the greatest single factor that engendered the violent anger of the Congress against him.

Many of the removals were made while Congress was in recess, and the political bombardment Congressmen got from constituents, stung deeply.[1] It went so far that Stevens openly accused Johnson of treacherous tactics in building up a party in opposition to the one that had put him in office.[2]

As he had done in the recess before the Congress met in 1865, when he conceived his Committee of Fifteen idea, Stevens the next summer developed what he thought was a method of curbing Johnson in his removals-from-office program. Rallying the offended Congressmen, on the first day of the session in December of 1866, he had no trouble in getting through his Tenure-of-Office Act. An alleged violation of this law on the part of the President gave the impeachment proceedings their only practical and legal foundation.

Johnson's consistent veto policy, in the latter part of the Thirty-Ninth and the early part of the Fortieth Congresses, gave the Radicals ammunition to support their charges that the President was studiously opposing the expressed will of the people. It was timely propaganda used mercilessly, and against which the President raised little defense.

Impeachment had been talked of over the country from the moment Johnson attempted his precipitate restoration a few months after he took office as President. Previously referred to, the first resolutions indicting the Executive were introduced in the House on

December 16, of 1866, by General Ashley of Ohio.

There was no mention of the President by name. The proposal was merely to have a Committee of Seven inquire if any acts of any officer of the Government of the United States "in contemplation of the Constitution, are high crimes and misdemeanors, and whether said acts were designed or calculated to overthrow, subvert, or corrupt the Government of the United States." On a test vote, the move was defeated ninety to forty-nine.

In January of the next year, a resolution to impeach "the officer now exercising the functions pertaining to the office of President of the United States of America," and remove him from "office upon his conviction," and another one in similar vein, were referred to the Judiciary Committee.[3]

At this time the House accepted by a vote of one hundred eight to thirty-nine, General Ashley's resolution to impeach "Andrew Johnson, Vice-President and acting President of the United States, of high crimes and misdemeanors," alleging usurpation of power, corruption of the appointing, pardoning and veto powers, the corrupt disposition of public property and the corrupt interference in elections. It was referred to the Judiciary Committee for investigation.

That group filed a brief report on the last day of February, in which it complained of being pressed for time, due to the expiration of the session on the fourth of March. No recommendation was made one way or the other, but it turned over to the Clerk of the House the testimony it had taken, "notifying the succeeding Congress of the incompleteness of its labors," and sug-

gesting "that they should be completed." The majority
report was signed by eight of the nine members of the
Committee, and a minority report setting forth "that
there is not one particle of evidence to sustain any of
the charges," was filed by the dissenting member.

Three days after the Fortieth Congress came into
being, Ashley again brought up the matter and the
House directed its Judiciary Committee to report on
the charges against the President on the first day after
recess.

The Committee showed unusual industry, hearing a
continuing stream of witnesses. Although accusations
and charges against Johnson were as easy to find as
sunshine, getting specific evidence to support impeachment was another matter.

In spite of the vigorous way the Committee was working, it had nothing to report in July, and continued its
labors on until the latter part of November. Then it
reported. Five of its nine members recommended impeachment, but the other four opposed the step in two
minority reports. On December 7, the House refused
to act under the majority report by a vote of one hundred eight to fifty-seven.[4]

The near two to one vote against them did not seem
to discourage those who wanted impeachment. Through
January, they kept hammering on. Late that month,
whether in collusion with Stevens or not is unknown,
Spalding under suspension of rules, had the House
pass a resolution authorizing Stevens' Reconstruction
Committee to inquire "what combinations have been
made or attempted to be made to obstruct the due execution of the law," and vesting the Committee "with

power to send for persons and papers, examine witnesses, and report" at any time to the House what action, if any, it might deem necessary.

These vigorous instructions had the practical effect of transferring impeachment matters from the Committee on the Judiciary into Stevens' immediate control.

Early in February, the Lancastrian had referred to his Committee the impeachment evidence taken by the Judiciary Committee. The next day, he had similarly referred the correspondence between General Grant and President Johnson. By now it was clearly evident that he was dissatisfied with the way the Judiciary Committee had handled the matter, and wanted it where he could give it closer attention. On February 13, when he brought impeachment to a vote before his Committee, six opposed it and only Boutwell and Farnsworth stood with him.[5]

In the meantime, those outside Congress were rapidly bringing that body and the Executive into open warfare. Stanton had turned against the President. By what might be construed as almost double dealing, he had for some time held a clandestine contact with the Radicals, all the while appearing friendly to Johnson.

Slow to sense Stanton's real position, and equally reluctant to believe it, the President was at last forced to realize that his Secretary of War was not only opposed to him, but came suspiciously near to actual betrayal. Still Stanton made no move to vacate his office.

Acting quite properly in the matter, Johnson, on the fifth of August, notified the War Secretary that his resignation would be accepted. But Stanton on the same day haughtily refused to resign. A week later,

Johnson did the only thing that any self-respecting President could do under the circumstances. He suspended Stanton and appointed Grant Secretary of War *ad interim.*

Under the Tenure-of-Office Act, it remained for the Senate to approve the President's order. Johnson notified that body on the twelfth of December of his action, and on the thirteenth of January, it refused to "concur in" Stanton's suspension.

The next day Grant wrote Johnson that he had received notice of the action of the Senate and his "functions as Secretary of War, *ad interim,* ceased from the moment of the receipt of" that notice. Accordingly, he relinquished the office to Stanton.[6]

This withdrawal on the part of Grant gave rise to a heated controversy between the President and himself, in which Johnson bitterly complained and attempted to prove, that Grant had been guilty of a breach of his word to the Executive. In some of this the President was supported by signed statements of his Cabinet officers, and altogether it seems the opinion of those who have given the incident careful study, that Grant had the worst of the encounter.[7]

However, Stevens viewed the controversy as of little public importance. It was a question of veracity between the two. "Both," said he, "may call each other liars if they want to; perhaps they both do lie a little or let us say 'equivocate,' though the President does seem to have the weight of evidence on his side. . . . If they want to settle the question between them, let them go out in any back yard and settle it."[8]

Johnson felt that as President he had the right to

demand and receive cooperation and support from members of his Cabinet and in that he was entirely correct. Stanton, emboldened by the attitude of the Senate, not only refused to cooperate and support the President, he engaged actively in embarrassing him. The situation was becoming intolerable for the Executive. On February 21, the President took the matter into his own hands by peremptorily removing Stanton from office and appointing Lorenzo Thomas, Adjutant General, Secretary *ad interim*.[9]

But, ignoring Johnson's order of dismissal, Stanton still occupied his rooms as Secretary of War and did not propose to be ejected except by a force greater than he was able to oppose. Possession of the office was of great strategic importance and with Stanton holding on, Thomas had to take the offensive. How he called upon Stanton, their conversations and the Secretary's refusals to vacate, are matters which have been so thoroughly treated that there is no necessity to repeat them here. Thomas showed himself no match for Stanton and his actions gave Johnson little help. The Secretary had the General arrested and much was made of the incident.

It gave Johnson and his very able legal advisers a rare opportunity to test the Constitutionality of the Tenure-of-Office Act and had they really wanted to proceed along that line, there should be some explanation as to why they took no advantage of it.

Instead of having Thomas surrender himself, they entered bail. They certainly had plenty of time to fully comprehend the situation, for the bail for Thomas was not posted until many hours after his arrest, and after

Johnson and his legal staff had been fully apprised of
what was intended.[10] This, of course, prevented their
asking for a Writ of Habeas Corpus on which the Constitutionality of the Tenure-of-Office Law could have
been tested.

When the news of Johnson's removal of Stanton
reached the Senate on February 21, it created consternation. A resolution was rushed through setting forth
"that the President has no power to remove the Secretary of War and designate any other officer to perform the duties of that office *ad interim*." [11] The strategy of the Senate leaders was quickly planned and
Sumner sent his laconic order to Stanton. It was one
word—"Stick!"

Impeachment threats stormed through the Senate with
renewed vigor. But impeachments are not made in that
forum. The action is laid in the name of the people
and it is consistent with the theory of our Government
that when resorted to, the House of Representatives
should invoke the process. There, also, no time was
lost. More than fifteen months had elapsed since Ashley had first formally demanded impeachment of Johnson, and the proponents had searched assiduously during all that time for evidence sufficient to ground the
action, but without avail. Now by a single act, the
President himself had furnished a basis which the Republican Party in the House believed was more than
ample. However, no attempt was made to get the Reconstruction Committee together on Friday the twenty-
first.

The country had been notified by telegraph of what
was expected, and many from the great cities of the

From Frank Leslie's Illustrated News, March 14, 1868.

Stevens Announcing Impeachment to the Senate and Notifying it to Make Preparation for the Trial of President Johnson

East flocked to the Capitol. In the early hours of Saturday morning men and women trooped by the hundreds through the snow-paved streets of Washington, to the House galleries. Many others, whose carriages had brought them, were there in fine clothing and furs.

Long before twelve, the seats were filled, the corridors packed, and the Capitol police had to be called in order to help the House Sergeant-at-arms stay the throng. When the clock showed high noon, there was a tensed anxiety. It was time for something to happen. But nothing did.

Stevens' Reconstruction Committee, contrary to the rules of the House, had gone into session shortly before,[12] and was wasting no time.

At twenty minutes to two, on that dreary February day, anniversary of the birth of George Washington, word went through the crowd with electric swiftness that the Committee had acted and was about to report. From the cloak rooms and the offices, there poured into the Floor of the House not only Congressmen, but most of the members of the Senate, which Body had adjourned in order to witness the tremendous event.

Surely this was Stevens' day, and anyone who reads his utterances of the time, cannot fail to be convinced that he believed with all the sincerity that was in him, that Johnson was trampling underfoot the will of the people, attempting to reform the Nation with all its old weaknesses, and might possibly be thinking of rebuilding the Government on a basis that would make the Congress and therefore the popular will, subservient.

Not only that; the Old Commoner feared that the Executive at the time was in a position so strong that there was grave danger of his succeeding in the effort.

What an opportunity were Stevens', could he have used it! To challenge the Chief Executive of a great nation for, as he held, betraying the people; to indict him in the House of Representatives; to try him in the great Court of the Senate with the Chief Justice of the Supreme Court of the United States presiding; to remove him from office and thereby vindicate our democratic form of Government—what an opportunity for any Commoner!

But the days of his strength were gone. The time had passed when that striking presence and devastating invective of his was the summons to a legislative body to surge over all before it. The years had taken their toll, and his emaciated frame could no longer support even verbal battle. Facing the death which he had already twice yielded to and then fought off, he showed no enthusiasm for the fray. Nothing, if not practicable, no one knew better than he that never again could he battle with his oldtime vigor.

With bagging clothes that loosely draped his bent frame, he hobbled in from the door behind the Speaker's desk to take his seat. The noise in the galleries subsided; talking on the Floor ceased, and a death-like silence fell over the Chamber.

All eyes were turned upon him as he rose. Even the Speaker was watching only him. He straightened himself and waited. Colfax, presiding, sternly announced that "if there shall be any manifestation of approbation or disapprobation" among the spectators "at the proceedings and actions of this House, the chair will instantly order that portion of the gallery so offending cleared and the doors of the chamber closed and locked."

He turned to serve an unusual notification upon the members themselves. If any of them "manifested approbation or disapprobation" or showed any disobedience of the rules of the House, he would call the person so offending by name, "the effect of which will be to bring the case before the House for such action as the House shall adjudge to be necessary for this contempt of its rules by a member."

Having, as he thought, properly prepared the Chamber for a pronouncement without parallel in the country's history, he solemnly recognized Stevens.

Pale, haggard and thoroughly spent, but with a penetrating dark eye that had not lost its luster, Stevens, in low voice, said simply, "I am directed by the Committee on Reconstruction to present to the House a report with an accompanying resolution which I ask the Clerk to read."

That officer took less than a minute to read the writing that the Old Commoner sent him. Seven of the nine members had joined in recommending a stupendous undertaking. Stevensesque, it was condensed to seventeen words, and read, "That Andrew Johnson, President of the United States, be impeached of high crimes and misdemeanors in office."

Leaning heavily on his stout cane, the Lancastrian said it was not his intention in the first instance to debate the question and "if there be no desire on the other side to discuss it, we are willing that the question should be taken upon the knowledge which the House already has." But if debate were insisted upon, he would "for the present give way and say what he had to say in conclusion." [13] Tired and broken he appeared "to speak as one from the very brink of the grave." [14]

The opposition, although outnumbered to the point of hopelessness, nevertheless determined to fight. Brooks, a member of the Committee, fully apprised in the preliminary meeting of what the majority party planned, took the Floor to deliver a solid speech in a vain hope of stemming the tide.

He and his associates would lay all possible obstruction "in the way of these high-handed proceedings," and if impeachment succeeded, he warned that the "hundreds of thousands and millions of the people of this country would never, never,—so help me God—never, never, submit!" He threatened that "four-fifths of the army of the United States now are composed of the democracy of the country" and if politics were introduced, it would bring the country to "the verge of vile revolution."

His barbs were aimed directly at Stevens whom he said had "upon the instant, impromptu, in a single day, in utter violation of the rules and ordinances of this House, summoned us here at once .. . . . to convict the President of crimes and misdemeanors because he honestly holds to one construction of the law while you hold to another." He did not aid Johnson's cause by his unusual construction that "the President is a primary judge of the Constitution."

When he finished, he had in no way curbed the temper of a determined House. Throughout the afternoon, the oratory went on, and after a short recess, the House reconvened for evening session.

The sick man from Lancaster sat patiently through

the deluge of fiery debate. He took no part; he spoke
no word, and the far away look in his eyes might have
indicated that his thoughts were on matters less ephemeral than even legal proceedings which rocked the
Nation.

Speakers on both sides delivered their arguments, but
the issue was never in doubt. The Commoner had decided the opposition should be given a brief period in
which to be heard, and then the formality of a vote
should come. All day Monday, the fleeting minutes
were charged with a heavy flow of words, but their
combined effect upon the inevitable was a nullity.

On Saturday the House had agreed that the vote
should be taken at five o'clock on Monday. Stevens
was to have a half hour to close the debate.

How little interest he showed in that debate is indicated by the fact that even after his time was beginning to run, he did not call it to the attention of the
House. Another Representative did, however, and
with but twenty-five remaining minutes in which to
close, Stevens willingly yielded a part of it to Washburn.

When he had finished, Stevens arose. "A climactic
sensation passed through the crowd" in a stillness that
almost could be felt. In a very matter of fact way, he
agreed with the prior "speakers that the matter before
the House was a grave subject and should be gravely
treated." It was important to the high official who was
the subject of the charges, and important to a Nation
of forty million people, then free.

The official character of the chief executive being thus
involved, the charge, if falsely made, was a cruel wrong;

but if on the other hand, the usurpations and misdemeanors charged were true, he was guilty of as atrocious attempts to usurp the liberty and destroy the happiness of the Nation as were ever perpetrated by the
most detestable tyrant who ever oppressed his fellow
men. He would, therefore, discuss the question "in no
partisan spirit, but with legal accuracy and impartial
justice."

The people desired no victim, but they would endure
no usurpation. With an outspoken honesty that
stunned the opposition, he agreed "with the other side
of the House" that the impeachment was "a purely
political proceeding." It was "intended as a remedy
for malfeasance in office and to prevent the continuance
thereof." Beyond that, it was not intended as a personal punishment for past offenses or for future
example.

He pointed out the difference between impeachment
under the United States Constitution and impeachment
under the English law. Furthermore, he felt that to
sustain the proceeding, it was not necessary to prove a
crime that was an indictable offense or any act *malum
in se.*

In the briefest manner possible, he reviewed Johnson's action relating to Stanton and concluded that it
was a clear violation of the Tenure-of-Office Act and
therefore, a basis for impeachment.

In the Executive's controversy with Grant, "if Andrew Johnson thought and told the truth, then he was
guilty of a high official misdemeanor for he avowed his
effort to prevent the execution of the law." If Grant
told the truth, then the President again was guilty of

high misdemeanor, for the General declared the same thing as the President, denying only his own complicity. If he and General Grant told the truth, then Johnson committed willful perjury by refusing to take care that the laws should be duly executed.

The managers would prove at the trial that the President was guilty of misprision of bribery, by offering to General Grant, if he would unite with him in his lawless violence, to assume in his stead the penalties and to endure the embarrassment resultant from acts denounced by the law.

Stevens' complaint was of greater consequence, however, than the technicality of the Tenure-of-Office Law violation. When the War ended, Johnson "with unblushing hardihood," undertook to rule the conquered states, and by his own power alone, "to lead them into full communion with the Union; told them" what governments to erect and what Constitutions to adopt and to send representatives and senators to Congress, according to his instructions.

In spite of the warning of Congress, he had continued his lawless usurpation. It was the Congressional duty to protect the liberty and happiness of a mighty people, and defend against every kind of tyranny. "As we deal with the first great political malefactor, so will be the result of our efforts to perpetuate the happiness and good government of the human race."

This was not to be the temporary triumph of a political party, but was to endure "in its consequence until this whole Continent shall be filled with a free and untrammeled people or shall be a nest of shrinking, cowardly slaves." His speech was ended and there yet remained some minutes before the fatal hour of five o'clock.

But no one sought the Floor, and after an ominous pause, Stevens called the question. One hundred twenty-six supported the impeachment resolution, forty-seven opposed it, and seventeen did not vote. In that solemn moment, a President of the United States was impeached; and impeached for a political reason as was the aim of his accusers.

Losing no time, Stevens moved for the appointment of a Committee to notify the Senate and for another to prepare Articles of Impeachment. Dilatory motions were interposed, but the rules were suspended by a three to one vote to clear the way for the rampant majority. Stevens and Bingham were immediately appointed a Committee to inform the Senate.

The minority, consisting of some half hundred Representatives, had failed even to delay the machine-like actions of the majority, and at twenty minutes after six, the formalities of indictment had been concluded and the House adjourned.

On Tuesday, the twenty-fifth, Stevens reported back to the House that in obedience to its order, he and Bingham had notified the Senate of the impeachment and that the Senate had answered that "order shall be taken." [15]

The other Committee lost little time and by the next Monday, it had prepared ten specific Articles of Impeachment against the President. The first nine complained of the peremptory removal of Stanton by Johnson, and the incidents surrounding it, while the tenth, citing parts of speeches made by the Executive, charged that his words had brought "the high office of the President of the United States into contempt, ridicule, and disgrace, to the great scandal of all good citizens," which, it was alleged was a high misdemeanor on the part of the President.

The Committee's Articles did not fully satisfy the Old Commoner. The President's usurpation, as Stevens called it, whereby Johnson, "assuming to establish an empire for his own control and depriving Congress of its just prerogative in the erection of North Carolina and other conquered territories into states and nations, giving them governments of his own creation, and appointing over them rulers unknown to the laws of the United States," were acts far more heinous.

Johnson's persistence in pursuing his course of action, ignoring Congress completely in the matter, was to the Lancastrian, "worse than sedition and little short of treason." Although these were "important fundamental offenses, and much more worthy of punishment because more fatal to the Nation," he believed the Committee had omitted them in their articles "because they were determined to deal gently with the President." And what the Committee had pointed out was enough, even "if half were omitted, to answer the great subject and purpose of impeachment."

That proceeding had as its aim only removal from office "and anything beyond what will effect that purpose, being unnecessary, may be looked upon as wanton cruelty."

Nevertheless Stevens wanted an added article, and although he had been unable apparently to convince the Committee of its importance, he brought the House to its acceptance. It was the most comprehensive of the violations charged.

Referring to Johnson's speech in August of 1866, wherein the President stated that the Thirty-Ninth Congress of the United States was not a Congress authorized by the Constitution, but on the contrary a Congress of only part of the states, Stevens' article held that his veto of subsequent legislation was a deliberate and premeditated scheme on Johnson's part to violate his oath to execute his country's laws faithfully.

The charge cited specifically the Tenure-of-Office Act, the Appropriations Act, and the Act to "provide for the more efficient Government of the rebel states" of March, 1867, all leading up to Stanton's removal in February. The Stevens' article was added to the Committee's ten and on those eleven charges the President was tried.

There seemed to be little of superstition in those who fixed the date of the trial, for it was set and actually began on Friday, the thirteenth of March, with Chief Justice Chase presiding.

Johnson entered his appearance by counsel, who asked for at least forty days to prepare their answer. The Senate allowed ten, and at one o'clock of Monday, March twenty-third, reconvened to move promptly into the hearing of the case.

At Chase's direction, the Sergeant-at-arms rapped for silence and then solemnly called the imposing Court to order, with his "Hear ye! Hear ye! All persons are commanded to keep silence while the Senate of the United States is sitting for the trial of the Articles of Impeachment by the House of Representatives against

Andrew Johnson, President of the United States."

The impeachment managers were announced, admitted, and in impressive silence, took the seats assigned them by the Senate. The President's counsel, led by his former Attorney General, Henry Stanbery of Kentucky, who had resigned to represent him, Curtis of Massachusetts, Nelson of Tennessee, Evarts of New York, and Groesbeck of Ohio, as able and distinguished an array of counsel as had ever represented a defendant on this Continent, "appeared and took the seats assigned to them on the right of the Chair."

The House of Representatives, headed by its Committee and with its Clerk, entered the Chamber.

Chase satisfied himself that all was in order and the impeachment trial was on. Although the President's counsel "profoundly regretted" that they had not been allowed more time, (they had "abandoned all other engagements," some quitting their Courts and cases, and their clients) by devoting "not only every hour ordinarily devoted to labor, but also those required for necessary rest and recreation," they were able to present their client's answer. Evarts read it. It was a carefully drawn, sweeping denial of the charges and indicated the line of defense.

The question of time to be allowed for reply was debated at length. The Senate showed its disposition to press on by refusing the thirty days asked for, granting but six.

On Monday, March 30, Butler opened for the managers with a lengthy speech, elaborating the charges and outlining the evidence which the House would present. He submitted a brief prepared by Congressman

Lawrence, of Ohio. As there was but little authority
in the American law, recourse was had to the impeachments of other nations, especially to those of England.
The rest of the day and a part of the next was devoted
to a reading of the documents supporting the Manager's case and on the next day, the first witness was
called.

With Stevens' life hanging by a thread the entire
time, he was able to take but a very minor part in the
work of the trial, and there is nothing to indicate that
he took any part of importance in the conferences of
the Managers, where procedural plans were made. Taking into account the tremendous significance of the case,
the large number of individuals who constituted the
Court, and the additional fact that most of them were
not skilled lawyers, it must be said that it moved with
surprising rapidity.

The Managers, of course, were anxious to get the
case to the Senate, for when the trial started, they were
confident that they had enough votes to convict. The
Senate itself had found Johnson practically guilty of
some of the charges in its resolutions wherein it held
that he had no legal right to remove Stanton, and the
sooner the vote could be asked for, so much greater
weight would that record have, and so much less would
Senators feel justified in reversing themselves if they
inclined to vote acquittal.

On Saturday, April 18, the defense closed its testimony, and on Monday, arguments began. Just a week
later, on April 27, Stevens attempted to deliver a closing address, in support of the articles.

He called all of his fast ebbing energies to the task,

but so frail was he that in spite of his great will, he could not finish the speech. Aware of his condition, he had written out his address. For a minute or two he stood and spoke. When unable to stand any longer, he was given permission to continue from his chair, and the official account says he read for nearly half an hour. Then his voice became too weak to be heard and the exhausted Old Commoner was forced to "hand over his manuscript to Mr. Manager Butler, who concluded the reading."

His speech is a gem of pure logic and clarity. Instead of covering the whole ground laid in the eleven counts, he confined himself to the single one which he "had the honor to suggest and was expected to maintain." That one charged Johnson with breach of his oath to take care that the laws were faithfully executed. He went directly to the issue in a frontal attack.

In March of 1867, Congress had repassed over the veto of the President, the Tenure-of-Civil-Offices Act. It provided that an office holder who had been appointed by and with, the advice and consent of the Senate, was entitled to hold his office until a successor was appointed and duly qualified, with the qualification that Cabinet officers should hold their offices for the term of the President by whom they were appointed, and one month thereafter, subject to removal by and with the advice and consent of the Senate.

When the Senate was in recess, the President was permitted to suspend an official until its next meeting, but was required within twenty days of its convening to notify that Body of the reasons for his act. If the Senate concurred the official was removed. But if the

Senate deemed the President's reasons for suspension insufficient, he was entitled to "forthwith resume the functions of his office."

Stevens reviewed the President's acts in his attempted removal of Stanton. Johnson's lawyers had contended that the proviso which embraced Cabinet officials did not include Stanton, because he was not appointed by the President in whose term the acts charged were perpetrated. Lincoln had appointed Stanton and when Johnson succeeded to the Presidency, he continued the War Secretary in office with no further formality.

Johnson's counsel insisted that the term of office referred to in the Tenure statute meant the time during which the President who made the appointment actually held. This, of course, would mean that Lincoln's term had expired with his death, and that Johnson was not serving for the remainder of it.

Stevens argued that under the Constitution, a President's term was four years, and cited passages of the document itself in support. Stanton had been appointed by Lincoln in 1862, and was still serving as his appointee. Otherwise, his commission was invalid, for it was the only one that had been approved by the Senate.

And the Lancastrian had another answer. The first section of the Tenure-of-Office Act provided that every person holding Civil office who had been appointed with the advice and consent of the Senate, should hold until a successor had been in like manner appointed and qualified, except as therein otherwise provided. Then came the qualification which Johnson's counsel said did not embrace Stanton, because he was not appointed by the President in whose term he was removed. Stevens argued that if Stanton were not embraced in the proviso, "then he was nowhere specially provided for" and was consequently embraced in Section 1, which declared that "every person holding Civil office not otherwise provided for" came within the provisions of the act. That seemed clear, accurate, and unanswerable.

One of the defenses raised by Johnson was that he had removed Stanton simply to test the constitutionality of the Tenure-of-Office Law. Showing a radical attitude which seemed to permit Congress to share an exclusive Court function, Stevens said, "the matter has already been tested and decided by the votes twice given of two-thirds of the Senators, and of the House of Representatives."

He used Johnson's own correspondence to strike at the President's defense. In his somewhat inconsistent answer, Johnson had contended that he had not removed Stanton under the Tenure-of-Office Law. But Stevens introduced the Executive's letter of August 14, to the Secretary of the Treasury, in which he stated, "in compliance with the requirements of the act entitled 'an act to regulate the tenure of certain civil offices,' you are hereby notified that on the twelfth instant, Honorable Edwin M. Stanton was suspended. . . ."

The Old Commoner went further than his broad charge that Johnson had been guilty of high crime in refusing to faithfully execute the laws after he had sworn so to do. He attempted to show that the Executive had himself deliberately moved to violate what he knew was then existing law.

In his letter to Grant on January 31, 1868, Johnson wrote, "you had found in our first conference 'that the President was desirous of keeping Mr. Stanton out of office, whether sustained in suspension or not.'" Surely, concluded Stevens, the President, by his own words, had clearly shown his intent to deliberately violate the laws of the country.

From the Johnson-Grant correspondence he thought no one could hesitate "to choose between the words of a gallant soldier and the pedagoguery of a political trickster. If either of these gentlemen has correctly stated the facts, the President has been guilty of violating the law and of misprision of official perjury."

It was easy to sweep away Johnson's contention that he had the right to remove heads of departments on the ground that his predecessors had done so. The Old Commoner pointed out that when former Presidents had so acted, there was no law of prohibition. When Johnson attempted it, there was a specific statute against it.

Stevens made no appeal to the Senators hearing the case, except to remind them that their vote on February 21 pronounced Johnson's "solemn doom." The Senate had then determined that "the President has no power to remove the Secretary of War." When they so voted, the Lancastrian contended Senators acted not only on the ground stated, but with the conviction that Johnson's procedure was a positive breach of law.

Altogether it was clear that Johnson had violated the Tenure-of-Office Act. Had he been unwilling to execute the statutes passed by the American Congress and unrepealed, his proper course was to resign "his office

From Harper's Weekly, August 29, 1868.

Death of the Old Commoner

which was thrown upon him by a horrible convulsion, and retire to his village obscurity. Let him not be so swollen with pride and arrogance which sprang from the deep misfortune of his country as to attempt an entire revolution of its internal machinery and the disgrace of the trusted servants of his lamented predecessor."

Under our Constitution, personal punishments like those existing in England for impeachment had been excluded. "Our Government would deal with the defendant just so far as the public safety required, and no further. It was our theory, therefore, that impeachment should apply simply to political offenses, and persons holding political positions."

He could not close without another word on Johnson's usurpation, repeating his charge that Johnson, without consulting the Congress, which was the real authority to readmit the States, had "seized all the powers of the Government within these States and had he been permitted, would have become their absolute ruler."

The address ended abruptly; probably because Stevens had been too weak to complete its writing.

What he thought as Butler read it for him can only be imagined. To him impeachment meant removal of one who had been attempting to thwart the will of the people, and as such, was of highest importance. He must have mourned within his lonely self the vanished strength that would have permitted him to lead the battle. But he made no comment.

Stanbery closed for the defense on May 1, and Bingham for the Managers on May 6. The Radicals soon sensed a weakening of Senate support, and delayed the vote in order to bring the wavering ones back into line.

Stevens was grievously ill.

On Saturday, May 16, with no one knowing how the matter would go, the ballot of the most impressive jury that had ever heard a case in this Hemisphere was called for.

The President was acquitted by a single vote.

Among many others, there were three outstanding reasons for Johnson's release. First, conviction would have upset completely the balance of our tripartite Government, making the Executive subservient to the Legislative Body. Many Senators who otherwise would have voted guilty, could not bring themselves to such a fundamental overturn.

Secondly, Thaddeus Stevens who led the impeachment as long as he was physically able, suffered complete collapse soon after the trial started. Secretary of the Navy Welles, who was very close to the situation and practically all of those taking part in it, seemed to think that had Stevens been in good health, there would have been no acquittal.[16]

A third fact of more weight than is usually given it, was the knowledge on the part of the Senate and the country that if Johnson were removed from office, Ben Wade would succeed him. He was neither the type nor the quality of man for President, and the whispered question, "Are you going to make Wade President?" was directed at wavering Senators with an effect that registered.

As we look at the matter today, we see it exactly as

Stevens described it—a political maneuver to remove an Executive who differed with the Congress on a matter of policy. The Old Commoner was honest enough never to give it any other cloak. Had Johnson been convicted, it is impossible to say just how far it would have remodeled our Governmental set-up, for among other things, it would have established that the Executive Department was answerable to the Legislative in matters of political policy with the President removable at its will. One of the singular circumstances of the proceedings is the fact that Stevens and his followers seemed entirely oblivious of the revolution the impeachment program contemplated.

Stevens went to his bed and for weeks, most of those who saw him thought he was dying. But slowly he retrieved himself sufficiently to be carried into the House for short intervals, and in July, delivered one of his longest Congressional speeches. Surprisingly, it was on the matter of impeachment. He had not given up. True it was, as he said, that the Senate had adjourned after a vote upon but a single article, but those close to the trial were convinced that the matter was dead.

The Old Commoner would revive it with five additional articles. The first charged Johnson in substance with making removals and appointments for no cause of merit or demerit, but for the purpose of building up a new party of his own.

The second reviewed his restoration acts, charging usurpation of the Congressional functions.

The third set forth that Johnson had indulged in corrupt practices in attempting to induce Senators-elect from Colorado to perjure themselves on a promise of admitting Colorado into the Union; that he pardoned deserters from the army upon condition that they would vote for the Democratic party in the ensuing election, and had paid a Democratic agent $1,000 in cash; that he appointed to office persons who could not qualify under the test oath; restored forfeited property contrary to law, and sold pardons for money.

In the next count, the President was accused of removing from the Treasury large tracts of land and large amounts of money contrary to law. The last was a broad indictment charging Johnson with usurping the powers of other branches of the Government in carrying out his restoration policies.

The Speaker decided the resolution was a question of high privilege and Stevens took the Floor. To him, the impeachment trial had been most unsatisfactory. The prosecutors had gone about gathering charges of small gravity, thinking to break the elephant's back by piling upon it straws and chaff bags. "These innumerable eggs were thrown into the nest of investigation until it was more than full, and there was great danger of their becoming addled."

But they had missed the real offenses. He had set them forth specifically in his additional articles. He took great pains to show that there was no necessity of proving an indictable offense in order to sustain an impeachment. There were quires of scandalous testimony to prove the respondent's depraved appetite and licentious habits. But he would turn to graver charges of embezzling or allowing others to embezzle the public property, and the abuse of the high prerogative of the pardoning power.

Johnson had violated the July law of 1862, which provided a punishment for treason, by pardoning many of the most guilty offenders. Furthermore, instead of confiscating their property as was directed, he permitted them to retain it. Stevens gave specific instances with names and amounts. Had Johnson not been guilty of official perjury, the "whole of the bonded debt which is now a lien upon every man's property, would have been paid."

He elaborated on the Executive's dogged persistence in attempting restoration when the country had ordered reconstruction, marking it as high tyranny. "This," said he, "may seem to be the argument of spleen, emitted by disappointment at recent events, but I disclaim any reference to those events, nor do I intend that they shall be made to apply to any fact or individual connected with recent transactions."

If this Government learned to punish her delinquent rulers and never depart from the principles of the Declaration of Independence, she could never take a step backward. But "trust could not be placed in Princes. Ambition should be flung away, and the rights of every human being, however lowly born or degraded, should be treated as inalienable. Ours might be a happy people" if this were done.

"My sands are nearly run, and I can see with only the eye of faith. I am fast descending the downhill of life at the foot of which stands an open grave." But, with a will to still carry on, he asked that his "resolutions be posted until next Monday," adding ironically, "certain gentlemen might wish to look at them." [17]

Again he returned to his bed. The following week,

when time for consideration of his resolutions came, he was too ill to attend. Within the month he died.

Impeachment was invoked under his leadership. Keenly aware from the outset of the difficulty of his position, he tried to explain time after time that he wanted no punitive measures against the President. Johnson occupied the highest office in the nation. Stevens believed it was the duty of that officer not only to execute the laws, but when policies must be applied not specifically covered by statute, it was his further duty to proceed in a manner consistent with the will of the people.

They had clearly ordered reconstruction; Johnson, in spite of that, insisted on restoration. Stevens would not tolerate such a condition of affairs. Had a similar situation arisen under English law, it could have been cleared quickly by the Parliament defeating the government, forcing it to resign and calling a new one in accord with the will of the people. In this country there was and is no machinery to accomplish such end. The President is elected for an arbitrary term of years. As long as he holds the support of majority public opinion, all is well; when he loses it, there is only one means of removing him. That is impeachment, and impeachment is a harsh process which Americans have been traditionally educated to view as a last resort.

We think of it as punitive and to be used more where the impeached has been guilty of misdemeanors or crimes in office. Stevens did not want Johnson punished any further than removal from office, and that explains his repeated statement that to justify conviction it was not necessary to prove Johnson guilty of any indictable offense. It was sufficient to show merely that he opposed the will of the people.

In other words, the Old Commoner wanted to substitute our impeachment process for a lack-of-confidence vote of more democratic governments where the chief officer is removed from office when he can no longer hold the majority support of the people's representatives. He would expand impeachment to make our governmental machinery more responsive to the popular will.

That in itself cannot be condemned by any one who believes in a democratic form of government. But the Senate was too conservative to adopt the Old Commoner's reform. They feared, and perhaps rightly so, that it might be opening the door to changes that would fundamentally modify our system of government.

Had he been in vigorous health to carry it through, this country today, in all likelihood, would have a different view of the impeachment process. But death came to Johnson's aid, and neutralized the power of Stevens.

The Old Commoner's fear that the people's will would be thwarted proved groundless. Six months after impeachment, Johnson was retired from office by the election of Grant. That he was not a candidate is significant evidence in support of Stevens' contention that he had lost the confidence of the people.

If Johnson's term had not expired within the year, the Senate might have voted differently. But Senators knew that by removing the President, they could anticipate the popular will by only a few months. In that short time, little injury could be done and under the circumstances, it was probably best to rest the decision in the hands of the people.

BOOK SEVEN
EPILOGUE

BOOK SEVEN—EPILOGUE

I

THE MAN

UP to Lincoln's election, Stevens had achieved but little national notice, and most of that was anything but commendatory. But with the cataclysm of War came his opportunity. Had he lived in a peace period, he probably would never have attained wide prominence. But it was his fate to be born in a time when a great political problem was to be determined. In such times it is not unusual for men to attain extraordinary power.

Stern times demand stern men. War leaders dare not falter. They must be men of action, resolute, intelligent, daring and strong. For such leadership, Stevens was eminently fitted.

There was not a single man in the Lower House of the Congress from 1858 to 1868 who could have filled the Old Commoner's place. Whether he proceeded in the best course possible is beyond the point. The record is irrevocably sealed, and the fates had decreed that it was to be done the way it was done. No man in all that decade achieved the power or wielded the influence that Stevens did. No Congressman in all our history rose to the heights of dictatorship that he did. To understand just how that came about is not easy.

As a politician, Stevens was an enigma. All power that he achieved was built upon his office as Representative. But if any other politician had attempted to treat his constituents and the people at large the way

Stevens did, he would have been quickly retired. Not so with the Old Commoner. He could hold his office as long as he chose in spite of his lack of deference to those who elected him.

In the early War, when huge revenues had to be raised, he was the author of a bill that placed a tremendously burdensome tax upon farmers, and farmers comprised a large part of his constituency. A fellow Representative brought this to his attention, but Stevens had no long explanation to make; he merely said he realized it would be hard upon the people in his district, but that was all. As he reasoned, it was wholly justified and if his people did not like it, they could show their displeasure at the next election.

Possessed with a capacity for exquisite humor, he used it solely for his own amusement. Had he desired to leave it in the record, he would have applied it in the discussion of great issues. He did just the opposite. Liberating it only when he was in easy frame of mind, and among his few intimates, it was not published and consequently has been lost almost entirely. One commentator who knew him well said, "no public man was ever more famous for his ready humor," adding that had the Lancastrian enjoyed a faithful Boswell, "the volumes containing his jokes and sayings would have constituted a precious legacy to his countrymen." [1]

In addition to his humor, he commanded a searing wit which, when he chose to unloose it, withered the most pretentious foe. His fellow-townsman, historian Harris, was an ardent Southern sympathizer and resented Stevens' bold Anti-slavery speeches. One day they met in a weed-grown path beside the street. One had to step aside so the other could pass, and Harris quickly resolved that he would not extend the courtesy. Walking close up to Stevens in a challenging manner, he looked squarely into the heavily-browed eyes of the Old Commoner, and said defiantly, "I never yield to a skunk." Stevens, taken somewhat by surprise, looked at him calmly for a moment and then quietly answered, "I always do," and proceeded to move around his challenger.[2]

President Johnson's friend, trying to convince Stevens one day that the President was not such a bad fellow, finally asked him if he did not think that the Tailor from Tennessee was a self-made man. Stevens answered, "I never thought of it that way, but it does relieve God Almighty of a heavy responsibility."[3]

On occasions he used an effective irony to batter down an opponent. In a House discussion of a measure looking toward the grant of some rights to the freed negro, Brooks of New York had discoursed for more than an hour upon the foot, heel, nose and skin of the blackman in an attempt to show that he was of a race apart from the white man.

Stevens listened patiently, and although most members believed him so weak as to be physically incapable of reply, he laboriously arose, and leaning heavily on his desk, reminded Brooks that in spite of the color of his hair and the size of his feet, the negro had an immortal soul which "God may damn" as well as his "if it deserved it." As to intellect, he said, "there are various degrees of it. In that regard, the gentleman from New York towers above the rest of us, though,

I fear, he sometimes abuses his superiority by the declamation which he travels out of his road to inflict upon us with regard to the various races of the earth. But that in intellectual gifts the gentleman stands above all of us, no man who has heard him today or heretofore can deny; and I do not, I assure you, sir, I do not speak this ironically, (laughter) for I do not know when I have heard anything more eloquent than the discourse which the learned gentleman has given us today. But I have one proposition to make. For the oratorical championship of America, I am willing to match Fred Douglass (Stevens' negro barber in Lancaster) against the gentleman from New York. I will allow the latter gentleman to select two out of three judges. Let the topic be anything the gentleman pleases, except the negro's skin, and if, at the end of the discussion, he does not 'throw up the sponge,' I will admit that the negro is an inferior animal—not only inferior to the gentleman from New York, but inferior to the rest of us."

The Old Commoner paused and slowly turned his pallid but determined face toward Brooks. That gentleman, completely vanquished, had no desire to continue in the fray wherein he was so badly outclassed. There was but one more sentence uttered. Stevens said, "I move the previous question," and the bill was passed.[4]

When an inexperienced newcomer to the Pennsylvania Legislature, anxious to enter into verbal combat with Stevens, had delivered what he thought was a most scathing and unanswerable denunciation of the Commoner, Stevens crushed him with the answer, "I hope

I may be credited with virtuous silence on this occasion;
let the wounds made by the gallant foe, wide gaping,
plead my cause." [5]

American history contains no better example of subtle
irony on a stupendous scale than Stevens' reference to
his measure to seize more than four hundred million
acres of Southerners' property as a "mild confiscation." He was never awed by dealings in grand
amounts. Equally competent to estimate accurately the
hundreds of millions of dollars that the country would
need in the War program, and the allowance to be
made a Pastor who offered prayer at the opening of a
Convention, he combined in an extraordinary manner
the qualities which made him an excellent Dictator in
the work of the House Committee on Appropriations.

One of the finest attributes of his character was his
charity. Even his enemies said that no request for aid
was ever made by one in need, whether friend or foe,
that was not immediately and cheerfully answered.
Many of his contributions were made privately, and
closely guarded, as was the case where he contributed
for a number of years to a crippled soldier whose pen-
sion was wholly inadequate to support himself and his
family. [6]

In December of 1867, when he at last found himself
unable to handle his correspondence by reason of his
exhausted energies and disease, in spite of the fact
that he was pressed under a tremendous burden of
work, he took the time to search out a crippled man
for secretary. [7]

He treasured throughout life the early religious training his mother had given him. But in his mature and

later years, he seemed to hold to it more from respect for her than from his own convictions. The year before he died, he wrote indifferently, "I was raised a Baptist and adhere to their belief." [8] While resident in Gettysburg, he was a constant attender of several churches and always held a pew in at least one.[9] In his early years in Lancaster, he was a member of the Presbyterian Church there. As time went on, the slavery problem became more and more acute, and it was frequently referred to by clergymen in their sermons. In the section where Stevens lived, the Ministers generally were apologists for the institution or, as Stevens called them, "doughfaces." [10] And inasmuch as he had no toleration whatever on the slavery subject, it was only to be expected that he would absent himself from church.

Through the years of his greatness, he had little if any actual contact with churches and was rarely seen at services. Jeremiah Sullivan Black, Attorney General in Buchanan's Cabinet, who knew him well, said that "his mind, as far as his sense of obligation to God was concerned, was a howling wilderness." [11]

Nevertheless, he seemed anxious as death drew upon him to discuss matters of after-life with all of the clergymen who called upon him. The McPherson collection contains a long report on the subject by someone who apparently visited him in those days.[12] He was always a substantial contributor to churches of all denominations, and in his Will, provided for assistance in building a Baptist Church in Lancaster County in memory of his mother.

On one occasion, when two negro Ministers had come

from Lancaster to ask his financial aid in restoring a part of their church that had been burned, they found that Stevens had left his home to spend the evening at the card table in one of the gambling places then so plentiful in Washington. They traced him and waited outside until he came. Approaching him, they explained their mission. Without ceremony or comment, the Old Commoner reached in his pocket and from a profusion of bills, picked and handed them one. They thanked him and turned away, but upon inspecting the contribution, found that it was a hundred dollar bill. Knowing that Stevens was far from a rich man, and quickly appraising the situation, they turned and ran after the old man, who was hobbling home. Catching up with him, they told him that he must have made a mistake, for the bill he had given them was of hundred dollar denomination. The fact was Stevens had intended to give them but $10, and in the near dark, had selected the wrong bill. But the cause was a worthy one, and the evening had not been entirely unprofitable. He refused to admit the error, commenting to the colored churchmen, "God moves in a mysterious way, his wonders to perform."

His charity was not confined to his private donations. Hospitals, asylums, or houses-of-refuge which opened their doors to any and all, regardless of class, color or religion, found in him not only a sympathetic friend, but a powerful proponent who would give his time and effort unstintingly to their aid. It was due to him more than any other that Government assistance was extended to the Columbia Hospital, the Soldiers' and Sailors' Home, the Deaf and Dumb Asylum, the Providence Hospital, and many other institutions that gave relief to the poor.

When the Sisters of Charity of the Roman Catholic Church sought his financial help for their commendable work among the poor, they received it so lavishly that before long, their establishment, which was at first no more than a shack, was soon raised to the status of a real hospital. They never forgot his kindness, and through his long illness, ministered tenderly and faithfully to him and were with him when he died.

In dealing with the public funds, he was ever alert in assisting those in need, and it mattered not whether they were on his side or opposed to him. When an amended Freedman's Bureau Bill, which was aimed primarily to give sustenance and shelter to the freed negroes, was under discussion, he showed that he not only knew that some of the monies were being diverted for the help of white people, most of whom were bitterly opposed to him politically, but that he was wholly satisfied with such diversion. When taken to task for the manner in which the appropriations had been used, Stevens answered, "all I can say is that nine out of ten of those who have been fed by the Freedman's Bureau have been disloyal men who have become poor." [13]

One of the most striking qualities of the Old Commoner was his aggressive and forward-looking attitude toward our theory of Government. To him, conservatism was "a vile ingredient." [14]

And no movement, however revolutionary, ever seemed to awe him. One month he could engage himself and his followers in a plan that would restrict the

Supreme Court to a field allowed it by a dominating Congress, and the next month, lead an impeachment against the President that would remove him from office, merely because he differed with Congress on a political question. That the inevitable result of such action would be to completely upset the tripartite basis of our Government, and irrevocably invalidate the fundamental theory of our Constitution, did not disturb him.

When Stevens was active in these causes, he was past seventy-five years of age and so ill that he expected death daily. But fearing to pass the gage to those about him, lest in weaker hands the battle be lost or the victory postponed, he drove himself to the task with a courage well nigh unmatchable. Carried to and from the House daily, in the feeling he could waste not a moment of the short space of life that remained to him, he did the work of two ordinary men there.[15]

While the impeachment trial was pending, a case of far-reaching importance that everyone realized might upset the whole military reconstruction was appealed to the Supreme Court of the United States. William H. McCardle was an Ex-Confederate Colonel who, after the War, became a publisher in Mississippi. Enraged by General Ord's stringent enforcement of the military reconstruction measures, he printed some stinging criticism of the program in his paper. The General promptly arrested him and held him in military detention on a charge of having published libellous and incendiary matter.

In a Federal statute passed February 5, 1867, the radical bloc in Congress had inserted a clause providing that "in all cases where any person may be restrained in his or her liberty in violation of the Constitution or any Treaty or law of the United States, an appeal" would lie to the United States Supreme Court. The provision had been included so as to prevent Southern State Courts from punishing unduly the so-called loyal people of the South. It was never intended to be used against those who exercised the Congressional power, but it was pertinent to McCardle's case, and he took advantage of it.

He asked the Circuit Court of the United States for a Writ of Habeas Corpus and on the hearing, General Ord admitted detention of the editor, resting his action on the military reconstruction law. That Court sustained the Government and the editor appealed to the Court of last resort. When the Government asked for dismissal of the appeal on the grounds that the case was wholly under military control and that the civil arm was therefore without jurisdiction, the Supreme Court, to the alarm of Stevens and his supporters, held that under the February statute, it was competent to hear the case and denied the motion to dismiss.

This brought the Constitutionality of the reconstruction acts squarely before the High Court.

There was great concern as to what that Court might say of the enactments which placed the South under martial law two years after the War had ended, while everywhere else the United States had returned to civil government authority. There was further alarm due to the fact that it was rumored in Congress that five of the nine Justices of the Supreme Court viewed the reconstruction acts as unconstitutional,[16] and the five to four decision in the Milligan case the year before seemed to corroborate this. Attorney General Stanbery, who ordinarily should have argued the case for the Government, refused to appear, stating that he had already given his opinion to the President that the reconstruction acts were unconstitutional and he would not, therefore, stultify himself by arguing otherwise.

Senator Trumbull of Illinois, was accordingly appointed to present the case for the Government, while Jeremiah Sullivan Black, Buchanan's Attorney General, acted for McCardle.

The dominant Congressional group was on notice that its military measures were seriously endangered and that expeditious action was necessary if they were not to be declared unconstitutional. Accordingly, no time was lost in rushing through both Bodies a bill repealing the appeal section of the February statute of 1867. It was unique in that it applied not only to all future litigation under the act, but to pending cases as well. Johnson, although on trial at the time, vetoed the bill but Congress promptly repassed it, notwithstanding the sound argument that the Executive gave for opposition to it. It was certainly a bold procedure on the part of the Legislative Department, but it was a thoroughly effective solution of the dilemma and that was all those challenged desired.

While the Congress was taking this action, the Supreme Court, although it had advanced the case on motion of General Black, seemed reluctant to proceed with it, presumably awaiting to see if Congress would pass the superseding legislation that was widely talked of. A study of the case and circumstances leads one to feel that the highest judicial body was surprisingly loathe to assert its vested authority in the field where the Constitution makes it supreme.

Just how much Stevens had to do with this action is not clear. He was grievously ill at the time and his only appearance of record was in a substitute measure that was offered in the House soon after the appeal got to the Supreme Court. But his liegeman Schenck, took a very active part and there is every reason to believe that he was acting under the directions of the Old Commoner.

In those days, Stevens was the absolute Dictator of the House. Sniped at by some of his fellow Representatives and made the target of many bitter newspaper attacks, he nevertheless exerted a strange influence upon his colleagues, seeming to gain more and more in their respect as physical disability grew. His speeches, more than ever, were terse and to the point. Whenever he arose, he had something of importance to say. In earlier years, the members had refrained from answering through fear of verbal chastisement, which everyone had learned Stevens could direct upon them at will. That withering scorn, with which he barbed his ironic wit, was more than anyone of them could stand, and although he used it only occasionally, his opponents and even those who generally worked with him, soon lost any desire to risk his barrage. But, as the Old Commoner's health declined, that is, from 1866 on, the House seemed to show a different attitude toward him.

In the allotting of seats, the member who drew the one Stevens was accustomed to occupy in the center aisle about one-third of the way back, whether he was friend or foe always graciously yielded it to the Old Commoner. Only on rarest of occasions would Stevens in his latter days vent his word-weapons upon a member. Slowly he was becoming the pleader, but that did not mean that his language was always gentle. When he detected some cowardly tactics on the part of a man, whether of his party or not, he directed a sally against him. But it was not in the bitter words of his years from 1859 to 1865. The House seemed to sense this change in the man, and although the opposition differed just as vehemently as ever, all of the members showed a deferential indulgence to everything he had to say. His voice was becoming weak, and could no longer be heard in the galleries, but whenever he got to the Floor, friend and enemy moved quietly to his chair to listen with a respectful interest.

A frequent line in the metropolitan newspapers, reporting a speech of his was "not a single member but drew near enough to catch the eloquence of the man whom all revere and respect." [17] Or, "all his friends and some of his enemies gathered around him (this is always the case when he speaks) and listened in perfect silence to every word he uttered." [18]

But more intensely than ever, he was the uncompromising Equalitarian. He appreciated as well as anyone, the unwavering and dogged persistence with which he drove forward in his cause. Asked on occasions to yield, it was his wont to reply in good humor, "my organism is not favorable to retreat, and I must leave to my friends the honors to be won by acts of locomotion backward." [19]

One of his outstanding characteristics was the ever

uniform gentleness with which he treated younger members of the bar. No matter how intensely a case might be tried, never was Stevens known to have shown even in the slightest way, any but the kindest attitude toward a young man beginning his work at the Bar.[20] If his adversary were well-able to take care of himself, Stevens as a rule showed little restraint, but if his opponent was either new in the profession or unable to return thrust for thrust, Stevens was most generous. That quality continued throughout his life.

In 1866, he had prepared an important speech outlining his policy of reconstruction. About the time he asked for the Floor to deliver it, a young Congressman requested the same privilege. Stevens, without comment, yielded graciously. When opportunity came several months later for the Lancastrian to release his remarks, he said merely that they might be considered a bit late, but as the man to whom he yielded was a "young member," he wished to give him an opportunity.[21]

Stevens may have been radical, but he was never rash. In the great consternation that followed Lincoln's death, President Johnson issued a proclamation in which a reward of $25,000 was offered for the arrest of Jefferson Davis and former United States Senator Clement C. Clay, Jr., of Alabama, on the ground that they were in some way connected with the assassination plot. Stevens was among the few who kept his head. When George Shea, one of Davis' counsel, called on the Lancastrian in Washington, Stevens advised him "that the Chief of the Military Bureau had shown him the 'evidence' upon which the proclamation issued." He told Shea that he had refused to give the matter any support, holding that "the evidence was insufficient in itself and incredible."

Referring to Davis and Clay, he continued, "those men are no friends of mine. They are public enemies and I would treat the South as conquered territory and settle it politically upon the policy best suited for ourselves. But I know these men, sir. They are gentlemen and incapable of being assassins." [22]

The Old Commoner's life was that of the politician. It was strikingly devoid of other phases. His lameness unbalanced and distorted his existence. The clubfoot prevented his taking part in social activities, and he felt that it made him especially unattractive to women. Consequently, he never sought their company. However, to say that he was not socially inclined would be to misrepresent him. The fact is, he craved the company of his kind and although he made but few intimates, no one enjoyed a chat or happy gathering more than he.

During his busy years in Washington, he permitted himself no relaxation except an occasional evening at the card tables where he lost himself in the fascination of his favorite game of euchre. Money never meant much to him and he was frequently prodigal in handling it. At the gaming table, one account records that he lost in a single evening approximately two thousand dollars, but the same record makes mention of the fact that whether he won or lost meant nothing to him. He played merely for the joy and the thrill of the contest. [23]

Although he had been accused of illicit relationships with women in his early life that knew no bound in color, during his later years there was laid against him but one, and that was his conduct with his negress housekeeper. Lydia Hamilton Smith came into Stevens' employ and life about 1848. He came to Lancaster in April of 1843, and soon after purchased a corner property which had been laid out for two adjoining homes. He remodeled the one for an office, and lived with his nephews, who later became members of the Lancaster County Bar, in the other. It, of course, was necessary that he employ a housekeeper and after several changes [24] he finally came upon Mrs. Smith. She was recommended to him by her cousin, whom the Old Commoner at first tried to engage. The cousin was about to be married, and so recommended her widowed relative. Stevens employed Mrs. Smith, and she, with her two children, moved into a small building in the rear of his property.

The negress lived there until her boys grew up and left, when she was given a room in Stevens' house. She continued to live under the same roof with the Lancastrian from then on until his death.

An unusually attractive woman, she was neat in appearance and well above average intelligence. Though she was at all times reluctant to speak of her former life and family connections her neighbors understood that she was born in the deep South and had come North while still a young girl. During her life in Lancaster she was a devout Catholic and rarely missed a religious service. Reputed to have been of Creole origin she was light complexioned with almost Caucasian features and her hair was nearly straight. Slightly under average size she gave great attention to her appearance and dress. One neighbor remembered that, without referring to

it, she took great delight in having clothes made to re-
semble Mrs. Lincoln. She was a woman of poise and
personal dignity. Industriously caring for Stevens'
home and managing his servants, she nevertheless found
time to perform a multitude of her own quiet charities.

During all her years in Stevens' employ she was
never known to eat at the same table with him. He
always addressed her as "Mrs. Smith." None of the
few surviving intimates of Stevens are able to recall
a time when Stevens and Mrs. Smith lived alone in the
House. For several years members of the Old Commoner's family lived there and always during Mrs.
Smith's residence one or more negro servants lived with
her in a separate wing of the home.

It was to be expected, however, that the vitriolic
hatreds which Stevens encountered would sooner or
later give rise to stories of irregularities with her. Some
of the newspapers went so far as to refer to her as
"Mrs. Stevens," [25] insisting that that was a frequent
title employed by some who knew the woman. Many
fine people of Lancaster who were intimately acquainted
with Stevens' home life, and who would not for a moment approve of any irregular relations between the
Old Commoner and the woman, always held the negress
in highest esteem. Whether or not the association was
more intimate than that of master and servant, there is
no shred of evidence to indicate, and, of course, the
gossip surrounding it is of no value in determining the
answer to the question.

Whatever her position, the woman was a most faithful servant of the old man, and apparently conformed to
all of the proprieties of her position. She was eminently

discreet. No information of the Commoner's conversations with his political affiliates was ever gleaned from her by the newspaper reporters who haunted his doorstep. On occasions, when he had evening visitors, she prepared and served refreshments, all the while scrupulously observing all of the etiquette of her station as servant. Never by look, word or deed, did she intimate to anyone any relationship with the Old Commoner other than a proper one. There remains today but a single writing of hers which is a report of the Lancastrian's condition, mailed to his nephew a few days before his death.[26]

In his Will, Stevens gave her the choice of $500 a year from his estate as long as she lived, or a lump payment of $5,000. He also noted that in his home she had some of her own furniture, which the Old Commoner, trusting to her "honor," allowed her to take "as she might claim, without further proof." In addition she was permitted to occupy Stevens' house for a year after his death. She survived her master sixteen years, and is buried in the St. Mary's Catholic Cemetery in Lancaster. Her tombstone bears the inscription, that she was "for many years the trusted housekeeper of Honorable Thaddeus Stevens." Buried beside her are her two children, William and Isaac, the former born in 1835 and the latter in 1847.

In his famous letter of September 14, 1867,[27] which Stevens designates as "a larger disclosure than" he had "ever made before of" his "private affairs," he states that so far as he knew, no child had ever been begotten under his roof. No accusation has ever been laid that any children were born to Stevens and his housekeeper, and it seems clear that both of Lydia Smith's children came with her when she entered Stevens' employ. These are the simple known facts of Stevens' relations with Lydia Smith. Anything further is merely guess work.[28]

Stevens never indulged more than temperately in the use of intoxicating liquors, and during the greater part of his life, was a total abstainer. In his early days in Gettysburg, he was known not only to take a glass of wine occasionally, but had some small stock in the cellar of his home. After a card party one night, one of the participants who had sat in the game and drunk quite heavily, was found dead. Stevens connected his fate with his drinking, and immediately resolved never to drink again. He destroyed the wines he had and soon became prominent in a temperance organization that was then being organized.[29]

Thereafter, and throughout life, he was incessantly active in the cause of temperance, frequently appearing on the platform of temperance societies and assisting in quiet way, publicly and privately, in the cause.[30] When the War broke out, he offered prizes to the commissioned officers of the companies of soldiers that were organized in his home county who would "sign a pledge on honor to abstain from all intoxicating drinks (except taken bona fide) for a period of nine months." The Old Commoner looked "upon it not only as a shame, but a crime for those having the lives of others under their charge to become intoxicated," and he presumed "there would be no difficulty in finding a number of officers willing to procure for their soldiers the comforts which these small sums would purchase."[31]

By that time, the misery that undue liquor indulgence

brings had struck in his own home. His nephew Thaddeus, a student in the University of Vermont, had become addicted to the habit. With all the interest that the father, who was Stevens' dead brother, could have shown, Stevens stood as kind and loving, although stern, parent. Having long since abandoned the hope of having children of his own, his hopes had centered upon his nephew to take his place. Zealously he guarded the boy's habits and by constant advice and counsel, sought to start him in the proper path. When the young fellow entered college, Stevens' first letter to him was well worthy of the Old Commoner.

"Your duties are now but just begun. You are only on the threshold of knowledge. It will require your close attention every hour that you can spare from sleep and necessary exercise, to put you on a standing with your studies that will be respectable.

"Mere meditating should not be your ambition. Be first in your class. You can if you will. It will take intense application, but the prize is worth all the toil. If you neglect the present opportunity, when you have reached active manhood, and mingle with men of mark, you will blush at your ignorance and regret that you have failed to acquire what was easily within your reach. The most studious man can find hours, weeks and years that he might have usefully employed, which he threw away in idleness and frivolous amusements. You ought to expect to occupy positions in future life that will bring you in contact with scholars and statesmen.

"Knowledge cannot be had per order when you want to use it, as you can order a dinner at a restaurant. Not only your classic, but general information should be mastered. History, biography, the whole circle of knowledge should be traversed while in college.

"I fear indolence is your besetting sin, for sin it is. But now in the midst of stimulants to effort, I trust you will raise your energies, and do honor to yourself. You need not partake of your grandmother's fear that you will be injured either in body or mind by close study. I have never known such a case. A handsome speaker has great advantages.

"Let strict morality guide all your actions, or your acquirements will be a curse. *Never* taste intoxicating drink—a little is folly—much is crime." [32]

But Thaddeus, Jr., did not seem to get along to the satisfaction of his Uncle, who wrote him frequently and plainly. Later, in addition to complaining of the nephew's laziness, he said:

"I fear also you love rum and sometimes drink it. If so, the sooner you are abandoned the better, as there is no hope for one who ever tastes strong drink."

He submitted these remarks with "pain," but admonished "your whole future life depends upon your present conduct." [33]

The young man answered with a weak attempt at explanation and a promise to retrieve himself. The Old Commoner's response is a fine example of his simple but stern honesty. Thaddeus, Jr., was his namesake; and all he could count upon in the next generation. But Stevens was a disciplinarian, and even though it hurt, he sent his rending ultimatum.

"I have read," he wrote in his own hand, "your letter with pain. It is grievous to lose near relatives by death. But it is still more painful to see them disgraced and worthless men.

"I foresaw that your indolence and habits would lead you to ruin unless reformed. It seems that instead of reforming, you have continued them, and they have produced the natural result. I know not what course you had better pursue now. Unless you intend to change your whole habits it matters but little what you do. Study, unless accompanied with ambition, is useless and unproductive. You will hardly be fit for a profession. Perhaps a trade would be best. If, however, you think of staying and struggling through the winter, you can study hard enough to regain your standing, and if you determine to do it, it had better be tried.

"I must say that until you have redeemed yourself from disgrace, I have no desire ever to see you."[34]

But he did see his nephew again, and made him the largest beneficiary under his Will. Young Thad apparently could not cure himself of the drink habit, and with that in mind, the Old Commoner wrote down the provision that "if at the end of any five years, Thaddeus (nephew) shall have shown that he has totally abstained from all intoxicating liquors during that time, the Trustees may convey to him one-fourth of the whole

From Harper's Weekly, August 29, 1868.

The Old Commoner's Body, Guarded by Negro Zouaves, Lies in State in the
Rotunda of the National Capitol

property." Total abstinence for another five years permitted the vesting of another fourth, and a third consecutive five year period of abstention would convey the whole estate "in fee simple." But, as might be expected, those conditions were too stringent and the estate of the Old Commoner went to the alternate residuary legatees, who established a home of refuge for indigent orphans.

The arts meant little to the Lancastrian. He was never known to sing or whistle. A musical friend once said to him, "Stevens, when you were young in Vermont, did you never go to singing school?" The answer was, "yes, and I could learn the tunes, but it is a very trifling affair." [35]

He deliberately directed his mind toward the practical things of life, to the exclusion of all others. Possessed by nature of an unusual capacity for sentiment, he strangled its every expression in the utter bitterness of the sorrow that his natural blemish inflicted upon him. Carl Schurz, unusually adept at character analysis and who had a long contact with Stevens, noted this trait in the old man. [36] Practically all his contemporaries would at times incorporate some lines of poetry into their speeches or writings. Stevens never did.

In his reading, of which we have an accurate partial record in books drawn from the Congressional Library, we know him as a student of politics. Familiar with the history of all great Governments, he had no trouble at any time in reaching back for precedent or example to sustain his proposition. He read Ellis on the "English Tariff;" Hume and Lingard on "History of England;" the Federalist Papers; Bancroft's histories; Cicero's orations; Headley's "Napoleon;" Lives of Washington and Jefferson; Bollingbroke's works; Arnold's "Rome" and his "Commonwealth;" Campbell's and Villet's "Lives of the Chief Justices;" The Laws of Henry the Eighth; McCauley's essays, and his "History of England;" Halleck's "International Law;" Fletchers' Poland; "History of the Bank of England," by Francis; "Bohns' Gaelic War;" Cinsara's "Education in Holland;" and many other substantial works.

In all the years that he drew books from the Library, there was only rarely a call for fiction. On two occasions, he borrowed Shakespeare's works, and in his last year, the two volume edition of Don Quixote, but as far as the record discloses, that was the extent of his deviation from history, biography and philosophy.

With Lincoln, Stevens was always kind, generous and gentle. He respected the character and quiet ability of the martyred President, and although he differed with him utterly upon many policies, their personal relations were always most cordial. When war began, the Old Commoner took Lincoln to task for declaring a blockade of the seceded states, pointing out that inasmuch as a Nation did not blockade its own ports, it was a tacit acknowledgment of the independence of the Southern States. "Yes," said Lincoln mildly, "that's a fact. I see the point now, but I don't know anything about the Law of Nations and I thought it was alright."

The Old Commoner returned dryly, "as a lawyer, Mr. Lincoln, I should have supposed you would have seen the difficulty at once." "Well," drawled Abe, "I'm a good enough lawyer in a western law court, I suppose, but we don't practice the Law of Nations up there, and I supposed Seward knew all about it and I left it to him. But it is done now and can't be helped. So we must get along as best we can." [37]

In 1864, when Lincoln insisted upon the nomination of Johnson as a representative of a Border State, Stevens grumbled to his companion, McClure, "can't you get a candidate for Vice-President without going down into a damned rebel province for one?" [38]

But when the "tailor from Tennessee" became President, Stevens treated him with the respect due his office. At times he opposed Johnson vigorously but always in a dignified way, and all of the personal recriminations that passed were uttered by the President. It was he who could work himself up to say to his audience, "why not hang Thad Stevens?" Of course, the Commoner could and did ridicule the President and his remarks, but he never showed heat when so doing. Whenever he spoke to the House of President Johnson the record is largely interspersed with inserts of "laughter."

On rare occasions when the two men met formally, they greeted each other and shook hands in kindly manner, as was done at Grant's reception. [39] Many believed incorrectly that Stevens harbored a personal hatred for Johnson, just as Johnson hated Stevens. In the Mc-Pherson manuscript is a letter addressed to Stevens from a Cumberland County, Pennsylvania, address, in which the writer sent "a few lines confidentially." He identified himself as the person "who rowed the boat for Andy Johnson" when the President went wild duck hunting. He had just received a letter from Johnson requesting him to go South with him on another trip.

He informed Stevens that he could swim "a half mile" but that Johnson could not swim "a first bit. Now, sir," he proposed, "if you will give me a purse of $10,000—$5,000 now right away and the other $5,000 after I give him a ducking, I will go with him and row him half a mile in the river, and upset the boat. I tell you, I will make him swim. If he cannot, I can. It will be an accident." [40]

His fellow townsman, James Buchanan had risen to the Presidency. But in the matter of politics, they were as far apart as the poles. The "Sage of Wheatland," ultra-conservative, compromising, and with decided Southern sympathies, Stevens abhorred as a weakling who was permitting the country to disintegrate. His lack of firmness when secession threatened, Stevens viewed as the gravest dereliction of duty. "Buchanan is a very traitor," he confided to his friend, McPherson, on December 19, 1860. [41]

When they met as they were bound to do, because of the nearness of their homes, Stevens always tried to be at least decent in that he would, even though quietly, pass the time of day with Buchanan. But the latter showed an attitude toward the Old Commoner of something between contempt and fear. Each had as his personal physician, a highly respected fellow townsman, Dr. Carpenter. Appraising the good in each of them, it grieved him to know that they were not friends. In the last public appearance that Buchanan made in Lancaster, the Doctor arranged to have the ex-President pass on the platform where Stevens was seated and had gotten Stevens to agree to extend his hand to

Buchanan as he passed. The Old Commoner carried out his part of the bargain, but the ex-President strode by without acknowledging it. They never met again. Whether Buchanan disdained Stevens' attempt at friendliness, or whether he did not see the extended hand of the Commoner is not known.[42]

Stevens was always scrupulously careful to see that the ex-President was informed of all important matters before the Congress by sending him the copies of the bills under discussion and many reports, circulars and messages. In 1850, Buchanan had frankly asked him to give assistance in getting his nephew into West Point. Stevens exerted every effort possible, but did not succeed. His letters show his sincere desire to accommodate his political enemy, and in fairness to Buchanan, it must be said that he showed appreciation of it.[43]

For a long time Stevens held little regard for Grant. He saw him as a successful General astute enough to await his opportunity and then overcome the enemy by weight of numbers, regardless of cost. Before impeachment, Stevens had fixed upon Chase as Republican candidate for President, but after the trial he switched definitely to the support of the soldier aspirant. He never accused Chase of bias in his rulings while presiding at the impeachment, but he felt that the Chief Justice used what influence he had to save the President. This might have cooled his ardor for Chase, and turned him to Grant.

A story is told of how the General approached the Old Commoner to enlist his support. In 1867, when the battle in Congress was at white heat and open war-

fare between that body and the Executive was immi-
nent, Grant, one night in September, came to Stevens'
house unattended. He was ushered into the Lancastrian's presence by Mrs. Smith. The General bolted
the door, and without waiting for the Old Commoner's
greeting of welcome, turned to him and said bluntly,
"Mr. Stevens, you are the leader of the Republicans in
Congress. I, as General of the Armies, have come to
assure you that I, like yourself, distrust 'the man at
the other end of the avenue'—Andrew Johnson, and it
is therefore due from me to you that I should say that
in the event of a collision between Congress and the
President, I will stand by Congress and against Andrew Johnson." [44] But however it might have come
about, by late spring of 1868, Stevens had centered
upon Grant and warmly aided him in every way he
could.

In spite of the ungentle way in which he sometimes
dealt with his constituents, it soon became apparent
that no one could defeat him for his seat in Congress
as long as he cared to hold it. The Lancaster County
district had become overwhelmingly Republican and
nomination by that party was practically equivalent to
election. In 1860, Stevens was reelected by a vote of
12,065 to 470.[45] Thereafter he regularly received party
selection without opposition, and his opponents viewed
the situation as so hopeless that no real contest was ever
made against him.[46]

Stevens died on Tuesday, August 11, 1868. The following Saturday was the day for nominations for his
Congressional office. When the news of his death
reached Lancaster, the party heads got together, and

although there was time to place upon the ballot the name of a substitute candidate, they decided unanimously that as a tribute to him, no other name would be submitted. While his body lay in state in the Nation's Capitol, thousands of ardent supporters of his made it their business to go to the polls on that election day to pay, by their vote, a last tribute to the crippled Yankee youth who had come to Pennsylvania years before, friendless and alone, to make his way to the most powerful place in the politics of the Nation.

A striking thing about the vote is that there were practically as many ballots cast as at the prior elections. There was not a single one that did not bear the name of him whose mortal remains were fast disintegrating in a satin-lined rosewood casket under the dome of the Capitol in Washington.[47]

Stevens was concerned largely with matters within his own country. But where a foreign policy had to be decided upon, he always acted in accord with his liberal principles. Among the first to recognize and applaud the emancipation of Russian serfs, he consistently encouraged the Republicans of Mexico, and with characteristic generosity, was willing to run the risk of endorsing their bonds to assist them in their struggle for free government.[48]

He was always ambitious for territorial expansion of the Nation. Alaska's purchase he mentioned as one of the big things of his life and hoped that Seward could also purchase Samana.[49] At the time there was widespread rumor that substantial monies were paid in order to get the appropriations for the purchase of Alaska voted through. Seward is quoted as authority for the statement that two thousand dollars had been given to Robert J. Walker, ten thousand to his partner, F. K. Stanton; ten thousand each to two members of Congress, and twenty thousand to Forney, who had suffered large loss through the defalcation of his clerk. It was planned to give another thousand dollars to "poor Thad Stevens, but no one would undertake to give it to him."

Before anyone could be found to attempt the delivery, the Lancastrian died. That is the only record that can be found where anyone so much as thought of offering Stevens a bribe for his vote, and that record itself is eloquent of his integrity, setting forth that not a single one of all the agile-minded lobbyists of the day could be found who would dare the old man's certain fury in the attempt.[50]

An illuminating comment on the character of the man was the manner in which he held on to life until satisfied his work was completed, and then quietly yielded to the inexorable demand of the death that for more than two years had called him. At the time there was no one who saw him who did not realize that his body had broken down completely and that the only thing that kept him alive was his indomitable will.

Those piercing dark eyes under their shaggy, overhanging brows, had retreated deeply into his head. Gone was the fire that made them sparkle in previous days on occasions when he saw battle ahead. The fulsome features that had given an impressive firmness to the countenance of his prime, had wasted away. An unusual sallowness and paleness had usurped the ruddy complexion of his virile manhood years, and the emaciated frame that had once stood boldly and defiantly upright, was pitifully bent.

For months prior to the impeachment, he was so feeble he could not walk, and it was a familiar sight to see his two negro servants carrying him to and from the Chamber. Even then his grim humor showed itself. On one of these occasions, with a trace of smile, he looked down on the stalwart shoulders of the young negroes, and in mock seriousness, asked, "what will I do for some one to carry me when you boys are dead and gone?" [51]

The impeachment was lost, but the Thirteenth and Fourteenth Amendments had been incorporated into the Federal Constitution, and his prognosis assured him that nothing could prevent the addition of the Fifteenth. His labors were done.

Slavery was forever eradicated from the United States, and every American was, or soon would be, on equal political footing. That, to him, was as near Utopia as the Nation could get in his day. He was satisfied. In spite of heavy strain upon it, his thin thread of life had carried him through the crisis, and he could expect no more.

For days he lay stricken in a little bedroom in his modest house at 279 South "B" Street, on Capitol Hill. There his faithful housekeeper, Lydia Smith, with the assistance of the Sisters of Charity, attended him day and night. By August 10, he could take nourishment no longer, but a piece of ice slipped between his lips seemed to assuage the fever that was rapidly consuming him. The Doctor called twice daily, but gave no hope.

On the afternoon of the eleventh, rumor got out that he was very much better but it had no basis in fact. Everyone about him knew that he would never again rise from his little old-fashioned bed, and by evening, he indicated to those about him that the end had come. He suffered fearful pain, but never did a single complaint escape from him. He had disciplined himself to travel his lonely way without sympathy, and even approaching death could not move him from his long acquired habit.

A few minutes before twelve o'clock he seemed relieved. The pain which had distorted his face apparently ceased and his countenance relaxed. Thad, Jr., sat fanning him upon the bed. The two negro Nuns kneeling beside him continued to read the prayers for a departing soul. Mrs. Smith, discreet and efficient, watched quietly, ready to answer the minutest desire of her dying master. Sister Loretta had asked permission to perform the Catholic Baptismal rite, and interpreting his silence for permission, she proceeded to perform the ceremony.[52]

As the distanced mellowed chimes of the great bells in St. Aloysius Church sounding midnight, registered musically upon the tired ears of the Old Commoner, death took its long evasive prey.

With an insinuation of a smile on his worn face, he had met the inexorable Summoner serenely. He died just as bravely as he had lived. Rest and peace and quiet were unknown to him in life, and even his last long illness had brought no surcease from his labors.

Although he passed in the dead of the night, the word spread rapidly about the Capitol, and the tele-

graphic wires soon carried the message to the further-
most parts of the country. Gone was the familiar figure of the hobbling and marble-faced Commoner from
his haunts about Washington. Silenced forever was
the unmusical voice of him who untiringly pled the
cause of the exploited.

The man in the White House, just retrieving himself from the ordeal of impeachment, sighed in relief.
He showed no magnaminity by the silence that he invoked. Thaddeus Stevens had been the Congressional
leader for years, and behind him was enlisted a majority following in the Nation. But that seemed of little
account to the President. He issued no word of notice
of the passing, nor did he proclaim any sign of national
mourning. Charles Lamb had said, "it is a trait of
human nature for which I love it, that man wars not
with the dead, for the dead are no man's enemies."
But if the man in the White House subscribed to that
sentiment, he gave no acknowledgment.

The body was embalmed by Surgeon E. F. Schof-
hirt, of the Medical Museum, and placed in a rosewood
coffin, adorned with silver handles and mounting, and
lined with white satin. Upon it was a silver plate,
bearing the simple inscription,
"THADDEUS STEVENS
Born 4th of April, 1792
Died 11th of August, 1868."
Negro Zouaves who immediately mounted a guard
of honor, had difficulty in handling the crowds that
flocked to view the remains. Next day, the body was
moved to the Capitol, where it lay in state in the rotunda, on the same catafalque that had supported the

casket of the martyred Lincoln. Thousands passed it in the quiet gloom of the late afternoon, and many of the vast banks of white flowers that were heaped high around the casket, had been placed there by black hands.

Two days later, Saturday, the body was placed in a special train for its last journey to Lancaster. Everywhere along the route, flags were at half mast and at every stopping point, throngs by the thousand turned out to pay their respects to the clubfooted Old Commoner.

Arriving in Lancaster late on Saturday night, the funeral train nevertheless was greeted by a large part of the population. Next day the body lay in the little shuttered front room parlor of the Stevens home on South Queen Street. In the sultry quiet of that August day, a deep gloom hung impressively over the city. The dead man's face was turning black, and the burial time came none too soon.

Special trains poured their multitudes into Lancaster. By two o'clock twenty thousand people had arrived for the funeral. Eight Protestant Divines officiated and whether deliberately or not the service in the home was mainly ceremonial, with but little eulogy. One pastor said, "during his long public life, exposed to every kind and degree of temptation, he never once swerved from the path of rectitude." Only a small fraction of the mourners could get in or even near the house, but they waited with respectful patience for a fleeting glimpse of the rosewood coffin.

As the stately procession moved in solemn dignity from the residence toward Center Square, up East King Street to Lime, out Lime to Chestnut and then down

Chestnut to the cemetery, it was noticed that every available foot of standing space was occupied and in some sections, the crowds stood five and six deep.

To all of them, the dead man had been merely rough "Old Thad." They had been accustomed to make no fuss of him, to address him familiarly, and treat him as just an ordinary citizen, away for a time in Congress. Of course, when they wanted something that he could get for them, they never hesitated to make their wishes known, for he seemed always not only ready, but anxious to do a favor and was easily imposed upon. While down through the years they had grown to think of him as not much more than a local politician, he was suddenly returned to them, dead, and to their surprise, mourned by the Nation as one of its great.

As a whole, they had never felt an affection for the old fellow, but there was something that not one of them could refrain from admiring in his rugged honesty, and his plain outspokenness. Surely they had heard of his many charities, but a man in public office who asked for the vote of the people every two years was expected to be liberal.

The great funeral procession included contingents from highest Commonwealth officials to colored delegations from the South. An ex-President of the United States had traveled that way two years before, but never had Lancaster shown sadness as profoundly as did those twenty thousand who cloaked the funeral movement.

At the grave, Reverend E. H. Gray, Chaplain of the Senate of the United States, delivered a brief eulogy, and prayed "God to give Vermont another son;

THADDEUS STEVENS

Lancaster another citizen; Pennsylvania, another statesman; the country, another patriot; the poor, another
friend; the freedmen, another advocate; the race, another benefactor; and the world, another man like
Thaddeus Stevens." There, as the shadows of a late
summer afternoon fell across the grave, tender hands
lowered the fast decomposing body of the Old Commoner.

At least half of those attending the ceremony were
negroes. The black people of America already realized
how largely responsible the Old Commoner had been
for bringing the country to act in their behalf. The
liberation which raised them from chattels to human beings, and the ingenious way in which it had been
accomplished, was in large measure attributable to the
dead man. Many of them had come under hardship
of long travel to mourn the loss of the man who had
done more for them than any other man in all the history of their race.[53]

But they could not lay exclusive claim to the old
man's life. The negro, because of black slavery here
existing at the time, benefited most from the Commoner's work, but he would include with the blackman,
the yellow serf, the white serf, and every other individual or group of downtrodden or exploited, whom-
soever they might be and wheresoever they might live.
Stevens did not confine his effort to a race; the field in
which he worked knew no boundary of race or geog-
raphy.

He believed in humanity and was willing to trust
the people with their own Government. Education was
the key. The heart and conscience of the masses when

they could comprehend the situation, would yield a fairer and more beneficial solution of the problems of Government than could otherwise be obtained. He had an abiding faith in the rightness of majority opinion. When he drew his Reconstruction Bill late in 1867, the first draft required more than half of all registered votes for passage. That was the way he would have it. The law would be the expression of the greater part of those on whom it acted. That was good theory, but difficult of application. His colleagues had to exert a great deal of effort to have him amend the measure so as to permit a majority only of votes cast to dictate the laws.[54]

At the time of Stevens' death, the policy of military reconstruction of the conquered states had been definitely decided upon and partially fulfilled. While he was alive, no one doubted but that it would be carried through to completion. But with the stimulus of the Old Commoner gone, some modifications might be effected. It was only natural, therefore, that his passing "furnished a topic for more general discussion than any other before the American public." [55]

Republican newspapers throughout the North in their partisan bias praised him unstintingly as one of the great of all time. Southern newspapers on the whole, although they showed no regret at his death, were loathe to express their relief at his passing.

The Richmond, Virginia, *Examiner* (Bloodhound of the Southern Press) gave a typical expression of the opinion in the South:

"The bitter animosity displayed by Mr. Stevens toward the people of the South has rendered it impossible that any of them should sincerely mourn his death, and they will not pretend to do it. Yet we cannot withhold from him a tribute to his honesty, which placed him far above the mean acts of the mere politician and made him boldly avow the wickedness of his purpose. He had the sense to perceive the end at which Radicalism was aiming, and the courage to avow it."

The Petersburg *Index* said mildly:

"The man must have had some good traits . . . He was by no means the worst man in the House."

The Richmond, Virginia, *Whig* saw him as:

"The very incarnation of sectional prejudice," and "although in him the North may have lost a friend and the negro an advocate, the South will feel that she had lost a bitter and implacable enemy. But he was an outspoken enemy, without Sumner's cant and cowardice, and without Butler's roguery and unspeakable nastiness.

"However varied may be the feeling inspired by his death in the two sections of the country and among the members of the two political parties, all will feel that a man, and a strong man, has gone from the earth, and that his departure is an event in the history of the Country."

The Richmond *Dispatch* regarded him as the:

"leader of the radicals and the best of them all. He was imbued with a very great virtue of sincerity which few of them had at all, and he was honest. He fought boldly and never resorted to hypocrisy."

Some, however, could not restrain themselves. The New Orleans *Bee* referred to him as "this malignant

Frank Leslie's Illustrated News, September 5, 1868.

Last Rites for the Old Commoner in the Little Lancaster Cemetery where Charter Rules Knew no Restrictions

old man." It gave him credit for no good qualities except candor, saying "our sphere is rid of a pest and a marplot," and felt certain that he was "now in the company of Lazarus." [56]

The *Planters Banner,* still seething in its hatred, said, "the prayers of the righteous have at last removed the Congressional curse. Brownlow, Butler, and all such political monsters," it hoped, would "soon follow the example of their illustrious predecessor. May his new works wean him from earth, and the fires of his new furnace never go out. The devil will get on a big bender now. With Thad Stevens in his Cabinet and Ben Butler in Washington, he can manage things in both kingdoms to his liking. Lucky devil!" [57]

The Amite City, Louisiana, *Times,* was just as bitter: "Thaddeus Stevens presented Articles of Impeachment to his Satanic Majesty. Hell is to be reconstructed. There will be five military districts. Griffin commands number one. Sheridan, Meade, Syckles and Mower are assigned command of the others, with leave of absence until the seventh of November. They will then report in person. At the same time, Grant will take command-in-chief with Stanton in the war office. Logan, Butler and Brownlow will be assigned to important duties. Tramp, tramp, tramp, the boys are marching! Cheer up, Thaddeus, they will come!" [58]

Harper's Weekly of August 29, reviewed newspaper and magazine comments, finding:

"great unanimity in the expression of the public judgment on the character of Thaddeus Stevens. Even the Democratic journals recognized his sincerity and independence, while the Republicans, praising his love of liberty, concede his lack of many essential qualities of a true statesman and leader of men."

Foreign papers made more than a casual note of his passing. In London, "Stevens' death created a most profound sensation, and all the morning journals have elaborate obituary notices." [59]

The *Times* gave an extended discussion of his connection with impeachment, and his views on the payment of the five-twenty bonds.

"His impeachment policy was of incalculable injury to his political party, and the financial dishonesty which he encouraged dies with him. He was a fanatical, bitter, and selfwilled man, but not mean or deceitful. He is the last of the leading Americans who had the courage to rise above political partisanship."

To the London *Morning Telegraph,* he was,

"neither good, wise nor generous. But in his time, he did signal service, and with all his faults, merits the famous phrase, 'that was a man.'"

There was no one to take the place the Old Commoner left vacant in Congress. For the greater part of a decade it, and especially the Lower House had been accustomed to act under the smart of his sharp words, and the force of his iron hand. No contender for his power had risen to challenge him. There was therefore no one prepared to take up his dictatorship. [60]

When he died, seven states had been readmitted to the Union; six of them while he was confined in his last illness. Military reconstruction continued on hap-

hazardly. Much of what was contemplated in the enactments was shamefully abused. But grass was growing on the grave of the Lancastrian before the Carpet-
Bag movement really started.

An impression has gained wide currency that Stevens,
in some way, was responsible for the wrongs attributed
to that group. Even if they were creatures of legislation passed during his life, no one can deny that they
were the products of its misapplication. Stevens never
would have tolerated the wild debaucheries of State
Governments that were perpetrated upon the areas in
the process of reconstruction. The outstanding life
record of his integrity is conclusive assurance that he
would have crushed them at the very outset of their
malpractices. With no responsible Congressional
leadership, the brigands were permitted to go their way
unchallenged. The man who would have assured the
South justice, even though a stern one, was gone and
no one in Congress was strong enough to deal effectively
with the turmoil.

Had Stevens lived but two years longer, undoubtedly
there would have been no reign of the Carpet-Baggers.

II

EQUALITARIAN

The aged Commoner was laid away in a secluded little cemetery in the quaint old town of Lancaster. Lancaster that he had early dreamed of as the real starting place of his life; Lancaster whose stolid aloofness and smug complacency had awed and frightened him to another and smaller town; Lancaster, which while his body lay in state as her first citizen, honored him with one of the most fulsome tributes a city ever paid to its heroic dead.

He had drawn his comprehensive Will just a year before he died, and added a codicil some four months later, but neither made mention of his burial. For many years he had owned a plot in the city in a quite pretentious cemetery. But shortly before death, he suddenly discovered that persons of color were not permitted burial there. He immediately disposed of his lot and purchased one in Schreiner's Cemetery, where he now lies beside his nephew, Major Thaddeus Stevens, the only one of his kin buried in Pennsylvania. There, the gates were open unrestrictedly to all.

No imposing shaft of marble marks the spot, but an unobtrusive monument raised there in the shadow of a willow tree shows through the iron fencework to the passerby on the quiet street. The inscription on the stone was penned by the Old Commoner himself shortly before he died.

"I repose in this quiet and secluded spot,
Not from any natural preference for solitude,
But finding other cemeteries

Limited by charter rules as to race,
I have chosen this that I might illustrate in
death
The principles which I advocated through a long
life,
Equality of man before his Creator."

In his public speeches, especially those in Congress, he had occasionally mentioned something concerning an epitaph. In answer to Pendleton's attack upon the proposed Thirteenth Amendment, in January of 1865, Stevens had said, "he may have his epitaph written, if it be truly written, 'here rests the ablest and most pertinacious defender of slavery and opponent of liberty'; but I will be satisfied if my epitaph shall be written thus, 'here lies one who never rose to any eminence; and who only courted the low ambition to have it said that he had striven to ameliorate the condition of the poor, the lowly, the downtrodden of every race and language and color.' " [1]

Later, he indicated that his mind was made up that if he had an epitaph at all, it would be written by another. "I ask none," said he, "and I shall have none. But I shall go with the pure consciousness of having tried to serve the whole human race and never having injured a human being." [2] Had that been carved on his monument, it would have fitted admirably.

He seemed, however, to have been upset by his discovery that only white persons could be interred in the cemetery where he contemplated burial, and reversing himself, he composed the above inscription. That it was done hurriedly or while his faculties were waning, is apparent from the writing itself. It stands in pitiable contrast to the clear-cut utterances of his prime.

The second verse is a weak attempt at humor, and the last, which he no doubt intended to be the important one, is a complete failure. What he advocated through life was not equality of man before his Creator, but equality of man before his fellowmen and the law. The fact is, the Commoner with civilized people in general, was satisfied that all men were equal before their Creator. He was a practical man and realized the utter futility of argument in that direction. His life work was to convince men that it was only fair and just to legislate civil equality on earth. More than once, he had said, "such is the law of God and should be the law of man." He expressed himself clearly in his speech supporting a reconstruction bill in January, 1867. "Every man," said he, "no matter what his race or color; every earthly being who has an immortal soul, has an equal right to justice, honesty, and fair play, with every other man and the law should secure him those rights." [3]

So the principles which he advocated through a long life were not appeals to the Supreme Being for equality of men before Him, but appeals to his fellow beings to establish earthly equality among themselves.

Stevens was the staunch supporter of the Declaration of Independence, and he believed the real object of the founders of the Republic was there accurately expressed. Early in life he concluded that the Constitution was the product of a compromise with slavery and as such, a distortion of the true purpose of American Government.

As early as 1838, he wrote, "the slaveholder claims

his prey by virtue of the Constitution, which contradicts the vital principles of the Declaration of Independence." [4] That conviction remained with him and was reasserted among the last of his public utterances. [5] He had studied, digested and understood what was said in the discussions and debates at the time the Nation was conceived, and no one of those who helped write the original document, believed more strongly than he what they had written. His life's work was to bring the Constitution and the laws up to the propositions set forth in the Declaration of Independence. Practical minded, he was willing to advance a step at a time. With an intellectual equipment that knew no superior, living at a time when War had produced a condition in which these changes could be lawfully effected, he was the ideal man to assume leadership.

Today amendments to the Constitution are thought of as normal modifications necessarily coupled with the advances and evolvements of Government. But in 1860, there was an entirely different attitude. For more than a half century the Constitution had not been tampered with, and propositions so to do were viewed with suspicion and sometimes alarm. The instrument seemed to have gained some kind of sanctity of parchment which made it nearly inviolate.

To bring the people to the idea of fundamental change of it was no inconsiderable task. Of course, the Commoner worked with and among the ablest abolitionist agitators. The great names that were coupled with that movement were his collaborators. Henry Winter Davis, Lovejoy, Wilson, and a host of others toiled incessantly to bring an end to American slavery.

In the Senate were several men who gave valiant support to the cause. Outstanding among these, of course, was Charles Sumner, but he, polished orator and ardent worker, was a theorist who lived apart from the world of actualities. Striking evidence of this is the manner in which he at first caused the defeat of the proposed Fourteenth Amendment in the Upper Body. His purpose, undoubtedly, was worthy, but he showed himself the dreamer and not nearly as able as was Stevens to deal with practicalities. Stevens and he probably aimed at the same goal. But the Senator would insist on a theory even if it meant defeat of his object, while Stevens, in workmanlike and masterful fashion would adjust theory to practice and achieve his end.

In him, there was that rare combination capable of conceiving the theory and then successfully applying and executing it. In his fertile and resourceful brain, the whole theory of the reconstruction was born; there originated the substance of the Fourteenth Amendment. He showed Lincoln the way to emancipation and invented the device of the Committee of Fifteen, which gained for him and his group dictatorial control of the method of reconstruction, relegating the opposition to utter subserviency.

All of these ideas developed while the old man, sick of body and weary of soul, sat alone and pondered in the summer shade of the little lawn in the rear of his Lancaster home. When the gavels fell assembling the different sessions of Congress, he metamorphosed from creator of ideas to lawmaker. Skillful expert in the handling of things as they were, he was the "greatest

Parliamentarian to whom the Congress ever bowed its knee." His most intensive and important work was done when he was well past seventy years of age; his body racked with pain and disease, and so weak that for months at a time, he had to be carried to and from the House. Fainting frequently in the Library and in the House, he sometimes lay prostrate for a whole day.[6] The almost unbelievable manner in which he repeatedly spurred his worn-out body to matchless action and his driving power in developing theories into realities, stand as monuments to his indomitable will.

Throughout life, he was the Equalitarian. From the very earliest record we have of him down to the date of his death, he was always the ardent proponent of the public school system as a great leveler. Mass education was to him the most efficient defense the people could raise against their own exploitation. Intense and sometimes vehement Anti-Mason, his feeling was but an outcropping of his innate hatred of every scheme that would permit preference or create inequality among men. He fought all secret societies, and centered his battle on Free Masonry only because it was the outstanding and by far the most powerful one of his day. Its name would not have mattered. He was opposed to all such organizations.

It was not a far cry from Anti-Masonry to Anti-slavery. The movements were similar in that they both were steps toward Democracy. They differed in that the former was an attempt to degrade an alleged aristocracy, the latter an effort to elevate a race. The ends were to put both groups on a level with ordinary citizens. The former gave Stevens his opportunity to

enter public life, and its early decadence forced his
political retirement. The latter made him a national
leader, wielding the mightiest power a legislator ever
commanded in the history of this Republic.

Advocate of honest financial measures, he labored
to have assessed against the poorer classes, only their
fair part of the money burden of the War. The rich
who, when drafted, could pay for a substitute, were not
reluctant to attempt to shift from themselves as much
of the resulting taxes as possible. Stevens, always on
guard to protect the mute masses, did valiant service
in shielding them from debts which the wealthy should
help pay.

Early in life his fearless championship of the masses
and the exploited, gained for him the name of Commoner. Monuments in our history on which his
name is blazoned in large letters in justification of that
title are the Public School System of his adopted state
of Pennsylvania, the Anti-Masonic Party, financial
measures of the War of the Rebellion, the Emancipation movement, the Thirteenth, Fourteenth and Fifteenth Amendments, and the foundations of early reconstruction.

Ardent Republican that he was, he was never the
blind and hidebound disciple of any political party.
True it is that under his severe discipline, the Republican Party rose to political power and by the vigor he
and his colleagues instilled, continued in control with
but two temporary interruptions for more than six decades. But he was Republican only because by necessity
he was forced to some party affiliation. He championed
that group because it furnished the channel most nearly

accommodating the expression of his policies. On the whole, he refused to be limited by any party platform, and it was only to be expected that he never had any large part in shaping one.

On the public debt question, he was a Democrat; on the tariff, a Whig Protectionist; on slavery, an Abolitionist; in name and affiliation only, a Republican. He was bigger than party. The deep and wide sweeping surges of his character demanded a platform as comprehensive as humanity itself.

His total indifference to fame and high office; his ever-apparent determination to speak the truth, no matter how or whom it offended; his lack of tact; his bitter wit; his unpleasing personality and his dogged refusal to answer or explain the accusations and anathemas that were hurled upon him, all combined against his reputation. Through seven decades of history he has been thought of as a ruthless, vindictive, immoral and desolate man, gnarled in mind as well as body.

But, as long as men deem it noble to defend the weak and exploited, to labor to free humanity from prejudices arising from the accident of birth, to give everyone endowed with a human soul a fair and equal chance in life, just so long will they continue to see the figure of a gaunt, bewigged and stern-visaged, clubfooted Commoner toweringly silhouetted against the background of Reconstruction.

THADDEUS STEVENS, EQUALITARIAN.

REFERENCES

Book I—Chapter I—Clubfoot

1. James Truslow Adams, 'The Epic of America,' 275.
2. New York World, August 13, 1868.
3. S. P. Bates, 'Martial Deeds of Pennsylvania,' 981.
4. New England Genealogical Register; Century Dictionary Encyclopedia; F. M. Eastman in 'Bench & Bar of Pennsylvania;' S. P. Bates, 'Martial Deeds of Pennsylvania,' 981.
5. Lloyd Lewis, 'Myths after Lincoln,' 269.
6. J. A. Woodburn, 'Life of Thaddeus Stevens,' 2. McPherson Mss., Vol. 16.
7. Anna Bowman Dodd, 'Talleyrand;' preface and introduction.
8. G. Lacour Gayet, 'Talleyrand,' Paris, 1928; 220.
9. Idem; 232.
10. Bernard De Lacome, 'La Vie Prince de Talleyrand,' Paris, 1910; 59.
11. G. Lacour Gayet, 'Talleyrand,' Paris, 1928; 303.
12. A brother Morrill obtained a fair education for those days and taught school for a number of years; Alanson became a physician and practiced for many years in Indiana.
13. Recollections of an old schoolmate of Stevens, S. P. Bates, 'Martial Deeds of Pennsylvania,' 981.
14. An observant older schoolmate believed the ridicule of his playmates hurt him so deeply that it accounted for his never returning to the house in which he was born. Idem; 981.
15. C. A. Bunker, '100th Anniversary of the Caledonia County Grammar School,' Peacham, Vermont, 1900.
16. McPherson Collection, Item No. 55295.
17. Alexander Harris, 'The Political Conflict in America,' 15.
18. C. A. Bunker, '100th Anniversary of the Caledonia County Grammar School,' Peacham, Vermont, 1900.
19. Idem.
20. Idem.
21. Idem.
22. Idem.
23. Note: In his will, Stevens takes no credit as founder of the Library, but makes only the modest reference quoted.
24. Note: This is their first record of the Dollar system.
25. Thomas Whitson to Stevens, McPherson Collection, Item No. 52688.
26. Barr Spangler to Thaddeus Stevens, McPherson Collection, Item No. 52912.
27. Author's correspondence with the College.
28. Mildred L. Saunders, Archivist, Dartmouth College, letter to the author. In those days, colleges adjourned through the winter months to permit their students to teach in the outlying districts.
29. Lancaster County Historical Society Reports, Vol. X, No. 10, "An Early Letter by Thaddeus Stevens." 398.
30. Alexander Harris, 'The Political Conflict in America,' 15.
31. Forney's Press, August 12, 1868.
32. Lancaster County Historical Society Reports, Vol. X, No. 7, 249, 'Thaddeus Stevens as a Country Lawyer,' by W. U. Hensel.

References

33. Alexander Harris, 'The Political Conflict in America,' 16.
34. History of Cumberland and Adams Counties, published by Warren, Beers & Co., 1886; 75.
35. Star and Banner of Gettysburg, October 2, 1816.
36. See letter of Henry Smyser, Star and Banner, July 30, 1833.
37. Christian Keesy vs. Jacob Koch, 28 November Term, 1816.
38. Donely vs. Galbreath, 35 January Term, 1817.
39. Alexander Harris, 'The Political Conflict in America,' 17.
40. June 18, 1817.
41. See Commonwealth vs. James Hunter, 1 Oct. Term, 1817.
42. Samuel W. McCall, 'Thaddeus Stevens' 26; McPherson Collection, Item No. 55439.
43. Alexander Harris, 'The Political Conflict in America,' 18.
44. McPherson Collection, Item No. 55439.
45. All figures in this connection are from the original records at Gettysburg.
46. It was not unusual there for lawyers to invest in real estate, and the older lawyers were substantial holders of real property.

Book I—Chapter II—Politics

1. S. P. Bates, 'Martial Deeds of Pennsylvania,' 981.
2. See Hunter murder case, previous chapter.
3. Congressional Globe, January 28, 1867.
4. Idem; March 10, 1866.
5. William M. Hall, 'Reminiscences and Sketches,' 11.
6. Idem; 15.
7. Editor Lefever of the Gettysburg Compiler.
8. Letter of Stevens to Governor Wolfe, August 27, 1831, in the Pennsylvania Archives at Harrisburg, with reference to the suit against Lefever.
9. Thaddeus Stevens letter to W. B. Melius, Sept. 4, 1867.
10. Idem; original of which was lately in the hands of Thomas Madigan.
11. Lancaster Examiner and Herald, quoted in Gettysburg Compiler, December 27, 1839.
12. Newspaper reports of early Anti-Masonic Conventions.
13. He was powerless in the Constitutional Convention of 1836; and also in the Anti-Masonic Convention of December 14, 1835.
14. American Historical Association Reports, by Charles McCarthy, 1902; Vol. 1, 24.
15. Pennsylvania House Journal, 1833-4, December 9.
16. American Volunteer, October 14, 1836, cited by Henry R. Mueller, 'The Whig Party in Pennsylvania,' 32, n.
17. Pennsylvania Reporter, January 8, 1836.
18. American Sentinel, May 6, 1836, and Pennsylvania Reporter, May 13, 1836. Also Adams Diary, Vol. 9, 273.
19. A. K. McClure, 'Lincoln and Men of War Times,' 287.
20. American Sentinel, August 31, 1840. Note: Because the paper was circulated in Adams County, Stevens instituted the process there.
21. Letter to John T. Keagy, January 23, 1862. Also William H. Hall, 'Reminiscences and Sketches,' 18.
22. Keystone, February 3, 1841.
23. Idem; January 30, 1841.
24. Idem; February 24, 1841.

References

25. North American, February 19, 1841.
26. A. K. McClure, 'Lincoln and Men of War Times,' 283.
27. Idem.
28. Keystone, February 6, 1841.
29. A. K. McClure, 'Our Presidents and How We Make Them,' 68.
30. American Sentinel, March 1, 1841.
31. Keystone, November 12, 1841.
32. McPherson Collection, Item No. 52530.
33. Idem; No. 52532.
34. Idem; No. 52535.
35. Keystone, November 24, 1841.

Book II—Chapter I—Anti-Masonry

1. Lancaster Anti-Masonic Herald, January 22, 1830.
2. S. U. Mock, 'Morgan Episode,' 18.
3. Idem.
4. See Egle papers, Archives, Pennsylvania State Library.
5. See list and dates in bibliography.
6. He was defeated by more than 1,500 votes.
7. O. J. Harvey, 'History of Lodge 61, F. & A. M.,' 86.
8. Pennsylvania Intelligencer, December 14, 1829.
9. Charles McCarthy, in 'American Historical Association Reports,' 1902; Vol. 1, 432.
10. Pennsylvania Reporter, February 9, 1830.
11. See correspondence in Adams Sentinel of Gettysburg, June 20, 1831.
12. Speech published in full in pamphlet 'Free Masonry Unmasked,' Library of Congress item HS527 S82.
13. Referring, no doubt, to the gossip connecting Stevens with the murder of a pregnant colored woman found dead near Gettysburg. See Stevens' letter to Governor Wolfe, August 27, 1831, in Pennsylvania Archives, at Harrisburg.
14. Referring to 'Old Dobbin'.
15. Referring to Washington's membership in the Masonic Order.
16. Repeated constantly in Gettysburg Star.
17. See original records.
18. See letter to Governor Wolfe, dated August 24, 1831, in which Stevens told the Governor he believed the Prosecuting Attorney to be one of the authors of this libel. Archives, Pennsylvania Library.
19. See William M. Hall, 'Reminiscences and Sketches,' 26.
20. Pennsylvania Reporter, March 2, 1830.
21. Charles McCarthy, in 'American Historical Association Reports,' 1902, Vol. 1, 435.
22. Albany Evening Journal, October 26 and November 11, 1830.
23. Pennsylvania Reporter, October 9, 1830.
24. Idem; December 10, 1830.
25. 1831.
26. Pennsylvania Reporter, October 28, 1831.
27. Idem.
28. Good Samaritan Lodge, F. & A. M., No. 200.
29. Adams Sentinel, May 13, 1833. It was not revived until January 23, 1860.
30. O. J. Harvey, 'History of Lodge No. 61, F. & A. M.,' 100.

References

31. Note: Wolfe received 91,235; Ritner 88,186. Pennsylvania Reporter, October 19, 1832.
32. Pennsylvania Reporter, October 19, 1832.
33. New York Commercial Advertiser, also Pennsylvania Telegraph, November 21, 1832.
34. Pennsylvania House Journal, 1834-5, Vol. 1, 369.
35. Pennsylvania Reporter, February 21, 1834.
36. See supra.
37. Pennsylvania House Journal, February 17, 1834-5, 414.
38. Report of the Stevens Committee, House Journal, 1834-5, Vol. 2, 735.
39. Pennsylvania House Journal, 1834-5, Vol. 2, 454.
40. On March 10, when more petitions to investigate Anti-Masonry were presented, Stevens consistently moved his same resolution which he used for both cases, that is, to refer all the petitions, to investigate both Masonry and Anti-Masonry, to a committee "with power to send for persons and papers." House Journal, 1834-5, Vol. 2, 551.
41. Note: The House, realizing that such authority would open the door to a line of testimony from renouncing Masons and Anti-Masons, which would be made to appear very pertinent and conclusive, voted down the motion 33-54. House Journal, 1834-5, Vol. 2, 552.
42. Wolfe, who had pardoned Lefever.
43. Lefever and others.
44. Stevens' report, House Journal, 1834-5, Vol. 2, 734, et seq.
45. Pennsylvania House Journal, 1834-5, Vol. 2, 856.
46. Idem; 861, et seq.
47. Pennsylvania Reporter, October 28, 1834.
48. By vote of 38 to 58, House Journal, 1834-5, Vol. 1, 45, et seq.
49. Idem; 557, et seq. Also Pennsylvania Telegraph, April 2, 1835.
50. Niles Register, Vol. 48, 198.
51. Pennsylvania Reporter, April 3, 1835, and Niles Register, 20.
52. Pennsylvania Reporter, May 6, 1835, and Niles Register, Vol. 48, 190.
53. Jackson's letter of July 1, 1835, cited by McCarthy, 468.
54. Ritner, 94,023 votes; Wolfe, 65,804; Muhlenberg, 40,586. Pennsylvania Reporter, October 30, 1835.
55. Pennsylvania Reporter, October 30, 1835.
56. Pennsylvania House Journal, 1835-36, Vol. 1, 86, et seq.
57. Idem; 11.
58. Idem; 39.
59. Idem; 112, and American Sentinel, January 21, 1836.
60. Note: The House Journal teems with his name from beginning to end of the session.
61. Pennsylvania House Journal, 1835-6, Vol. 1, 230.
62. Idem; 1835-6, Vol. 2, 245, et seq.
63. Idem; 240.
64. Pennsylvania Reporter, Jan. 22, 1836.
65. Pennsylvania House Journal, 1835-6, Vol. 2, 253.
66. Harrisburg Chronicle, Jan. 18-21, 1836.
67. American Sentinel, January 23, 1836.
68. Niles Register, Vol. 49, 481; Franklin Depository, Jan. 10, 1836.
69. Pennsylvania House Journal, 1835-6, Vol. 2, 319.
70. American Sentinel, February 29, 1836.
71. Harrisburg Chronicle, March 10, 1836.
72. Pennsylvania House Journal, Mar. 5, 1836,

References

73. Speech delivered at Lancaster, 1836, American Sentinel, Oct. 9, 1838.
74. Anti-Masonry.
75. Gettysburg Sentinel, Sept. 12, 1836.
76. Idem.
77. Governor's Annual Message, House Journal, 1837-8, Vol. 2, 17.
78. McPherson Collection, Item No. 54503.

Book II—Chapter II—Anti-Slavist

1. Habeas Corpus case of James Somerset.
2. American Archives, Fourth Series, 696, 735 and 1136.
3. Note: The indictment was stricken out before the draft was submitted to the Congress.
4. H. A. Herbert, 'Abolition Crusade and its Consequences,' 52, and Sharpless, 'History of Pennsylvania,' 312.
5. Note: In 1790, in the eight Southern States, there were 657,527 slaves, which number, by 1810, in the then eleven Southern States, had increased to 1,163,854. Larned's History, Volume 5.
6. Ames State Documents, on Federal Relations, 203.
7. Gettysburg Star and Banner, July 27, 1835.
8. Memorial Addresses on the Life and Character of Thaddeus Stevens, delivered in the House of Representatives, Wash., D. C., Dec. 17, 1864. Remarks by Mr. Orth, 53.
9. William M. Hall, 'Reminiscences and Sketches,' 22.
10. Same as 8 supra, 54.
11. People's Press, September 18, 1835; and also Star, October 19, 1835.
12. Idem.
13. Pennsylvania House Journal, 1835-36, Vol. 1, Index, 99.
14. Idem; 1835-36, Vol. 2, 804, et seq.
15. The vote was forty-two to thirty-seven. House Journal, 1835-36, Vol. 1, 1353.
16. Gettysburg Star, June 27, 1836; National Gazette, June 1 and 15, 1836.
17. Christian Cynosure, April 5, 1883.
18. Some as 8 supra, 52.
19. Gettysburg Star, March 20, 1837.
20. Same as 8 supra, 23. In Blanchard's report of the matter, he says the mob would have injured him had not someone intervened.
21. Christian Cynosure, April 5, 1883.
22. Idem. Note: In describing Stevens' speech, Blanchard said that "giving his words as a report of it, without his overwhelming, crushing looks and intonations, seems like pointing to a slivered tree as a description of a thunderstorm."
23. Gettysburg Star, quoted in Keystone, March 15, 1835.
24. See Blanchard's Great Commoner. Christian Cynosure, April 5, 1883. Note: Democratic newspapers reported the matter less favorably to Stevens. Keystone, May 3, 1837, American Sentinel, May 4, 1837.

Book II—Chapter III—Constitutional Convention

1. Henry R. Mueller, 'The Whig Party in Pennsylvania,' 33.
2. Idem; 34.
3. On July 21, 1837.

REFERENCES

4. Note: The Democratic Keystone of May 3, 1837, accused the Whigs and Anti-Masons of calling a caucus beforehand for the purpose of organizing the Convention.
5. National Gazette, May 18, 1837. Also Proceedings and Debates of the Convention of the Commonwealth of Pennsylvania to propose Amendments to the Constitution commenced and held at Harrisburg on the second day of May, 1837, Vol. 1, 41.
6. Keystone, May 3, 1837.
7. Star, May 1, 1837.
8. Stevens was reputed to be a champion of banks, but see his proposal for absolute prohibition of State Banks in Pennsylvania. Because his whole interest centered on a Federal institution, and he supported the United States Bank of Pennsylvania only as second choice, the matter is treated in the Chapter on the ''United States Bank and 'Tapeworm'.''
9. See William Meredith Speech.
10. Note: Early that year he had introduced a resolution in the State Legislature "that Congress does possess the Constitutional power and it is expedient to abolish slavery and the slave trade within the District of Columbia." Harrisburg Chronicle, June 2, 1836.
11. Proceedings and Debates of the Convention, etc., Vol. 2, 37, et seq.
12. Idem; Vol. 2, 40.
13. Idem; Vol. 2, 98.
14. Idem; Vol. 2, 387-8, and 65.
15. Keystone, June 7, 1837.
16. Note: Not all of this speech is in the official reports.
17. Proceedings and Debates of the Convention, etc., Vol. 2, 110.
18. Idem; Vol. 3, 611.
19. Idem; Vol. 2, 400.
20. Idem. The vote was 61-59.
21. National Gazette, June 17, 1837, Vol. 2, 401.
22. Proceedings and Debates of the Convention, etc., Vol. 2, 397.
23. Idem; Vol. 2, 40.
24. Idem; Vol. 2, 384.
25. Idem; Vol. 2, 252 and 389.
26. Idem; Vol. 1, 117; Vol. 2, 32; and 295; Vol. 3, 518, et seq.
27. Idem; Vol. 2, 219.
28. Idem.
29. Idem; Vol. 5, 317.
30. Idem; Vol. 6, 5.
31. Idem; Vol. 3, 581.
32. Idem; Vol. 3, 519.
33. Note: The Democratic Newspapers called attention to the omission and one referred to it as "Stevens' Hypocrisy." Keystone, July 19, 1837.
34. Proceedings and Debates of the Convention, etc., Vol. 3, 666.
35. Idem; Vol. 2, 200-202.
36. Idem; Vol. 3, 369.
37. Idem; Vol. 4, 127.
38. Idem; Vol. 3, 685-686.
39. Journal of the Committee of the Whole, 85.
40. Proceedings and Debates of the Convention, etc., Vol. 10, 106.
41. Idem; Vol. 9, 218.
42. Idem; Vol. 13, 256, et seq.
43. Keystone, August 15, 1838, quoting Bedford Gazette.

References

Book II—Chapter IV—Buckshot War

1. Note: United States Senators were then elected by the Legislature.
2. Keystone, June 20, 1837; Pennsylvania Reporter, September 7, 1838, and issues of both papers between those dates.
3. Also American Sentinel, June 5 and June 12, 1838.
4. Pennsylvania Reporter, September 28, 1838. Also Keystone, September 19, 1838, and Gettysburg Compiler, September 18, 1838.
5. Pennsylvania Reporter, November 16, 1838.
6. Gettysburg Star, American Daily Advertiser, Pennsylvania Telegraph and Pennsylvania Intelligencer for the period July to October, 1838.
7. Pennsylvania Telegraph, August 15, 1838.
8. Idem.
9. Pennsylvania Telegraph, October 1, 1838.
10. Idem; September 10, 1838.
11. Keystone, November 7, 1838.
12. The York Republican says: "The most stupendous system of betting on elections was practiced during the late contest in Pennsylvania that was ever known." Also Pennsylvania Telegraph, October 24, 1838.
13. Pennsylvania Telegraph, September 26, 1838.
14. Pennsylvania Reporter, September 26, 1838.
15. Keystone, September 26, 1838.
16. Pennsylvania Telegraph, September 26, 1838.
17. See Testimony, Pennsylvania Senate Journal, 1838-9. Note: If the amendments had been accepted, the Governor should not have been inducted into office until January.
18. Pennsylvania Senate Journal, 1838-9, Vol. 2, 832.
19. Testimony before the House Investigating Committee, printed in Pennsylvania House Journal.
20. See Report of Senate Committee on Disturbances at the seat of Government, Pennsylvania Senate Journal. Also read in House of Representatives, June 24, 1839.
21. When criticized for not incorporating the full returns in their report, they answered that they had been refused permission to see the record returns of the majority of the Board.
22. In some places referred to as "Ritner Central State Committee."
23. See Burrowes' full letter, in Pennsylvania Senate Journal, 1838-9, 975.
24. They were, of course, acting with the Anti-Masons.
25. See Harrisburg Chronicle, October 31, 1838. Also Testimony taken by Senate. See Senate Journal.
26. Pennsylvania Reporter, November 3, 1838.
27. Letter of Representative R. P. Flenniken, Democratic (VanBuren) representative from Fayette County, Senate Journal, 972, et seq. This, with his other correspondence written at the scene of the disturbance, is of importance and may be taken as a fair presentation of the facts, because he later served on the House Committee to investigate the trouble and assisted the Democrats in endeavoring to maintain their position that the turmoil, if any, was of mild nature and without serious threat. All of Flenniken's letter appears in the Senate testimony.
28. See testimony of John Ash, before Senate Committee. Pennsylvania Senate Journal, 993.

References

29. For example, there were groups from Luzerne County. See testimony in Pennsylvania Senate Journal.
30. Stevens' testimony before the Senate Committee.
31. Stevens' letter in Pennsylvania Telegraph, January 17, 1839.
32. Note: J. J. M'Cahen who although not a member of either House, acted as general for the Democratic forces, was accused of having brought "one hundred Philadelphia toughs to Harrisburg." And an equal number were there from Lancaster and "not less than five hundred" more were on the way. See Senate Testimony. Also Flenniken's letter, December 3.
33. See testimony in Pennsylvania House Journal and 'Political Conflict in America,' by A. H. Harris, 47.
34. Stevens' letter, Pennsylvania Telegraph, January 17, 1839.
35. See Senate testimony.
36. See Senate testimony. Also Stevens' letter, Pennsylvania Telegraph, January 17, 1839.
37. Stevens' speech, Pennsylvania Telegraph, January 17, 1839.
38. Testimony, Senate Journal. Note: The time was set, Stevens said, so as not to conflict with the meeting of the Hopkins House.
39. Testimony of Stevens before the Senate Investigating Committee.
40. Penrose's version of the affair. See Library of Congress pamphlet F 153, 39.
41. See testimony, Senate Journal, 824, 875, 894, and 993.
42. Idem.
43. See Senate Journal, testimony, 876.
44. Majority Senate Report, 12.
45. Note: This probably refers to the delay of the assassins, when their curiosity led them to watch the "fracas" referred to in the Senate Journal testimony, 876.
46. McPherson Collection Item No. 55309.
47. Majority Senate Report, 14.
48. Idem.
49. See testimony, Senate Journal.
50. Official document, Archives of Pennsylvania.
51. Senate Journal, 973.
52. His official correspondence, see Senate Journal, 158, et seq.
53. For complete official correspondence between the Governor and Major General Patterson, see House Journal 1838-9, Vol. 2, Pt. 2, 245, et seq.
54. See testimony, Senate Journal.
55. See official correspondence.
56. Gettysburg Star, January 1, 1839. Also House Journal, 1838-9, Vol. 2, 294.
57. Stevens' letter to his constituents of May 3. Also his letter of December 6 published in Pennsylvania Telegraph, December 11, 1838.
58. Adams Sentinel, January 7, 1839.
59. Letter of Stevens dated May 3, Gettysburg Star, May 7, 1839.
60. Star, May 13, 1839. The membership of this committee was changed slightly by resignation, but the majority at all times consisted of Stevens' political opponents.
61. See House Journal, 987, et seq.
62. Gettysburg Compiler, May 7, 1839.
63. Stevens' letters, May 13, 1839. Gettysburg Star, May 28, 1839.

REFERENCES

64. House Journal, Vol. 1, 992.
65. Note: A minority report of the committee was "not received" by the House and referred back because it "reflected upon the majority of the committee." House Journal, 1838-9, Vol. 1, 1028.
66. Gettysburg Star, May 28, 1839.
67. McPherson Collection, Item No. 52502.
68. Keystone, April 24, 1839.
69. Idem; November 27, 1839.
70. Idem.
71. Idem; December 10, 1838; and Pennsylvania Reporter, December 14, 1838.

Book II—Chapter V—Educator

1. James Pyle Wickersham, 'History of Education in Pennsylvania,' 256.
2. Benjamin Franklin's, in 1743; Dr. Rush's, in 1786, and others.
3. Gettysburg Sentinel, March 23, 1825.
4. Idem; March 2, 1825.
5. Idem; March 23, 1825.
6. Gettysburg Compiler, July 29, 1826.
7. Sentinel, December 31, 1828.
8. Gettysburg Star, January 21, 1834.
9. Sentinel, December 31, 1828.
10. Idem; January 28, 1829.
11. Idem; February 10, 1830.
12. Idem; September 21, 1835.
13. Pennsylvania House Journal, January 21, 1834.
14. Sentinel, February 10, 1834.
15. Note: Stevens estimated that more than fifty thousand persons had signed these repeal petitions and accounted for the difference by explaining that some of them did not reach the Committee. See S. P. Bates, 'Martial Deeds of Pennsylvania,' 982.
16. S. P. Bates, 'Martial Deeds of Pennsylvania,' 983.
17. A. H. Hood, 'Biographical History of Lancaster County,' 578; and Pennsylvania Reporter, April 15, 1835.
18. Pennsylvania Senate Journal, April 10, 1835.
19. Pennsylvania Reporter, April 15, 1835.
20. Alexander Harris, 'Political Conflict in America,' 27.
21. Idem; 28.
22. Idem.
23. B. A. Hinsdale, 'James Abraham Garfield,' Vol. 1, 134.
24. McPherson collection, Item No. 54471.
25. Note: Stevens said his colleague, McSherry, told him on his return from Philadelphia, that three-fourths of their constituents had petitioned for repeal. S. P. Bates, 'Martial Deeds of Pennsylvania,' 982.
26. Report of the Secretary of State who was also Superintendent of Schools. February Files, 1837.
27. Proceedings and Debates of the Constitutional Convention, etc., Vol. 5, 288, 334, and 347.
28. Idem; 300.
29. Idem; 383.
30. See Stevens' letter as President of the Board of Canal Commissioners, addressed to all contractors, Sentinel, (Gettysburg), September 3, 1838.

References

31. McPherson manuscript, undated item.
32. Memorial Addresses on the Life and Character of Thaddeus Stevens, delivered in the House of Representatives, Washington, D. C., December 17, 1868. Remarks of Representative Orth, 50.

Book II—Chapter VI—U. S. Bank and "The Tapeworm"

1. Reginald C. McGrane, 'Correspondence of Nicholas Biddle,' 245.
2. Henry R. Mueller, 'The Whig Party in Pennsylvania,' 23.
3. National Gazette, October 20-21, 1835.
4. See draft of Biddle's letter to Committee, Reginald C. McGrane, 'Correspondence of Nicholas Biddle,' 246, and Pennsylvania House Journal, 1836-7, Vol. 2, 745-757.
5. Pennsylvania House Journal, 1835-6, Vol. 1, 279.
6. Idem.
7. American Sentinel, February 1, 1836.
8. Reginald C. McGrane, 'Correspondence of Nicholas Biddle,' 258.
9. Pennsylvania House Journal, 1836-7, Vol. 2, 769, et seq.
10. Idem; Vol. 1, 407.
11. American Sentinel, January 30, 1836, and Biddle's papers, Vol. 57, No. 1964.
12. Biddle papers, Vol. 57, No. 11951.
13. American Sentinel, February 8 and 11, 1836.
14. Biddle Papers, Vol. 58, Nos. 12080, and 12156.
15. Bedford Gazette, quoted in Pennsylvania Reporter, February 6, 1836.
16. Henry R. Mueller, 'The Whig Party in Pennsylvania,' 26.
17. American Sentinel, January 30, 1836. The same paper attempts to identify the Representative as one from Allegheny County. See also issue February 15, 1836.
18. Idem; February 2, 1836.
19. Pennsylvania Senate Journal, 1835-6, Vol. 2, 650.
20. Note: The Governor signed it on February 18, 1836, Pennsylvania House Journal, Vol. 1, 556.
21. Henry R. Mueller, 'The Whig Party in Pennsylvania,' 28.
22. National Gazette, February 1, 1836. This is probably the matter referred to in the Senate Investigation Committee's Report.
23. Proceedings and Debates of the Convention of the Commonwealth of Pennsylvania to propose Amendments to the Constitution commenced and held at Harrisburg on the second day of May, 1837, Vol. 1, 543.
24. Idem; Vol. 7, 158.
25. Idem; Vol. 1, 543, et seq.
26. Idem. Vol. 7, 154, et seq.
27. Pennsylvania Reporter, December 29, 1837, and August 17, 1838.
28. Idem; December 29, 1837.
29. Idem.
30. Laws of Pennsylvania 1836-7, 44.
31. Keystone, April 19, 1837, and Compiler, September 4, 1838.
32. Keystone, April 19, 1837.
33. Gettysburg Compiler, September 4, 1838; Pennsylvania Reporter, September 7, 1838; Keystone, September 22, 1841; See vote of Millerstown District, Keystone, April 10, 1839.
34. Keystone, October 12, 1838.
35. Idem.

References

36. Pennsylvania Reporter, September 14, 1838.
37. Pennsylvania House Journal, 1837-8, Vol. 2, 477, et seq.
38. Idem.
39. Keystone, June 20, 1838.
40. American Sentinel, September 10, 1838.
41. Keystone, July 10, 1839.
42. American Sentinel, June 5, 1838.
43. Keystone, September 28, 1842.

Book III—Chapter I—Lancaster

1. Blanchard correspondence. See Christian Cynosure, April 5, 1883.
2. Author's notes of conversation with the late Justice J. Hay Brown.
3. "Liberty Party" was the designation adopted by a group with radical tendencies in the Northwestern part of the United States around the year 1830. The movement spread slowly eastward and into it were merged many Whigs.
4. McPherson Collection, Item No. 52544.
5. Idem; No. 52546.
6. Lancaster Examiner and Democratic Herald, August 10, 1842.
7. Alexander Harris, 'Political Conflict in America,' 86.
8. W. U. Hensel, "Thaddeus Stevens as a Country Lawyer," 'Lancaster County Historical Society Papers,' Vol. X, No. 7, 264 and 282.
9. Alexander Harris, 'Political Conflict in America,' 87.
10. Idem; 93.
11. Idem; 95.
12. Lancaster County Historical Society Reports, Vol. X, No. 7, 278, 'Thaddeus Stevens as a Country Lawyer,' by W. U. Hensel.
13. Lancaster County Court Records.
14. Lancaster Examiner and Herald, Sept. 27, 1848.
15. American Press and Republican, July 1, 1848.
16. American Press and Republican, July 8, 1848.
17. Idem; August 12 and 26, 1848.
18. Idem; August 24, 26, 28, 1848.
19. Idem; August 26, 1848.
20. Lancaster Intelligencer, August 29, 1848.
21. Samuel W. McCall, 'Thaddeus Stevens,' 65.
22. Lancaster Intelligencer, November 14, 1848.

Book III—Chapter II—In and Out of Congress

1. Congressional Globe, December 13, 1849.
2. Idem.
3. When the House organized, there were one hundred five Whigs, one hundred twelve Democrats, and thirteen Free-Soilers.
4. George W. Julian, 'Political Recollections,' 109. Note: His sole appointment of any importance was membership in the Judiciary committee.
5. Congressional Globe, February 20, 1850.
6. Pittsburgh Daily Gazette, February 26, 1850.
7. Congressional Globe, Thirty-first Congress, Appendix, 4450.
8. Congressional Globe, February 12, 1850.
9. Idem; March 5, 1850.

References

10. The Pennsylvanian, Feb. 26, 1850, March 1, 1850.
11. Public Ledger, Feb. 22, 1850.
12. Pittsburgh Daily Gazette, Feb. 26, 1850.
13. National Era, Washington, D. C., March 7, 1850.
14. Congressional Globe, Appendix, 765, et seq.
15. Idem; Appendix, 769.
16. Idem; Appendix 1218.
17. Idem; Appendix, 1401.
18. Idem; Appendix, 1102.
19. McPherson Collection Item No. 52609.
20. Idem.
21. Lancaster Examiner and Herald, June 17, 1850.
22. Lancaster Intelligencer, June 25, 1850.
23. Lancaster Examiner and Herald, August 21, 1850.
24. Idem; October 16, 1850.
25. Congressional Globe, June 11, 1852.
26. Idem; August 12, 1852.
27. See letter of Scott to J. P. Atkinson, Feb., 1843.
28. Congressional Globe, August 12, 1852.

Book III—Chapter III—Back Home

1. Congressional Globe, March 3, 1853.
2. Lancaster County Historical Society Reports, Vol. X, No. 7, 272, 'Thaddeus Stevens as a Country Lawyer,' by W. U. Hensel.
3. Lancaster Examiner and Herald, September 18 and October 1, 1851.
4. Idem; October 8, 1850.
5. Note: W. U. Hensel, who made an extensive study of the case, was unable to give a reason for this, but he believed that it was merely for "prudential reasons."
6. Lancaster County Historical Society Reports, Vol. X, No. 7, 271, 'Thaddeus Stevens as a Country Lawyer,' by W. U. Hensel.
7. Idem; 281.
8. Idem; 266.
9. Dobbins vs. Stevens, 17 Sergeant & Rawle, (Pennsylvania Reports) 13.
10. William M. Hall, 'Reminiscences & Sketches,' 27.
11. Specht vs. Commonwealth, 8 Pennsylvania, 312.
12. Lancaster County Historical Society Reports, Vol. X, No. 7, 276, 'Thaddeus Stevens as a Country Lawyer,' by W. U. Hensel.
13. Idem; 279.
14. Alexander Harris, 'Political Conflict in America,' 164.
15. Library of Congress, Abraham Lincoln Collection.

Book IV—Chapter I—Eve of the Crisis

1. Congressional Globe, December 5, 1859.
2. November 16, 1859.
3. Congressional Globe, December 6, 1859.
4. Idem.
5. On January 31, 1866, Stevens used the words "* * * for men like Barksdale whom I have seen in this Hall draw their bowie knives on the Representatives of the people." See Congressional Globe of that date, also of January 31, 1865 and May 10, 1866.

References

6. L. Q. C. Lamar, Congressional Globe, December 7, 1859.
7. Referring to Stevens' escape from assassins through a washroom window. See Chapter on the "Buckshot War."
8. Lancaster Daily Express, February 20, 1861.
9. Congressional Globe, Jan. 3, 1860.
10. Idem.
11. January 25, 1860.
12. Anti-LeCompton Party.
13. Congressional Globe, January 25, 1860.
14. Told to author by a son of a Representative who heard it; see also George F. Hoar, 'Autobiography' Vol. 1, 268.
15. Congressional Globe, May 7, 1860, 1956, et seq.
16. Congressional Globe, February 25, 1860.
17. Idem; April 19, 1860.

Book IV—Chapter II—Secession

1. James D. Richardson, 'Messages and Papers of the Presidents,' Vol. V; 626, et seq.
2. December 13, 1860. See John W. Burgess, 'Civil War and the Constitution' Vol. 1, 102.
3. Alabama, Arkansas, Florida, Georgia, Louisiana, Mississippi & Texas.
4. New Mexico.
5. Representative Corwin.
6. Note: Lincoln is said to have admitted he acted in the matter without fully understanding the merit of Stevens' position. See text, 578.
7. John Brown.
8. Note: There had been recent efforts to reopen the slave trade.
9. Congressional Globe, Speech of January 29, 1861.
10. John W. Burgess, 'The Civil War and the Constitution,' Vol. 1, 101.
11. Congressional Globe, January 25, 1860, also, January 29, 1861.
12. Stevens' House Speech of January 29, 1861.

Book IV—Chapter IV—Leader

1. Congressional Globe, July 4, 1861.
2. John W. Burgess, 'Civil War and The Constitution,' Vol. 1, 148.
3. Congressional Globe, July 9, 1861.
4. Idem; July 11, 1861.
5. Idem.
6. Idem.
7. Idem; July 29, 1861.
8. Idem; July 17, 1861.
9. Idem; July 19, 1861.
10. Idem; July 22, 1861.

Book IV—Chapter V—Financier

1. Stevens' Speech, Congressional Globe, February 6, 1862.
2. Chase's Report, page 6, R. A. Love, 'Federal Financing,' App. Table No. 4; D. R. Dewey, 'Financial History of the United States,' 272.

REFERENCES

3. 'Bolles' Financial History, 1861-1865,' 103, and Report of the Treasurer, July 4, 1861, Congressional Globe, Thirty-seventh, First Session, Appendix 7.
4. See Chase's resignation from the Senate sent to the Governor of Ohio.
5. Globe, Thirty-seventh Congress, First Vol., App. 2. Note: Chase reduced this about eighty-two and one-half million dollars in his detailed estimates. Treasury Reports, Thirty-seventh Congress, First Session, App. 4.
6. William H. Stewart, 'Reminiscences,' 204; James G. Blaine says Stevens was a natural leader who assumed his place by common consent. 'Twenty Years of Congress', Vol. 1, 235.
7. Congressional Globe, Thirty-seventh Congress, First Vol., Appendix, 7.
8. James G. Blaine, "Twenty Years of Congress,' Vol. 1, 286.
9. R. A. Love, 'Federal Financing,' 76.
10. See Bankers' Magazine, February, 1862, cited by James Albert Woodburn, 'The Life of Thaddeus Stevens,' 246.
11. J. F. Rhodes, 'History of the Civil War,' 145.
12. Note: The December report provided that but ninety million dollars be raised by taxation.
13. Senator William P. Fessenden. See Congressional Globe, February 12, 1862.
14. Wesley C. Mitchell, 'History of Greenbacks,' 46.
15. Morrill of Vermont and Pendell of Ohio.
16. Morrill.
17. Pendell.
18. Congressional Globe, February 6, 1862.
19. February 6, 1862.
20. Congressional Globe, February 6, 1862.
21. Congressional Globe, February 24, 1862.
22. Lancaster Intelligencer, July 28, 1868.
23. Idem: February 20, 1862.
24. All these references are to Stevens' speech of February 24, 1862.
25. Stevens' speech, Congressional Globe, December 19, 1862.
26. Forney's Press, quoted in Lancaster Daily Express, December 11, 1862.
27. Idem.
28. Lancaster Express, December 11, 1862.
29. Note: Stevens' theory here should not be confused with the one sometimes advanced that where capital is invested for a long and indeterminate period, the quality of principal redemption is not as important as the quality of interest payments. That theory can, of course, be applied reasonably where there is little present concern with actual repayment of the principal. Here the principal had to be repaid, and that as soon as possible.
30. Congressional Globe, January 20, 1863.
31. J. Cooke. See Congressional Globe, January 23, 1863.
32. Speech of Representative Stratton and discussion, Congressional Globe, January 23, 1862.
33. Congressional Globe, March 16, 1864.
34. William G. Sumner, 'A History of American Currency,' 208.
35. Daily National Intelligencer of Washington, December 13, 1864, New York Tribune of December 10, 1864.
36. Congressional Globe, January 4, 1865, et seq.
37. William G. Sumner, 'A History of American Currency,' 211.

References

38. See Secretary McCulloch's Report, December 4, 1865.
39. Congressional Globe, March 16, 1866.
40. Idem; December 19, 1862.
41. McCulloch's Report, November 30, 1867.
42. Speeches of February 6 and February 20, 1862.
43. Congressional Globe, July 22, 1868.
44. Washington Daily Intelligencer, July 24, 1868.
45. Congressional Globe, July 17, 1868.
46. New York Tribune, quoted in Washington Daily National Intelligencer, July 24, 1868.
47. Lancaster Intelligencer, July 24, 1868.
48. Idem.
49. Washington Daily National Intelligencer, July 24, 1868.
50. Lancaster Daily Express, July 25, 1868.
51. Lancaster Intelligencer, July 28, 1868.
52. New York World, July 23, 1868.
53. Letter to John Gyger, Lancaster Examiner and Herald, August 5, 1868.
54. E. G. Spalding, 'Financial History of the War.'
55. Otto Gresham, 'The Greenbacks,' 147; see also Sumner's 'A History of American Currency,' 198.
56. Congressional Globe, December 23, 1862.
57. Idem; March 16, 1864.
58. Lancaster Intelligencer, July 28, 1868.
59. See Gyger letter, Lancaster Intelligencer, July 28, 1868.
60. Congressional Globe, February 20, 1862.
61. Idem; March 16, 1864.
62. Letter to Gyger, Lancaster Intelligencer, January 28, 1868.

Book V—Chapter I—The Constitution

1. Congressional Globe, August 2, 1861.
2. Idem; December 9, 1862.

Book V—Chapter II—Emancipation

1. Congressional Globe, January 25, 1860.
2. Speech of August 2. 1861. See Congressional Globe of that date.
3. Idem.
4. Idem.
5. A. K. McClure, 'Lincoln and Men of War Times,' 98.
6. Congressional Globe, December 3, 1861.
7. Congressional Globe, January 22, 1862.
8. Congressional Globe, March 6, 1862.
9. His remark caused great laughter. Congressional Globe, March 11, 1862.
10. Congressional Globe, March 12, 1862.
11. Congressional Globe, April 11 and May 9, 1862.
12. New York Herald Tribune, August 22, 1862.
13. Don C. Seitz, 'Lincoln The Politician,' 333.
14. Idem; 339; Speech to visitors.
15. Idem; 340.
16. Congressional Globe, July 5, 1862.

References

17. Stevens' Lancaster Speech, September 16, 1862. See Boston Liberator, September 19, 1862.
18. Lancaster Speech of September 19, 1862.
19. Lancaster Daily Evening Express, October 2, 1862.
20. Idem.
21. This author is not convinced that international considerations played any substantional part in Lincoln's decision to emanicipate.
22. A. K. McClure, 'Lincoln and Men of War Times,' 98.
23. Lincoln's Emancipation Proclamation freed slaves only beyond the Union lines.
24. Record of a conversation with Governor James A. Bramlette, of Kentucky, Senator James Dixon of Connecticut, and A. G. Hodges, reduced to writing on April 4, 1864. Quoted by Don C. Seitz, 'Lincoln the Politician,' 352 and 353.
25. Idem.
26. Congressional Globe, February 24, 1863.

Book V—Chapter III—Restoration Under Lincoln

1. Virginia was not included because the Pierpont Government there had already been recognized.
2. See Lincoln's letter, November 14, 1864. Works of Lincoln, Vol. 2, 597, cited by J. A. Woodburn, 'Thaddeus Stevens,' 200.
3. Alexander Harris, 'The Political Conflict in America,' 363.
4. Congressional Globe, December 7, 1863.
5. Idem.
6. Idem.
7. Idem; December 14, 1863.
8. Idem.
9. The official record notes "laughter" at the remark.
10. Congressional Globe. December 14, 1863.
11. Idem; May 4, 1864.
12. Idem.
13. See Stevens' letter of July 10, 1864, in McPherson Collection.
14. New York Herald Tribune, August 5, 1864.
15. A. K. McClure, 'Old Times Notes of Pennsylvania,' Vol. 2, 33.

Book V—Chapter IV—Restoration or Reconstruction

1. Congressional Globe, March 19, 1867.
2. James Albert Woodburn, 'The Life of Thaddeus Stevens', 600.
3. Arnold's 'Life of Lincoln' Vol. 4, 462. See also George W. Julian, 'Political Recollections,' 249.
4. George W. Julian, 'Political Recollections,' 249.
5. Idem.
6. George H. Haynes, 'Charles Sumner,' 295.
7. John W. Burgess, 'Reconstruction and the Constitution,' 37.
8. Stevens' letter to Sumner, May 10, 1865, Harvard Library.
9. Idem.
10. Idem; letter dated June 14, 1865.
11. Idem; letter dated August 17, 1865.
12. Idem; letter dated August 26, 1865.
13. Sumner Mss. and correspondence, Harvard Library.
14. George H. Haynes, 'Charles Sumner,' 297.

REFERENCES

15. Letter to Sumner, May 10, 1865, Harvard Library.
16. Johnson Mss., Item Number 8054.
17. James G. Blaine, 'Twenty Years of Congress,' Vol. II, 192.
18. Benjamin B. Kendricks, 'Journal of the Reconstruction Committee', 139.
19. Welles Diary, Vol. 2, 387. Note: Some scholars, for example, Claude Bowers in his 'Tragic Era,' 87, and George Fort Milton, in his 'Age of Hate,' 266, seem puzzled that Raymond who on occasions when he wished had no trouble making himself heard, sat quietly by while Stevens had the caucus approve his resolution. Perhaps the answer to this is that with some powerful argument or other means, Stevens had priorly taken the matter up with Raymond and gained his acquiescence, if not his positive support of the measure. The New York World, before the convening of the Congress of December 4, reported that Raymond had "already joined hands with" Stevens to throttle plans for an immediate restoration of the Union.
20. New York World, December 4, 1865.
21. McPherson Collection, Item No. 53297.
22. McPherson Collection, letter to Stevens of December 6, 1865.
23. New York World, December 4, 1865.
24. National Intelligencer, December 4, 1865.
25. Issue of December 7, 1865.
26. Congressional Globe, December 18, 1865.
27. James G. Blaine, 'Twenty Years of Congress,' Vol. II, 128.
28. Idem; 130.
29. See also draft of this speech in McPherson Collection, Item No. 53656, which is more conciliatory than the speech itself.
30. George Fort Milton, 'The Age of Hate,' 291.
31. Idem.
32. Idem.
33. Edward McPherson, 'History of the Reconstruction,' 63.
34. Idem; 61.
35. Congressional Globe, January 31, 1866.
36. Edward McPherson, 'History of the Reconstruction,' 62.
37. Congressional Globe, January 8, 1866.
38. Idem; March 10, 1866.
39. Edward McPherson, 'History of the Reconstruction,' 84 et seq.
40. Idem; 61, reporting President Johnson's Washington Birthday Speech of 1866.
41. Congressional Globe, Thirty-Ninth Congress, Appendix, 300 et seq.

Book V—Chapter V—The Decision

1. James Ford Rhodes, 'History of United States,' Vol. 5, 616.
2. Idem; 618.
3. Howard K. Beale, 'The Critical Year,' 315.
4. Edward McPherson, 'History of the Reconstruction,' 135.
5. See text, 437, et seq.
6. Seward's remarks in introducing President Johnson when he delivered his St. Louis speech.
7. Lancaster Speech, September 27, 1866. See also Lancaster Daily Evening Express, September 29, 1866.
8. See text, 437 et seq.

References

Book VI—Chapter I—Beginnings of Reconstruction

1. Congressional Globe, January 5, 1867.
2. Idem; December 3, 1866.
3. Idem; January 5, 1867.
4. Idem.
5. Idem; February 7, 1867.
6. Idem; February 13, 1867.
7. Idem.
8. Idem; February 18, 1867.
9. Idem; March 2, 1867.
10. Idem; December 11, 1866.
11. Idem; Feb. 18, 1867.

Book VI—Chapter II—Confiscation

1. McPherson Collection, Item No. 53509.
2. Lancaster Examiner Herald, May 1, 1867.
3. Lancaster Speech September 6, 1865. See New York Herald Supplement, December 13, 1865.
4. See his calculations in McPherson Collection.
5. Note: Later he changed slightly his basis of exemption. See speech of March 19, 1867, in Congressional Globe.
6. Lancaster Speech, September 6, 1865. See New York Herald Supplement, December 13, 1865.
7. McPherson Collection, Item No. 53565.
8. Congressional Globe, March 19, 1867.
9. McPherson Collection, Item No. 53509.
10. New York World, September 10, 1866.
11. Idem.
12. New York Herald, February 7, 1866; see also Congressional Globe, January 22, 1864.
13. Third Dallas, 22, Jones vs. Hilton.
14. Congressional Globe, March 19, 1867.
15. Washington Morning Chronicle, March 21, 1867.
16. Idem.
17. Harper's Weekly, May 18, 1867.
18. Augusta, Georgia, Constitutionalist, Sept. 7, 1867.
19. Issue of December 31, 1865.
20. Told the author by Lancaster County Court House official who knew Stevens.
21. Letters to Simon Stevens, July 6 and 11, 1863, in McPherson Collection.
22. Congressional Globe, March 19, 1867.

Book VI—Chapter III—13th Amendment

1. Congressional Globe, March 28, 1864.
2. Idem; January 31, 1865.

Book VI—Chapter IV—Fourteenth Amendment

1. Article I, Section II.
2. James G. Blaine, 'Twenty Years in Congress,' Vol. II, 129.

References

3. Speech of December 18, 1865. See Congressional Globe of that date.
4. Congressional Globe, January 22, 1866.
5. Idem; January 31, 1866.
6. Idem; January 22, 1866.
7. Idem.
8. Idem.
9. Idem; January 31, 1866.
10. Idem.
11. Idem.
12. Idem.
13. Idem.
14. Idem.
15. Issue of February 7, 1866.
16. Congressional Globe, May 8, 1866.
17. Speech of June 13, 1866. See Congressional Globe of that date.
18. Idem.
19. Congressional Globe, June 13, 1866.
20. Section III, see Congressional Globe, April 30, 1866. Section I, II and IV, see Congressional Globe, December 5, 1865.
21. John W. Burgess, 'Reconstruction and the Constitution,' 81.
22. Idem.
23. Idem; 106.

Book VI—Chapter V—Fifteenth Amendment

1. Dred Scott decision.
2. Justice Taney.
3. Congressional Globe, December 18, 1865.
4. Congressional Globe, May 8, 1866.
5. Idem; January 31, 1866.
6. Idem; March 28, 1868.
7. McPherson Collection. Several letters of similar contents filed in years of 1865, 1866 and 1867.
8. John W. Burgess, 'Reconstruction and the Constitution,' 106.
9. Congressional Globe, March 28, 1868.
10. Lancaster Daily Evening Express, September 29, 1866.
11. Congressional Globe, January 3, 1867.
12. Congressional Globe, January 3, 1867. Also Philadelphia Press, October 30, 1867, Pfeiffer letter.
13. Congressional Globe, March 18, 1868.
14. Idem.
15. Lancaster Intelligencer, March 19, 1868.

Book VI—Chapter VI—Impeachment

1. See text 458 and Congressional Globe, January 5, 1867.
2. Congressional Globe, February 1, 1867.
3. Idem; January 7, 1867.
4. Idem; December 7, 1867.
5. Edward McPherson, 'History of the Reconstruction,' 265.
6. Idem; 261, et seq.
7. The incident has been fully treated by several writers, including two recent reports of it. See Claude G. Bowers, 'Tragic Era,' and George Fort Milton, 'Age of Hate.'

[623]

REFERENCES

8. New York World, February 14, 1868.
9. Edward McPherson, 'History of the Reconstruction,' 265.
10. John W. Burgess, 'Reconstruction and the Constitution,' 172.
11. Congressional Globe, February 21, 1868.
12. Idem; February 22, 1868.
13. Idem.
14. New York Independent, February 27, 1868.
15. Congressional Globe, February 25, 1868.
16. Gideon Welles, 'Diary,' May 7-18, 1868.
17. Congressional Globe, July 7, 1868.

Book VII—Chapter I—The Man

1. Philadelphia Press, August 12, 1868.
2. Author's Lancaster Notes.
3. Colonel James S. Scovel, National Magazine, October, 1903.
4. New York Independent, December 26, 1867.
5. J. B. Grinnell, 'Reminiscences,' 187.
6. McPherson Collection, Item No. 54537.
7. Idem; No. 54520.
8. Letter of Stevens. See William M. Hall, 'Reminiscences & Sketches,' 18.
9. Idem; 20.
10. Idem.
11. Lancaster County Historical Society Reports, Vol. X, No. 7, 279, 'Thaddeus Stevens as a Country Lawyer,' by W. U. Hensel.
12. Note: Because the author cannot be identified and the writing is of doubtful authenticity, it is not treated here.
13. Congressional Globe, March 20, 1867.
14. McPherson Collection, Item No. 52525, letter to Simon Stevens, November 17, 1862.
15. Philadelphia Evening Star, August 12, 1868.
16. George Fort Milton, 'Age of Hate,' 543.
17. New York Tribune, June 14, 1866.
18. New York Independent, January 10, 1867, see also New York Tribune, August 13, 1868.
19. J. B. Grinnell, 'Reminiscences,' 186.
20. Lancaster County Historical Society Reports, Vol. X, No. 7, 281, 'Thaddeus Stevens as a Country Lawyer,' by W. U. Hensel.
21. Congressional Globe, March 10, 1866.
22. Southern Historical Society Papers, Vol. 1, 325.
23. McPherson Collection, Item No. 55313. Also James Albert Woodburn, 'The Life of Thaddeus Stevens,' 597.
24. McPherson Collection, Item No. 54523.
25. Note: One of his correspondents referred, in writing to Stevens, to Lydia Smith as "your good lady." See McPherson Collection, letter dated July 2, 1866, written by one John H. Quarles.
26. McKibben Collection.
27. McPherson Collection, Item No. 54523.
28. Note: In his personal investigation in Gettysburg, the author was told that a mulatto man who lived just outside the town frequently claimed that Stevens was his father. The author interviewed the fellow and several people who knew him, and is convinced that the statement has no basis in fact, and was

indulged in only when the man, was under the influence of liquor. Furthermore, if the boast were true, the man would be at least seventy years of age, and his appearance is that of a much younger person.

29. McPherson Collection, Item No. 55297. Also William P. Hall, 'Reminiscences and Sketches,' 31.
30. Idem.
31. McPherson Collection, Item No. 53625.
32. McKibben letter, Stevens to nephew, August 30, 1853.
33. Idem; October 23, 1854.
34. Idem; December 4, 1854.
35. McPherson Collection, Item No. 55323.
36. Carl Schurz, 'Reminiscences.'
37. New York Herald, July 8, 1867.
38. A. K. McClure, 'Old Time Notes of Pennsylvania,' Vol. 2, 141.
39. C. R. Williams, 'Rutherford B. Hayes, Diary & Letters,' Vol. III, 22.
40. McPherson Collection, Item No. 55437.
41. Idem; Item No. 52631.
42. Told author by several Lancastrians who had reputable knowledge of the incident.
43. See correspondence between the two from July 31, 1850 to August 10, 1850, in the McPherson Collection.
44. J. M. Scovel, National Magazine, October, 1903.
45. Boston Liberator, September 19, 1862.
46. Philadelphia Press, August 12, 1868.
47. Idem; August 15, 1868.
48. Idem; August 12, 1868.
49. Idem; August 14, 1868. Also cited by James Albert Woodburn, 'Life of Thaddeus Stevens,' 585.
50. John Bigelow, 'Retrospections of an Active Life,' Vol. 4, 217.
51. New York Herald, August, 1868.
52. Note: The Catholic Church denied through its official journal in firm language that the old fellow had been baptised under its authority. "Baptism to adults," it said, "is not given on the grounds of 'no objections' but on their asking of the Catholic Church for faith to lead them to life eternal, and professing their desire to be baptised." Freemen's Journal, (Roman Catholic), cited in Lancaster Intelligencer, August 25, 1868.
53. A description of the funeral is taken from the New York and Lancaster newspapers which gave elaborate accounts of their reporters who attended the ceremonies.
54. New York Tribune, December 20, 1867.
55. Philadelphia Press, August 15, 1868.
56. Quoted in Philadelphia Press, August 14, 1868.
57. Idem.
58. Idem.
59. London telegrams to Philadelphia Press. See issue of August 15, 1868.
60. There were many able men in the House at the time, but either through lack of desire or capacity, no one made any effort to succeed him. It should be noted, however, that the crisis in which his peculiar type of dictatorship could function had passed, and it is doubtful. if anyone with similar characteristics could have moved into his role.

REFERENCES

Book VII—Chapter II—Equalitarian

1. Congressional Globe, January 13, 1865.
2. Speech at Great Union mass meeting, Lancaster, September 27, 1866.
3. Congressional Globe, January 3, 1867.
4. Letter to Committee, see Pennsylvania Reporter, June 8, 1838.
5. Idem; March 18, 1868.
6. Washington Daily Morning Chronicle, February 22, 1867.

BIBLIOGRAPHY

Following are some of the books, writings and records which should be studied to obtain a trustworthy impression of the subject of this volume. A comprehensive list would be unduly long for insertion here.

Much of what the author examined has but an indirect bearing on the work and was considered mainly for background. This list has been restricted to the material which has been found most useful in throwing some direct light on the subject, his actions or his character.

The Edward McPherson manuscript collection of Stevens' writings in the Library of Congress is the logical framework on which to build a biography of the Old Commoner. The writings are chronologically arranged as far as possible in some sixteen volumes, and comprise the largest known group.

The Pennsylvania Historical Society at Philadelphia has a limited but valuable assortment of letters to and from Stevens that are useful in the study of his earlier life.

Harvard University has a small assembly of Stevens manuscript and Dartmouth University owns a few of his letters.

The Frank P. McKibben material, priorly inaccessible, furnishes a valuable insight into Stevens' relations with his nephews.

The author's collection consists of some two hundred holograph writings of the subject, covering his activities from his entrance into the Pennsylvania Legislature until his death.

BIBLIOGRAPHY

There are a few minor collections scattered throughout the country, but none of any great historic value. There are manuscripts of several contemporaries of Stevens in the Library of Congress, and a Sumner collection at Harvard, where an occasional letter from Stevens or a copy of one to him is found. But with the exception of those referred to in the text, none are of great importance.

BOOKS, REPORTS AND PAMPHLETS

A Candid Statement, Respecting the Philadelphia County Ticket, Philadelphia, 1839.

ADAMS, ALICE D., *"The Neglected Period of American Anti-Slavery,"* 1808-1831, Boston, 1908.

ADAMS, CHARLES FRANCIS, *"An Autobiography,"* (1835-1915) Boston, 1916.

ADAMS, JOHN QUINCY, *"Letters on the Masonic Institution,"* New York, 1847.

ADAMS, JOHN QUINCY, *"Memoirs,"* edited by Charles Francis Adams, 12 vols., Philadelphia, 1876.

ALTEE, BENJAMIN C., *"Thaddeus Stevens and Slavery,"* Lancaster County Historical Society Reports, Vol. XV, No. 6, Lancaster, 1911.

American Colonization Society Annual Reports, 1818-1910.

Annual Reports of American Anti-Slavery Society, 1834-1839.

Appeal of Forty Thousand Citizens, Threatened with Disfranchisement, to the People of Pennsylvania. Philadelphia, 1838.

Appleton's Proceedings of the Senate sitting for the trial of Andrew Johnson, Appleton's Annual Cyclopedia, New York, 1871.

ARMOR, WILLIAM C., *"Lives of the Governors of Pennsylvania, with the Incidental History of the State from 1609 to 1872,"* Philadelphia, 1872.

BACON, GEORGE W., *"Life and Speeches of President Andrew Johnson,"* London, 1865.

BANCROFT, FREDERICK, *"William H. Seward,"* 2 vols., New York, 1900.

BARNES, THURLOW W., *"Memoirs of Thurlow Weed,"* 2 vols., Boston, 1884.

BIBLIOGRAPHY

BARNES, WILLIAM H., *"History of the Thirty-Ninth Congress of the United States,"* Indianapolis, 1867.

BARRET, DONALD C., *"The Greenbacks and Resumption of Specie Payments,"* 1862-1879.

BARTLETT, MARGUERITE G., *"The Chief Phases of Pennsylvania Politics in the Jacksonian Period,"* Allentown, 1919.

BATES, SAMUEL P., *"Martial Deeds of Pennsylvania,"* Philadelphia, 1875.

BAUSMAN, LOTTIE M., *"A Bibliography of Lancaster County, Pa., 1745-1912,"* Philadelphia, 1917.

BEALE, HOWARD K., *"The Critical Year,"* New York, 1930.

BEALE, H. S. B., *"Letters of Mrs. James G. Blaine,"* 2 vols., New York, 1898.

BIDDLE, NICHOLAS, *"Correspondence of Nicholas Biddle, 1786-1844,"* edited by Reginald C. McGrane, Boston, 1919.

BIGELOW, JOHN, *"Retrospections of an Active Life,"* 5 vols., New York, 1909-1913.

Biographical Annals of Lancaster County, Pa., Chicago, 1903.

BISHOP, AVARD L., *"The State Works of Pennsylvania,"* (in Connecticut Academy of Arts and Sciences Transactions), Vol. 13, 1907-8.

BLAINE, JAMES G., *"Twenty Years of Congress: From Lincoln to Garfield,"* 2 vols., Norwich, Connecticut, 1884.

BLAINE, JASPER G., *"Political Discussions, Legislative, Diplomatic and Popular,"* 1856-1886, Norwich, Connecticut, 1867.

BOLLES, ALBERT S., *"Financial History of the United States,"* New York, 1896.

BOUTWELL, GEORGE S., *"Reminiscences of Sixty Years in Public Affairs,"* New York, 1902.

BOWEN, HERBERT W., *"Recollections, Diplomatic and Undiplomatic,"* New York, 1926.

BOWERS, CLAUDE G., *"The Tragic Era,"* Cambridge, Massachusetts, 1929.

BRAWLEY, BENJAMIN G., *"Short History of the American Negro,"* New York, 1913.

BREEN, MATTHEW P., *"Thirty Years of New York Politics,"* New York, 1899.

BROWN, HENRY, *"Narrative of the......Kidnapping and Presumed Murder of William Morgan,"* Brookfield, New York, 1827.

BROWN, HENRY, *"Narrative of the Anti-Masonic Excitement,"* Batavia, New York, 1829.

BIBLIOGRAPHY

BUCHANAN, JAMES, Works, (Comprising his speeches, state papers and private correspondence, edited by John Bassett Moore), Philadelphia, 1908-11.

BURGESS, JOHN W., *"Reconstruction and the Constitution,"* New York, 1902.

BURGESS, JOHN W., *"The Civil War and the Constitution,"* 2 vols., New York, 1901.

BURTON, THEODORE E., *"Financial Crises and Periods of Industrial and Financial Depression,"* New York, 1909.

BUTLER, BENJAMIN F., *"Autobiography of Personal Reminiscences,"* (Butler's Book) Boston, 1892.

BUTLER, BENJAMIN F., *"Private and Official Correspondence of General Benjamin F. Butler,"* (during Civil War) 5 vols., privately printed, 1917.

Caledonia County Grammar School, Peacham, Vermont, 1900.

CALLENDER, EDWARD BELCHER, *"Thaddeus Stevens, Commoner,"* Boston, 1882.

CARROLL, EBER MALCOLM, *"Origins of the Whig Party,"* Durham, North Carolina, 1925.

CATTERALL, RALPH C. H., *"The Second Bank of the United States,"* Chicago, 1903.

CHADSEY, CHARLES ERNEST, *"The Struggle Between President Johnson and Congress over Reconstruction,"* studies in History, Economics and Law, edited by the Faculty of Political Science of Columbia University, Vol. 8, No. 1, 1896.

CHANNING, EDWARD, *"A History of the United States,"* New York, 1921.

CHASE, SALMON P., *"Diary and Correspondence,"* American Historical Association Report, 1902, II.

CHESTNUT, MAY BOYDEN, *"A Diary from Dixie,"* New York, 1905.

CLARE, ISRAEL SMITH, *"History of Lancaster County, Pa.,"* Lancaster, Pa., 1892.

CLARK, JOHN A., *"Pennsylvania Law Journal Reports,"* (containing cases decided by the Federal and State Courts of Pennsylvania) 5 vols., Philadelphia, 1872-73.

CLAY, MRS. VIRGINIA CLOPTON, *"A Belle of the Fifties,"* New York, 1904.

CLAYTON, MARY BLACK, *"Reminiscences of Jeremiah Sullivan Black,"* St. Louis, 1887.

CLEMENCEAU, GEORGE, *"American Reconstruction, 1865-1870,"* Baldensperger, 1928.

BIBLIOGRAPHY

COFFIN, LEVI, *"Reminiscences of Levi Coffin,"* (reputed President of the Underground Railroad) Cincinnati, 1880.

CONKLING, ALFRED R., *"Life and Letters of Roscoe Conkling,"* New York, 1889.

COPE, GILBERT and J. SMITH FUTHEY, *"History of Chester County, Pa.,"* with Genealogical and Biographical Sketches, Philadelphia, 1881.

Correspondence of Robert Toombs, Alexander H. Stephens and Howell Cobb, (American Historical Association Annual Report, 1911).

COWAN, FRANK, *"Andrew Johnson, Reminiscences of his Private Life and Character,"* by one of his secretaries, Greensburg, Pa., 1894.

COX, SAMUEL S., *"Eight Years in Congress, from 1857 to 1865,"* New York, 1865.

COX, SAMUEL S., *"Three Decades of Federal Legislation, 1855 to 1885,"* (personal and historical memories of events preceding, during and since the American Civil War) Providence, Rhode Island, 1885.

CRANDALL, ANDREW WALLACE, *"The Early History of the Republican Party, 1854-1856,"* Boston, 1930.

CROCKETT, WALTER H., *"Vermonters,"* Brattelboro, Vt., 1930.

CROOK, WILLIAM H., *"Through Five Administrations,"* New York, 1910.

CULLOM, SHELBY B., *"Fifty Years of Public Services,"* Chicago, 1911.

CURTIS, BENJAMIN ROBERT, *"Memoir, with Some of his Professional and Miscellaneous Writings,"* edited by B. R. Curtis, Boston, 1879.

CURTIS, FRANCIS, *"The Republican Party,"* 2 vols., New York, 1904.

CURTIS, GEORGE TICKNOR, *"Life of James Buchanan,"* 2 vols., New York, 1882.

DANA, CHARLES A., *"Lincoln and his Cabinet,"* New York, 1896.

DANA, CHARLES A., *"Recollections of the Civil War,"* New York, 1902.

DEPUE, CHAUNCEY M., *"My Memories of Eighty Years,"* New York, 1922.

DEWEY, DAVIS RICH, *"Financial History of the United States,"* New York, 1922.

DEWITT, DAVID MILLER, *"The Impeachment and Trial of Andrew Johnson,"* New York, 1903.

BIBLIOGRAPHY

DICK, THOMAS, *"The Mental Illumination and Moral Improvement of Mankind,"* (dedicated to Stevens) Philadelphia, 1836.

DuBois, JAMES T., AND GERTRUDE S. MATHEWS, *"Galusha A. Grow,"* Boston, 1917.

DuBois, WILLIAM E. B., *"A Select Bibliography of the Negro American,"* Atlanta University Publications, No. 10, 1905.

DuBois, WILLIAM E. B., *"Philadelphia Negro,"* Philadelphia, 1899.

DuBois, WILLIAM E. B., *"The Suppression of the African Slave Trade to the United States of America, 1638-1870,"* New York, 1896.

DUNNING, WILLIAM A., *"Essays on the Civil War and Reconstruction and Related Topics,"* New York, 1904.

DUNNING, WILLIAM A., *"Reconstruction, Political and Economic, 1865-1877,"* New York, 1907.

ELLIOTT, EDWARD GRAHAM, *"Biographical Story of the Constitution,"* New York, 1910.

ELLIOTT, RICHARD SMITH, *"Notes taken from Sixty Years,"* St. Louis, 1883.

ELLIS, JOHN B., *"Sights and Secrets of the National Capital,"* New York, 1869.

ELLIS, FRANKLIN AND SAMUEL EVANS, *"History of Lancaster County, Pa.,"* Philadelphia, 1883.

EVANS, SAMUEL AND FRANKLIN ELLIS, *"History of Lancaster County, Pa.,"* Philadelphia, 1883.

FERTIG, JAMES W., *"The Secession and Reconstruction of Tennessee,"* Chicago, 1898.

FESSENDEN, FRANCIS, *"Life and Public Services of William Pitt Fessenden,"* 2 vols., Boston, 1907.

FIELDER, HERBERT, *"Life, Times and Speeches of Joseph E. Brown,"* Springfield, 1883.

FLACK, HORACE E., *"Adoption of the Fourteenth Amendment,"* Johns Hopkins University Studies, Extra Volume 26, 1908.

FISH, CARL RUSSELL, *"The Rise of the Common Man,"* 1830-1850, Vol. VI in a History of American Life, New York, 1927.

FLEMING, WALTER LYNWOOD, *"Documentary History of Reconstruction,"* Cleveland, 1906.

FLEMING, WALTER LYNWOOD, *"The Sequel of Appomattox,"* (Chronicles of American Series, Vol. 32) New Haven, 1919.

FLOWER, FRANK A., *"Edward M. Stanton, Autocrat of Rebellion,"* Akron, Ohio, 1905.

BIBLIOGRAPHY

FORD, WORTHINGTON C., *"Letters of Henry Adams,"* New York, 1930.

FORNEY, JOHN WIEN, *"Address on Religious Intolerance and Political Proscription,"* Lancaster, Pa., 1885.

FORNEY, JOHN WIEN, *"Anecdotes of Public Men,"* New York, 2 vols., 1873-1881.

FOX, HONORABLE JOHN, *"Opinion Against the Exercise of Negro Suffrage in Pennsylvania,"* 2 vols., Harrisburg, 1838.

FOX, EARLY LEE, *"The American Colonization Society, 1817-1840,"* Baltimore, 1919.

Free Masonry Unmasked: or Minutes of the trial of a suit in the Court of Common Pleas of Adams County, wherein Thaddeus Stevens, Esq., was plaintiff, and Jacob Lefever defendant. Gettysburg, Pa., 1835.

FUTHEY, J. SMITH, AND GILBERT COPE, *"History of Chester County, Pa.,"* Philadelphia, 1881.

GARFIELD, JAMES A., Works, edited by Burke A. Hinsdale, 2 vols., Boston, 1882.

GARNER, JAMES W., *"Reconstruction in Mississippi,"* New York, 1901.

GARRISON, WENDELL P. AND FRANCIS J., *"William Lloyd Garrison, the Story of his Life as told by his Children,"* 4 vols., 1885-1889.

GOEBEL, DOROTHY B., *"Life of William Henry Harrison,"* Indianapolis, 1926.

GODCHARLES, FREDERIC ANTES, *"Daily Stories of Pennsylvania,"* prepared for publication in the leading daily newspapers of the state, Milton, Pa., 1924.

GODCHARLES, FREDERIC ANTES, *"Influence of Lancaster County on Pennsylvania Frontier,"* Lancaster County Historical Society Papers, vol. 24, 1920.

GODCHARLES, FREDERIC ANTES, *"Pennsylvania; Political, Governmental, Military and Civil,"* 5 vols., American Historical Society, 1934.

GORHAM, G. C., *"Life and Public Services of E. M. Stanton,"* 2 vols., Boston, 1899.

GRANT, U. S., *"Personal Memoirs,"* 2 vols., New York, 1917.

GREELEY, HORACE, *"Recollections of a Busy Life,"* New York, 1868.

GRESHAM, OTTO, *"The Greenbacks,"* Chicago, 1927.

GRIFFIN, GRACE G., *"Writings in American History,"* Washington, Government Printing Office, 1908.

BIBLIOGRAPHY

GRIMKE, ARCHIBALD H., "*Charles Sumner,*" New York, 1892.
GUROWSKI, ADAM, "*Diary,*" 3 vols., Boston, 1862.

HALL, WILLIAM M., "*Reminiscences and Sketches,*" Harrisburg, 1890.
HAMLIN, C. E., "*Life and Times of Hannibal Hamlin,*" Cambridge, 1899.
HARDEN, ROBERT B., "*Account of the Private Life and Public Services of Salmon Portland Chase,*" 1874.
HARDING, SAMUEL B., "*Select Orations,*" Indianapolis, 1908.
HART, ALBERT BUSHNELL, "*Salmon Portland Chase,*" Boston, 1909.
HART, ALBERT BUSHNELL, "*Slavery and Abolition,*" Vol. 16, American Nation Series, New York, 1906.
HARRIS, ALEXANDER, "*A Review of the Political Conflict in America,*" New York, 1876.
HARRIS, ALEXANDER, "*Biographical History of Lancaster County, Pa.,*" Lancaster, 1872.
HARVEY, OSCAR JEWELL, "*History of Lodge No. 61, F. & A. M.,*" Wilkes-Barre, 1897.
HAY, JOHN, "*Abraham Lincoln,*" 12 vols., New York, 1905.
HAYES, RUTHERFORD B., "*Diary and Letters,*" edited by Charles Richard Williams, 5 vols., Columbus, Ohio, 1922-1926.
HAYES, RUTHERFORD B., *Diary and Letters,* edited by William and Charles Richard, 5 vols., Columbus, Ohio, 1922.
HAYNES, G. H., "*Charles Sumner,*" Philadelphia, 1909.
HAWORTH, PAUL LELAND, "*Reconstruction and Union, 1865-1912,*" New York, 1912.
HELPER, HINTON ROWAN, "*The Impending Crisis of the South: How to Meet It,*" New York, 1860.
HENSEL, W. U., "*Christiana Riot and the Treason Trials of 1851,*" Lancaster, 1911.
HENSEL, W. U., "*Thaddeus Stevens as a Country Lawyer,*" Lancaster, Pa., 1906.
HERBERT, H. A., "*The Abolition Crusade and its Consequences,*" New York, 1912.
HERBERT, H. A., "*Why the Solid South, or Reconstruction and its Results,*" Baltimore, 1890.
History of Cumberland and Adams Counties, Warner, Beers & Co., Chicago, 1866.
History of the Rise, Progress and Downfall of Know-Nothingism in Lancaster County, By two expelled members, Lancaster, 1856.

BIBLIOGRAPHY

HOAR, GEORGE F., "*Autobiography of Seventy Years*," 2 vols., New York, 1903.

HOCKEY, JOHN L., "*Pennsylvania's Free School Laws of 1834 and their Defender, T. Stevens*," (Lebanon County Historical Society Papers, Vol. 7, No. 10.)

HOLLISTER, ORLANDO H., "*Life of Schuyler Colfax*," New York, 1886.

HOOD, ALEXANDER H., "*Biography of Stevens*," Lancaster, Pa., 1872.

HOWARD, OLIVER O., "*Autobiography*," 2 vols., New York, 1907.

HOWE, JULIA WARD, "*Reminiscences*," 1819-1899. Boston, 1899.

HOWE, JULIA WARD, "*Reminiscences*," by L. E. Richards and M. H. Elliott, 2 vols., Boston, 1915.

HOWE, M. A. DE WOLFE, "*Life and Letters of George Bancroft*," 2 vols., New York, 1908.

HULME, JOHN F., "*The Abolitionists*," (a defense of the Abolitionists), 1905.

HURD, JOHN CODMAN, "*Law of Freedom and Bondage in the United States*," 2 vols.,

JENKINS, HOWARD MALCOLM, "*Pennsylvania*," 3 vols., Philadelphia, 1903.

JOHNSON, RICHARD M., "*Alexander H. Stephens*," Philadelphia, 1878.

JONES, JAMES S., "*Life of Andrew Johnson*," Greenville, Tennessee, 1901.

JONES, LEONARD AUGUSTUS, "*Index to Legal Periodical Literature*," 2 vols., Boston, 1891.

JORDAN, DONALDSON, "*Europe and the American Civil War*," Boston, 1931.

JULIAN, GEORGE W., "*Political Recollections, 1840-1872*," Chicago, 1884.

KELLEY, WILLIAM D., "*Speeches, Addresses and Letters on Industrial and Financial Questions*," Philadelphia, 1872.

KENDRICK, BENJAMIN B., "*Journal of the Select Committee of Fifteen*," Columbia University Studies, LXII, New York, 1914.

KLEEBURG, GORDON S. P., "*The Formation of the Republican Party as a National Political Organization*," New York, 1911.

Lancaster County Historical Society Reports, Lancaster, Pa.

LANDIS, CHARLES I., "*T. Stevens, a letter written to the Daily News Era*," Lancaster, Pa., 1916.

[635]

BIBLIOGRAPHY

LANDIS, CHARLES I., *"Refutation of the slanderous stories against the name of T. Stevens placed before the public by Thomas Dixon,"* Lancaster, Pa., 1924.

LEE, JOHN HANCOCK, *"The Origin and Progress of the American Party in Politics,"* Philadelphia, 1885.

LEE, STEPHEN D., *"The South Since the War,"* Atlanta, 1899.

LEISLER, JACOB, *"Letters to the People of Pennsylvania on the Political Principles of the Free Soil Party,"* Philadelphia, 1850.

LOCKE, MARY S., *"Anti-Slavery in America,"* Boston, 1901.

LOGAN, JOHN A., *"The Great Conspiracy,"* New York, 1886.

LOVE, ROBERT A., *"Federal Financing,"* London, 1931.

MACY, JESSE, *"Political Parties, 1846-1860,"* New York, 1900.

MACY, JESSE, *"The Anti-Slavery Crusade,"* New Haven, 1919.

MATHEWS, GERTRUDE S., AND JAMES T. DUBOIS, *"Galusha A. Grow,"* Boston, 1917.

MAY, SAMUEL J., *"Catalogue of Anti-Slavery Publications in America,"* 1883.

MAY, SAMUEL J., *"Fugitive Slave Law and its Victims,"* New York, 1861.

MAY, SAMUEL J., *"Some Recollections of our Anti-Slavery Conflict,"* 1869.

MACDONALD, WILLIAM, *"Select Statutes, 1861-1898,"* New York, 1903.

MCCALL, SAMUEL WALKER, *"Thaddeus Stevens,"* Boston, 1899.

MCCARTHY, CHARLES H., *"Lincoln's Plan of Reconstruction,"* New York, 1901.

MCCARTHY, CHARLES H., *"The Anti-Masonic Party,"* Annual Report, American Historical Association, Washington, 1903.

MCCLURE, ALEXANDER K., *"Our Presidents and How We Make Them,"* New York, 1900.

MCCLURE, ALEXANDER K., *"Recollections of Half a Century,"* Salem, Massachusetts, 1902.

MCCLURE, ALEXANDER K., *"Lincoln and Men of Wartimes,"* Philadelphia, 1892.

MCCLURE, ALEXANDER K., *"Old Time Notes of Pennsylvania,"* 2 vols., Philadelphia, 1905.

MCCULLOCH, HUGH, *"Men and Measures of Half a Century,"* New York, 1888.

MCDOUGALL, MARION G., *"Fugitive Slaves, 1619-1865,"* Fay House Monographs, No. 3, 1891.

BIBLIOGRAPHY

McMASTER, JOHN BACH, *"A History of the People of the United States during Lincoln's administration,"* New York, 1927.

McPHERSON, EDWARD, *"The Political History of the United States of America during the Great Rebellion,"* Washington, D. C., 1882.

McPHERSON, EDWARD, *"The Political History of the United States of America during the Period of Reconstruction,"* Washington, D. C., 1871.

Memorial Addresses on the life and character of Thaddeus Stevens, delivered in the House of Representatives, Washington, D. C., December 17, 1868, Government Printing Office, 1869.

MERIAN, EDWARD, *"A History of American Political Theories,"* New York, 1920.

MILTON, GEORGE FORT, *"The Age of Hate,"* New York, 1930.

MITCHELL, WESLEY C., *"A History of the Greenbacks,"* Chicago, 1903.

MORISON, SAMUEL E., *"Oxford History of the United States,"* Oxford University Press, 2 vols., 1927.

MOORE, JOHN B., *"Works of James Buchanan,"* 12 vols., Philadelphia, 1911.

MUELLER, HENRY R., *"Whig Party in Pennsylvania,"* New York, 1922.

NEEDLES, EDWARD, *"An Historical Memoir of the Pennsylvania Society for Promoting the Abolition of Slavery,"* Philadelphia, 1848.

NEVINS, ALLAN, *"The Emergence of Modern America,"* New York, 1927.

NICOLAY, JOHN G., *"Abraham Lincoln,"* 10 vols., New York, 1890.

OBERHOLTZER, E. P., *"A History of the United States Since the Civil War,"* 3 vols., New York, 1917.

OBERHOLTZER, E. P., *"Jay Cooke,"* 2 vols., Philadelphia, 1907.

OGDEN, ROLLO, *"Life and Letters of Edwin L. Godkin,"* 2 vols., New York, 1907.

OLBRICH, EMIL, *"The Development of Sentiment on Negro Suffrage to 1860,"* Madison, 1912.

PARKE, JOHN E., *"Recollections of Seventy Years and Historical Gleanings of Allegheny, Pennsylvania,"* Boston, 1886.

PENROSE, CHARLES B., *"Address of, together with speeches of Messrs. Fraley, Williams, Pearson and Penrose, on the sub-*

BIBLIOGRAPHY

ject of the insurrection at Harrisburg, in December of 1838," Harrisburg, 1839.

PERRY, BENJAMIN FRANKLIN, "Reminiscenses of Public Men, with Speeches and Addresses," Greenville, S. C., 1889.

PERRY, BENJAMIN FRANKLIN, "Biographical Sketches of Eminent American Statesmen," Philadelphia, 1887.

PHILLIPS, ULRICH B., "American Negro Slaves," New York, 1918.

PHILLIPS, ULRICH B., Introduction to first two volumes of "Documentary History of American Industrial Society," Cleveland, 1810.

PIERCE, EDWARD L., "Memoirs and Letters of Charles Sumner," 4 vols., Boston, 1877-1893.

POLK, J. K., "Diary," Chicago, 1910.

POORE, BEN PERLEY, "Perley's Reminiscences of Sixty Years in the National Metropolis," 2 vols., Philadelphia, 1886.

PRAY, ISAAC C., "Memoirs of James Gordon Bennett and His Times," New York, 1855.

PRATT, EDWIN J., "Europe and the American Civil War," Boston, 1931.

Proceedings of American Anti-Slavery Convention at Philadelphia, Philadelphia, 1833, (Misc. pamphlets, Vol. 295.)

Proceedings of American Anti-Slavery Society, Philadelphia, 1853.

Proceedings of Pennsylvania Society for Promoting the Abolition of Slavery, Centennial Anniversary, 1875, Philadelphia, 1876.

RANDALL, JAMES G., "Constitutional Problems under Lincoln," New York, 1926.

REID, WHITELAW, "After the War," Cincinnati, 1866.

Report of the Pennsylvania Society for Promoting the Abolition of Slavery: The Present State and Condition of the Free People of Color of Philadelphia, Philadelphia, 1838.

Report of the Select Committee of Managers of Impeachment, (raising money to be used in impeachment) Washington, D. C., 1868.

RHODES, JAMES FORD, "A History of the United States from the Compromise of 1850," New York, 1900.

RICHARDSON, JAMES D., "Messages and Papers of the Presidents, 1789-1897," Washington Government Printing Office, 1897.

RIDDLE, ALBERT G., "Life of Benjamin F. Wade," Cleveland, 1886.

BIBLIOGRAPHY

RIDDLE, WILLIAM, *"The Story of Lancaster: Old and New,"* Lancaster, 1917.

ROBINSON, EDGAR E., *"Evolution of Political Parties in the United States,"* New York, 1924.

ROBINSON, JOHN BELL, *"Pictures of Slavery and Anti-Slavery,"* Philadelphia, 1863.

ROSS, EDMUND GIBSON, *"History of the Impeachment of Andrew Johnson,"* Sante Fe, New Mexico, 1896.

RUSSELL, R. R., *"Economic Aspects of Southern Sectionalism, 1840-61,"* Urbana, Illinois, 1924.

SARGENT, NATHAN, *"Public Men and Events from the Commencement of Mr. Monroe's administration in 1817 to the close of Mr. Fillmore's administration in 1853,"* 2 vols., Philadelphia, 1875.

SAVAGE, JOHN, *"Public Services of Andrew Johnson,"* New York, 1866.

SCHIEFFELIN, S. H., *"The President and Congress,"* Philadelphia, 1867.

SCHOFIELD, JOHN M., *"Forty-six Years in the Army,"* New York, 1897.

SCHOULER, JAMES, *"History of the United States Under the Constitution,"* 7 vols., New York, 1894.

SCHUCKERS, J. W., *"The Life and Public Services of Salmon P. Chase,"* New York, 1874.

SCHURZ, CARL, *"Reminiscences,"* (with sketch of his life and public services from 1869 to 1906 by Frederick Bancroft and William A. Dunning), 3 vols., New York, 1908.

SCHURZ, CARL, *"Speeches, Correspondence and Political Papers,"* edited by Frederick Bancroft, 6 vols., New York, 1913.

SCOTT, EBEN G., *"Reconstruction During Civil War,"* New York, 1895.

SEIBERT, WILLIAM H., *"The Underground Railroad,"* New York, 1898.

SEWARD, WILLIAM H., *"An Autobiography from 1801 to 1834,"* (with memoirs of his life and selections from his letters, 1831 to 1856, by Frederick W. Seward), New York, 1891.

SEWARD, WILLIAM H., Works, edited by George E. Baker, 5 vols., Boston, 1884.

SHARPLESS, ISAAC, *"Two Centuries of Pennsylvania History,"* Philadelphia, 1900.

SHERMAN, JOHN, *"Recollections of Forty Years in the House, Senate and Cabinet,"* 2 vols., Chicago, 1895.

BIBLIOGRAPHY

Sherman letters, (correspondence between General and Senator Sherman, from 1837 to 1891, edited by Rachel S. Thorndike, New York, 1894.

SHERMAN, GENERAL, *"Home Letters,"* edited by M. A. DeWolfe Howe, New York, 1909.

SHERMAN, GENERAL WILLIAM TECUMSEH, *"Memoirs,"* 2 vols., New York, 1886.

SIMPSON, ALEX, *"A Treatise on Federal Impeachments,"* Philadelphia, 1916.

SMEDLEY, R. C., *"History of the Underground Railroad in Chester and the Neighboring Counties of Pennsylvania,"* Lancaster, 1883.

SMITH, THEODORE CLARKE, *"Life and Letters of James A. Garfield,"* 2 vols., New Haven, 1925.

SMITH, THEODORE CLARKE, *"The Liberty and Free Soil Parties in the Northwest,"* New York, 1897.

SPALDING, E. G., *"History of the Legal Tender Paper Money Issued During the Great Rebellion,"* Buffalo, 1875.

STANWOOD, EDWARD, *"A History of the President,"* 2 vols., Boston, 1928.

STEPHENS, ALEXANDER H., *"Constitutional View of the Late War Between the States,"* 2 vols., Philadelphia, 1868.

STEPHENS, ALEXANDER H., *"Recollections and Diary,"* New York, 1910.

STEPHENSON, NATHANIEL WRIGHT, *"Lincoln,"* Indianapolis, 1922-1924.

STEWART, WILLIAM M., *"Reminiscences,"* edited by George Rothwell Brown, New York, 1908.

STILL, WILLIAM, *"Underground Railroad,"* (revised edition), Philadelphia, 1883.

STOREY, MOORFIELD, *"Charles Sumner,"* Boston, 1900.

STOVALL, PLEASANT A., *"Robert Toombs,"* New York, 1892.

STRYKER, LLOYD P., *"Andrew Johnson, a Study in Courage,"* New York, 1929.

STURTEVANT, PELEG, *"The Buckshot War,"* or *"The Last Kick of Anti-Masonry,"* Harrisburg, 1839.

SUMNER, WILLIAM G., *"History of American Currency,"* New York, 1878.

SWIFT, LINDSAY, *"William Lloyd Garrison,"* Philadelphia, 1911.

THAYER, WILLIAM ROSCOE, *"Life and Letters of John Hay,"* 2 vols., Boston, 1915.

BIBLIOGRAPHY

TAILOR, RICHARD, *"Destruction and Reconstruction,"* New York, 1879.

TURPIE, DAVID, *"Sketches of My Own Times,"* Indianapolis, 1903.

TURNER, EDWARD RAYMOND, *"The Negro in Pennsylvania, 1639 to 1861,"* Washington, 1911.

WALLACE, JOHN WILLIAM, *"Cases in the Circuit Court of the United States for the Third Circuit,"* 3 vols., Philadelphia, 1849-71.

WALSH, LOUISE & MATTHEW J., *"History and Organization of Education in Pennsylvania,"* Indiana, Pa., 1930.

WASHBURN, E. B., *"Stevens and Convention of 1856,"* The Edwards Papers,

WATTERSON, HENRY, *"Marse Henry,"* (An Autobiography) 2 vols., New York, 1919.

WATSON, J. S., *"Stories of Pennsylvania,"* New York, 1897.

WATTS, F., *"Reports of Cases in the Supreme Court of the State of Pennsylvania,"* Philadelphia, 1850.

WEED, THURLOW, *"Autobiography,"* edited by Harriet A. Weed, Boston, 1884.

WELLES, GIDEON, *"Diary,"* 3 vols., New York, 1911.

WHEELER, J. H., *"Reminiscences,"* Columbus, Ohio, 1884.

WHITE, ANDREW D., *"Autobiography,"* New York, 1907.

WHITE, HORACE, *"The Life of Lyman Trumbull,"* Boston, 1913.

WICKERSHAM, J. P., *"A History of Education in Pennsylvania,"* Lancaster, 1886.

WILSON, HENRY, *"History of the Anti-Slavery Measures,"* Boston, 1865.

WILSON, HENRY, *"History of the Reconstruction Measures of the Thirty-Eighth and Thirty-Ninth Congresses,"* Chicago, 1868.

WILSON, HENRY, *"History of the Rise and Fall of the Slave Power in America,"* 3 vols., Boston, 1872-7.

WILLEY, AUSTIN, *"The History of the Anti-Slavery Cause in State and Nation,"* Portland, Me., 1886.

WINSTON, ROBERT W., *"Andrew Johnson,"* New York, 1928.

WISE, HENRY A., *"Seven Decades of the Union,"* Philadelphia, 1872.

WOODBURN, JAMES ALBERT, *"American Political History,"* 2 vols., New York, 1905.

WOODBURN, JAMES ALBERT, *"The Life of Thaddeus Stevens,"* Indianapolis, 1913.

BIBLIOGRAPHY

NEWSPAPERS AND PERIODICALS

Advocate, The, Lewistown, Pa.
American Advertiser, Baltimore.
American Advocate, Philadelphia.
American Historical Magazine.
American Historical Review, "Is the Political Diary of Gideon Welles Reliable?" by Howard K. Beale, XXX 1925.
American Historical Review, "The Attitude of Thaddeus Stevens toward the Conduct of the Civil War," by James Albert Woodburn, XII, No. 3, April, 1907.
American Historical Review, "The Purchase of Alaska," by Frank A. Golder, April, 1920.
American Historical Review, "Notes of Colonel William George Moore, Private Secretary to Johnson, 1866-1868," Vol. XIX, No. 1, October, 1913, 98.
American Journal of Education.
American Law Review.
American Press and Republican, Lancaster, (weekly).
American Sentinel, Philadelphia.

Blackwood's Magazine.

Centinal, Gettysburg.
Century Magazine.
Chautauquan.
Chicago Tribune.
Christian Cynosure.
Christian Witness, Pittsburgh (almanac).
Cincinnati Daily Gazette, Cincinnati.

Daily Advertiser, Boston.
Daily Evening Express, Lancaster.
Daily National Intelligencer, Washington.

Evening Bulletin, Philadelphia.
Evening Star, The, Philadelphia.
Evening Transcript, Boston.

Franklin Repository, Chambersburg, Pa.
Franklin Whig, Chambersburg, Pa.

Galaxy.
Gettysburg Compiler, Gettysburg.

BIBLIOGRAPHY

Harper's Weekly.
Harrisburg Argus, Harrisburg (weekly).
Harrisburg Chronicle, Harrisburg.
Harrisburg Daily Telegraph, Harrisburg.
Hazard's United States Commercial and Statistical Register,
  Philadelphia.

Independent, The, New York.
Inland Daily, Lancaster.
Intelligencer, Lancaster, (weekly).

Keystone, The, Harrisburg, (weekly).

Lancaster Examiner and Herald, Lancaster, (weekly).
Lancaster Union and Tribune, Lancaster, (weekly).
Lancasterian and Chronicle of the Times, Lancaster.
Liberator, The, Boston, 1831-1865.
Leslie's Magazine, (weekly).
Lippincott's Monthly Magazine.

Magazine of Western History.
Morning Courier and N. Y. Enquirer.

Nation, The, "Thaddeus Stevens," by E. L. Godkin, Vol. 7,
  August 20, 1868.
National Enquirer, Philadelphia, 1838. (almanac).
National Era, The, Washington.
National Gazette, The, Philadelphia.
National Intelligencer, Washington.
National Quarterly Review.
New York Daily Tribune, New York.
New York Evening Post, New York,
New York Herald, New York.
New York Morning Express, New York.
New York Times, New York.
New York World, New York.
Niles Weekly Register.
North American and Daily Advertiser, Philadelphia.
North American Review.
North American and United States Gazette, Philadelphia.

Pennsylvania Emancipator, Coatesville, Pa., (almanac).
Pennsylvania Intelligencer, Harrisburg.

BIBLIOGRAPHY

Pennsylvania Inquirer, Philadelphia.
Pennsylvania Magazine of History and Biography.
Pennsylvania School Journal, "Stevens and Education," article by Alexander H. Hood, January, 1891.
Pennsylvania Telegraph, Harrisburg, (weekly).
Pennsylvanian, Philadelphia.
Philadelphia Daily News, Philadelphia.
Philadelphia Press, Philadelphia.
Pittsburgh Daily Gazette, Pittsburgh.
Political Science Quarterly, "Paying for Alaska," by William A. Dunning, September, 1912.
Public Ledger, Philadelphia.

Richmond, Whig.

Scribner's Monthly, XX (1880). Extracts from Journal of Henry J. Raymond.
Star, Gettysburg.
Star and Sentinel, Gettysburg.
Star and Republican Banner, Gettysburg.
Sun, The, Philadelphia.

United States Gazette, Philadelphia.

Washington Chronicle, Washington.
Washington National Republican, Washington.

PUBLIC DOCUMENTS

Congressional Globe, 1849 to 1853 and 1859 to 1868, including the Senate and House Executive documents for those periods, the Reports of Committees of the House of Representatives, Impeachment Investigation—testimony taken before the Judiciary Committee of the House; investigation of charges against Andrew Johnson. (40th Cong., 1st Sess., Ser. No. 1314, Doc. No. 7.)
Journal of the Convention of the State of Pennsylvania, to propose Amendments to the Constitution, 2 vols., Harrisburg, 1837-1838. This contains the minutes of the Committee of the Whole of the Convention.
Memorial Addresses on the Life and Character of Thaddeus Stevens, delivered in the House of Representatives, Washington, D. C., December 18, 1868. Washington Government Printing Office, 1869.

[644]

BIBLIOGRAPHY

Messages and Papers of the Presidents, compiled by James D. Richardson, Government Printing Office, 1897.

Pennsylvania Archives, Harrisburg, Pennsylvania.

Pennsylvania House and Senate Journals, and Executive Documents.

Pennsylvania State Reports.

Pennsylvania Superior Court Reports.

Proceedings and Debates of the Convention of the Commonwealth of Pennsylvania to propose amendments to the Constitution, commenced and held at Harrisburg on the second day of May, 1837. 14 vols., Harrisburg, 1837-1839.

INDEX

Abolition movement, leaders speak in Pennsylvania, 92; Stevens takes bold position in support of, 102; in District of Columbia, 205, 372; gains support during emancipation movement, 369.

Act to provide for the more efficient Government of the rebel states, cited in Stevens' Impeachment charge, 538.

Adams, Charles Francis, Stevens' friend, 290.

Adams County Bar, Stevens' first cases before, 25.

Adams County Court, admits Stevens to practice, 24.

Adams, John Quincy, referred to by Stevens as center of abuse in House, 223.

Alaska, purchase of approved by Stevens, 583.

Allyn's Ritual (on Masonry) arouses people, 84.

American colonies, recognize slavery, 85; separation between Great Britain and colonies commented on by Chief Justice Chase, 479.

Anderson, George W., of Missouri, suggests meeting of various parties to agree upon House organization, 261.

Anti-Masonry, its party principles adopted by Stevens, 35; Whig Party grows out of, 36; campaign against, 37; Harrison believes in its principles, 38; chapter on, 49-84.

Anti-Slavery movement, beginnings, 87; agitation takes new life in early 1830's, 486; amendment abolishing slavery underway, 489.

Annual Catalogue of Dartmouth College, Stevens' name appears in, 18.

Archer, Stevenson, Esq., applies for Stevens' admission to Harford County Bar, 22.

Arch Priest of Anti-Masonry, Stevens referred to as, 74, 79.

Arnold, Isaac N., of Illinois, proposes amendment abolishing slavery, 489.

Arm in Arm Convention, 447, 448.

Articles of impeachment, prepared, 536; Stevens prepares second set, 547 et seq.; see Impeachment.

Ashley, James M., of Ohio, his impeachment resolution defeated, 4; his amendment to Stevens' resolution, 417; his impeachment resolution first, 522, 523; House accepts his resolution, 523.

Asylums, Stevens contributes to, 561.

Appropriations Act, cited in Stevens' charge, 538.

Auburn, New York, Journal, comments on Stevens' ability, 201.

Averett, Thomas H., of Virginia, asks Stevens if New England did not sell slaves, 227.

Baker, Jehu, of Illinois, chides Southern members, 209.

Baltimore, placed by Lincoln under military rule, 302.

Bancroft, George, historian adviser, writes Lincoln, 361.

Baptist, Stevens' mother as devout, 11.

Barksdale, William, of Mississippi, draws knife, 259.

Batavia Lodge, its members blamed for Morgan incident, 50.

Battocks, Judge John, Stevens starts his legal studies under, 20.

Bee, New Orleans, comments on Stevens' death, 592.

Beecher, Henry Ward, comments on Stevens' school speech, 169.

Bernard's Light on Masonry, arouses people, 84.

Biddle, Nicholas, President of United States Bank, 173, 174; commends Stevens on his able handling of bill, 176.

Bingham, John A., Stevens comments on his attempt to modify reconstruction measure, 31; is appointed with Stevens as a Committee to notify Senate of House action on impeachment of President, 537.

Black codes in South, 413, 495, 512.

Black, Jeremiah Sullivan, Attorney-General under Buchanan, 272; says Stevens' mind "as far as his sense of obligation to God" concerned, was a "howling wilderness," 560; acts for McCardle in case before Supreme Court, 565.

Blaine, James G., attempts to modify Stevens' bill governing insurrectionary states by amendments, 465, 466.

Blair, Francis, Jr., 300; enemy of Stevens, 339; is nominated by Democrats for Vice-Presidency, 339; called to order by Stevens in Thirty-Eighth Congress, 397; comments on Stevens' reconstruction speech, 429.

Blanchard, Reverend Jonathon, sent to Gettysburg as abolition leader, 92; declines at first Stevens' financial aid, 92; is made unwelcome in Pennsylvania, 93; attends convention to amend State Constitution and gives his version, 194, 195; suggests Chase contact Stevens, 191.

Blockade of South, criticized by Stevens, 285; 578.

Index

Board of Canal Commissioners, 115; reasons why Stevens made member of, as seen by Democrats, 171.

Board of Trustees, of Peacham Academy, 14, 15, 16.

Bocock, Thomas S., of Virginia, Democratic nominee for Speaker in 1859, 256.

Borough Council of Gettysburg, elects Stevens as member, 28; Stevens resigns from Council to become school director, 148.

Bray, Charles, claims Burrowes' election returns "false," 124.

Breckenridge, John C., his defeat believed by Stevens to be for best, 287.

British Government, Talleyrand is obnoxious to, 8.

Brown, Charles, Democratic contender for Philadelphia seat in Senate, 128; addresses Senate, 128, 129.

Brown, John, "raid" on Harper's Ferry, 256.

Brooks, James, of New York, 395; protests omission of Maynard's name, 416; makes address after Clerk reads Stevens' report from Committee on Reconstruction recommending impeachment, 532; fails to curb determined House, 532; his address attempting to show black of race apart from white man is ridiculed by Stevens, 557.

Buchanan, James, laborious preparation of speeches, 35; advises Stevens to support Jackson for Presidency, 35; charged by Stevens with delaying House organization, 264; attempts to appease South by condemning North, 272; his "explanatory amendment," 273; his fourth annual message, 273; his statement attacked, 281; favors a Thirteenth Amendment recognizing property right in slaves, 486; is called "a very traitor" by Stevens, 580; ignores Stevens' attempt at friendliness, 580, 581; asks Stevens' aid in entering his nephew at West Point, 581.

Buckshot War, 40; grows out of encounter for control of Lower House, 118; threatening situation at Harrisburg, 128, 129, 130, 131, 132, 133; War over, 134; defendants in action brought by Stevens are discharged, 140; chapter on, 114-141.

Burrowes, Thomas H., heads delegation to urge Stevens' appointment to Cabinet position under Harrison, 42; as Secretary of State receives minority returns, 120; Chairman of Whig Central State Committee, 120; makes statement, suggests investigation, 121; gives official returns to Clerk, 124; escapes with Stevens and Penrose, 129; resides at Lancaster, 195.

Butler, Benjamin F., opens for Managers in impeachment trial, 539; submits brief written by Congressman Lawrence, of Ohio, 539, 540; concludes reading Stevens' speech in support of articles when strength fails him, 541.

Caledonia, home county of Stevens, 12; ore mines and smelting plants at, 481; burned by rebels, 482; Stevens claims no remuneration for losses at, 484.

Calhoun, John C., speech of March 4, 1850, 203.

California, wants to be admitted to Union, 204; amendment for admission under consideration, 230.

Capitol, people flock to, 528; crowds there await Committee's report on impeachment, 529; police called to keep order, 529; Stevens' body is moved to, 587.

Capitol Hill, Stevens' home at 279 South "B" Street, 585.

Carpenter, Rev., Stevens' studies under, 18.

Carpenter, Dr., attempts to make Buchanan and Stevens friends, 580.

Carpet Baggers, movement not started until after Stevens' death, 595.

Cassett, David, Stevens forms contact with, 20.

Catholic Baptismal rite, administered to Stevens on death bed, 586.

Caucus, Republican, 412.

Chase, Salmon P., becomes interested in Liberty Party, 191; writes Stevens, 191; accepts Treasury Portfolio under Lincoln, 307; slowly gains stride in new office, 309; his plan advocates borrowing in toto to cover War expenditures, 310, 311; as Chief Justice comments on separation between Great Britain and colonies, 479; presides at impeachment trial, 538; Stevens at first supports him for President in 1864, 581.

Chambersburg Whig, comments on Stevens' report, 92.

Chicago Tribune, thinks West alone could win War in two or three months, 296.

Christiana Riot, 241.

Civil Rights Bill, 437.

Clark, James B., of Mississippi, precipitates trouble caused by Helper's "Impending Crisis," 256, 257.

Clay, Clement C., Jr., of Alabama, Johnson's proclamation offering reward for arrest of, 568.

Clay, Henry, possible candidate against Van Buren for Presidential election of 1836, 37, 38, 199; accused of influencing Harrison concerning non-appointment of Stevens to Cabinet position, 43; charged by

teenth, 511; Stevens' offered resolution is one of forerunners of finally adopted amendment, 519; resolution embodying amendment passed
by Congress, 519.

Finck, William E., of Ohio, says
Stevens' bill governing insurrectionary states important measure, 463.

Flenniken, Robert P., Democratic legislator, comments on trouble in Harrisburg, and escape of Stevens,
Burrowes and Penrose, 130; writes
constituents of threatening situation, 132.

Foreign papers, note death of Stevens, 594.

Forney, John W., publisher of Philadelphia Press, Stevens writes to him
concerning universal suffrage, 519.

Fort Sumpter, captured by Confederates, 295, 296, 298.

Fourteenth Amendment, o r i g i n a l
framework of, 496; changes made
by Senate on proposed sections, 501,
502, 503, 504; passes Senate, 504,
505; Senate changes reviewed by
Stevens, 505; passes House, 506;
contrasting set-up as proposed by
Stevens and as finally adopted, 507,
508; Congressional improvements
over Stevens' plans outlined, 508,
509; proposed amendment rejected
by every State which had seceded.
513.

France, Count Talleyrand returns to,
8.

Free Masonry, power in England, 49;
condemned as unfit for "professing
Christians," 49; "immoral and irreligious," 57.

Free School Law, Commonwealth
forced to vote against, 5; repealer
against, 159, 160; supported by
Stevens' speech, 160-168; f r e e
schools become popular under, 169.

Free Soil Party, nominates Hale, 238.

Free State Convention, held by Louisiana, 394.

Freedman's Bureau Bill, 430, 432,
444; Stevens comments on diverted
appropriations under amended bill,
562.

French Revolution, 85.

Fugitive Slave Acts, lawful procedure
under, 88; South believes they are
being nullified, 205; motion to lay
new bill on table defeated, 232;
measure passes, 232; better enforcement advocated by Lincoln,
382.

Garfield, James A., has part of Stevens' school speech placed on record,
169; claims Stevens intended five-
twenty bonds to be paid in gold,
339.

Georgia Convention, protests against
slavery, 86.

Gettysburg, 12; Stevens approaches,
23; lawyers practicing in, 24; near-
by murder, 26; Stevens owns house
and lot in, 28; Stevens leaves, 46;
Masonic Lodge disbands, 63; meeting to express slavery sentiments, 89.

Gettysburg Compiler, comments upon
Stevens' appointment as Chairman
of Scott State Central Committee,
45.

Giddings, Joshua, votes Stevens for
Speaker, 211.

Gilbert, Amos, comments on Stevens'
personality while beginning law
studies, 21; his opinion vindicated,
22, 23.

Gilmer, John A., of North Carolina,
offers substitute for Clark's resolution, 257; on ballot for Speaker, 260.

Gorsuch, Edward, slave owner, killed,
240.

Great Britain, abolishes slave trade,
87; her national debt in comparison
to that of United States, 472;
separation from colonies commented
upon by Chief Justice Chase, 479.

Granger, Francis, is appointed to
Cabinet position promised Stevens,
43.

Grant, Ulysses S., appointed Secretary
of War ad interim in place of
Stanton, 526; writes Johnson re-
linquishing office, 526; calls upon
Stevens to solicit his support in
Presidential campaign, 581, 582.

Greeley, Horace, 291, 299; accuses
Stevens of perpetrating "gigantic
fraud," 341.

Grinell, Josiah B., of Iowa, attempts
to explain his vote on Wade-Davis
Bill, 400.

Groesbeck, William S., of Ohio, one of
Johnson's counsel for impeachment
trial, 539.

Grotius, Hugo, authority on Law
of Nations quoted by Stevens, 479.

Grow, Galusha A., nominated for
Speaker, 1859, 256; elected, 300.

Gyger, banker friend of Stevens, 341.

Hagerstown, Md., races attended by
Stevens, 29; Stevens speech at, 55,
56.

Hahn, Michael, Free State Governor
of Louisiana, 394.

Hale, John P., of New Hampshire,
Free Soil Presidential candidate,
238.

Halleck, Henry Wager, used by Stevens as authority on compensation by
vanquished belligerent for war expenses, 476.

Hamlin, Hanibal, Lincoln writes to,
377.

Hanway, Castner, abolition sympathizer, participates in and is ar-

to Gettysburg after learning of Blanchard's reception, 93; ignores M'Giffin's attempt to make him ineffective at coming Convention, 94; attends Convention, makes speech, 94, 95; his procedure overcomes M'Giffin faction, 96, 97; delegate to Constitutional Convention, 98; his group in control, 99; his good work in organizing assembly, 100; takes bold abolition stand in Constitutional Convention, 102; loses support of Whigs, 103; battles with Meredith, 104, 105; drops proposal to limit representation, 106; convention adopts his amendment, 107; is ridiculed and defeated in Convention, 108; asks pay for Clergymen at Convention, 109; dubs Convention "sluggish body," 109; presents his suggestions, 110; but all are ignored, 111; made President of Board of Canal Commissioners, 115; accused by Democratic papers of importing workers for additional votes in October elections, 116, 117; threats of violence against him before convening of Legislature preceding Buckshot War, 122; abuse heaped upon him, 123; makes sound proposals for House organization, 125, 126; escapes with Penrose and Burrowes, 129; is called "arch conspirator," 130; denies being compromiser, 132; unwilling to admit defeat after "War" is over, 134; absents himself from Harrisburg, 135; believes Hopkins House "usurping body," 135, 136; resolution against his taking seat in House presented by McElwee, 136; comments on remarks of McElwee's resolution, 137; is accused of fornication and bastardy while home, 137; is reelected to House, 138; denies charges on which he is indicted, 139; loses in charges made against Democrats, 140; ruin brought upon him by Buckshot War, 141; agitates for municipal instruction in Adams County, 145; supports Gettysburg College appropriation while in Legislature, 146; answers party threat to defeat him because he supports college appropriation, 147, 148; uses all possible influence to further education, 148; makes grant to Pennsylvania College, 149; believes schools as essential as food, 149; makes answer to Patterson who opposes grant, 150; active in bettering educational institutions, 151; addresses House against repealer on Public School Act, 153, 154, 155, 156, 157; compares schools of Pennsylvania with those of New England, 158, 159; continues address, 160; attempts to rally support to sustain 1834 law, 161; rebukes Anti-Masonic Party for yielding principle to popularity, 161; attacks Representatives on stands held on education, 162, 163;

tells Representatives it is their duty to make laws creating and sustaining educational institutions, 164; counsels fellow Legislators, 165; concluding remarks, 166, 167; Upper House supports his substituted amendment, 168; "Father of Common School System," 169; supports bill to establish School of Arts, 170; active as Canal Commissioner, 171; agitates for schools in District of Columbia, 172; endows Juvenile Library Association, 172; his bill to form Bank, 174; rushes through legislation containing school and railroad provisions, 175; engineers his bill through, 176; it becomes a law, 177; proposes amendment that no branch of State Government have power to establish banks, 178; agitates for railroad near Gettysburg, 182; bill passed and work started, 183; his railroad dies, 186; his interest in iron business, 189; reasons for return to Lancaster, 190, 191, 192, 193; asked by Chase to bring Anti-Masons to Liberty Party, 192; is not sympathetic toward Liberty Party principles, 193; leaves Gettysburg for Lancaster, 194; opens law office in Lancaster, 195; accepted by new Bar as lawyer and gentleman, 196; among leading lawyers, 197; political labors, 198; campaigns for Clay, 199; aids young men seeking law as profession, 200; states position he would take if elected to Congress, 201; supports Taylor for Presidency, 201; nominated for Thirty-first Congress, 201, 202; irregular procedure in Thirty-first Congress irritates him, 210; is nominated for Speaker 211; addresses Congress defending North on slavery position, 212, 213, 214, 215, 216; answers Meade, 216; his speech stuns Southern members, 217; Southerners accuse him of insulting language in his speech, 218; rebuked by newspapers for speech, 219; recognized as leader of Antislavery in Congress, 220; makes speech on Congressional authority to legislate for territories and admit new States, 221; charges purpose of obtaining new territory is to enlarge slave domain, 221; disagrees with Clay's principles on slavery in territories, 222; argues on slave's "inalienable right to liberty," 222; makes answer to assaults, 223, 224; "He hath made of one blood all Nations of men," 225; cites 1808 statute of Virginia, 226; comments on Clay's Compromise Bill, 227; ridicules Clay and Webster and Act of 1793, 228; cites case of escaped slave family, 228; will not agree to admission of any state where slavery prevails, 230; opposes Congressional approval of Texas claim, 231; defends President

INDEX

INDEX

INDEX

Venable, Abraham, W., of North Carolina, pledges himself to vote for no Free Soiler or Abolitionist for Speaker, 206.

Vermont, birthplace of Stevens, 5; freed from winter bound isolation, 7; Stevens decides to emigrate from, 19; abolishes slavery, 86.

Virginia, legalizes slavery, 85; her Assembly searches for way to be rid of "great evil," 86; example of retrogression of slavery, 214; 1808 statute cited by Stevens, 226; Legislature passes secret session ordinance, 353; its Pierpont Government recognized by Johnson, 406.

Virginia Examiner, Richmond (Bloodhound of the *Southern Press*) comments on Stevens' death, 591.

Wade, Benjamin, expresses faith in Johnson, 406, 409; would have been successor to Johnson if latter convicted, 546.

Wade-Davis Bill, provisions of, 398, 399; vetoed by Lincoln, 400, 401; its authors enraged by Lincoln's action, 401.

Washburne, Elihu B., his resolution acted upon, 416; is allowed few minutes of Stevens' time to discuss report recommending impeachment. 533.

Webster, Daniel, possible candidate against Van Buren for Presidency in 1836, 37, 38; accused of influencing Harrison concerning non-appointment of Stevens to Cabinet position, 43; his charges of aggression of North ridiculed by Stevens, 228.

Weeds, political party, 64.

Welles, Secretary of Navy, accompanies Johnson in "swing around the circle," 449; thinks that had Stevens been in good health, Johnson would have been convicted, 546.

West Indian slaves, freed, 87.

West Point, Stevens attempts to enter Buchanan's nephew at, 581.

Wheaten, Henry, used by Stevens as authority on compensation by vanquished belligerent of war expenses, 476.

Whig Party, gains support, 36; ridicules M'Giffin's idea, 94; bent on keeping right of suffrage as extended by State Constitution, 111; holds National Convention in 1839, 42; challenge that members "will have seats," 122; Convention assembles, 233; permits members to differ on slavery opinion, 236; torn by opposing sections, 238; choses Scott as its Presidential candidate, 238; old Whigs join new Republican Party, 249.

Whig, Richmond, Virginia, comments on Stevens' death, 592.

Whitney, Eli, invents cotton gin, 86.

Wilmont Proviso, voted down, 205.

Wilson, James F., of Iowa, Judiciary Committee member, 499; collaborator of Stevens, 599.

Windom, William, of Minnesota, offers amendment resolution to Senate Judiciary measure, 489.

Winthrop, Robert C., nominated for Speaker, 210.

Wirt, William, nominee for Presidency of National Convention of 1831, 62.

Wolfe, Governor George, opposed by Stevens, 53; pardons Lefever, 60; successful in 1832 elections, 63; Stevens' committee plans to examine him concerning Masonic principles, 69; subpoenaed to testify as Mason, 77; writes letter to committee refusing to appear, 78; signs Public School Act of 1834, 152.

York, former teacher of Stevens moves to, 19.

York County Bar, takes steps to prevent Stevens' admission, 21.

Young Men's Colonization Society meeting, attended by Stevens, 88.

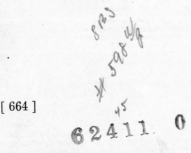

62411. 0